And No One
CHEERED

And No One
CHEERED

Federalism, Democracy and the Constitution Act

Edited by
Keith Banting and Richard Simeon

 Methuen

Toronto New York London Sydney Auckland

AND NO ONE CHEERED

Canadian Cataloguing in Publication Data

Main entry under title:
And no one cheered

ISBN 0-458-95950-2

1. Canada - Constitutional history - Addresses,
essays, lectures.   2. Canada - Constitutional law -
Amendments - Addresses, essays, lectures.   I. Banting,
Keith G., 1947–   II. Simeon, Richard, 1943–

JL27.A52   342.71′029   C83-094091-X

Printed and bound in Canada

1 2 3 4 5   83   88 87 86 85 84

TO OUR CHILDREN,
who will live with the consequences.

Contributors

Keith Banting is a member of the Department of Political Science at the University of British Columbia. A specialist in comparative public policy, he is the author of *Poverty, Politics and Policy: Britain in the 1960s* and *The Welfare State and Canadian Federalism*. During 1982–83, he is Associate Director of the Institute of Intergovernmental Relations, Queen's University.

Gérard Bergeron teaches at the École nationale d'administration publique of the Université du Québec. A leading member of the political science community in Quebec, his publications include contributions both to political theory, especially his *La Gouverne Politique*, and to debate on contemporary political issues, such as his *L'Indépendance Oui Mais . . .* and *Syndrome Québécois et Mal Canadien*.

Alan Cairns is a member of the Department of Political Science at the University of British Columbia. He is one of the pre-eminent students of Canadian politics, and has written widely on federalism and the constitution. During 1982–83, he is Mackenzie King Visiting Professor of Canadian Studies at Harvard University.

Pierre Fournier is chairman of the Département de science politique at the Université du Québec à Montréal. A specialist on Quebec economic and political life, his publications include *The Quebec Establishment*.

Roger Gibbins teaches in the Department of Political Science at the University of Calgary. A leading student of the politics of regionalism, he is the author of *Prairie Politics and Society: Regionalism in Decline* and *Regionalism: Territorial Politics in Canada and the United States*. He has also been active in discussions on constitutional reform, both as a Research Associate with the Canada West Foundation and as an advisor to the federal government.

Chaviva Hošek is a member of the Department of English at the University of Toronto, and an editor of *A Festschrift in Honour Northrop Frye* and *Lyric Poetry: After the New Criticism*. For the past decade, she has been active in the voluntary feminist movement, and in 1982–83 is Vice-President of the National Action Committee on the Status of Women.

Raymond Hudon teaches political science at the Université Laval, and is a specialist in the political economy of Canada and Quebec and in their relations with the continental and world economy. He has written several articles on Quebec politics, and is co-author of *Patronage et Politique au Québec, 1944-1972*.

Daniel Latouche teaches political science at the Centre d'Études canadiennes françaises at McGill University and has written widely on Quebec politics. In addition, he served for several years as an advisor in the office of Premier René Lévesque.

William Lederman is a member of the Faculty of Law at Queen's University. One of the country's leading experts in constitutional law, he is the author of *The Courts and the Canadian Constitution* and *Continuing Canadian Constitutional Dilemmas.*

Gil Rémillard is a member of the Faculté de droit at the Université Laval. A specialist in Canadian constitutional law, his publications include *Le Fédéralisme Canadien.*

Peter Russell teaches in the Department of Political Science at the University of Toronto. He is a leading student of the judicial process in Canada and the author of the widely used text, *Leading Constitutional Decisions.* He recently served as Director of Research for the Royal Commission on the RCMP.

Douglas Sanders is a member of the Faculty of Law at the University of British Columbia. A specialist in native legal issues, he has served both as a consultant and as counsel for a number of aboriginal organizations, including the National Indian Brotherhood/Assembly of First Nations, the Native Council of Canada, and the World Council of Indigenous Peoples.

Richard Simeon is the Director of the Institute of Intergovernmental Relations, Queen's University. A leading student of Canadian politics, he is the author of *Federal-Provincial Diplomacy* and co-author of *Small Worlds: Provinces and Parties in Canadian Political Life.*

Donald Smiley teaches political science at York University. The dean of students of Canadian federalism, his many publications include the widely used text, *Canada in Question.*

Walter Tarnopolsky is a member of the Faculty of Law and Director of the Human Rights Research and Education Centre at the University of Ottawa. In addition, he is the author of *Discrimination and the Law in Canada* and editor of *The Canadian Charter of Rights and Freedoms: A Commentary.*

Reg Whitaker is a member of the Department of Political Science at Carleton University. A specialist in Canadian politics and political theory, his publications include *The Government Party: Organizing and Financing the Liberal Party of Canada.*

George Woodcock is one of Canada's leading men of letters, having written extensively on a wide range of subjects: political philosophy, the arts, Canadian history and politics. His many books include *Anarchism; A History of Libertarian Ideas and Movements; Canada and the Canadians;* and *Peoples of the Coast.*

Contents

Preface, xi

Part I/Introduction 1
Chapter 1/Federalism, Democracy and the Constitution, 2
Keith Banting and Richard Simeon

Part II/Federalism and Constitutional Change 27
Chapter 2/The Politics of Constitutional Conservatism, 28
Alan Cairns

3/Quebec in Isolation, 59
Gérard Bergeron

4/A Dangerous Deed: The Constitution Act, 1982, 74
Donald Smiley

5/The Constitutional Misfire of 1982, 96
Daniel Latouche

6/Constitutional Politics and the West, 119
Roger Gibbins

7/Quebec, the Economy and the Constitution, 133
Raymond Hudon

8/The Future of Quebec Nationalism, 154
Pierre Fournier

Part III/The Courts in the Constitutional Process 175
Chapter 9/The Supreme Court of Canada and Basic
Constitutional Amendment, 176
William Lederman

10/Legality, Legitimacy and the Supreme Court, 189
Gil Rémillard

11/Bold Statescraft, Questionable Jurisprudence, 210
Peter Russell

Part IV/Democracy and the Constitution 239
Chapter 12/Democracy and the Canadian Constitution, 240
Reg Whitaker

13/The Constitution and Human Rights, 261
Walter Tarnopolsky

14/Women and the Constitutional Process, 280
Chaviva Hošek

15/The Indian Lobby, 301
Douglas Sanders

16/Confederation as a World Example, 333
George Woodcock

Part V/Conclusion 347
Chapter 17/Federalism, Democracy and the Future, 348
Keith Banting and Richard Simeon

Appendix: Constitution Act, 1982, 361

Preface

In this book, seventeen Canadian scholars of varying backgrounds, disciplines and languages seek to come to terms with the nature and significance of the recent struggle over constitutional reform and its results as embodied in the Constitution Act, 1982. How did we get here? Why this result, and not others? What does the struggle and its outcome tell us about Canadian federalism, and about how Canada's language groups and regions can continue to share together the northern half of a continent? What does it reveal about the character of Canadian democracy? About individual rights and the position of minorities within our community? What does the constitutional settlement tell us of the future? Will the cold words on a printed document come to life and help shape Canadian society? Or should we look elsewhere for guidance about the years ahead?

These questions are addressed in different ways in the pages that follow. There is no common vision of Canada here. But there is a common thread running through the volume, sometimes flashing in anger, sometimes showing as quiet regret: we could have done better, say these authors. None finds his vision of what Canada should be in the settlement. Some express muted satisfaction that the constitution has been patriated, or give qualified approval to the new Charter of Rights and Freedoms. But none really finds real cause for national celebration in the Constitution Act, 1982. Hence our title.

Others may find more to cheer about. But the book does demonstrate how a broad-ranging group of scholars assesses the meaning and implications of what has been done.

This book has a long ancestry, and reflects a continuing preoccupation of the Institute of Intergovernmental Relations at Queen's University. In 1972, concerned that Canadians must better understand and come to terms with Quebec nationalism, R.M. Burns edited a collection of essays entitled *One Country or Two?* In 1977, following the election of the Parti Québécois, that challenge was posed with fresh urgency, and Richard Simeon edited *Must Canada Fail? (Le Canada face à son destin)*. The present volume extends the tradition, and expands upon it in several ways. Both earlier volumes were written exclusively by English Canadians hoping to encourage a dialogue between the two major language groups. This book, by contrast, brings English- and French-Canadian scholars together between a single set of covers. In addition, the constitutional challenge to which the earlier volumes responded was pre-eminently a crisis of federalism. While that continued to be a central element in our latest constitutional battles, the agenda had also broadened to include new issues and new participants. This book reflects the wider agenda, both in its selection of authors and in the questions they address.

Many people made this volume possible. We thank first the authors, who responded with admirable speed to our requests for contributions and who took our editorial suggestions with good heart. We thank also the translators, Terrance Hughes and Agnes Whitfield, for their skill and care. The staff of the Institute of Intergovernmental Relations, especially Patricia Candido, Gerry Ketchum and Lilian Newkirk, helped in many phases of the preparation of the manuscript. And Peter Milroy of Methuen Publications has given us unfailing support and encouragement.

The constitutional debate posed difficult and profound questions for all Canadians. We hope that the effort of these authors to think through what it all means will help readers to come to their own assessments.

KEITH BANTING
RICHARD SIMEON

Part I/Introduction

Chapter 1/Federalism, Democracy and the Constitution
Keith Banting and Richard Simeon

On April 17, 1982 the new Constitution Act, 1982 was formally proclaimed by the Queen on the lawn of Parliament Hill. By that act, Canada patriated its constitution, sweeping away a final vestige of its colonial past, established an amending formula to govern future changes in its constitutional framework, and entrenched a Canadian Charter of Rights and Freedoms. Moreover, the ceremony capped one of the most tumultuous periods in the political life of the country, a period which will leave its mark on virtually every part of Canadian society for generations to come.

The struggle over the constitution revealed much about the political life of the country. Canadians and their governments debated profound questions about the basic nature of their country: about how its regional and linguistic divisions should be managed; about majority rule and minority rights; about consent and legitimacy; about the roles of governments and the public in the process of democratic change. The political struggle over these issues was unparalleled in its drama and intensity. In its final stages, the battle raged simultaneously on many fronts—in the byzantine world of federal-provincial negotiations, on the floors of Parliament and provincial Legislatures, and in the courts. The battle even flowed beyond the nation's borders, embroiling British parliamentarians and courts in Canadian discord. The climax finally came at the First Ministers' Conference in November 1981. Against a background of high drama and intense political intrigue, nine provinces and the federal government compromised, often radically, on the future they would like to have seen for Canada, in order to reach an Accord on constitutional reform.

Canadians are still grappling with the significance of the constitutional struggle and the provisions that emerged from it. At the conclusion of the November conference, many of the participants were euphoric. Premier Peckford of Newfoundland proclaimed it to be "a great day for Canada." There was, according to Premier Davis of Ontario, only one winner—the country. Premier Bennett of British Columbia claimed to see a new, more harmonious spirit sweeping the country. But the euphoria was far from universal. Premier Lévesque angrily denounced the Accord and the betrayal of Quebec. Even Prime Minister Trudeau was subdued. "We'd better grab the signatures and run," he observed, "before anyone changes his mind." The ambivalence within the conference chamber itself was magnified a hundredfold during the following days and months as Canadians from coast to coast debated what their governments had agreed to in their name, and often found it wanting. Native and women's groups were outraged, and had to mobilize anew to reinstate their claims in the constitutional package. And although thousands of Canadians did eventually gather on Parliament Hill to witness the royal proclamation, one remains struck by the lack of widespread public enthusiasm. Indifference, relief that the battle was finally over, and confusion about precisely what had been accomplished seemed to mingle equally in the public response.

In this book, a distinguished group of students of Canadian politics and law also grapple with the significance of the titanic political struggle and the changes to the constitution that resulted from it. They examine the dynamics of the constitutional debate of the last two decades and attempt to anticipate, however tentatively, the implications for the future of our political and social life. Once again, the conclusions are decidedly unenthusiastic. While some express muted satisfaction that the constitution has been patriated or give qualified approval to the Charter of Rights and Freedoms, the all-pervading sense is one of intense disappointment and wasted opportunities. None of the contributors finds cause for great celebration or national self-congratulation in the constitutional settlement.

The struggle over the constitution was shaped by dreams and compromises. The participants brought to the negotiations a complex mix of goals and dreams, only some of which are visible in the final outcome. For some dreams, especially those of Quebec nationalists, the constitutional settlement represents an historic defeat. For others, the settlement represents a sweeping compromise. But even here, the very word "compromise" is double-edged. On one hand, it means concessions and accommodations in a mutual effort to reach agreement. This, many political leaders proclaimed at the time, was the "Canadian way." On the other hand, "compromise" also reflects something less benign, something lost or tarnished. As these essays reveal, the competing dreams of Canada were compromised in both senses.

This first chapter seeks to provide a general overview of the constitutional experience and to capture the common themes that pervade the book. First, it briefly surveys the history of events that lead up to the constitutional settlement, and describes the specific nature of the reforms enacted. Then, it examines the central questions involved in an evaluation of the constitutional process and outcome, and highlights the fascinating ways in which the various contributors have responded to them.

The Politics of Constitution-Making
In one sense, constitutional debate has stretched over most of this century, especially in the unsuccessful search for an amending formula. The contemporary debate, however, with its pervasive criticism of our political institutions and sweeping proposals for change, is much more recent in origin. Indeed, as Don Smiley argues in his essay, for much of Canada's first century there was little sense that the constitution itself stood in the way of legitimate purposes which individuals and groups might wish to pursue.

The current debate really originates in the 1960s, with the growth of a secular Quebec nationalism that transformed the society of that province and brought demands for major reforms in the structure of Canadian federalism. In the 1970s, this pressure for change was reinforced by growing regional conflict, especially between the West and central Canada, which increasingly came to take the form of demands for constitutional change. Western provinces, as well as Newfoundland in the East, became central participants, and the constitutional agenda became increasingly crowded.

Constitutional negotiations have gone through four distinct cycles over the last two decades, with the range of issues under debate widening with each new cycle. In the early 1960s, negotiations over the procedures for amending the constitution failed when the Quebec government vetoed the proposed Fulton-Favreau formula. A second set of discussions began in the late 1960s, but again collapsed in 1971 when Quebec rejected the Victoria Charter, a package of proposals including an amending formula, entrenchment of certain rights, and minor adjustments to the division of powers. Then, in 1975, Prime Minister Trudeau initiated a third effort, which quickly widened to cover more aspects of the division of powers, but again without success. The final and most intense cycle was triggered by the election of the Parti Québécois in November 1976.

The advent to power of a government committed to Quebec independence sparked a frenzy of debate about the future. Citizen groups sprang up everywhere to voice their concern and offer suggestions; academics debated an ever-growing array of constitutional possibilities; political parties cautiously issued discussion papers; and governments appointed advisory councils of wise men and women to guide them. While numerous groups tried to focus discussions around their own proposals, the debate remained defiantly multi-facetted. At the federal level, a Task Force on Canadian Unity toured the country and issued its blueprint for a reformed Canada.[1] But the Liberal government remained cool to it. The government's own ideas had been introduced in June 1978 in the form of a draft Constitutional Amendment Bill (Bill C-60), which sought a more limited measure of reform in the structure of the central government. But the bill was widely criticized, and it suffered a mortal wound in 1979 when the Supreme Court of Canada ruled that Ottawa did not have the constitutional authority to alter unilaterally the powers and membership of the Senate. By then, however, the federal strategy had already been put in abeyance. Constitutional conferences in the fall of 1978 and in early 1979 had failed to make progress on the intergovernmental front, and the Liberals had been defeated in the election of May 1979. In the months following, the Progressive Conservative minority government struggled to formulate its own approach. Within Quebec, meanwhile, the battle-lines were forming. In November 1979 the Parti Québécois published its outline of "sovereignty-association," and the Quebec Liberal Party replied with its own distinctive approach to reform.[2] Canadians thus faced a veritable kaleidoscope of constitutional options as they entered 1980, one of the most eventful years in their history.

In a few short months, the constitutional debate was sharply narrowed and focussed by electoral politics. At the federal level, the sudden defeat of the Progressive Conservatives in the House of Commons and the re-election of a strong Liberal majority government strengthened Liberal self-confidence. While federalism and the constitution had been muted themes in the 1980 Liberal campaign, Prime Minister Trudeau had vigorously championed the role of the federal government during the 1979 election, and there was a renewed sense of assertiveness in Ottawa. Even more important were electoral fortunes within Quebec. In May 1980 came the defeat of the referendum in which the Parti Québécois had sought a mandate to negotiate "sovereignty-association." Federal leaders, especially Justice Minister Chrétien and the prime minister himself, had played a central role in the campaign, and the victory strengthened their conviction that a strong defence of the federal government was possible. Their opportunity to do so was increased significantly the next April, when the Parti Québécois defeated the Quebec Liberal Party led by Claude Ryan in a provincial election. The defeat of both sovereignty-association and Ryan's proposals for radical reform within the federal system dramatically weakened the bargaining strength of the government of Quebec in the constitutional bargaining that was to follow. The Parti Québécois government was left virtually paralyzed, and the federal Liberals seized their opportunity.

The renewed federal drive began immediately after the referendum.[3] The prime minister called the premiers together to establish a timetable and an agenda for rapid agreement, with the threat that if it were not reached, Ottawa would proceed unilaterally to patriate the constitution and to redeem the "promise" made to Quebecers that a "no" to the Parti Québécois was a "yes" to some unspecified form of renewed federalism. There followed a summer of intensive negotiations between federal and provincial ministers and officials on a twelve-point agenda. The federal government withdrew some concessions it had earlier been prepared to make, and placed a number of new issues on the table, notably the questions of "powers over the economy," which were designed to limit provincial capacity to erect internal barriers to the Canadian common market. Federal officials also made a brilliant distinction between their agenda of "powers for the people," which was to include patriation and the Charter of Rights, and "powers for governments," including the division of powers and the reform of federal institutions. No longer would Ottawa countenance sacrificing the former for the latter; it would not trade "rights for fish." Or so it argued.

The summer negotiations culminated in a First Ministers' Conference in September 1980 in which the competing federalist and provincialist visions of Canada were stated more sharply and more uncompromisingly than ever before. After five days of bitter debate the result was impasse once again. The federal response was then to assert that provincial agreement was not necessary after all, and that the federal government had the power unilaterally to bring about constitutional change. Politically, federal officials believed that public impatience, together with the undoubted popularity of a constitutional Charter of Rights, would give it the political strength to succeed.

Nevertheless, unilateral action represented a major political gamble. In virtually all constitutional discussions until then, all political leaders had presumed that substantial, probably even unanimous, federal-provincial agreement was essential. In 1980, however, only two provinces—Ontario and New Brunswick—supported the federal initiative. The others argued that Ottawa's action was a fundamental denial of the federal nature of Canada, tantamount to a constitutional *coup d'état*. So six, later eight, provinces moved to challenge Ottawa in three provincial appeal courts. The "gang of eight," as they came to be known, devised their own constitutional package, calling for patriation of the constitution and specifying an amending formula clearly designed to protect provincial rights. They also campaigned vigorously for public support and pursued an effective lobby with British parliamentarians, arguing that Britain had a residual responsibility to safeguard the federal principle which they claimed lay at the heart of the constitution. British misgivings were, in fact, to grow as opposition within Canada increased. These intensified after a British parliamentary committee issued a report, known as the Kershaw report, concluding that the federal action was unconstitutional and that Britain did have an obligation to protect provincial interests.[4]

Once Ottawa had decided to act on its own, a Resolution was introduced to Parliament. The federal Cabinet hoped for a short debate in order to move quickly and avoid the mobilization of widespread opposition. In the event, however, parliamentary debate stretched into the spring. This had contradictory effects. On one hand, the Progressive Conservative Party rejected the Resolution, thus denying it the legitimacy and nation-wide support it might otherwise have had. More importantly, through highly effective parliamentary strategy the Tories were able to extend the debate, giving the provinces more time to organize, and in particular, giving time for the legal challenges to work their way through the courts. In other respects, however, the parliamentary debate also mobilized considerable support behind the federal initiative. The most important forum was the Special Joint Committee of the Senate and House of Commons, whose deliberations were televised and extended over several months. The committee provided a platform for numerous public groups to express their views. While many, especially civil libertarians and native peoples' groups, were highly critical of the federal Resolution, their efforts greatly strengthened the federal bargaining hand; most of the groups focussed their arguments not on the propriety of change without provincial consent, but on the need to improve and tighten the Charter of Rights, thus legitimizing and building a vocal constituency for the federal proposals. The Liberals further nurtured this constituency by accepting many of the suggestions for strengthening the Charter, and by the time the governments came together again in the fall of 1981, it was politically unlikely that the Charter would be completely jettisoned.

The provincialist coalition relied for its defence increasingly on the courts. The federal government argued throughout that the issue was political, not legal, and that it was convention, not law, which required that provincial consent be obtained. First to decide was the Manitoba Court of Appeal, in a split decision favouring Ottawa. But a few weeks later, the Newfoundland Court of Appeal concluded that the federal initiative was unconstitutional. From that point, it was clear that Ottawa could not proceed in Parliament until the Supreme Court of Canada had decided the issue once and for all. The court heard the case in the spring, a case unprecedented in many ways. Never before had the Supreme Court been drawn so firmly into the heart of a political crisis of the first order. As Peter Russell observes in his essay, "never had the mainstream of national political life flowed so relentlessly up to a Supreme Court decision." The decision would be critical. Could judges resolve conflicts that the politicians clearly could not? The court's judgement was rendered in September 1981, and was received with cameras rolling and television commentary reminiscent of an election night.

In a complex judgement, which is analyzed carefully in Part III of this book, the majority held that it was technically legal for Parliament to petition Britain without provincial consent, but that such action was unconstitutional in a conventional sense.[5] Convention and law, the majority argued, were equally necessary to establish constitutionality. The court also held that while convention required "substantial consent" of the provinces, it did not require unanimity. The court thus threw the ball back to the governments and forced them to return to the bargaining table. But the court had also altered the ground rules in ways that maximized the costs of intransigence for both sides. While the judgement had upheld the strict legality of federal unilateralism, its reflections on the importance of conventions enhanced opposition to such a procedure within Canada and greatly compromised its chances in Britain. Greater provincial consent was politically essential. But the Court had also opened up the possibility of establishing sufficient legitimacy to proceed without unanimous provincial agreement, thereby eliminating the capacity of a single province to block the process, and putting much greater pressure on the internal cohesion of the gang of eight. From that moment, the stage was set for the isolation of the Parti Québécois government.

The fateful First Ministers' Conference was held five weeks later. After four tense days of conflict and intrigue, an Accord was reached in what Alan Cairns aptly describes as a "blunt and brutal compromise." Essentially, the road to patriation was reached by the federal government agreeing to adopt a revised version of the gang of eight's amending formula on the one hand, and the provinces agreeing to accept a revised version of the federal government's Charter of Rights and Freedoms on the other.

Quebec was isolated from the Accord. Later, the province returned to the courts to assert that its consent was a necessary element of any constitutional change, but this did not prevent the Resolution proceeding to Britain. Nor did the British respond to Quebec pleas to hold up passage until the Canadian courts had resolved its claim. Women and native groups had also expressed outrage at the way in which the Accord watered down or eliminated protections they had fought hard to have included in the federal Resolution. In an unprecedented display of public protest, described fully in the essays by Chaviva Hošek and Douglas Sanders, they mounted campaigns across the country that forced the governments to restore at least partially the rights they had been denied. But the main lines of the constitutional change had been set by the first ministers on November 5. Canada's long constitutional struggle had reached a conclusion, however temporary.

The Settlement

Before evaluating the Accord, it is necessary to describe its contents. The Constitution Act, 1982 first brings about patriation, ending the holdover from the colonial past. The constitution of Canada is no longer made up of statutes of the British Parliament. No future Act of the British Parliament will apply to Canada, and all future constitutional amendments will be achieved through a domestic political process. These changes are given symbolic expression as well in the renaming of the British North America Act of 1867 and its later amendments as the Constitution Acts.

Second is the amending procedure. The basic mechanism for future change is a purely intergovernmental one: most amendments require assent of the federal Parliament and at least two-thirds (seven) of the provinces, comprising 50 percent of the total population. However, where an amendment so decided takes away from the legislative powers, proprietary rights, or "any other rights and privileges" of a province, then a dissenting province may declare the amendment does not apply to it. And where such an amendment touches on provincial powers respecting education "or other cultural matters," a province that opts out shall receive financial compensation from the federal government. Unanimity is required for amendments affecting the monarchy, representation in the House of Commons and Senate, the Supreme Court and use of the English and French languages. Amendments affecting only some provinces require their assent. Both Ottawa and the provinces may unilaterally amend the constitution as it affects their internal operations. Finally, the Senate is to have only a suspensive veto over constitutional change.

Third, the Act for the first time entrenches in the constitution a Canadian Charter of Rights and Freedoms, which is far more detailed and comprehensive than earlier proposals. It embodies guarantees of fundamental freedoms such as conscience, speech and association, the right to vote, legal rights such as the right to counsel, and protection against arbitrary arrest or self-incrimination. It guarantees the right of citizens to live and work anywhere in the country, together with protection against numerous forms of discrimination. Moreover, it empowers the courts to provide remedies to those whose rights are infringed.

The rights of Canada's native peoples were, and remain, matters of bitter contention. The Charter now states that the rights in it shall not be construed so as to derogate from any existing treaty rights or rights acquired in future land claims settlements. In addition, the Constitution Act requires the holding of a constitutional conference within one year of its proclamation, at which native rights are to be on the agenda and native representatives are to be present at the table. The rights of women were also a prominent feature of the debate, and the Charter states that the rights and freedoms in it "are guaranteed equally to male and female persons."

The Charter is, however, hedged with significant qualifications. Section 1 states that the rights and freedoms it establishes are subject "only to such reasonable limits prescribed by law as can be demonstrably justified in a free and democratic society." Governments are also given the power to set aside fundamental freedoms, legal rights and equality rights by passing legislation which expressly declares it will operate "notwithstanding" the provisions of the Charter. Provinces with lower-than-average employment rates are expressly permitted to give preferential treatment in hiring to their own residents. And the Charter delays the coming into force of some sections for three years, to permit governments to adjust their legislation to the new regime.

Fourth, the constitution now embraces a number of linguistic rights. It constitutionalizes English and French as the official languages of Canada and New Brunswick, and ensures that their governments will function in both languages. Similar linguistic obligations on Quebec and Manitoba in the former BNA Act remain. The Charter also provides educational rights for English and French minorities in all provinces. Citizens (but not landed immigrants) in all provinces are guaranteed the right to have their children educated in their own official language, at public expense, subject to the condition where "the number of those children so warrants." There is a small concession to Quebec's position, in that one part of the language of education section, dealing with the children of citizens who did not receive their education in Canada, does not come into force in that province until authorized by its government or Legislature.

Fifth, the Act contains a determination by all governments to promote equal opportunities and reduce regional disparities, including an unspecified federal "commitment to the principle" of equalization payments to ensure that all provinces are able to "provide reasonably comparable levels of public service at reasonably comparable levels of taxation." Thus the concept of "sharing" between richer and poorer regions is entrenched—at least symbolically.

Sixth, the only section of the Act touching directly on the division of powers is a strengthening of provincial control over natural resources. A new section 92A gives the provinces exclusive power over exploration, development, conservation and management of natural resources and electrical energy. Provinces are also empowered to make laws respecting export of natural resources to other provinces, so long as they do not discriminate in price or supply against other regions. Parliament has the power to override such laws. In another response to Saskatchewan in particular, provinces are now allowed to impose indirect taxes on natural resources.

The Accord thus achieves some long-standing objectives. Patriation and an amending formula have been goals at least since 1927, and a constitutional bill of rights and stronger guarantees of Canadian bilingualism have been central objectives of the federal government since the late 1960s. But other goals have been ignored, in whole or in part. How, then, are Canadians to evaluate this package of constitutional reforms?

Federalism, Democracy and the Accord

A collective experience as complex as constitution-making can be evaluated from a wide variety of perspectives. This book approaches the struggle over the constitution and the Constitution Act itself by assessing them according to two basic concerns of Canadian political life: federalism and democracy. The particular concerns and viewpoints of the contributors differ, often pointedly. But over and over the discussion returns to two fundamental questions. First, do the constitutional process and settlement represent an effective response to the underlying stresses and strains within the federation, which gave rise to the debate over the constitution in the first place? Second, what does the constitutional battle itself tell us about the quality of democracy in Canada, and will the new provisions enhance or diminish the quality of democratic life in this country?

In addressing these questions, the book focusses on both the way in which the constitution was changed and the substance of the reforms. The legitimacy of constitutional change is always tightly interwoven with the process through which it is accomplished. Most countries have established special procedures for constitutional reform, which require especially broad agreement, some special majority greater than that needed to enact changes in ordinary laws. The recent Canadian debate was made infinitely more complex and bitter, however, by disagreement on the amending process itself. Clearly, a bare majority in the two Houses of Parliament would have been a perilously narrow basis on which to carry through controversial changes. But how much wider an agreement was needed to ensure the legitimacy of the new provisions? Given Canada's federal nature, what was the necessary level of agreement among the federal and provincial governments, and was it legitimate to proceed over the opposition of the government of Quebec? Given Canada's democratic nature, what role should have been played by ordinary Canadians and public groups in the process of re-designing the instrument that is to regulate their future life together?

The substance of the Constitution Act is examined as well from the same perspectives of federalism and democracy in order to assess its implications for the decades to come. First, do the changes represent a new reconciliation between anglophones and francophones, between region and region, between government and government within the federal system? Or do they at least provide a better framework within which these conflicts can be managed in the future? Second, does the Constitution Act, with its amending formula and Charter of Rights and Freedoms, add a new dimension to the meaning of democracy in this country? These may not be the only questions that can be asked about the constitution, but they are profound ones, the answers to which would tell us much about our political system and its future.

Federalism and Constitutional Reform: Two great questions have underpinned the constitutional controversy of the last twenty years, each growing out of the primary cleavages and conflicts that have dominated Canadian politics since Confederation. One is dualism, the political relationship between French- and English-speaking Canadians, and the second is regionalism, the enduring tension between the national political community and the provincial or regional communities. Does the Constitution Act represent an effective response to these twin challenges to the federal system? The authors in this volume are agreed that it does not. The Accord did not resolve these central problems, and the manner of its creation may have exacerbated them dangerously.

The challenge posed by a linguistically divided society has been at the core of constitutional debate since the "Quiet Revolution" of the 1960s, and during that time two starkly contrasting visions of the relationship between anglophones and francophones have competed for dominance. The first view has been expressed in one form or another by every recent Quebec government, from Jean Lesage with his slogan *maîtres chez nous*, to Daniel Johnson with "equality or independence," to René Lévesque with "sovereignty-association." Quebec, this view says, is a distinct society or nation. Its national government, its primary political expression, the one political instrument that Quebecers alone control, is the government of Quebec. That is to be the tool to develop, protect and expand the society and culture. Furthermore, Canada itself should be understood as a partnership between two nations: relations between French and English Canada, therefore, are to be found in relations between Quebec and Ottawa.

The constitutional agenda of successive Quebec governments has flowed directly from these premises. Quebec needs greater financial and jurisdictional autonomy; the central government must not be able to impose the values of the English-speaking majority on the Quebec people; and internally, Quebec must be a French-speaking society. During the 1960s, this thrust remained largely within the context of a federal system, to be achieved either through a general decentralization of the federation, or through some form of special status in which Quebec would exercise wider powers than other provinces. During the 1970s, the Parti Québécois extended this basic logic one large step further, by arguing that Quebec must be fully sovereign to fulfill its historic mission, and that future economic relations with Canada must be based on the principle of equality between nations. But the general assumptions underlying the Quebec-centred vision remain common to all provincial political parties in that province.

To the symbolic appeal of a Québécois society and state, the federal government posed another ideal: a bilingual Canada in which franco-phones could feel at home from sea to sea. This second conception reflects fundamentally different assumptions about the nature of Canada, one which rejects the equation of French Canada with Quebec and envisages two major language groups spreading across the land. The constitutional implications of this view run directly counter to the proposals advanced by successive Quebec governments. Language should be a matter of individual choice, not collective determination. Canada should be a fully bilingual country, with entrenched protections for linguistic minorities wherever they live. Transfers of additional powers to the Quebec government are not essential to the preservation of a French-speaking community there, and would simply initiate a politically irresistible slide into formal separation.

As the constitutional debate became increasingly polarized between these antithetical views, and personalized in the leadership of Prime Minister Trudeau and Premier Lévesque, many Canadians searched for some form of "third option" that would respect the aspirations underlying Quebec's view and accommodate them within a reformed federal system. This was the basic thrust of the Task Force on Canadian Unity, chaired by Jean-Luc Pépin and John Robarts, and of the Quebec Liberal Party's "Beige" Paper, *A New Canadian Federation*. This was also the vague common ground on which federalist political forces within Quebec grouped, under the banner of "renewed federalism," to fight separatism during the referendum. But in the *realpolitik* of the constitutional battle in the succeeding months, this intellectual mid-point dissolved, and the polar positions re-asserted themselves in sparkling and dangerous clarity.

The final settlement reached in those early November days gave nothing to the Quebec view of Canada. The very way in which the decisions were made was the greatest blow, as the constitution was changed despite the passionate opposition of the government of Quebec. Twice before—in 1965 and 1971—Quebec alone held out against an Accord, and no one then had even suggested proceeding without its agreement. The legitimacy of the decision to proceed in 1981-82 despite Quebec's position is hotly contested in the chapters that follow. In his essay, Don Smiley adopts the three tests employed by the Supreme Court to identify constitutional conventions and argues that Quebec's consent was, in fact, constitutionally required, thereby qualifying the new provisions as illegitimate. Not surprisingly, however, the most hostile judgements come from Quebecers themselves, especially Gérard Bergeron, Pierre Fournier, Raymond Hudon, Daniel Latouche and Gil Rémillard. Their essays all reflect a deep sense of betrayal. Quebecers are bitter, Bergeron writes, that critical choices were made "not only against their wishes, but without their even being present" during the decisive nocturnal bargaining. While the various authors from Quebec differ on what might constitute an ideal relationship between their society and the rest of Canada, they are as one in angrily rejecting a process that has entrenched an outcome that no Quebec government could have supported. Indeed, in an essentially philosophical essay, Rémillard goes as far as discussing whether civil disobedience is warranted. Although he concludes it is not, the fact that the question arises at all reveals clearly the profound sense of illegitimacy that surrounds the outcome within the intellectual community of Quebec.

The substance of the Accord also gives nothing to the Quebec view of this country. There was no decentralization of power; the Charter threatens important Quebec legislation, including its language laws; with one minor exception, the new amending formula treats Quebec like any other province. As Daniel Latouche concludes, "however one looks at it, the Quebec approach to constitutional change has failed." By contrast, Prime Minister Trudeau won important parts of his agenda for French-English relations. Admittedly, the victory was incomplete and compromised. Full bilingualism is constitutionally entrenched in the federal and New Brunswick governments, but Ontario refused to declare itself bilingual. The education rights of linguistic minorities are guaranteed, but only "where numbers warrant." The Charter of Rights and Freedoms, with its national symbolism and mobility rights, is entrenched, but important parts of it are subject to a legislative override which the Quebec government is determined to utilize fully. Nevertheless, the battle over Canadian dualism has been resolved, temporarily at least, largely on Prime Minister Trudeau's terms.

This outcome is paradoxical, dangerously so. The growth of Quebec nationalism was the driving force behind the long constitutional debate. Yet the response to that movement has been to reduce that province's powers. As Gérard Bergeron observes, "those who instigate hostilities are often doing the dirty work for others when it is time to untangle the spoils." The isolation of Quebec poses difficult moral and political questions. Does this outcome really constitute the "renewed federalism" promised Quebecers by the federalist forces during the referendum campaign? The authors here register a decisive "no." Donald Smiley concludes bluntly, "this electorate has been betrayed," and the Quebec contributors agree in even stronger terms. Even if greater benefit of the doubt is given to federal leaders, can one comfortably accept a conception of Canada that so totally denies Quebec's position as the primary government of Quebecers, with a special role to assert and protect a distinct society? Can one comfortably accept the imposition of a settlement repugnant to both major parties in Quebec provincial politics?

Canada remains far from a resolution of the historic conflict between its French- and English-speaking parts. The Parti Québécois was re-elected in 1981 with a greater share of the vote than before. The party has turned its back on the *étapiste* strategy for independence and is pledged to fight the next election on the issue of outright independence. It is also considering participating in the federal electoral process. Clearly, the Constitution Act is only one episode in a continuing struggle between the two images of Quebec and Canada.

The second great question underlying the constitutional debate has been the relationship between the national community and the regional communities, which together constitute Canadians' sense of place. Regional conflict has been a constant feature in our history since well before Confederation, but it has reached new heights in the last two decades. Like dualism, regionalism has spawned two very different conceptions of how Canada should be governed: a "provincialist" and a "centralist" view of the country. The provincialist view rests on some key assumptions: that the strength of Canada lies in its regional diversity; that regional communities and identities are at least as important as national ones; and that the central government as currently constructed cannot hope to respond to the needs and aspirations of a country as varied as Canada. Responding to regional needs is the natural role of provincial governments, this view holds, and the secret to a more harmonious balance between state and society lies in strengthening provincial influence over the patterns of public policy in this country. At its extreme, the provincialist view sees Canada as a true confederation, a compact among provinces, with Ottawa as their creature. More commonly, it argues that sovereignty is *shared*, that each order of government is sovereign in its own jurisdiction, and Canada as a whole is a partnership between both its federal and provincial sides.

This vision of Canada underpinned the constitutional agenda of the coalition of eight provinces. In varying degrees they called for greater provincial jurisdiction in several areas, especially those crucial to economic development; for cast-iron protection of provincial control over natural resources, including those off-shore; and for an amending formula that treated all provinces equally and guaranteed their rights and powers. They called for limitations on the very broad powers the constitution now gives Ottawa to intervene in areas of largely provincial jurisdiction—the spending power, the emergency power, and the declaratory power. Finally, there was the view that provinces should have a greater voice in national decision-making and national institutions, a view expressed most forcefully by British Columbia. The national interest was not Ottawa's alone to enunciate; it must be the collective will of all governments.

The provincialist conception was opposed with equal passion by a centralist view of the appropriate response to Canadian regionalism, a view that asserted the primacy of the national community and government. This view insisted that Canadians' primary commitment is, and must be, to the country as a whole. It is on the broad national scene, Canada from sea to sea, that Canadians can best maximize their freedom and opportunity. Canada is more than the sum of its parts, more than a "community of communities." The primacy of the national interest implies also the primacy of the national government, which alone can speak for it. Only Ottawa, in this view, can manage the national economy, re-distribute wealth among regions, or ensure national standards in areas such as health care. Parliament must be supreme and have the ultimate power to act in cases of conflict with narrow, regional interests. From this perspective, the proper response to regional concerns and identities is not to transfer greater power to provincial governments, but to strengthen the attachments of Canadians to their national government. Reinforcing the symbols of nationhood and ensuring that regional interests can be readily expressed and accommodated within national institutions are the keys to a more balanced Canada.

The federal Liberal government, determined to reverse the trend to decentralization in the last two decades, seized on part of this agenda. Patriation itself was to be a symbolic capstone of national independence. But more important would be the Charter of Rights and Freedoms. By vesting the rights of citizens in a national document, held by virtue of their membership in the national community and protected by a national court, loyalty and identity with Canada would be strengthened in the long run. Moreover, the Charter, with its abstract, universalistic values, might in the long run be a device to check regional cultural differences. The federal government did not seek many new powers, but it did insist on strong measures to protect the Canadian common market, and served notice that it was prepared to exercise much more vigorously the powers the BNA Act gave it.

These two conceptions of the nature of this country underlay the intense intergovernmental struggle over the *process* of constitutional change. Ultimately, the federal government argued, sovereignty lies in the Parliament of Canada, the only body elected by all Canadians. Legally, there was no barrier to Parliament unilaterally petitioning Britain to amend the constitution; and there was, Ottawa asserted, an absolute obligation on Britain to accede to any such request. The provinces, on the other hand, insisted that unilateralism violated the essential nature of federalism—the divided nature of sovereignty—and that agreement of both levels of government was absolutely required. The battle over procedure, in Alan Cairns' words, "helped turn the constitutional process into a brutal power struggle which undermined civility and trust."

These conflicting visions of Canada lay at the heart of the submissions made to the Supreme Court in the constitutional reference. In grappling with this controversy, the court was confronted with a fascinating array of basic issues in constitutional doctrine: the relationship between law and convention; the nature of Canadian federalism; and the proper role of the courts in the political life of the nation. Seldom has a single case raised such an imposing set of theoretical issues. The complexities of these issues and the nature of the court's response to them are evaluated thoroughly by William Lederman, Gil Rémillard and Peter Russell.

The Supreme Court's carefully balanced judgement and the Accord that followed represented a fundamental trade-off between these competing visions of Canada. Perhaps the greatest victory for the provincialist view was the blocking of unilateral patriation itself and achieving judicial endorsement of the view that Canadian federalism implies shared sovereignty. As Lederman concludes, the majority opinion of the court held, in effect, that Canada was essentially a classical federation, with equally sovereign levels of government. In the settlement itself, the major provincialist victory was the new amending formula, three aspects of which reflected provincialist assumptions. First, no single province is privileged with a formal veto, as Ontario and Quebec were in earlier proposals. Second, the "opting-out" provision means that any province can protect its powers and resources against any national majority. Third, the amendment procedure remains restricted to governments. The original federal Resolution had included a referendum procedure, by which Ottawa (but not provinces) could call a referendum if governments were not able to agree. Provinces feared that such a device could have been used to exploit a transient popular mood to bring about major change in the federal-provincial relationship.

The most obvious centralist victory was finally to have brought about patriation and to have won consent for a Charter, albeit one modified substantially to allay provincial concerns. But equally important, Ottawa had succeeded in blocking much of the provincialist agenda advocated in recent years; there was no transfer of powers to the provinces, and no provincial limitations on the broad discretionary federal powers.

So the settlement was a compromise between competing dreams of Canada. It did not reconcile those views. As Alan Cairns predicts, those who search for some single vision animating the Constitution Act will search in vain. The settlement did not provide a new consensus on the balance between region and nation, and represented only a temporary cease-fire in the struggle between governments. The federal government continues to battle the provincialist trend of post-war history, and has sought to assert its policy influence in a wide array of policy fields. But the federal capacity to act as a national government is weakened, perhaps fatally, by its lack of a truly national base. Authority can be meaningless without political support. Regional discontents remain intense, as the election of a western separatist to the Alberta Legislature underscored shortly after the Accord was signed. Yet our central political institutions do not fully reflect regional interests, and nothing in the settlement changed that sad fact. Among the authors represented here, Roger Gibbins is the most forceful exponent of the need for a major re-vitalization of our national institutions. Rather than providing for representation of all regions at the centre of power in Ottawa through electoral reform or a new Senate, Gibbins fears that the constitutional struggle itself left many Canadians in this country's diverse regions with an even more tenuous national sense of Canadian life.

Thus the Constitution Act did little to resolve the major strains within the federal system which launched the search for renewal in the first place. The challenges posed by dualism and regionalism survive almost untouched. The setttlement was not a great act of nation-building; it established no new consensus at the heart of Confederation. Probably it was unrealistic to hope for a lasting reconciliation of the conflicting views of Canada. But, more seriously, the Accord did not even provide a framework within which the continuing tensions between French and English, region and nation, government and government, might be better managed in the future.

Democracy and Constitutional Reform: For Canadians, democracy is an essential and unquestioned principle, the very foundation of their political community. Yet democracy is a concept that has been given many meanings, and nations that pronounce themselves to be democratic often conduct their political affairs very differently. What, then, is the Canadian conception of a democratic society? For several contributors to this volume, the constitutional experience, especially the role of the public in it and the debate over the protection of rights, provides revealing answers to this fundamental question.

This is hardly surprising. The constitution is the basic framework of our political system, defining many of the relationships between different units of government, and between government and citizens. Surely the ways in which such fundamental elements of government are changed, and the content of those changes, should provide an ideal test case of our ideas about democracy. Moreover, the constitutional debate that Canada has just undergone was so broad that it touched the interests of virtually every Canadian and every major group in the country. Who participated, in what way, and with what effect surely must speak loudly about how we conceive of power and authority.

Democratic theorists have long differed over the extent of public involvement in a truly democratic polity. Advocates of the representative conception of democracy argue that in modern societies democratic government is essentially a mechanism by which the public selects representatives to rule in its name through periodic, competitive elections. In effect, the public's role is to choose whom it will consent to obey. Advocates of direct or participatory democracy, on the other hand, contend that reliance on representative institutions alone drains democracy of its central ideal—the continuing involvement of an informed public in its own governance—and legitimates elitist patterns of politics. While there are no pure direct democracies in modern nations, proponents of this conception insist that a truly democratic society is one that strives to enhance public participation and consultation wherever possible.[6]

Measured against these two standards, the constitutional struggle reveals Canadian politics to be a process of democratic elitism tempered by occasional populist anger. In this, our present is largely an extension of our past. Constitution-making in this country has always been an elite process. The negotiations that shaped the BNA Act in the mid-1860s were conducted by colonial leaders and imperial officials, and their creation was never submitted to any form of popular legitimation. Indeed, some of the Fathers of Confederation took great pains to avoid an electoral, or even legislative ratification, for fear that their careful compromises would be defeated. This tradition has survived in only slightly modified form the transition to modern politics. With the exceptions of Newfoundland's referendum on entry into Confederation and Quebec's referendum on withdrawal from it, constitutional deliberations have been the preserve of political leaders, operating often behind closed doors.

The roots of this tradition extend deep in Canadian political thought. Gil Rémillard sees it as the modern reflection of the ancient British doctrine that sovereignty lies in the Crown-in-Parliament, contrary to the French and American traditions, which invest sovereignty in the people. Reg Whitaker agrees, and adds that this conception of sovereignty was reinforced by profoundly anti-democratic strains in the political ideology of nineteenth-century Canadian political leaders such as Sir John A. Macdonald. Approaching the same conclusion from below rather than above, George Woodcock attributes the survival of an elitist constitutional politics to "the lack of a true insurrectionary tradition in Canada."

Populist resistance did emerge in the farmer and Progressive movements, and in the rebellions of the Métis, but it was clearly sporadic and outside of the mainstream of Canadian political development.

Institutional barriers to popular sovereignty have reinforced these ideological traditions. The modern parliamentary system concentrates power in the hands of the Cabinet and creates a relatively closed policy process, with direct participation limited to ministers, senior civil servants and well-organized interest groups. In comparison, Parliament and provincial Legislatures, poorly organized groups, and the broad public can only exhort from outside. Federalism reinforces this pattern. The complexity of intergovernmental relations confuses and weakens the lines of accountability between governments and the electorate, and the critical policy issues are often hammered out in secret negotiations between Ottawa and the provinces.

Indeed, more generally, federalism raises profound issues for democratic discourse. As Whitaker argues, the division of powers between co-ordinate governments "in effect, denies the universal efficacy of the national majority as the embodiment of the sovereign democratic will." The critical question in federations becomes: Which majorities, for which purposes? For some, ultimately it is the Canada-wide majority which must prevail.[7] For others, including many contributors to this volume, a truly democratic Canada must at least respect the need for a double majority of English and French Canada in major questions. And for George Woodcock, majoritarian democracy can only work in small communities; hence his proposals for radical decentralization. Federalism thus creates deep ambiguities for majoritarian notions of democracy, and has complicated the appeal of popular sovereignty in Canadian life.

The elitist tradition of Canadian politics has had, according to some of the contributors here, corrosive consequences for the vitality of both the Canadian nation and contemporary constitutional discourse. Whitaker argues, for example, that the lack of a commitment to popular sovereignty has undermined the nation-building efforts of successive federal governments since 1867, and has impoverished Canadian political debate, diverting attention away from major philosophical questions of liberty, equality, obligation, and relations between citizen and state. For Woodcock, the lack of public involvement has sapped our constitutional experience of any sense of historic mission, of any feeling that through their constitution Canadians are making a collective statement about themselves and their conception of the good society.

But the recent constitutional battle also reveals the modern version of populist resistance to elitist traditions. The public's impatience with its own exclusion from the drafting of a new constitution became marked as the process ground on. Repeated calls for a popularly elected constituent assembly reflected a pervasive assumption that constitutional renewal was too important to be left to ministers and officials operating in the twilight of Cabinet secrecy. The local citizen groups that sprang up spontaneously after the election of the Parti Québécois in 1976 could find no channel through which to express their concerns, and the federal government had to create the special Task Force on Canadian Unity to listen to them. Later in the process, the women's movement and the native organizations faced even more intense frustrations. Indeed, Chaviva Hošek argues that the very fact that women had to operate as an "interest group" testifies eloquently to "the failure of our national institutions to represent the specific concerns of women as women adequately." Her dismissal of the elaborate system of federal-provincial bargaining is blunt: "Anyone watching a First Ministers' Conference sees no women in the sea of grey and blue three-piece suits." Natives faced similar barriers. Despite repeated, formal assurances of participation in the process of constitutional revision, meaningful consultations never took place. As Sanders observes, in the real world of federal-provincial warfare, there was little room for the first Canadians.

This pent-up pressure flooded forth when the Special Joint Committee began its hearings, as public groups and individual Canadians stepped forward to involve themselves in the process of constitutional renewal. The contrast in priorities between the intergovernmental and the public agendas was stark. While governments focussed primarily on competing amending formulae and divisions of power, the committee deliberations were monopolized by the Charter of Rights and Freedoms. Moreover, as the papers by Hošek and Sanders reveal, public groups brought to the debate some of the idealism, some of the sense of mission and of a better society that was so lacking, at least in English Canada. The outrage that greeted the Accord's watering down of the formal protections for women and natives, and the unprecedented cross-country campaigns that forced first ministers to reinstate them at least in part, stand as dramatic evidence of the contradiction between an elitist politics and an age of heightened democratic expectations.

The lack of formal public legitimation of the constitutional changes through a referendum or special election is also lamented most interestingly by Gil Rémillard. Drawing on French philosophical tradition, he sees a written constitution as a social contract that guarantees order and justice, and insists that "a democratic government cannot pretend to act democratically by changing the terms of the social contract of a society without the latter's express consent." The need for public legitimation was most acute in his own Quebec, since the social contract was being altered against the wishes of the provincial government and in ways that did not reflect most Quebecers' understanding of the renewed federation they had been promised during the referendum. For Rémillard, the constitutional *fait accompli* will, as a result, be forever tainted with illegitimacy, a stain that cannot be washed away by subsequent elections. "Canada's leaders in

1981," he concludes, "made the same mistake as Sir John A. Macdonald and Sir Georges-Étienne Cartier who, in 1865, called upon the sovereignty of Parliament in order to avoid consulting the people."

The fate of the federal government's proposal to include a referendum in the procedures governing future constitutional reforms is one more graphic indicator of the nature of Canadian democracy. Prime Minister Trudeau had defended this idea as a symbolic means of embedding sovereignty not in the institutions of government, but in the people. The vigorous opposition to the use of referenda to amend the constitution, and its elimination from the Accord, represented another classic re-affirmation of our elitist constitutional traditions. The question posed by Whitaker, however, is whether such traditions are worth cherishing.

The second dimension of the constitutional process that revealed much about our democratic traditions was the debate over the Charter of Rights and Freedoms. The Charter stands out as the single most important innovation in the new provisions. It may well also stand as the most enduring contribution of Prime Minister Trudeau's long tenure in office, for there is no doubt that his personal commitment was crucial to its adoption. The lack of an entrenched bill of rights was not pushed onto the constitutional agenda by pressure from the public. On the contrary, as Chaviva Hošek's comparison between Canadian and American feminist movements reveals, many social groups who were battling for a more equal place in Canadian life were ambivalent or internally divided over the importance of a constitutional statement of rights. The Charter was placed firmly on the political agenda by the federal government alone. In part, as we have seen, this had a strategic value in the intergovernmental wars. But the Charter also reflected Trudeau's long-standing commitment to individualist values and to their entrenchment in the constitution of the land.

The Charter was, and is, the subject of intense controversy, a controversy which was again rooted in part in conflicting visions of the ideal system of government. Traditions of the supremacy of Parliament and of the people's elected representatives clashed with an insistence on formal limitations on the state. These disagreements are reflected throughout the essays in this volume. While none of the contributors rejects the basic principle of entrenched rights, they divide sharply on the adequacy of the new Charter itself. Don Smiley and Reg Whitaker, for example, disagree on whether the Charter should have been limited solely to basic political and legal rights, or extended to incorporate a much wider array of social or equality rights—a disagreement flowing in part from different conceptions of a just democracy. But more revealing is that great compromise between parliamentary sovereignty and liberalism, the *non obstante* clause. For some, this clause symbolically gutted the Charter at the moment of its birth and confirmed rather than altered Canadian political practice. Others, including Walter Tarnopolsky, are more optimistic. The best defence of human rights is a vigilant and informed public, he insists; if the electorate does not act as the ultimate guarantor of human rights, then "bills of rights and Supreme Courts will be irrelevant."

The full impact of the Charter will only become apparent over several decades, as courts and citizens adjust to the new legal order. Both Tarno-polsky and Smiley suspect that the Supreme Court will be inclined to interpret the Charter's provisions cautiously, and avoid supplanting legislators as the primary policy-makers in the field of human rights. But the impact of the Charter will also depend on the response of individuals, groups and corporations to this new avenue for political action. Will Canada become a more litigious society, as some have predicted? Will the Charter become an instrument of greater cultural integration, as Canadians from coast to coast take pride in their common rights? Or is the defence of individual and group rights an inherently fragmenting rather than unifying process, one premised on conflict rather than co-operation, as Smiley speculates? Brave indeed is the person who seeks to prejudge history decisively on such questions.

Our constitutional life thus reveals much about the nature of Can-adian democracy. Champions of representative democracy can rest assured that those historic traditions have been preserved with only minor challenge. Those who yearn for greater public participation in political life, on the other hand, will agree that both the process by which we changed our constitution and the substance of the changes themselves fall far short of their aspirations for a democratic Canada. They may, however, take hope that the experience of the Special Joint Committee and the angry mobilization following the November Accord will ensure that constitu-tion-making will never again be allowed to be a purely governmental process.

Lost Opportunities
Despite the specific gains represented by patriation, the amending formula and the Charter, a sense of lost opportunities still pervades the constitu-tional settlement. At moments during the long debate, especially in the aftermath of the first election victory of the Parti Québécois, there was a widespread sense of openness to change, an unprecedented acceptance that significant reform was necessary. A wider and wider range of possibilities was enthusiastically debated, and heady expectations about the future flourished. November 1981 brought a thousand hopes crashing to the ground. In Daniel Latouche's words, "Now we know. There will be no new Canada."

Disappointment permeates most of the essays that follow. Different authors see the missed possibilities in various ways. Gérard Bergeron insists that the federal government wasted a unique chance to lead Quebec away from its penchant for independence, adding ominously that "opportunities like the post-referendum period do not occur every day." Roger Gibbins laments "a lost opportunity, perhaps tragically so, to re-vitalize national institutions and political life." While some authors do see gains for human rights, Reg Whitaker saw his hopes for a more thoroughly democratic Canada dashed in the final Accord. Donald Smiley can find "little cause for self-congratulation in the Constitution Act." Even Alan Cairns, perhaps the most enthusiastic, can manage only "a restrained half cheer." There are, he concludes, "no constitutional utopias. We have to be satisfied with the stumbling efforts of imperfect men."

Disenchantment has been the bitter product of what was clearly, in retrospect, a collective national illusion about the ease with which political institutions could be re-designed. The major lesson to be drawn from recent Canadian experience is the supreme difficulty of achieving sweeping constitutional reform. Even though all parties to the dispute agreed on the need for significant changes, and even though they engaged in an effort at constitution-making unparalleled in its intensity since 1867, the settlement represents a modest adaptation of the existing constitution. Continuity, not change, was the primary victor.

The explanation for the limited nature of the Constitution Act is to be found in the intractability of the underlying conflicts and in the complexity of the procedures through which change had to be enacted. Regional and linguistic conflict were firmly rooted in Canadian society and could not be eliminated by institutional tinkering. The rules governing constitution-making ensured that the federal and provincial governments, the primary exponents of sharply conflicting visions of Canada, had to be the central participants in the process. Because each side preferred the existing constitution to the other's vision of the future, they vetoed each other, each cancelling out the reformist impulses in the other.

The difficulty of securing reform does not mean, however, that the final outcome was inevitable or predetermined by some irresistible historical or social forces. The constitutional Accord was a delicate compromise, the product of an often chaotic struggle in which political leaders repeatedly had to make difficult choices, fashioning and re-fashioning their positions on reform and their strategies for battle. Different outcomes at key turning-points could have altered the constellation of interests in play: a "oui" vote in the referendum; the retention of power by the Clark government in Ottawa or the election of a Ryan government in Quebec City; a different emphasis in the Supreme Court judgement; and so on.

Just how much freedom of choice political leaders really did enjoy during the constitutional debate is the subject of interesting differences in the papers that follow. Raymond Hudon and Pierre Fournier, for example, strongly emphasize the role of the economic realities of Canada in shaping the alignment of the federalist and provincialist camps. The federal government's general economic strategy, the National Energy Policy and its proposals for strengthening the economic union transformed the constitutional deliberations into an economic struggle, they insist. Economic interest defined government positions. The industrial centre of the country, represented by the federal and Ontario governments, was pitted against the resource-dependent peripheries, whose provincial governments struggled to control the economic destinies of their regions.

Other contributors place their primary emphasis on the freedom enjoyed by political leaders and the importance of their choices. Alan Cairns confronts this issue head on: "The constitutional struggles of the sixties and seventies do not lend themselves to explanations of social forces bending men and institutions to their dictates." Daniel Latouche and Roger Gibbins also emphasize the role of political visions and strategies, attributing the limited outcome to the failures of the principal challengers to the federal system—Quebec and the West. In a paper which he himself describes as having "the aura of a confession" from an active and *indépendantiste* intellectual, Latouche places much of the blame for Quebec's continued lack of success in constitutional discussions since 1960 on its own failure to establish a consensus internally on specific constitutional goals and to pursue them consistently and effectively. Constant ambiguity and a reluctance to conclude any agreement were the consequences. Similarly, Gibbins argues that, historically, western political protest never generated a constitutional vision that came to grips fully with the region's minority status within national politics, leaving westerners poorly equipped for the battles of the last decade. "Lacking an alternative constitutional vision, western provincial governments fell into a largely defensive posture, protecting an institutional status quo that should never have been defended, not in its present form, and not by the West."

Strong personalities also figure largely in the pictures that emerge in this book. Even some contributors who usually see political life as tightly constrained by economic and social pressures provide highly personalized accounts, depicting the constitutional controversy as a titanic struggle between strong-willed politicians. Some see Prime Minister Trudeau's icy determination to break the impasse, through the "Gaullist" act of unilateralism if necessary, as providing the traumatizing momentum essential for some kind of settlement; others see the evolution of Quebec nationalism as torn between contradictory loyalties to two charismatic leaders: Prime Minister Trudeau and Premier Lévesque. Attributing such importance to particular personalities implies that change in the cast of central actors could usher in a new era in Canadian federalism. For Gérard Bergeron, for example, another prime minister "could entirely change the situation."

Yet while changes in the personalities and the proposals at the heart of the battle could well have altered the details of the outcome, perhaps significantly, they would not have eliminated the fundamentally difficult nature of extensive constitutional change. The experience of other countries in recent decades suggests that our limited successes are hardly unique. During recent years, efforts to change the basic institutions and rules of political life have become a recurring feature in many western countries, including some whose political structures have been stable over long periods of time. Belgium, France, Great Britain, Spain, the United States and West Germany have all debated reforms in their constitutions during the last decade. While demands for change abound, however, examples of major constitutional change are rare. Countries facing the prospect of a complete breakdown in the old political regime can sometimes dramatically transform their constitutional order, as did Spain in the aftermath of Franco's death. But the predominant pattern elsewhere is one of frustrated, or only partially fulfilled expectations, not wholesale renewal.[8]

An inevitable dynamic underlies this. The demand for constitutional change itself reflects lack of consensus about some important aspect of the political system. But the norms governing constitutional reform normally require a high degree of consensus on the changes to be enacted and therefore make it difficult to mobilize sufficient agreement to succeed. Lack of consensus makes constitutional change necessary. The same lack of consensus makes constitutional change particularly difficult. Canadian experience certainly conforms to this pattern. Broader constitutional agreement could only have followed from a prior consensus. However, once the constitutional genie was out of the bottle—once its legitimacy had been called into question—then it could not be put back. Because the constitution lacked consensus, it had to be debated. But the same lack of consensus made it impossible to agree on a new one.

Notes

1. Canada, Task Force on Canadian Unity, *A Future Together: Observations and Recommendations* (Ottawa: Supply and Services, Canada, 1979).
2. See Quebec, *Québec-Canada: A New Deal* (Québec: Editeur officiel, 1979); and Quebec Liberal Party, Constitutional Committee, *A New Canadian Federation* (Montreal: 1980).
3. For detailed summaries of events from the publication of the Parti Québécois' White Paper on Sovereignty-Association to the hearing before the Supreme Court, see Ronald J. Zukowsky, *Struggle over the Constitution* (Kingston: Institute of Intergovernmental Relations, 1981). For events from the Supreme Court decision to the Accord of November 1981 and after, see Sheilagh M. Dunn, *The Year in Review, 1981* (Kingston: Institute of Intergovernmental Relations, 1982).
4. Britain, House of Commons, First Report from the Foreign Affairs Committee, Session 1980–81, *British North America Acts: The Role of Parliament*. The Canadian federal government attacked the Kershaw Report in *The Role of the United Kingdom in the Amendment of the Canadian Constitution*, Background Paper (Ottawa: Publications Canada, 1981). For the British committee's

reply, see Second Report from the Foreign Affairs Committee, Session 1980–81, *Supplementary Report on the British North America Acts: The Role of Parliament.*

5. For another set of commentaries on the reference case, see Peter Russell *et al.*, *The Court and the Constitution* (Kingston: Institute of Intergovernmental Relations, 1982).

6. See Carole Pateman, *Participation and Democratic Theory* (Cambridge: Cambridge University Press, 1970) for a discussion of these themes.

7. See, for example, Garth Stevenson, *Unfulfilled Union: Canadian Federalism and National Unity*, rev. ed. (Toronto: Gage Publishing, 1982).

8. For a comparative view of constitutional change, see Keith Banting and Richard Simeon, eds. *Redesigning the State: The Politics of Constitutional Reform* (London: Macmillan Press, forthcoming); and Edward McWhinney, *Constitution-making: Principles, Processes, Practice* (Toronto: University of Toronto Press, 1981).

Part II/Federalism and Constitutional Change

Chapter 2/The Politics of Constitutional Conservatism

Alan C. Cairns

> Tradition means giving votes to the most obscure of all
> classes—our ancestors. It is the democracy of the dead. Tradi-
> tion refuses to submit to the small and arrogant oligarchy of
> those who merely happen to be walking around.
>
> — G.K. Chesterton

The dust is slowly settling on the battlefield of intergovernmental warfare over a new or revised constitution. The truce called the Constitution Act has produced an uneasy peace. The retrospective stage, of the use and abuse of history, is now upon us. The search for truth and the search for partisan advantage vie for our attention. The race is on between those who seek to uncover what happened and those who prefer to conceal yesterday's realities, and so plant false clues to mislead the unwary. For, as always, there are votes to be won, reputations to be made and destroyed, and causes to be served. In these matters truth is not always as serviceable as fiction, and may be jettisoned by the politically minded if it gets in the way of advantage. It is, accordingly, not much easier to keep one's feet on the ground now that the first phase of our constitutional renewal has begun to fade into history than it was when we were caught up in the drama of its unfolding.

Those who profess objectivity may only be practising a more subtle partisanship, possibly unbeknownst to themselves. Academics, who pride themselves on being above or outside politics, may be caught up in a war of the schools in their own discipline and thus suffer from their own special brand of disrespect for what really happened, and why. So, in what follows, we are treading on treacherous ground. There is no other place to walk.

This chapter has two objectives. First, it will underscore and attempt to explain the conservatism of the Canadian constitutional system, man-ifested in the remarkable difficulties it places in the way of advocates of formal change. Second, it will also argue that the package of changes which finally got over all the hurdles, and which emerged as the Constitution Act, cannot be explained in any deterministic fashion as the result of some inexorable unfolding, but on the contrary was the precarious result of a byzantine process in which accidents, personality, skill and sheer will-power were central to the final outcome.[1]

Introduction

There is no lack of competing perspectives that can be fruitfully employed in attempting to make sense of our recent constitutional struggles. Perhaps the most obvious approach is to focus on the modifications to the constitution made by the Constitution Act and to seek their explanation in terms of various antecedent conditions and the strategies of the main actors. This emphasis on change, especially congenial to the social science community, is unquestionably a necessary part of an inclusive assessment of the great chess game of constitutional politics that both entertained and exhausted Canadians in recent years. The package of changes now embodied in the revised constitution, particularly the Canadian Charter of Rights and Freedoms and a new amending formula, clearly surpasses in significance any previous amendment in Canadian history. It is not unacceptably far-fetched, therefore, to suggest that the 1982 additions to the constitution will have major effects on the Canadian polity.

Nevertheless, an exclusive stress on change and its determinants has serious drawbacks. It too easily leads to an overlooking of the constitutional continuities which dwarf change in extent and significance. Certainly the recent constitutional changes, if not trivial or minuscule, seem relatively modest when placed alongside the slowly evolving traditions and long-established constitutional practices deriving from Confederation and before. Our constitutional system was only modified, not overthrown by our recent constitutional renewal.

The limited nature of the change is readily apparent from several perspectives. The twelve-item constitutional agenda established by the first ministers after the Quebec referendum proved to be far too ambitious. Of the twelve items, only resource ownership and interprovincial trade, equalization and regional disparities, the Charter of Rights, and patriation with an amending formula got past all of the roadblocks to achieve some kind of constitutional resolution. Eight other items—communications, the Senate, the Supreme Court, family law, fisheries, off-shore resources, powers over the economy, and a statement of principles—were put aside for the future.

Not only did this twelve-item agenda experience severe attrition as the constitutional process developed, but it was originally said to represent only the first of a several stage process of constitutional reform. Now, with only a limited portion of the first stage achieved, the momentum for a further major burst of constitutional renewal seems all but dissipated. The requirement to hold a constitutional conference by April 1983, with the accompanying requirement of an agenda item "respecting constitutional matters that directly affect the aboriginal peoples of Canada," is unlikely to elicit extensive further constitutional change.

This limited outcome, it must be stressed, was achieved after constitutional efforts unparallelled in Canadian history. No other period since Confederation manifested a concentration of energy on constitutional reform even remotely equivalent to that of the past few years.

Furthermore, the constitutional system possessed by Canadians at the time of the Quebec referendum, and which still survives in its essentials, had been the subject of widespread denigration and scorn from a variety of actors and commentators for the previous two decades. Few would have speculated only a few years ago that the Canadian constitution, never endowed with the symbolism and majesty of the American constitution, could have emerged so relatively unscathed from the battering of so many diverse opponents. Then, too, especially in the sixties when worlds were made and unmade by pamphleteers and gurus, constitutional change seemed so easy, little more than a matter of good intentions, a pencil and a note pad. Against such facile assumptions the revealed reality of the almost impregnable barriers to large-scale formal change attests to the discrepancy between the flexibility of language and the inflexibilities of the world to which it is addressed.

In retrospect, it is evident that the constitutional process had a remark-able capacity to elicit a striking diversity and extent of proposals for constitutional change. By comparison, the constitutional thinking of the thirties was cribbed and confined. Equally striking in our recent efforts, however, was the ruthless winnowing process which resulted in such a limited constitutional outcome. No extraordinary insight is required to observe how much remains the same, to assert that our major constitutional problems survive almost untouched, and to note with varying degrees of surprise, sadness, or anger that the Parti Québécois government of Quebec, whose accession to power in 1976 was the major catalyst of the drive for constitutional change, was left embittered on the sidelines when the constitution came home, deprived of its veto and with a weakened jurisdiction.

The Parti Québécois goal of sovereignty-association was never dis-cussed at the bargaining table as the Quebec electorate decisively refused to authorize the provincial government to see what terms, if any, could be struck with the other governments of the country it hoped to leave. The competing Quebec constitutional proposals of the provincial Liberal Party never attained the status of an official government position, as Claude Ryan was unable to unseat the Lévesque government. Thus the behaviour of the Quebec electorate in defeating the Parti Québécois' sovereignty-association proposals, but refusing to elect a provincial Liberal govern-ment with alternative proposals, greatly reduced the Quebec impact in the constitutional discussions that followed the referendum. By a profound irony, which may have long-run tragic consequences, the decisive stages of a process of constitutional renewal originally undertaken primarily to respond to Quebec had only an ineffectual provincial representation from Quebec. Lévesque and his colleagues were on the defensive, toothless tigers in the struggle for a renewed federalism they neither believed in nor thought attainable.

The Quebec experience is not unique. It is not only sovereignty-association and Quebec independence that were jettisoned in the confusing march to the Constitution Act. The road is littered with proposals that fell by the wayside, reflecting aspirations raised and then shattered in a bruising process of accommodation to the narrow limits of the attainable. The proposals of the Task Force on Canadian Unity (Pépin-Robarts), in spite of praise from various political commentators, languished on the sidelines as they never received endorsement from any of the governments that dominated the process. Fifth region status for British Columbia, a transformed Senate, proportional representation, a referendum role for the people in the amending procedures, Supreme Court reform, and innumerable other projects and proposals have been put back on the shelf to await the political maestro of the future once again capable of breathing life into them.

The major lesson to be drawn from recent Canadian constitutional experience, then, is the truly impressive capacity of the existing constitutional system to survive, to outlast its detractors, and to frustrate those who seek its fundamental transformation. The constitutional exercise of recent years is a practical lesson in the politics of constitutional conservatism, which deserves no less explanation than the politics of constitutional change. Each interacts with the other, and neither can be understood in isolation from the other. However, in spite of the general academic predisposition to be more attracted to understanding the exciting phenomenon of change than the stodginess of stability, the next two sections of this paper seek to explain why there was so little formal change when so many were convinced that the Canadian constitutional system was about to be turned upside down, and so many directed their efforts to extensive reform.

Sources of Conservatism

Conflicting Objectives: The capacity of the constitutional system to survive in spite of widespread dissatisfaction with its functioning was partly due to basic divergences of opinion over the desired direction of change. This served the interests of the status quo. The constitutional goals of the competing governments and the incompatibility of many of their objectives have been described elsewhere[2] and need not be given detailed repetition here. An illustration of the extent and nature of the profound differences that surfaced in the constitutional struggle is, however, necessary to an understanding of the barriers to consensual change.

At the very core of the intergovernmental conflict was a profound difference of opinion over the relation of constitutional change to the societies and economies of the country, and over the direction in which the federal system should go. A pervasive assumption, verging on a new conventional wisdom, was that the federal government had lost contact with the vigorous nationalism of post-Duplessis Quebec and the only slightly less demanding regionalism of English Canada in the sixties and seventies. From this perspective, constitutional renewal was designed to make the federal system more congruent with the underlying realities of a politically assertive Quebec and a provincialized English Canada. This perspective was also fed by the widespread belief that Canadian federalism was in a long-run decentralizing phase due to a variety of socio-economic, cultural and political considerations. The task of constitutional renewal was to accommodate these underlying forces. Society was the master, the political system was the superstructure. Accordingly, the new federalism had to be a positive response to the province-building forces based on the powerful realities of dualism and regionalism.

Since the reality of the country had come to be defined in terms of a developing re-alignment of social forces behind provincial governments, proposals for accommodative constitutional change inevitably favoured the provinces. This was most strikingly the case with respect to Quebec. The fact that the Parti Québécois was committed to independence logically seemed to imply that a constitutional response within federalism, and responsive to Quebec concerns, would result in enhanced jurisdiction for the Quebec government. So powerful and widespread was this climate of opinion that it was almost universally assumed that the unspecified constitutional renewal promised by Trudeau in the 1980 Quebec referendum would mean more power for the Quebec government.

There was, however, a competing definition of an appropriate constitutional response to provincial aggressiveness. From the perspective of the federal government under Trudeau, although not under the short-lived Clark government, the purpose of constitutional change was to strengthen Ottawa by giving it new resources to overcome the centrifugal tendencies threatening to break up the country. Thus the federal proposals for constitutional change from the late sixties to the First Ministers' Conference in 1981 were consistently informed, not by a desire to respond in an accommodative fashion to provincialism, but to weaken it, and to build a resurgent Canadianism and a stronger Ottawa to fight it.

The task of constitutional change from this perspective was not to transform the constitutional system to make it more consonant with the allegedly dominant regionalism of Canadian society. Instead, the challenge was, by an act of political will, supported by all the jurisdictional levers commanded by Ottawa, to transform Canadian society in support of federal ambitions to be once again the senior government in Canadian federalism. This posture was given an extra stimulus by the return of the Liberals to power in 1980, followed shortly after by the decisive defeat of the Parti Québécois referendum. As Bruce Doern astutely observed, this federal effort at re-assertiveness was not confined to the constitutional front, but was also displayed in the energy field, in intergovernmental fiscal relations, and elsewhere. The 1981–82 Liberal spending priorities reflected "what is perhaps the most coherent assertion of political belief and principle by the Liberals since the early years of the Pearson Government." The guiding Liberal belief was simply "that there is a sense of Canadian nationhood and that it is fundamentally based on an identification by individual Canadians with their national institutions, including the federal government."[3] The task of government policy, accordingly, was sedulously to foster and cultivate that identification. In the constitutional field the Liberals acted on the premise that the provincial governments were far more weakly rooted than the strident provincialism of provincial premiers suggested, and that a coast-to-coast nation was struggling to find a constitutional expression that Ottawa was more than willing to provide.

This general federal-provincial conflict was supplemented by an additional conflict over the appropriate future relationship of the anglophone and francophone communities to the governments of the federal system. Ottawa sought to define Canada as a coast-to-coast community in which the French language was not confined to Quebec, but had a national extension, and the English language was equally protected and thriving in Quebec. This Liberal vision of Canada required for its implementation a profound wrenching of Canadian history in a new direction, resulting in serious confrontations with many of the provinces. It required the provinces to adopt a national perspective in their provincial language policies.

The difference in federal-provincial perspectives was cogently summed up by the Pépin-Robarts commission:

> Canada, seen from the federal government's perspective, is a linguistically dual federal state composed of two societies—one French-speaking and one English-speaking—which extend geographically beyond the borders of any one province. Thus the federal government believes that it is necessary that this linguistic duality be more fully reflected in Canada's central political institutions and in federal policies and programs.
>
> To the provincial governments, the picture is different. With one exception [New Brunswick], each of them serves a provincial population whose vast majority shares one language.[4]

The Trudeau objective of protecting and fostering linguistic duality at the provincial level, specifically in education and in the use and enjoyment of a range of provincial government services, required the provinces to be subordinated to certain national principles. This necessarily precluded a sensitive response by provincial Cabinets to the cues and pressures deriving from their own provincial milieus. Parliamentary supremacy and majoritarianism at the provincial level were to be restrained in the interests of official language minorities. Provincial governments were to become servants of national purposes. This bilingualism goal required the successful imposition on the provinces of English Canada of a limited acceptance of dualism, which was far more natural to any federal government than to provincial political elites and electorates outside of New Brunswick and, possibly, Ontario. The Liberal goal of fostering linguistic duality within Quebec also directly confronted the persistent thrust of a succession of

Quebec governments in the sixties and seventies to secure and extend the primacy of the French language. The differences between the Liberals and the Parti Québécois over the nature of community within Quebec spilled over into differences over the linkages between francophones inside and outside Quebec. The Parti Québécois objective was to separate francophones in Quebec, re-labelled Québécois, from French Canada as a whole. The federal Liberal goal was to keep the concept of French Canada alive, for it had the useful property of crossing provincial borders and linking francophones together regardless of their provincial location. It was thus hostile to Quebec nationalism.

At the heart of the Quebec-Ottawa confrontation was a basic difference of assumption as to the boundaries of linguistic communities in Canada and their relationship to the governments of the federal state. The Parti Québécois, in its pursuit of sovereignty-association, sought total political responsibility for the preservation and nourishment of the French fact in an independent Quebec. The goal of the federal Liberals was to protect French Canadians throughout the country by means of entrenched constitutional rights binding on all levels of government. In its purest form, the Parti Québécois goal required the elimination of the federal government role in Quebec. In its more restricted form after the referendum defeat, the Lévesque government sought to ensure that Quebec was the primary government of the Québécois nation it was fostering. The Liberal goal, by contrast, required a reduction in the power of the Quebec government to shape the linguistic evolution of Quebec, by constitutionally shoring up the existence of the anglophone community in the demographic heartland of French Canada. The overall federal purpose was thus clear, consistent and public. Ottawa sought to preserve linguistic duality in Quebec in order to counter tendencies to equate Quebec exclusively with its francophone majority, and to keep alive the possibility of a French Canada not confined to Quebec, but vital and flourishing in Ontario, New Brunswick and, possibly with more hope than realism, in small pockets of settlement elsewhere.

These profound differences in the major premises of the desirable shape of future government-society relationships constantly got in the way of reaching a constitutional agreement. The compromises that can be fairly easily developed when differences concern matters of technique or detail are much less attainable when large issues of principle animate the parties seeking agreement.

The Procedural Bottleneck: The procedures available for constitutional change compounded the difficulties deriving from competing government objectives. The possibility of reaching an acceptable compromise was indelibly affected by the ill-defined procedures for constitutional change bequeathed to the main constitutional actors by their predecessors. The inability of previous generations to regularize, and thus constitutionalize, the amending procedure had an overwhelmingly deleterious effect on the constitutional renewal process. The available procedures for formal change were made up of a cluster of accepted rules and an uncharted, shadowy area where conflicting opinion was rife. The ambiguity of the amending procedures helped to turn the constitutional process into a brutal power struggle which undermined civility and trust. The disagreement over what was included under the domestic amending authority available exclusively to Ottawa under section 91(1)[5] of the British North America Act, and the contradictory assertions of what degree of prior political consent was necessary to legitimate a federal request to Westminster for constitutional change falling outside of section 91(1), profoundly embittered the reform process and eventually turned the courts into prominent participants.

The uncertainty attending the amending process was, of course, far from being total. It was less serious and less pervasive with respect to the domestic amending authority available to Ottawa than with respect to the amending route that involved Westminster. For the former, controversy was relatively focussed and, at least in terms of legality, restricted to rival interpretations of the precise scope of an explicit amending authority possessed by Ottawa. The capacity of Ottawa to stray beyond the core of meaning of section 91(1) was limited and, in relative terms, fairly easily controllable by the courts.

The Westminster route was much more contentious, partly because the scope of the amending authority here was much more threatening to the provinces, and partly because it involved competing interpretations of convention. The stakes were higher, and the procedures were cloudier—an almost certain recipe for tension and bitter disagreement. Acrimony was also heightened over the British route to constitutional change because the ultimate federal resort to unilateralism in the autumn of 1980 was a clear rebuff to the provincial governments, who had been intimately involved with Ottawa over the previous four months in a co-operative intergovernmental search for constitutional agreement.

Somewhat paradoxically, uncertainty and conflict over the method of obtaining constitutional change increased rather than diminished with the passage of time, and reached its highest levels in the post-referendum period. This was partly because the main federal government effort in the period leading up to the referendum was its draft Constitutional Amendment Bill (Bill C-60), which in its first stage was based on section 91(1) rather than on the potentially much more contentious resort to the British Parliament. Although in the seventies there were several federal trial balloons intimating the possibility of a unilateral approach to Westminster, these did not erode the widespread assumption that unanimous provincial consent was required for constitutional changes which affected the division of powers and the rights or privileges of the provinces.

The assumption that unanimity prevailed in these crucial areas had a decisive centrifugal effect, for by giving a veto to each government, it undermined the possibility of any overarching focus on a set of commonly agreed problems requiring solution. It gave each government the option of total selfishness without having to pay a price. It discouraged compromise by not penalizing obstinacy. It made the possibility of agreement conditional on the support of the most recalcitrant or demanding government, and since one government was committed to removing its province from Canada, any adherence to unanimity was a recipe for stalemate. Unanimity, which maximized the power to block, provided an almost unbeatable defence of the existing system wherever it could be invoked. Ironically, this made it most useful to the government least committed to Canadian federalism, for it gave the Quebec government the power to block any possible changes that might tie its people more effectively to Canada and to Ottawa.

Ottawa's search for constitutional change in the period following the election of the Parti Québécois in 1976 until the Quebec referendum was governed by the necessity of avoiding a Quebec government veto. On two previous occasions—the Fulton-Favreau amending formula of the mid-sixties and the Victoria Charter of 1971—Quebec alone dissented, and Ottawa had not proceeded with the proposed constitutional amendments. There was no reason to believe that a Quebec government seeking independence would be more co-operative than the previous Liberal administrations of Lesage and Bourassa. Lévesque, it could reasonably be assumed, was not going to co-operate in any scheme of renewed federalism which would disprove his criticism of the rigidities and insensitivities of the existing system and thus weaken the case for sovereignty-association in the build-up to the referendum. In any event, Trudeau's preferred brand of renewed federalism was essentially hostile to the interests of the Parti Québécois governing elite, for it did not stress the jurisdictional aggrandisement of the Quebec government, the only kind of constitutional change within federalism of any interest to Lévesque and his supporters.

The federal Liberal government response to this limitation on its manoeuvrability had several facets. One was to chip away at the concept of unanimity as an impossible and unacceptable straitjacket, and thus to pave the way for a full-fledged future assault should that prove necessary. This was coupled with a floating of the idea that referenda might be an acceptable alternative to intergovernmental agreement for constitutional change, for Ottawa believed with some justification that the people were more likely to be supportive of federal government ambitions than were the provincial governments. Lurking in the background was the possibility that Ottawa might petition the United Kingdom unilaterally for those amendments incapable of being implemented by Ottawa's domestic amending authority under section 91(1). Although different versions of this approach surfaced intermittently in the last half of the seventies, the possibility acquired its greatest prominence after the return of Trudeau to power in 1980.

The federal government made two major, explicit efforts to escape the paralyzing consequences of the unanimity requirement. In its first effort in 1978, with Bill C-60, Ottawa tried to achieve a limited measure of reform under the domestic authority it had under section 91(1). The constitutional matters covered by the bill included a revised Senate, to be called the House of the Federation, the Supreme Court, certain aspects of the federal executive, a preamble to the constitution and a statement of aims, and a Charter of Rights and Freedoms.

There was a certain awkwardness and incompleteness to the 1978 federal proposals, not only in what was excluded, but even with respect to what was ostensibly included. For example, initially the Charter of Rights and Freedoms would be binding only on the federal government. It would become applicable to the jurisdiction of a province only when adopted by that province, and would become entrenched only when endorsed by a formal amending process. Similarly, the provisions relating to the Supreme Court would be part of the constitution upon enactment of the bill, but would become entrenched only after appropriate constitutional amendment processes involving the provinces had been undertaken. Even the proposed preamble and the statement of aims would become entrenched only after provincial approval, although they would become part of the constitution and applicable to Ottawa on passage of the bill.

There were additional complications attendant upon Ottawa's choice of this route to constitutional renewal. In an attempt to maximize its freedom of action, Ottawa was induced to assert a very generous interpretation of what was within the latitude of its domestic amending power, where it could act alone. On the other hand, and revealing the political complexities of the process, Ottawa agreed to discuss its proposals with the provinces while simultaneously denying that any provincial agreement was necessary on those aspects of the bill it claimed fell under section 91(1). Consultation with the provinces was defined as a political courtesy, and not as a recognition of any formal provincial right to veto the federal proposals.

The most controversial component of this 1978 package was the inclusion of a complex scheme of Senate reform. Sufficient doubts existed about the legality of attempting Senate reform, which obviously directly concerned the provinces, without their concurrence that Ottawa agreed reluctantly to refer the matter to the Supreme Court. Long after the federal proposals had been sidelined by political opposition in Parliament and from the provincial governments, and when the Liberal government was no longer in office, the Supreme Court ruled that the Senate reform proposal was not within the scope of Ottawa's domestic amending authority.

This attempt to bypass the provinces had the inevitable effect of skewing the contents of the federal package in a particular direction, thus avoiding many of the issues on the constitutional agenda of the provinces, particularly the division of powers. Central to the federal effort here, of course, was the necessity of making a response to the people of Quebec which did not require the consent of the government of Quebec.[6]

The procedures of constitutional change and the controversies that surrounded them thus had a significant influence on what reforms it was feasible to pursue. To the extent that Ottawa tried to avoid provincial consent by utilizing the amending authority it possessed under section 91(1), it had only a very restricted range of manoeuvre. Many of the weaknesses and awkward features of Bill C-60 reflected Ottawa's tortuous efforts to squeeze the maximum amount of constitutional reform out of section 91(1). To the extent that resort to Westminster was the preferred strategy, the subject matter of potential amendments was greatly increased. But if unanimity was respected as an unbreakable rule, this version of the amending process tilted the scales in favour of conservatism and against significant reform.

The frustrations that flowed from unanimity were most pronounced for the federal government. Unanimity deprived Ottawa of the leadership role in constitutional change which the national government felt was rightfully hers. Furthermore, no one questioned the existence of a federal veto over constitutional change.[7] So Ottawa, secure in its legal ability to prevent constitutional change it disliked, was concerned to reduce impediments to change it sought. Accordingly, it was in Ottawa's interest to downgrade any requirement of provincial consent preceding resort to the British Parliament to a mere convention, or occasional practice, and certainly not binding.

Federal government frustration was also fed by the commitment it had given to the Quebec electorate in the referendum to achieve some measure of unspecified constitutional renewal. Consequently, once the September 1980 First Ministers' Conference had ended in a failure which Ottawa could partially attribute to the unanimity assumption, there were powerful incentives for the Liberal Cabinet to commence a process of unilateral patriation and limited amendment. Ottawa sought to exploit its privileged access to Westminster for amendments by claiming the unilateral right in law to request the British Parliament to amend the BNA Act, with no questions asked, in a manner dictated by the federal government, with or without provincial consent.

Ottawa's willingness to resort to unilateralism was also based on a developing mistrust of and retreat from executive federalism. Co-operative federalism seemed to be long ago and far away as Ottawa mandarins and ministers came to view intergovernmental diplomacy, especially of first ministers and before television cameras, as a no-win situation for the federal government. It was a forum in which they were publicly lambasted on national television by provincial governments whose appetites for "more" were considered insatiable.

This attempted unilateralism, described by the prime minister as a necessary act to break the logjam of unanimity, had convulsive effects on intergovernmental relations, on the subsequent development of the constitutional struggle, and on the contents of the package which ultimately gained the agreement of all provinces but Quebec more than a year later.

Once the federal government decided to proceed with less than unanimous provincial consent, the constitutional reform process fragmented. For the dissenting provinces, questions of substance were replaced by controversy about the methods by which the proposed reforms were being pursued. Thus those provinces opposed to the idea of a Charter, which was consistently supported by decisive majorities of the Canadian electorate, focussed their criticisms not on the Charter itself, but on the safer ground of the unilateralism by which it was to come into effect. On the other hand, the unilateral reform process elicited a very different response in the Special Joint Committee of the Senate and the House of Commons, to which the federal resolution was sent for examination. In the committee, whose proceedings were televised, questions of substance almost completely displaced concern for the procedural constitutionality of Ottawa's methods.

The fragmentation of the reform process engendered by Ottawa's push for unilateral change produced a partial division of constitutional labour which was to have a profound impact on the final constitutional package. The dissenting provinces, initially six, then eight, not only tried to block the federal effort, but also undertook the refinement of an alternative amending formula, based on earlier Alberta proposals, so that their efforts would not appear totally negative.

Throughout the autumn and winter of 1980–81, two distinct constitution-making arenas emerged with separate personnel and only partly overlapping agendas. The go-between, compromise role attempted by Saskatchewan and the sideline role of Nova Scotia could not survive the polarization between the two camps, and both ultimately joined what then came to be known as the provincial "gang of eight." In this provincial arena, where there was no public input and no federal presence, the Alberta amending formula was worked on, refined, and eventually subscribed to by the eight provinces as their constitutional Accord. The gang of eight then invited Ontario, New Brunswick and Ottawa to join and thus end the constitutional impasse. The Accord, which was simply an amending formula which as a by-product would allow patriation, was unquestionably constructed as a protective device to defend the interests of provincial governments. When released in a staged television ceremony in April 1981, it was savagely criticized by federal spokesmen as viewing Canada as no more than a nation of shopping centres. Generally, the media treated this achievement of the gang of eight with little enthusiasm and much derision.[8]

Little is known about the politics of the constitutional Accord, which was fashioned in secret meetings. But its workings were probably governed by an implicit veto based on the need to appear united in the face of the federal juggernaut, and to respond to Trudeau's reiterated taunts that the gang of eight could not agree on anything. Furthermore, it would have been politically impossible for the eight provincial premiers to have insisted on a unanimity requirement for eleven governments to proceed to Westminster if they could not attain it in the less demanding context of eight allegedly like-minded governments. The unanimity assumption had the inevitable effect of giving strong leverage to the most provincialist-minded members of the shaky coalition—Alberta, Manitoba and Quebec. The influence of Quebec in toughening the Accord was enhanced after the decisive re-election of the Lévesque government just a few days before the Accord was to be publicly released. Some of the premiers had tried to make it more difficult for provinces to opt out of future constitutional amendments by requiring a two-thirds' vote of the provincial Legislative Assembly, a requirement which would have made the amending formula somewhat more attractive to Ottawa. Lévesque, fresh from a decisive election victory, led the fight against the two-thirds' rule, which was defeated, and a simple majority requirement for opting out was retained.[9] Several months later, Premier Bennett of British Columbia noted that Quebec had been far more amenable to compromise after the Parti Québécois loss in the referendum than it was after Lévesque won the subsequent provincial election a year later.[10]

The need for unanimity of the gang of eight also precluded a more comprehensive approach to constitutional reform, for any attempt to widen the provincialist agenda would generate fissures in the provincial camp and thus be counterproductive. Thus a response to the federal desire for a Charter was incompatible with the continued allegiance of several provinces, particularly Manitoba and Quebec, to the provincialist front.

The provincial constitutional Accord, fashioned without any public input, with no federal government involvement, and without the moderating influence of the two provinces (Ontario and New Brunswick) closest to the federal position, inevitably reflected a provincialist vision of Canada. The eight provincial signatories were further pulled away from compromise by the need to placate the most unyielding of their colleagues: Alberta and Quebec on the amending formula, and Premier Lyon of Manitoba on the Charter. The possibilities of an olive branch being offered to Ottawa were further damaged by the political weakness of Premier Blakeney, the most plausible candidate for a mediating role, whose provincialist credentials had been sullied by his flirtations with Ottawa. Accordingly, the constitutional Accord, which was essentially a province-protecting amending formula, contained nothing to entice Ottawa to give up its unilateral drive. By its nature and its limits the Accord revealed the fragility of the gang of eight, whose precarious unity was based more on opposition to a common federal enemy than on any overriding constitutional vision capable of encompassing national as well as provincial concerns.[11]

In the highly visible federal arena of Parliament and the Special Joint Committee, an alternative constitutional package, reflecting the interests of a different set of actors, took shape. Building on the original Liberal government resolution, the overt parliamentary process, supplemented and partly orchestrated by the behind-the-scenes manoeuvres of the federal Cabinet and officials in the Federal-Provincial Relations Office and the Department of Justice, worked on the Charter, an amending formula, the taxation and regulation of provincial resources, and several other items. The original federal amending formula was modified slightly in deference to provincial concerns, particularly those of Saskatchewan, and clauses dealing with the regulation and taxation of natural resources were inserted to maintain the parliamentary support of the New Democratic Party and to go some way towards appeasing the Western provinces.

Overall, however, the federal political process, especially in the Special Joint Committee, focussed on the Charter. The form of the Charter originally presented to Parliament was weak and conciliatory to its provincial government opponents, reflecting both the lengthy inter-governmental constitutional process from which Ottawa had just emerged and the continuing federal hope that some provincial governments might yet come on side. But the dissenting provinces did not respond to this implicit concession, and Ottawa was in danger of antagonizing its potential civil rights constituency. Far better to offend the provinces and gain the support of the aggressive lobbyists for a stronger Charter, who had negligible concern for provincial rights or for abstractions such as parliamentary supremacy.

Four provincial premiers appeared before the committee, while four other provincial governments submitted briefs. Several provincial opposition parties also presented their views to the committee. On the whole, however, the provincial perspective was distinctly in the minority of the 97 witnesses who gave evidence to the committee, and the 962 written submissions made to it.[12] The complete federal package, therefore, and particularly the Charter and the amending formula, reflected a vision of the country insensitive to the expressed wishes of eight provincial governments. Ottawa, intent on exploiting the loophole of unilateralism, preferred to respond to its own pan-Canadian vision of the country, supported by the lobbyists for a tougher Charter, than to the provincial premiers it considered to be balkanizing a people aspiring to clothe itself in national garments.

When the Supreme Court decision threw the two sides back together, there was a confrontation of two antithetical philosophies of federalism embodied in two explicit constitutional reform packages. Given the intense pressure to compromise, and the different components of the two packages, the most plausible bargain was a provincial concession on the Charter, to which Ottawa was wedded, and a federal concession on the amending formula, which was the only developed proposal to which the gang of eight was committed. But given the long build-up of antipathy between the two groups, the hothouse atmosphere of the bargaining, and the uncompromising stance of Quebec, one more failure was a distinct possibility and was only narrowly averted. The federal government gave up its amending formula and injected some national concerns into an amending formula originally tailored with provincial interests in mind. The dissenting provinces, with Quebec left out, succeeded in weakening a nation-building Charter to make it more compatible with their desires to be as unhampered as possible in their pursuit of policy goals. They saw the Charter less as an attack on parliamentary supremacy at the provincial level than as an attack on the ongoing creation of provincial diversities by the exercise of provincial jurisdiction. The language of parliamentary supremacy was a rhetorical device to protect province-building against the nationalizing philosophy of the Charter. Thus the basic compromise resulted in the partial provincialization of a nationalizing Charter, and the partial nationalizing of a province-protecting amending formula.[13]

The impact of the process on the outcome was complex. In general, the curious mix of rigidities and ambiguities in the reform process had a profoundly dampening effect on the scope and substance of constitutional change it was possible to pursue. It deflected immense resources and psychic energy away from the substance of change to an exhausting controversy about the legitimacy of the process. On the other hand, given the political context, the availability of a questionable right of unilateralism had a catalytic effect that produced a degree of constitutional change that otherwise would almost certainly not have been achieved.

The final package sent to Westminster and subsequently enacted is a strikingly inconsistent document which reflects the competing visions of Canada that went into its making. Its two basic components—the Charter and the amending formula—emerged through different routes and were the creation of different actors. They were brought together in a blunt and brutal compromise in which each was tugged marginally in the direction of the spirit that animated the other. However, the last-minute concessions produced a very particular kind of compromise. A different kind of compromise, which would doubtless have reflected a more philosophically integrated view, would have emerged had the final package been the end product of a series of piecemeal adjustments in an ongoing bargaining process.

The constitutional package reflects the cumulative biases built up in two separate arenas, in each of which the main actors proceeded with negligible attention to the sensitivities of the other side. In each arena there was a certain congealing and consolidation of a one-sided perspective from the time the federal government decided to proceed unilaterally to the final crash course in constitution-making more than a year later, in four days in November 1981. By this time, positions were too entrenched and time was too short for a fundamental change of direction by either the gang of eight or the "gang of three"—New Brunswick, Ontario and Ottawa. Consequently, those who seek the guiding spirit or the real intentions of the Fathers of our limited re-Confederation will search in vain for a dominant animating vision. There is none to be found. The Constitution Act does not transcend competing visions of the country; it only entrenches them in the constitution and provides new arenas in which the battles of the future will be fought. Our constitutional discontents are not yet behind us, although the exhaustion of the actors and the imperatives of a collapsing economy may produce a lull of considerable duration.

Opposition Within: The conservatism of the reform process was based not only on the struggles between governments in the context of unwieldy and unsettled procedures for amendment, but also on the power of interests and institutions within governments to block change they considered repugnant. These intragovernmental barriers to reform were most evident on the federal side, especially with respect to Senate reform and, although the issue was not pressed and is not formally constitutional in nature, with respect to electoral reform.

Since the late sixties, the Senate has been high on the list of candidates for reform, but it has possessed an almost invincible resource—the capacity to veto any change not to its liking. The federal 1978 Bill C-60, which recommended extensive changes in Senate representation and a reduction of its veto power to a delaying power of sixty days, was given severe treatment by the senators, and it was far from clear that it would have passed the Senate hurdle had it not been dropped for other reasons. It is also widely understood that one reason Trudeau was reluctant to embrace Senate reform in the summer of 1980, although it was strongly demanded by some provinces, was his unwillingness to take on the Senate again and thus risk the delay or thwarting of his plans in other areas more central to his objectives. The power and willingness of the Senate to block any changes designed to diminish its influence was further revealed when the Liberal government attempted in its parliamentary resolution of October 1980 to reduce the Senate's participation in constitutional amendments from its existing veto to a delaying power of ninety days. This was not major Senate reform as such, but it would have paved the way for future Senate reform without Senate concurrence. The opposition of an organized minority of Liberal senators to this proposed reduction in their power and influence led to an unsuccessful government attempt at appeasement by doubling the time of the suspensive veto to 180 days. When it remained unclear that this revision would placate the Senate, the Liberal government re-introduced the absolute veto the Senate had historically possessed. The government was unwilling to jeopardize its larger package by risking a confrontation with the Senate for the sake of a secondary aspect of its constitutional proposals. The situation was graphically, but not inaccurately, described by Svend Robinson, an NDP committee member, as follows:

> [The Senate,] this nonelected body, this house of patronage accountable to no one, in a final stab at self preservation had made it very clear, apparently, that they do not intend to tolerate any interference with their powers; and that the only way this resolution will pass through Parliament is if there is a Senate amendment, a Senate preservation amendment appended.[14]

The remarkable capacity of the Senate, an institution widely considered to be without roots in Canadian society, to protect itself was built on the entrenched position derived from its veto power. Its veto gave it much greater defence against unwanted change than the Supreme Court possessed. The Supreme Court, unlike the Senate, had many defenders but a much more limited capacity of self-defence from its position on the sidelines.[15] The resistance of the Senate was finally overcome when the limitation of its veto power in amendments, which was built into the provincial constitutional Accord, survived the November 1981 First Ministers' Conference and was contained in the final agreement of the ten governments. From the perspective of the Trudeau Cabinet, it was a happy circumstance to be able to include an elimination of the Senate's protective veto in a larger constitutional package which no Senate, at this culmination of years of constitutional effort, could afford to block.[16]

While electoral reform, technically speaking, is not constitutional reform, Prime Minister Trudeau has viewed a measure of proportional representation as part of his overall political strategy to make the central government more representative of the regions of the country. Here, too, the power of interests built up around the existing system, which it is the function of reform to reduce, threatens to block reform. Electoral reform has to run the gauntlet of the very biases in House of Commons representation which it is designed to overcome. While a generalized affection for the traditional ways of electing members has been a not unimportant support for the existing electoral system, the deepest opposition to change comes from Liberal members of Parliament from Quebec and Conservative MPs from the prairies. On this matter the New Democratic Party is a party like the others. At its 1981 national convention the NDP, whose leader, Ed Broadbent, was publicly in favour of a limited use of proportional representation, voted against electoral reform at the behest of its western members who were fearful that such reform would reduce their party's power in the West, and the power of the West in the party.

Thus the biases in the representative system that it is the purpose of proportional representation to alleviate are kept alive by the beneficiaries of those biases. Those who would benefit from the change are present neither in caucus nor in the House of Commons to argue their case. The goals of a strengthened Ottawa and national integration are clearly secondary concerns to those who are asked to make sacrifices. If the issue ever reaches the House of Commons, the prairie Liberals, Quebec Conservatives, and NDP supporters east of Ontario that electoral reform is designed to represent in the House will not have votes on the proposed measure.

In summary then, the conservative resistance of the existing constitutional system to change was truly impressive. It derived from the conflicting goals pursued by the contending governments, the limitations and uncertainties of the amending procedures, and the veto power of particular interests within the federal government. In spite of these formidable barriers, some constitutional change was nevertheless achieved. Detailed examination of the particulars of that change is beyond the purview of this paper. What the next section attempts is not to provide additional historical analysis of the making of the Constitution Act, but to provide a perspective which stresses the essential arbitrariness and chancy nature of what has been newly added to the constitution to bind future generations of Canadians.

Determinism, Contingency and Personality

A focus on the politics of constitutional change invites us to look backward from the particulars of the recent Constitution Act to the factors that went into its making. Such an approach subtly tempts the researcher to find an underlying determinism which inexorably led to what happened. That same determinism applied to the policies and proposals that failed to survive to the implementation stage explains their rejection as equally the result of some historical juggernaut, which cast them aside as inappropriate to the needs of the time, or some other alleged economic or social imperative.

To some twenty-first century historian, falsely assuming that the passage of time and the cooling of passions have contributed to an Olympian objectivity which allows truth the more easily to be discerned, the constitutional struggles of the last fifteen years may seem to fall into place as the inevitable working out of some deterministic process. Such an interpretation, however plausible its neat and tidy patterns may appear, will be false to the historical record. The Constitution Act resulted from a chaotic process dominated by titanic contests of political will. It was deeply influenced by the byzantine procedures from which it ultimately emerged, and it was profoundly marked by the personalities of the key actors, by the skills they employed and the blunders they perpetrated, and by various historical accidents and ephemeral considerations. At every stage and in every arena the developing constitutional package was tugged and pulled by competing interests seeking advantage. In its final form it is a composite creation whose imperfections and contradictions reflect the compromises of the exhausted opponents who fashioned it.

To suggest that no other outcome was possible is to ignore the fragility of the delicate and precarious balance of interests which shaped the final agreement. It is also to overlook the chaos and contradictions, the accidents and miscalculations, which were an integral part of the long constitutional struggle, not only from the Parti Québécois victory in 1976, but going back to the 1960s.[17]

Prior to the November 1981 First Ministers' Conference which frantically pieced together a constitutional package, it was quite unclear what agreement, if any, would be reached; and failing agreement, it was not clear what would have happened to the federal patriation package in the United Kingdom had the Liberal government proceeded unilaterally. Unilateralism, still available to Ottawa after the Supreme Court decision, might well have been accepted, albeit reluctantly, by a weary Westminster, resulting in a very different amending formula and Charter for the country. On the other hand, an attempted federal unilateralism in the face of extensive provincial opposition in the United Kingdom could have been defeated, either because of an ultimate failure of federal nerve, or a firm, if unenthusiastic Westminster acceptance of a trusteeship role on behalf of the provinces. Either of these outcomes would have embittered federal-provincial relations for years to come.

The particular outcome of the Constitution Act, therefore, was underdetermined. Slight or major differences in one or more of dozens of prior events or political decisions could have nudged the constitutional process onto a different path, which would have led the country to another constitutional destination. The retention of power by the Clark government, a Parti Québécois referendum victory or the replacement of the Lévesque government by the Ryan Liberals, the non-leaking of the Kirby memorandum, a different Supreme Court decision which, given the general surprise that greeted its actual decision, can scarcely be rejected as a possibility[18]— any one of these or various other no less plausible happenings could have re-shuffled the actors in the game, the resources at their disposal, and their perceptions of the possible. The constitutional struggles of the sixties and seventies do not lend themselves to explanations of social forces bending men and institutions to their dictates. The constitutional conflict occurred largely at the elite levels of the political system itself. The key actors were political leaders making choices and pursuing strategies in a situation of considerable fluidity.

The observations of Edward McWhinney, while somewhat cynical and even exaggerated, do not entirely miss the mark. The patriation exercise, he wrote, seems to have been less a clash of contending, clearly defined, historical forces or of rival ideologies—a genuine dialectical operation—than an exercise in political theatre in which personalities were often more important than the ideas they claimed to represent. If it was not, at times, a dress rehearsal in the theatre of the absurd, some of the players seemed casual characters wandering on and off the stage in search of an author and a script, without always being certain about their lines or why they were there in the first place.[19]

This attribution of extensive happenstance to the final constitutional package is supported by the considerable discretion, autonomy, and manoeuvrability possessed by the leading political actors. The constitutional controversy was not rooted in enduring constellations of economic interests which dictated the constitutional options pursued by political elites. The relevant economic concerns were those defined by political elites who dominated the process. There was negligible constitutional input from the big battalions of management and labour.[20] While this partly reflected the particular issues on the agenda, several of the issues were far from irrelevant to the major actors in the economy. The issues on the twelve-item agenda in the summer of 1980 included resource ownership and interprovincial trade, communications, fisheries, off-shore resources, powers over the economy, and equalization and regional disparities, subjects which by no stretch of the imagination could be defined as matters of indifference to corporate managers and union leaders. The federal paper on powers over the economy[21] introduced into the 1980 discussions was of great significance to the economic elites on both sides of the industry bargaining table. Yet even here business and labour elites, possibly due to internal divisions in their national organizations, were more akin to Wimbledon spectators than to backroom puppeteers manipulating federal and provincial Punch and Judies in a make-believe performance. The constitutional struggles, therefore, seem peculiarly resistant to any Marxist explanation that denies extensive autonomy to state political elites.

While the relative freedom of the political actors, which contributed to the unpredictability of the process, was partially due to the exclusion of established economic interests, it was also due to intragovernmental bureaucratic considerations. Particularly in the decisive unilateralism period, the items on the agenda were such that operating departments, with their normal bureaucratic goals of self-preservation and imperial expansion, and with ongoing programs linked to specific clientele groups, were shunted to the background. The stage was occupied by prime ministers and premiers, ministers of intergovernmental affairs, attorneys general, and other officials and ministers with jurisdiction-wide concerns. The issues of patriation, an amending formula, and the Charter were issues of high politics, of concern to governments as governments, and thus relatively insulated from the more specialized bureaucratic constraints that a constitutional agenda focussing on the division of powers might have elicited.

Policy proposals pertaining to these highly political areas, as well as to the Senate, the Supreme Court, equalization, and a constitutional preamble, often had an idiosyncratic quality, although they seldom conflicted with some conception of jurisdictional gain or defence. They are best seen as the products of particular political elites and their key advisors, rather than the inescapable consequences of viewing the world from the vantage point of Manitoba, British Columbia, or some other jurisdiction. Much of Manitoba's position, especially on the Charter, was due to the particular incumbency of Sterling Lyon rather than to some basic values in the Manitoba political culture. The defeat of the Lyon government in November 1981 was partly attributed to "his negative position on the charter of rights." The defeat also "had a profound effect on the style of federal-provincial relations conducted between the province and Ottawa. . . . Lyon's outspoken opposition to Ottawa's constitutional proposals" contrasted with his successor, "Premier Pawley [who] ushered in a policy of friendly, co-operative dealings with Ottawa."[22] A British Columbia government led by Opposition Leader Dave Barrett would almost certainly not have ended up with the specifics of the constitutional positions so vigorously espoused by Premier Bill Bennett. To Bennett, Senate reform was the centrepiece of the British Columbia proposals. To Barrett, "the best reform of the Senate is to abolish it."[23] Barrett was a passionate supporter of the Charter, Bennett a cool defender of the British tradition of parliamentary supremacy.[24] The accident of who was in office made its own contribution to the dynamics of constitutional renewal.

The staggered process of constitution-making which Canadians have experienced since the mid-sixties, and especially since the election of the Parti Québécois in 1976, was an unusually hazardous undertaking for the participants. No single actor possessed sufficient power to ensure a favourable outcome. The possibility of a devastating defeat no matter how skilfully one played the game was a recurrent nightmare. The knowledge that even the shrewdest strategies might backfire accompanied each actor on his constitutional rounds.

The vagaries and waywardness of the process put an extraordinarily high premium on such traits as political skill, intelligence[25] and willpower. The political game of constitution-making and unmaking did not have clear rules, with the result that the key actors devoted much effort to trying to get their definition of the game accepted. This involved various attempts to define who were the other relevant actors, what were the legitimate arenas, and what were the rules. Successful re-definitions of the game could greatly enhance one's bargaining position, increase the possibility of victory, and diminish the likelihood of defeat.

Given the conflicting objectives of the competing governments, acceptance of the unanimity requirement for constitutional change was, as already noted, a virtual guarantee of stalemate. Thus the two governments which combined an especially strong concern for constitutional change sought to re-define the nature and rules of the game by taking charge, developing momentum on their side, and reducing the capacity of their adversaries to block their way. The two major efforts of this kind were the attempt of the Parti Québécois to break out of Canadian federalism by the use of a referendum, and the strategy of unilateralism announced by Trudeau four and a half months after the referendum defeat.

The Parti Québécois under Lévesque brilliantly re-defined the rules of the Canadian constitutional game by asserting a self-declared right to a unilateral exit from the Canadian Confederation after a process of democratic consultation with its own electorate, a process in which Canadians outside of Quebec were turned into onlookers while one province pursued its own destiny. The Parti Québécois gained considerable support for the idea that should the Quebec people decide to leave Canada after an open and fair consultation of their opinions, force would not be used to prevent such an outcome.

This Quebec unilateralism, to be based on an act of collective will, was not justified by any reference to the extant procedures for constitutional change. To break up a country has its own imperatives, and they clearly would not include the requirement of unanimous consent of the other ten governments. Thus, in the period from 1976 to 1980, Quebec operated in terms of two sets of rules. With respect to the existing constitution Quebec conducted herself in the traditional way, as possessed of the historic right of veto which she had exercised against the Fulton-Favreau amending formula and against the more comprehensive Victoria Charter. With respect to her proposed future exit from the constitution, Quebec asserted a unilateral right of departure. The legitimacy of secession, should events come to that, was founded almost entirely on plebiscitary consultations with the Quebec people, not on some explicit constitutional right of self-determination sanctioned by the existing constitution.

Quebec also pushed the view of Ottawa as the government of English Canada, and hence as the only government with whom an independence-seeking Quebec would have to deal in attempting to work out the sovereignty-association it was pledged to seek after a positive referendum result. The referendum defeat, however, produced a remarkable transformation of the Parti Québécois government's definition of the rest of Canada. The provinces of English Canada, treated prior to the referendum as little more than irrelevant subdivisions of an English Canada led from Ottawa, were transformed into the provincial brothers of a beleaguered Quebec badly in need of allies as a new round of constitutional discussions got underway. Devoid of any plans of its own for a renewed federalism, and hostile to the plans of Trudeau, the Parti Québécois government had no alternative but to adopt a defensive strategy in which safety lay in numbers. According to Claude Morin, the "no" vote left Quebec with no other choice but to "try and block Ottawa and form a common front with the other provinces. . . . Giving us a 'no' vote meant sending us to Ottawa with a terrible handicap."[26] Thus Quebec, for more than a year, and for strategic reasons, became a "province like the others." The Quebec bargaining position was simply to protect all existing rights and to repeat the "traditional" demands of previous Quebec governments.

The behaviour of the Quebec government in the constitutional discussions can only be understood in the light of the extremely difficult political position in which the Lévesque Cabinet found itself. As Zukowsky succinctly expressed it,

> the Quebec government's options were quite limited. On one side, its representatives were constrained by their ideals and by their membership in a party dedicated, not to renewing federalism, but to sovereignty-association. On the other side, they were constrained by their role as representatives of a people who had just rejected sovereignty-association. Thus, if the Quebec government could not appear to its party to be actively pursuing renewed federalism, neither could it be seen by the provincial electorate to be actively obstructing it. Only in this way could the PQ leaders retain the confidence of their party and maximize their chances for success in the next provincial election.[27]

With its own unilateral assault on federalism shattered by the Quebec electorate, the Lévesque government returned to the provincial fold as a stout defender of whatever federal principles could be mustered in her defence. The Quebec willingness to return to the provincialist camp and play the federal-provincial game once again required the acceptance of the Lévesque government as a legitimate partner and reliable colleague by at least some of the provincial governments of English Canada. Throughout the lengthy interministerial discussions in the summer of 1980, the Quebec delegation guided by Claude Morin carefully cultivated the other provincial delegations. By the time of the September 1980 First Ministers' Conference, Quebec was a prominent actor in orchestrating the strategies designed to thwart Trudeau's plans. Quebec was influential in presenting an overwhelmingly provincialist package to Trudeau as the collective wishes of the provinces, a package so clearly destined for rejection that it seemed to have been designed with failure in mind.[28] In the subsequent unilateralism period, Quebec was a leading participant in the provincial camp which fought Ottawa's unilateralism before courts and before the public in Canada and in Great Britain. This dramatic and successful *volte face* by Quebec was a brilliant example of effective federal-provincial diplomacy. Seven of the English Canadian provinces which had formed a common front with Ottawa against sovereignty-association moved into a provincialist camp whose main objective was to block Trudeau's version of constitutional renewal.

If the pursuit of the constitutional goals of the Quebec government in both pre- and post-referendum periods was the result of choices made by a small group of political actors, particularly Lévesque and Morin, federal goals and strategy were equally influenced by a small group of individuals, led by Prime Minister Trudeau. The constitutional vision pursued by Trudeau was not simply an automatic consequence of scanning the federal system from the vantage point of Ottawa. While it was clearly designed to serve federal government interests, it also reflected the particular view of federalism developed by Trudeau in an unusual sequence of theory and practice as he moved from the world of scholarship and political journalism to the world of action.

The indispensability of the role of particular individuals in explaining the constitutional outcome is highlighted by the federal decision in the fall of 1980 to pursue constitutional change unilaterally. While the availability of unilateralism as a possibility was an historical accident, the seizure of this device to break the deadlock was a Gaullist act which found in Trudeau a willing agent. "Don't underrate the guy's commitment on the constitution," a senior federal advisor said of Trudeau. "He's not obsessed, he's monomaniacal."[29]

In the decisive post-referendum phase of the constitutional struggles, the Trudeau Liberal government's high morale and aggressiveness reflected the party's unexpected return to power in February 1980 and the extent of the referendum defeat of the Quebec government's appeal for a mandate to negotiate sovereignty-association. From the federal perspective this conjuncture of events provided an unanticipated opportunity to redress the centrifugal drift of Canadian federalism towards a progressively weaker Ottawa. The defeat of the Progressive Conservatives was turned into a repudiation of Joe Clark's concept of Canada as a "community of communities." The referendum, which was to give the Lévesque government a mandate to dismember Canada, was interpreted as a mandate for the Trudeau government to re-structure Canadian federalism in pan-Canadian terms and to define dualism on a country-wide basis, thus denying Quebec the exclusive role as spokesman of one-half of the Canadian duality. More generally, the federal government under Trudeau decided to act on the assumption that there was no irresistible determinism in the centrifugal trends which the conventional political and academic wisdom assumed must carry the day.

When the processes of executive federalism, with their assumption of a necessary unanimity of agreement, failed to produce an outcome acceptable to Ottawa, the decision was made to break with the past and proceed unilaterally. Federal government unilateralism, with the support of Ontario and New Brunswick, provided the dynamism in the face of massive opposition for fourteen months—from October 2, 1980, when Trudeau announced unilateral action, to early December 1981, when the constitutional package received final parliamentary approval after receiving support from nine provincial governments.

In its unilateral efforts Ottawa and its two provincial allies were deflected but not sidetracked by the Supreme Court decision of September 28, 1981. Although its ruling on convention gave ammunition to the provinces, the Supreme Court sustained the legality of Ottawa's efforts. Furthermore, by its pointed unwillingness to support the proposition that unanimous provincial consent was necessary, the court changed the context of the next round of intergovernmental bargaining. By preserving the legal possibility of unilateralism and refusing to support a conventional requirement of provincial unanimity, the court greatly diminished the probability that unilateralism would be necessary. The tyranny of unanimity which had been used as a justification for unilateralism by Ottawa, and which had frustrated the possibilities of intergovernmental agreement, no longer existed as a cohesive force to keep the dissenting provinces in a common front of opposition. Unanimity had become, in Blakeney's words, no more than a "ghost of conferences past."[30] The disappearance of the unfettered power to block was replaced by the disturbing possibility of being left out. Furthermore, the overwhelming pressure of public opinion for an agreement, coupled with the evident willingness of Ottawa and her allies to compromise in this final bargaining session, made some of the premiers of English Canada fearful of being blamed for a breakdown of the talks. The federal capacity to split the gang of eight was thus enhanced, while the ability of Quebec and other hard-liners to keep the gang united was gravely attenuated. The conflicting purposes which had found a temporary home in the gang of eight and the provincial constitutional Accord could no longer be submerged once there was a return to the bargaining table, and unilateralism had been at least temporarily checked. "It's one thing to try to get 11 people to agree," stated Premier Blakeney, "but if only seven or eight have to agree and three can disagree then it makes for very, very different negotiations."[31]

The re-alignment of Ottawa and the nine provinces behind a compromise agreement which Quebec refused to sign was not inevitable, but it quickly emerged as one of several highly plausible outcomes. The final agreement can be explained in many ways. McWhinney's somewhat unfashionable judgement that Lévesque had simply been "out-smarted,"[32] is not the kind of explanation customary in social science analysis, but in this case it has the virtue of reminding us of the significance of key individuals and the decisions they made.

The ethics of unilateralism in the Canadian federal context, and the judgement of the future on the quality of the constitutional achievement to which the threat of its employment contributed—two separate strands of evaluation which cannot be entirely disentangled—will be the subject of scholarship and political controversy for decades to come. Those evaluations will be unable to ignore the indispensability of unilateralism to any constitutional renewal in the post-referendum drive for constitutional change.

The major impact of unilateralism on the constitutional process is inexplicable without recognizing the support the Charter gave to the federal initiative. Bereft of the Charter, unilateralism would have been reduced to a simple power play lacking in popular support for the substance of the federal efforts. The immense popularity of the idea of a Charter gave the federal government a crucial support base in the country. In political terms this helped to compensate for the public disquiet over the procedure of unilateralism and greatly complicated the opposition of the gang of eight. The vulnerability of Ottawa in the area of procedure was counterbalanced by the vulnerability of the dissenting premiers who, however much they proclaimed their defence of the federal principle, could not claim to be representing the majority wish of their provincial electorates for a Charter.

The Charter and unilateralism were Siamese twins. Without the Charter the federal unilateral effort would surely have foundered. On the other hand, unilateralism, by removing the Charter from the intergovernmental arena where it had languished in the summer of 1980 and making it the centrepiece of the federal proposals before the Special Joint Committee, mobilized both diffuse and specific support for the Charter. When the parliamentary package returned to the chambers of executive federalism after the Supreme Court decision on constitutionality, the Charter enjoyed too much momentum to be totally emasculated, even in private, by the provincial advocates of parliamentary supremacy. If the Charter kept the federal unilateral process alive, it is equally true that the political salvation of the Charter was the political support developed on its behalf by that same unilateral process.

Conclusions

What was in happier days described as the "living Canadian constitution" still lives, modified in some ways, but still essentially much as before. Its survival is due at least as much to the difficulties of change and the profound disagreement about the desirable direction of change as to any massive support by elites or masses for the particulars of the existing constitutional system. It survives because no other constitutional option enjoys enough first choice support to replace it. It survives because in competition with its rivals it alone possesses the supreme advantage of existence, and its continuation does not spell chaos for the private and public interests whose affairs it regulates and channels.

If the existing constitutional system which confronted the blueprints of its adversaries had been itself only a blueprint confronting some other historical, established reality, its triumph would have been unlikely. For in that case those interests which attach themselves to any reasonably successful ongoing system would have been ranged against it. It is not, therefore, the abstract qualities of the Canadian constitutional system, its theoretical virtues so to speak, which account for its durability, but simply its mono-polistic occupation of the field and the resultant advantage this gives it over all contenders.

The conservatism of the constitutional system and its marked resistance to far-reaching change are not due to an exalted reverence in which it is held, nor to any special logical consistency of its parts, nor even to some mystic entity called traditionalism whose enveloping spirit erodes the will of would-be reformers. A more basic explanation resides in the prosaic fact that any developed constitutional system acquires numerous supporters in the varied interests which have adapted themselves to it, and which resist change detrimental to themselves.

The prime interests, of course, are the federal and provincial govern-ments, often radical in what they seek, but always bulldog-like in self-defence of what they have. The reiterated accusation that some of the provinces wished to barter their support for the symbol of patriation for increased provincial powers, or their acceptance of the Charter for jurisdic-tion over fisheries, was both true and not surprising. The guiding strategy here was to employ the blocking power derived from the claimed require-ment of unanimous consent to advantage oneself elsewhere. Ottawa's veto power was no less selfishly employed in self-defence, as in the dismissal of the loose interprovincial Accord presented by all provinces to Ottawa at the close of the September 1980 First Ministers' Conference.

On occasion, the conservatism of the process resulted not from the self-interest of government in some unitary sense, but from the capacity of particular institutions with key blocking power to defend themselves against unwanted change. Thus the Senate, as already noted, fully exploited its central position in the amending process to beat back changes detrimental to its own preferred image of its future role. Only when the pressures were irresistible, when the elimination of its veto on future amendments was embodied in a package which it would have been suicidal to resist, did its string of successful opposition finally run out. The defen-sive capacity of strategically-placed institutions is not confined to the Senate. Reform of the House of Commons by proportional representation will undoubtedly encounter opposition from the parliamentary bene-ficiaries of the regional imbalances in the party system which it is intended to alleviate.

This conservatism and general resistance to major change can be dressed up in the language of functionalism. It can be viewed uncritically by admirers as a highly appropriate protective reaction of an integrated interdependent system preserving its clockwork harmony against barbarian *ad hocery*. Less false to reality is to view the conservatism as deriving from the mutually cancelling tendencies of competing powers with divergent goals. The result is a system in which the capacity to resist major constitu-tional change has far more leverage than can usually be mustered by the forces of innovation.

This conservatism means, however, not that constitutional change is impossible, but that it is supremely difficult. In the period of constitutional turmoil just ended, an idiosyncratic combination of circumstances, which included an almost obsessive firmness of constitutional purpose in Ottawa, was required to generate the limited breakthrough of November 1981. While Ottawa hoped to employ the strategic advantages of unilateralism to generate an amending formula and Charter significantly beneficial in both practical and psychological terms to its long-run interest, such was not to be. Unilateralism was constrained by the politics of provincial opposition before the courts and the public. In the resultant compromise, no government enjoyed an undiluted victory, although the Parti Québécois government of Quebec was a clear loser. Thus, while change is possible, it requires Herculean efforts, and the outcome may be seriously disappointing. While the new amending formula will at least provide a set of known rules which can be followed, formal amendments will doubtless continue to be infrequent events in the evolution of Canadian federalism.

Constitutional change is seldom intended to be easy. The bias of established systems is to favour continuity. The existing system thus illustrates the reach of the past into the present. In the same way, the new amending formula, the Charter, and other components of our recent constitutional change will be our gift to our successors and will confront future generations as givens, incapable of easy modification.

These evolving constitutional givens can, at the extreme, be viewed either as a prison from which escape is unlikely, or as a rich tradition to be worked and cultivated. At the present juncture, the recent ferment of the search for change lends little credence to the idea that Canadians see themselves as the happy inheritors of a rich tradition. Eulogies seem fanciful and strained. On the other hand, at least in English Canada, it seems no less exaggerated to describe our constitutional situation as a prison.

In French-English relations, Quebec-Ottawa relations, and federal-provincial relations more generally, there is no resting place, no end to tensions and frustrations. There are no constitutional utopias. We have to be satisfied with the stumbling efforts of imperfect men to keep our problems at bay. From that perspective a restrained half cheer may be suggested as the appropriate response to the new Canadian constitution. It is the only constitution we have.

Notes

1. Several paragraphs and phrases in this article are taken from an earlier article by the author in "The Magazine" section of the *Vancouver Province*, April 18, 1982.
2. See Alan Cairns, "Constitution-Making, Government Self-Interest, and the Problem of Legitimacy in Canada," in Allan Kornberg and Harold Clarke,

eds., *Political Support in Canada: The Crisis Years* (Durham, N.C.: Duke University Press, forthcoming).

3. G. Bruce Doern, "Spending Priorities: The Liberal View," pp. 1 and 9, in G. Bruce Doern, ed., *How Ottawa Spends Your Tax Dollars: Federal Priorities 1981* (Toronto: James Lorimer, 1981).

4. Canada, Task Force on Canadian Unity, *A Future Together: Observations and Recommendations* (Ottawa: Supply and Services Canada, 1979), p. 48.

5. Section 91(1) gave the federal Parliament exclusive legislative authority over "the amendment from time to time of the Constitution of Canada, except as regards matters coming within the classes of subjects by this Act assigned exclusively to the Legislatures of the provinces, or as regards rights or privileges by this or any other Constitutional Act granted or secured to the Legislature or the Government of a province . . ." and other matters not germane to this particular federal-provincial controversy.

6. The federal position was explained by Marc Lalonde, minister of state for federal-provincial relations, when he placed the bill in the context of "the decision that will have to be taken by the people of Quebec in the course of the coming months as to whether they want Quebec to continue to be a part of Canada or not." He continued: "Some of the changes would be of concern to the provincial governments, especially those relating to the House of the Federation and the Supreme Court. Obviously, agreement on them, as well as on other provisions, would be desirable. However, to be realistic, it is most unlikely that agreement is going to be given to these or to any proposals by all provincial governments. Premier Lévesque and his government have never concealed their objective. It is not to improve the Constitution of Canada so that Quebec can be more comfortable within it; it is not to make Canada a more effective union or a place where French Canadians will be more content; it is to get Quebec out of Confederation. They are not likely to agree on constitutional changes for which a major objective is to keep Quebec a part of Canada. So what are we to do? Are we to be paralyzed? Are we to say that federal jurisdiction under Section 91(1) cannot be exercised if *any* province disagrees—even if it is a matter clearly within federal jurisdiction? The federal government is not prepared to accept such a proposition. . . . Parliament must be able to act, in the national interest, in areas where it legally can—with agreement of the provinces if at all possible, but without being the helpless prisoner of a province if agreement is impossible. To fail to act, in the face of a national crisis, could be irresponsible." *Statement by the Honourable Marc Lalonde . . . to the Joint Parliamentary Committee on the Constitution*, August 15, 1978, pp. 1 and 4.

7. Except of course for a possible unilateral secession by Quebec after some acceptable democratic process of consultation with the Quebec people.

8. Michael Valpy described the meeting at which the Accord was released "as one of the funny curiosities of Canadian history—like the Canadian Army's 1920s battle plan to attack America." From "A Somewhat Mediocre Bunch," *Vancouver Sun*, April 20, 1981, p. A4.

9. *Toronto Globe and Mail*, May 7, 1981. See Ronald J. Zukowsky, *Struggle over the Constitution* (Kingston: Institute of Intergovernmental Relations, 1981), p. 110, for the main differences between the Accord and the earlier proposal discussed at the September 1980 First Ministers' Conference, which in turn was based on the Alberta amending formula.

10. Ian Mulgrew, "Moratorium on patriation urged before top court ruling," *Toronto Globe and Mail,* August 15, 1981. See also the report of Robert Sheppard who, after stating that some provinces had tried to toughen up the opting out provisions, continued: "Provincial sources say that Premier René Lévesque, bullish from a smashing electoral win in Quebec earlier in the week, insisted on redrafting many of the provisions that had been agreed to informally by provincial representatives in Winnipeg a few weeks ago." *Toronto Globe and Mail,* April 17, 1981.

11. See Edward McWhinney, *Canada and the Constitution, 1979-1982* (Toronto: University of Toronto Press, 1982), pp. 101, 119, for an acerbic critique of the gang of eight.

12. See Zukowsky, *op cit.,* pp. 71-86, for a good discussion of the committee.

13. For the details see Sheilagh M. Dunn, *The Year in Review 1981: Intergovernmental Relations in Canada* (Kingston: Queen's University, Institute of Intergovernmental Relations, 1982), pp. 27-28, 31-32.

14. *Minutes of Proceedings and Evidence of the Special Joint Committee of the Senate and of the House of Commons on the Constitution of Canada,* No. 52, February 3, 1981, p. 91.

15. On the other hand, although the court lacked a veto, it was not, apparently, entirely without influence and persuasive powers. During the September 1980 First Ministers' Conference, a columnist for the *Toronto Star* asserted that any enlargement of the court was unlikely. "Part of the reason for this is the quiet but efficient lobbying of the present members of the court, who feel that expansion is neither necessary nor desirable." Andrew Szende, "Conference Notebook," *Toronto Star,* September 12, 1980. That same month, while the Trudeau government was pondering its course of action, Chief Justice Laskin gave two interviews with the *Financial Post,* which constituted a defence of the existing court. *Financial Post,* September 20, 1980 and September 27, 1980. See also *Financial Post,* March 21, 1981, p. 9, for an editorial, "Don't fiddle with the Supreme Court," commenting on a vigorous defence of the Supreme Court by the Chief Justice before the Empire Club in Toronto.

16. Although an unsuccessful attempt was made at the last minute by Conservative senators to retain an absolute Senate veto. In November 1980 a subcommittee of the Standing Senate Committee on Legal and Constitutional Affairs issued a *Report on Certain Aspects of the Canadian Constitution* (Ottawa: Minister of Supply and Services, 1980) which, among other proposals, recommended the replacement of the Senate's absolute veto by a six months' suspensive veto. Correspondence from Senator Maurice Lamontagne and former Senator Eugene Forsey makes it clear that the suspensive veto was intended to apply to the Senate's role in constitutional amendments.

17. Edward McWhinney has suggested that several weaknesses in the Constitution Act were due to oversight, haste and confusion, partly reflecting the perils of the "telex diplomacy" of the period between the November 1981 First Ministers' Conference and the final debate in Parliament. McWhinney, *op. cit.,* pp. 106, 109.

18. See, however, the prescient comment of the Kirby memorandum, "Report to Cabinet on Constitutional Discussions, Summer 1980, and the Outlook for the First Ministers' Conference and Beyond," August 30, 1980, p. 51, that the court "might very well . . . make a pronouncement, not necessary for the decision, that

the patriation process was in violation of established conventions and therefore in one sense was 'unconstitutional' even though legally valid."

19. McWhinney, *op. cit.*, p. 118.
20. There was some business input into the Special Joint Committee, but negligible participation from labour interests. Zukowsky, *op. cit.*, pp. 73-76.
21. Subsequently published as Jean Chrétien, *Securing the Canadian Economic Union in the Constitution* (Ottawa: Supply and Services Canada, 1980).
22. Dunn, *op. cit.*, pp. 214-15. See also *Vancouver Sun*, November 29, 1980, p. A6, for an analysis of the discrepancy between the positions of Lyon and the Manitoba public on the Charter.
23. *Vancouver Sun*, September 16, 1980, p. B14.
24. See *Vancouver Sun*, October 28, 1980, p. A9 for Barrett's opposition to the bulk of the Social Credit government's constitutional position.
25. See the Kirby memorandum, "Report to Cabinet on Constitutional Discussions. . . ." for an excellent example of political intelligence.
26. *Toronto Globe and Mail*, January 8, 1982, p. 8.
27. Zukowsky, *op. cit.*, p. 37.
28. See *ibid.*, pp. 53-55 for a discussion. Premier Blakeney's assessment was that "the basic problem . . . was an inability on the part of Mr. Trudeau and Mr. Lévesque to agree on some things. That was an aftermath of the referendum that had not yet disappeared. Mr. Lévesque, as it developed, had not yet reached the conclusion that his best interests and those of the PQ lay with getting a settlement." Joan Sutton, *Toronto Star*, September 25, 1980, p. A10.
29. John Gray, *Toronto Globe and Mail*, September, 29, 1981, p. D4.
30. Dunn, *op. cit.*, p. 23.
31. "Constitution: Quick reaction from regions," *Financial Post*, October 3, 1981, p. 7.
32. McWhinney, *op. cit.*, p. 102.

Chapter 3/Quebec in Isolation*

Gérard Bergeron

The editors of this book asked me for an analysis of "the outcome from Quebec's perspective." In particular, they were expecting "a piece which reflects on the implications of the present constitutional struggle for the future of Quebec nationalism and for relations between English and French Canada." In short, I must attempt to question the future in an unpromising present in order to acknowledge some rosy time to come.

For any political analyst from Quebec, regardless of his or her political preferences, such a subject is hardly comforting at the moment. It is predicated on the forced isolation in which Quebec finds itself after struggling for nearly twenty years. Successive Quebec governments have carried on the battle with remarkable perseverance, almost single-handedly most of the time. However, in the final phase, all Canadian governments have inevitably become involved in it. The rest of Canada could have done without this reform for some time to come, but the Quebec election on November 15, 1976, and the referendum on May 20, 1980 in particular, hastened events.

Without bothering to distribute the blame or make accusations at this juncture, we are confronted with the isolation, if not the exclusion,[1] of *la province pas comme les autres*, which should have been avoided at all costs. It will soon become untenable not just for Quebec, but for all concerned. The awareness of this isolation, or exclusion, is accompanied by the feeling of having been misled all along by Prime Minister Trudeau, and especially of having been ridiculed in the end by those provincial premiers who had joined with Quebec in their emergency coalition in order to resist Ottawa's attempted constitutional reform. I am referring to the "day of the dupes,"[2] November 5, 1981, when in the dark of night, in some prosaic back room, three "conspirators" (Jean Chrétien, Roy McMurtry and Roy Romanow) concluded a sort of horse traders' deal, while deliberately excluding Quebec's representatives, to save "the last-ditch attempt" to reach a consensus.

However, we must look beyond this nocturnal *climax*, which at least one provincial premier saw as the ultimate example of the *Canadian way* of doing such things. Above all, we must take into account the scope of the constitutional reform movement launched by the federal government after the May 20 referendum in Quebec. A different federal approach might have produced an outcome that even a *péquiste* Quebec government could not have refused, instead of the agreement reached by nine provinces and

---

*Translated from the French by Terrance Hughes.

Ottawa, which not even a federalist Quebec government could have accepted in its present form. It is simply not true that the Parti Québécois government's negotiators intended, or had the means, to wreck the constitutional reform. In its position of both weakness (since the loss of the referendum) and strength (since its recent re-election in April 1981), the Quebec government wanted a basic, albeit inevitably temporary and incomplete, agreement even if that entailed having to explain itself subsequently to vigilant, demanding party militants, to which it had been accustomed for some time! The federal government's constitutional reform movement missed the perhaps unique opportunity to make Quebec relinquish its penchant for sovereignty-association, independence, secession, or even separation, once and for all.

The thoroughly abusive manner in which the entire round of constitutional negotiations was carried out by Ottawa after June 1980 is sufficient to fuel the anti-federalist feeling of Quebecers indefinitely. This sentiment has always been the dialectical prop and rhetorical inspiration of the penchant mentioned earlier. Indeed, any constitutional gain by Ottawa at the expense of the Quebec government does not produce a comparable gain in the political consciousness of Quebecers. Precisely the opposite may be true in the long run.

Of course, it was Claude Ryan and the Quebec Liberal Party who lost the election on April 13, 1981. However, Pierre Elliott Trudeau also contributed to keeping the Parti Québécois in power less than a year after its disastrous referendum defeat, through the perverse effect of his constitutional pressure. Imposing a constitution unacceptable to *any* Quebec government might seem to weaken the PQ, but it also meant wounding Quebecers, less through lost illusions than through their yet unsurrendered pride. I would even be tempted to risk taking a shortcut: it was a strategic victory, yes, but an historic defeat, even if this will only become evident later. Opportunities like the post-referendum period do not occur every day.

Other contributors to this book analyze how the unleashing of regional sensitivities in the 1970s made the federal government's attempt at constitutional reform even more difficult. It is now possible to ascertain how each of the regions profited by it, in one way or another, with the exception of Quebec, which is not just another region. "Those with an axe to grind won, the others lost," Jean Paré abruptly concluded.[3] "The others" making up the troop of losers include Quebec society, French-speaking Canadians outside Quebec, women and Amerindians. As history clearly demonstrates, those who instigate hostilities are often doing the dirty work for others when it is time to untangle the spoils of participants in unstable coalitions arising out of exceptional circumstances.

The constitutional battle had lasted long enough, so it was essential to reach an agreement among practical people whose interests could seriously be taken into account. Agreement was indeed reached, but without the government which had enunciated principles and which was tactically excluded from the decisive nocturnal pact. How could some Quebecers not be inclined to take this exclusion personally, when matters of such importance could be decided in the absence of their representatives?

These perceptions of Quebecers serve as a point of departure.[4] There is a sort of fate in our history which once again has shown that "Canadians have a very special propensity for failing to create great national symbols, which are necessary popular references in any political society."[5] In this instance, Canada obtained a new constitution in the absence of Quebec. The project is, to say the least, incomplete. Perhaps that was inevitable, but it is virtually self-destructive if it continues in its present unfinished state.[6]

Everything really started with the psycho-political shock of the Quebec election on November 15, 1976. The political situation was unprecedented not only in Canada, but probably in the world: a secessionist party came to power in a federal state strictly on the condition of not seceding from it! However, under the terms of a sort of electoral pact, the Parti Québécois promised to hold a referendum on its constitutional option. Moreover, the idea would be complex: secession would only occur, or *sovereignty* would only be achieved, contingent upon a new agreement "between equals" being reached, including a new *association* with the federal state. Such a program was equally unprecedented. The process of association, which is frequent nowadays, results from invariably difficult negotiations between established sovereign states, which accept some degree of self-limitation for the convergence of common interests. In this case, association was to be achieved following a complex operation which would have initially granted sovereignty. This is tenable in terms of pure logic; but in terms of the extremely practical logic that would prevail during possible negotiations between antagonistic and unequal parties, it implied taking a great deal about human nature for granted.

A party following such a program must be particularly concerned with calculating its risks. As long as its logic was that of a potential negotiator, it was rational: first take power in order to hold a referendum whose result would probably provide a strong mandate for future negotiations. However, such logic was based on a victory which did not occur. With the loss of the referendum, the Parti Québécois' negotiating potential collapsed, and its overall credibility was shaken. In an extraordinarily rapid recovery following such a defeat, it was returned to power less than a year later. Thus continued the series of mutually supportive Quebec paradoxes.

The Parti Québécois had wanted to pursue its "grand design" step by step. In this perspective, the referendum was put off as long as possible. Opinion polls, which provide the party in power with a basis for wisdom, indicated that the government was not sure of winning even with a flexible question, such as a request for a simple mandate to demand the opening of constitutional negotiations. Could the government have avoided holding the referendum? It had promised one, but are those in power bound to fulfill all their promises, especially the risky ones? Had there not been a referendum, what would have become of its constitutional plan? Would it not have provided proof that it was being abandoned for want of sufficient popular support? It may sometimes be desirable for a government to lose a referendum: to confound adversaries who demand perilous or insufficiently thought out measures, to decline an overly controversial responsibility by counting on inconclusive results, or simply to take care of other matters.

When a government has an interest in winning a referendum, it only embarks upon it with victory assured or, at least, in circumstances and conditions which seem the most favourable to it. The Lévesque government found itself under the obligation (more moral than strategic) to hold its referendum. As it had been announced so long before, the militant wing of the Parti Québécois and various party officials had it prominently on their minds; people on the outside talked to them about it constantly, in a challenging and accusing way. It will always be to their credit that the party leaders dared to fulfill their solemn promise without being sure of winning. They deemed the risk of losing a first battle smaller than that of avoiding the battle already announced.

The militant wing of the party was a little more optimistic. Why would Quebecers act differently from other peoples by "voting against themselves?" Does not history show that the positive outcome of referenda on independence is almost always a foregone conclusion? Indeed it does, for such referenda by definition are held just before or just after independence is achieved. In the case of the Quebec referendum, such a moment was far off; the government was asking for a simple mandate to negotiate, while promising a second referendum in the event of changes to the constitution. One might also have considered the referendum as a sort of initiation, carried out as an educational measure ("don't pull up the plant to hasten its flowering," as the proverb would have it) to help develop the idea of sovereignty in the minds of Quebecers by providing them with the opportunity to get used to it gradually. Moreover, was not sovereignty presented in a reassuring way through its being necessarily linked to association—a measure Canada could not refuse to examine.

On the other hand, it would be impossible to lose completely, since at worst the confrontation between two preponderant factors would continue to thrive: the gradual but laborious progress of the idea of independence among Quebecers, and the exasperating slowness of the renewal of Canadian federalism. This line of reasoning was also widespread among Quebecers who were more favourably disposed to the renewal of federalism than to Quebec's independence, and who claimed to support a strategic "yes" vote. This calculating attitude was aimed at putting the Quebec government in a strong position to negotiate at least a hypothetical form of "neo-federalism," if not sovereignty-association.

During the referendum campaign, public opinion was polarized very quickly and in an overly simplified manner. The "no" forces succeeded in dramatically diminishing the impact of the question. It was not a matter of replying to it as such, in its complex formulation, but rather of replying to the question behind the question: whether to leave the federation or remain in it, whether to break up Canada or isolate Quebec, and so forth. Thus it might be maintained that it was the *péquiste* option that was defeated, not the question as such. This phenomenon was predictable. Prior to the referendum various commentators had maintained that the question, regardless of how it was worded, would have little effect on the polarization of public opinion. This was true, but two nuances should be added. The wording of the question was important insofar as it provided arguments for the "no" camp to denounce its "hypocrisy," or to claim just as vigorously that there would be no negotiation, because Quebec's partners would refuse. The complex text submitted to the electorate was also designed to facilitate a much higher score on the "yes" side, through the addition to the *indépendantiste* votes of a considerable number of affirmative ballots from those claiming to be strategic "neo-federalists."

Had the electorate actually replied to the question *as such* (an impossibility given the passionate circumstances), the "yes" vote would have won by a substantial margin. Had the Parti Québécois' fundamental option been the object of the question, the "no" forces would have achieved a much higher score than they did.

Two conclusions can be drawn from this. First, the Parti Québécois made the best possible choice, considering the unfavourable situation in which its premature electoral success had placed it. Having come to power too soon, it also had to hold its referendum too soon. The second conclusion, as certain as the first, is the existence of the hope among most Quebecers for a renewed federalism. Both the committed advocates of independence and those satisfied with the status quo are in a minority. A large central block formed; through contradictory replies it expressed the same hope for a new federalism. Thus it might be surmised that a third, specifically "neo-federalist" result appeared, composed of almost equal numbers of "yes" and "no" votes. What was readily apparent during the referendum campaign was confirmed by various analysts after May 20, 1980.

The "too soon" that qualifies the taking of power by the Parti Québécois and, consequently, the holding of the referendum almost became a "too late" with respect to the political destiny of Pierre Elliott Trudeau. The predictable surprise of November 15, 1976 revived his political fortunes, which had been uncertain for some time. Even more dramatically than in 1968, he again became the man to deal with the situation.

He had, with little conviction, agreed to set up the Task Force on Canadian Unity in response to considerable pressure from the population at large and various elites. He did not wait for the task force to produce its report before launching his own reform program in *A Time For Action* and with Bill C-60 in 1978. Confronted with unanimous objections from the provincial governments and the relative indifference of the population, he was obliged to retreat. When the Liberals were defeated at the polls in July 1979, he was forced to contemplate the collapse of his life's dream—the modernization of the Canadian constitution.

However, fortune, which "looks kindly upon the audacious," may also end up being indulgent towards those who persevere. As a result of parliamentary in-fighting, the Conservative minority government was defeated in the House of Commons. Two months later, in February 1980, Trudeau was brought back to power. He was to receive an historic and unexpected last chance. He would seize upon it with the cold determination of a volunteer to whom destiny has just made an ironic, but imperious last sign.

Trudeau regained power while avoiding any mention of the constitution during the 1980 election campaign. To persistent journalists, he simply replied, "You know my ideas!" Earlier the prime minister had dissociated himself from the report of the Task Force on Canadian Unity and *A New Canadian Federation*, the Quebec Liberal Party's Beige paper. It later became evident that the only ideas he retained on the constitution were his own. Returned to power just before the referendum, he resolutely awaited the unique opportunity that his perennial constitutional adversary was about to offer him. During the campaign he made few public declarations, but those he did make were masterful and effective. Quebecers believed his solemn promise to undertake the great constitutional reform expected, even if it meant putting his party's seats at risk. He had promised nothing else, nor anything more explicit: a victory for the "no" forces would signal the immediate implementation of a vast constitutional reform. It was then that his remark of the previous year ("You know my ideas!") should have come to mind. Strictly speaking, he did not mislead anyone, although he consciously and effectively played on ambiguity. Shortly thereafter, all Quebecers who had justified their vote as a means of hastening the implementation of a new federalism became disenchanted, whether they were in the "no" or the "yes" camp.

These Quebecers were expecting other measures than those announced —patriation (unilateral if necessary), the adoption (imposed if necessary) of an amending formula, and the granting of a Charter of Rights (written by federal civil servants). Many ideas on basic reform had been circulating since the publication of the report of the Task Force on Canadian Unity and the Beige paper of the Quebec Liberal Party, not to mention Trudeau's *A Time For Action*, which had bluntly posed the question of reforming federal government institutions. Yet immediately following the referendum, nothing was proposed that would satisfy the diffuse but real expectations of the great majority of Quebecers. In its very principle, the federal constitutional offensive took on the aura of a misappropriation (in the legal sense) of the outcome of the referendum. On this point many Quebec federalists were, and still are, just as bitter as the *péquistes*.

The constitutional offensive was carried out at a diabolical pace for eighteen months, except for a brief respite during which the Supreme Court studied the legality of the constitutional reform proposed by Ottawa. The brutal attack inexorably followed its course within the ministerial committee during the entire summer of 1980, at the constitutional conference in September, in the House of Commons, and within the Special Joint Committee of the Senate and House of Commons. It was, for all intents and purposes, a constitutional "coup." The abuse lay not only in Ottawa's arbitrariness, but also in the dubious principles upon which such an operation was based. Without even the appearance of having a mandate for this purpose, and with very uneven regional representation, the Canadian government, temporary as all governments are, assumed a sort of new, unlimited constituent power. In doing so, it pushed aside parliamentary minorities while maintaining that it could act without the support of a clear majority of provincial governments, and even force Westminster's consent. When the Supreme Court finally brought down its judgement on the unconstitutionality of the reform, the Trudeau government had no other basis for its actions than that of a narrow formal legality through the simple presumption of explicit non-illegality. Moreover, the Supreme Court noted that this "silence" might "just as well have indicated the opposite."

Because so many hopes were dashed, particularly in Quebec, there was even more reason to resolutely oppose such a brutal offensive. While Liberal MPs from Quebec suffered pangs of conscience which, with a few rare exceptions,[8] they had to stifle under the inflexible rule of party discipline, Liberal MNAs in Quebec City experienced an acute crisis from which they have not yet recovered. After its crushing referendum defeat, the Parti Québécois government's only choice, and duty, was to play the federalist card by allying itself with other provinces. It did so without excessive enthusiasm, but scrupulously, largely supported in this respect by a strong majority of the electorate and most of the media. In a difficult manoeuvre, it even received the almost unanimous support of the National Assembly, with the exception of nine Liberal MNAs, most of whom were English-speaking and who could hardly have been expected to support the government's motion.

The Lévesque government thus emerged from its isolation. It could now conduct its struggle within a broad coalition with seven other provincial governments representing the majority of Canadians. The Lévesque government no longer had the air of a "black sheep returning (pitifully) to the fold," well supported as it was by public opinion in

Quebec, and participating as it did in such an extensive resistance on the part of the provinces. The Quebec government participated actively in the common front, adhering to the terms of the celebrated "agreement of the eight" signed only three days after its re-election in April 1981; however, the recollection of its recent tumultuous past prevented it from assuming a clear leadership role. This agreement would later turn against it with respect to its traditional veto, which Trudeau claimed it had relinquished for an illusory "hill of beans."[9]

Debate on this provincial agreement, reached in April and more particularly, on the federal-provincial conference at the beginning of November 1981, continues. The politicians involved have given disparate accounts of these events, particularly in the interpretations of former ministers Roy Romanow of Saskatchewan and Claude Morin of Quebec.[10] It is impossible to know precisely what happened. My comments must be limited to recalling how this time of great confusion, resulting in such an abrupt clarification, was perceived in Quebec. According to this still-lingering perception, the Quebec negotiators were misled and duped; not only did other negotiators in the gang of eight break their promise, but they failed to respect what was for Quebec the essential clause in the agreement of the previous April. This view is held not only by the leaders and members of the Parti Québécois, but also by the majority of Quebecers, including many "sincere federalists."

In a short period of time Quebecers had been subjected to the misappropriation of the meaning of the referendum's outcome, followed by a prolonged constitutional "coup" on the part of the federal government. Then, at a critical moment, they saw their negotiators, who had acted in good faith, abandoned and literally duped by their provincial allies. That was all it took for them to start thinking they were beginning to pay a high price for their daring at the time of the referendum, without going so far as to ask themselves what would have transpired had they voted "yes" in this first exercise of their right to self-determination. Quebecers still do not generally accept such a *dénouement*. While there is no shortage of more down-to-earth preoccupations to distract them, will they ever forget it?

The Parti Québécois took the final course of events even harder than its referendum defeat. Officially, it could once again maintain that Quebec is always the loser in federalist machinations! The party congress in December 1981, immediately after the constitutional conference, gave rise to an extraordinary "collective letting off of steam."[11] Following such excesses, René Lévesque, who is both premier and president of the Parti Québécois, was on the verge of resigning, and finally resolved to hold an "in-house referendum" in order to re-establish the party's traditional line.

Many Quebecers are still bitter that decisions respecting the constitution with such important implications for their future were made not only *against* their wishes, but *without* their being present during the decisive nocturnal back-room dealing. It is possible that the Quebec negotiators lacked prudence and tactical acumen under the circumstances. They could and should have been more wary. Even if it were natural (if not astonishing) that the emergency common front of the eight provinces be formed, it was inconceivable that it could endure even up to the scuttling of any constitutional reform. The seven other provinces would not sacrifice the ultimate chance of an agreement simply out of a spirit of solidarity with the desires of an ally with a well-established reputation for recalcitrance, and even dissidence. Be that as it may, it is probably the first time in the history of our constitution that Quebecers displayed even stronger political resentment against the other provinces than that which they traditionally harbour against the federal government.

The more basic question of how a secessionist government within a federal state can profit by a constitutional reform aimed precisely at consolidating the federal state was scarcely asked. On the other hand, had the November 1981 conference ended in a general agreement, what sort of reception would the Quebec negotiators have received upon their return from Parti Québécois supporters, already unenthusiastic about, and even suspicious of, a "federalist" compromise? For the sake of preserving the sovereignty option, it was perhaps best that the "neo-federalist" adventure of the PQ government end in such a rout. Nevertheless, it is not good for the political climate in Canada that a feeling of humiliation persist in Quebec, affecting many others besides the fervent, intractable proponents of independence. It would be unhealthy that Ottawa's severity be perceived as punishing the people of Quebec, guilty of not electing the right government!

After such a long struggle, which its governments have conducted almost single-handedly most of the time, it is already clear that Quebec has gained nothing for itself, while seeing certain of its powers diminished. Even if one believed that a PQ government was doomed in any event to finding itself alone at the end of such an undertaking, the fact remains that Quebecers cannot accept for long their exclusion from arrangements which may affect them profoundly. In one way or another[12] it will be necessary to find a way of resolving the inextricable dilemma—either conform or remain isolated—in which Quebec finds itself. We have not lost a sense of proportion and will readily admit that the experience of Quebecers is not as dramatic as that of the Poles, that Trudeau has not imposed the same fate on Lévesque as Jaruzelski has on Lech Walesa. Moreover, Quebecers currently have many other reasons besides the constitution to be morose; it does not head the list of their daily anxieties. However, this persistent malaise may still mask a "time-bomb," as Mr. Lévesque warns. In the meantime the *legal* civil war between Ottawa and Quebec has begun.[13]

When Quebec has emerged from this sort of "double protectorate," simultaneously maintaining Lévesque in Quebec City and Trudeau in Ottawa, the federal system will have to find a different equilibrium. A

Canadian prime minister who is not of French origin and a leader of the Parti Québécois who does not have the same sense of his duties as the present one could entirely change the situation. Meanwhile, both men may stay at the helm for several more years, which will certainly be decisive ones. Pierre Elliott Trudeau and René Lévesque are not just complementary adversaries; they are also synchronous. Neither seems to be able to decide on the end of his career before the other leaves. Lysiane Gagnon expressed the fate to which we must resign ourselves with this note of ironic tenderness: "Both our charismatic leaders cause us a lot of concern: one, in Quebec City, threatens to leave, while the other, in Ottawa, threatens to stay!"[14] If it is difficult to imagine one leaving without the other, the aftermath of their departure is even harder to envisage.

There are many uncertainties. Both the federal Conservatives and Quebec Liberals have been beset with leadership crises. A Progressive Conservative government might be more flexible and accommodating. Quebec Liberals under new leadership may re-open the "renewed federation" of the Beige paper, but that is not yet clear. Nor is it clear whether either the leaders or the people will wish to re-dedicate themselves to the broad constitutional questions, since they have become deeply bored by the interminable debate and increasingly preoccupied by more pressing economic problems.

In history there are no conclusions. At best, one can only note results, few of which subsequently prove to be irreversible. However, two undisputed historical facts are noteworthy. First, the Quebec government was defeated twice: on May 20, 1980, and on November 5, 1981. Second, in the intervening period the federal government managed to force the writing of appendices which were still missing from the Statute of Westminster passed in 1931. It took more than half a century to bring up-to-date a text which was already more anachronistic than innovative. Both events have important consequences, but they are difficult to discern. The most substantial and difficult part of the constitutional reform has yet to come. Indeed, it is the *reform* itself which has yet to come. What has changed is that it can take place. But my bet is that it will not take place. The *Canadian way* is too slow and too "impractical" to effect the necessary constitutional reforms in time.

Quebec's setbacks are, above all, those of a government which performed no better on the defensive at the beginning of November 1981 than it did on the offensive eighteen months earlier. In a broader sense they are also the reverses of a society which, in the first instance, showed too little inclination toward complete self-determination to change the basic rules of the game. In the second instance, it lacked a capacity to block the outcome of a complicated game which finally turned against its representatives, and the society itself.

Not long before, Quebec society, through its government, had been able to hinder reform *in extremis,* as it did when the Lesage government rejected the Fulton-Favreau formula, or more recently when the Bourassa government refused to adhere to the Victoria Charter. The Quebec government's veto can only be recognized conventionally, not legally. Only limited satisfaction, or rather the cause of new resentment, can be derived from it, and both are purely symbolic. Such a legal opinion would be perceived as the solemn consecration of another form of impotence in isolation.

The constitutional and legal philosophy of Quebecers has always rested essentially on the conventional inspiration of British public law. They have been forcefully brought around to the austere conception of a strict legalism which suddenly engulfed the notion of a federal regime based on two nations, which they had hitherto nurtured. Until very recently, in the name of their cultural specificity, they felt relatively strong because basic decisions respecting the constitution could not be made against them. They now know that such questions can be settled without them, from a strictly legal viewpoint, even when Westminster and the Queen's signature are involved (Her Majesty reportedly felt "sad" about Quebec's isolation). With respect to supra-legal protection, Quebecers will only receive it as individuals, just as other Canadian citizens do, under the general terms of the Charter of Rights or through the promotion of official bilingualism. Outside Quebec, their linguistic and cultural compatriots will, insofar as their system of education is concerned, have to rely on the increasingly ineffective principle of "where numbers warrant."

Nationalism flourishes in a mythical universe, but thrives just as naturally on broken hopes. It may intensify through the shattered images of a future over which it has less and less control. Is Quebec nationalism, which is currently undergoing a difficult phase, doomed to further decline? Even if the reply is affirmative, this would be the time to ask if the present situation does not conceal something obscure, and probably explosive. For the moment it would seem that the beautiful dream of independence, shared fervently by about a quarter of all Quebecers, has vanished. What is undoubtedly more serious for the stability of the regime is that "neo-federalist" nationalists are not satisfied with the recent constitutional arrangements imposed on Quebec. As there is no question of retreating into the only French society in North America, nothing will be able henceforth to alter the conscience of a society which for nearly twenty years has defined itself less and less as a minority in Canada, but more and more as a majority in Quebec. This deep-seated phenomenon must be considered irreversible.

The most tenacious myth arising from Quebec nationalism has been the belief in one, and only one, English-language society in Canada. The most mature and politically effective of Quebec nationalisms—that espoused by the *péquistes*—has proved to be just as unrealistic. Its proposition, commodious in terms of its program, of an agreement as equals is directed to *one* Canada, when in fact there are at least five of them: those of the four regions and that of the central government which unifies them. May 20, 1980 indicated that Quebecers still did not feel strong enough to challenge *that* Canada. November 5, 1981 proved the forced reduction of Quebec's status to that of one province in ten. In the near future the other partners will have to be made aware of the fact that this is an unhealthy situation which cannot endure.

Will a Parti Québécois government be able to continue opposing federalism without having the strength to take Quebec out of Canada? One can imagine many possible scenarios for the transformation or dissolution of the party. However, this sort of speculation, like that on the possible recovery of the Quebec Liberal Party, does not deny the persistence, or even the necessity, of Quebec nationalism. The party, or parties, which might replace the Parti Québécois in the public's mind or in the Quebec government will always advocate a strongly autonomist nationalism. Even more so than in the past, the dividing line will be not between nationalism and non-nationism, but between a nationalism which encompasses sovereignty, and another which does not go that far.

What currently makes it difficult to measure the dynamics of Quebec nationalism is that it is still functioning in unequal systems, under double leadership. This will be the case for as long as so many Quebecers continue to recognize themselves in René Lévesque, while contemplating their image in Pierre Elliott Trudeau. It was completely suicidal to hold a referendum on Quebec's fate while a Quebecer was prime minister of Canada. Just imagine a referendum proposing the same question with the equivalent of a Diefenbaker and a Lesage in each capital. Quebec nationalism continues to justify and sustain itself through its contradictory loyalties to two superb politicians operating at different levels. The deep political commitment of each of them rests on a great illusion which neither has yet succeeded in converting into reality: Lévesque's illusion of one English Canada reduced to the necessity of negotiating sovereignty-association corresponds to Trudeau's illusion that Quebecers might ultimately be content with a bilingual and bicultural (or more precisely, "multicultural") Canada. Lévesque's instinctive but calculating nationalism complements Trudeau's broad, institutionalized variety. Thus one homogeneous cultural group, a small minority in a heterogeneous ensemble into which it is integrated, can only exude one form or other of a defensive, if not emancipating, nationalism. Because of the voluntarist "illusions" of the two leaders, this nationalism, when detached from an illusory Quebec, is shunted towards a no less illusory Canada.

Being hardly inclined to play Cassandra or Candide, I do not know how to conclude. Therefore, I will take the easy way out by quoting two short, complementary texts drawn from very disparate sources, which I read during the course of preparing this essay. Both quotations are by

Quebec poets. Perhaps they can better express what analytical language can only clumsily and ineffectively articulate—the sort of dialectical tension between the referent of *otherness* and the affirmation of *identity* in the experience of French-speaking Quebecers. Precisely because of this frame of reference, it can never give rise to a proclamation of *exclusivity:*

> (*nous autres*
> dit couramment ce peuple
> à propos de lui-même
> marquant ainsi d'un mot
> l'intime ambiguïté
> de son identité . . .)
> —Michèle Lalonde*

> Québec, coeur originel.
> L'amande la plus dure
> et la plus profonde.
> Le noyau du temps premier.
> Tout autour, neuf autres
> provinces forment la
> coque de ce fruit encore amer
> qui a nom Canada.
> —Anne Hébert.**

---

*(*nous autres* / this people frequently / calls itself / thus indicating with a word / the intimate ambiguity / of its identity. . . .) Excerpted from "Allusion permanente," published in *Defense et illustration de la langue québécoise* (Paris: Editions Seghers Laffont, 1979).

**Québec, primordial heart. / The hardest, deepest / kernel. / The nucleus of time immemorial. / Around it, nine other / provinces form the / husk of this still bitter fruit / called Canada.

Notes

1. In an editorial entitled "Le Québec exclu et isolé" (Quebec excluded and isolated), Jean-Louis Roy, director of *Le Devoir*, wrote on November 6, 1981, p. 8: "Relegating the definition of a new constitution to the level of an ordinary political undertaking, the provincial and federal governments succeeded in completely isolating Quebec."

2. This event has occasionally been characterized in Quebec as "the night of the long knives," although this is inaccurate and exaggerated. We prefer to evoke the "day of the dupes" on November 11, 1630, when Richelieu, upsetting the manoeuvres of Marie de Médicis, reversed the situation in his favour even though everybody, believing him disgraced, had begun to rally the rival clan.

3. Editorial by the director of *L'Actualité*, January 1982, p. 7.

4. Letter from Richard Simeon to the author, dated March 5, 1982: "Clearly, any attempt to evaluate the constitutional battle must focus on the dynamics of Quebec's views."

5. Gérard Bergeron, *Syndrome québécois et mal canadien* (Québec: Les Presses de l'Université Laval, 1981), p. 243, which gives other inglorious examples from Canadian political history (pp. 243-44).

6. This idea of "incompletion" was often mentioned in editorial comments: "The unfinished country," *The Gazette*, April 17, 1982, p. B2; "Requiem pour un pays inachevé," *La Presse*, April 19, 1982, p. A6. Michel Roy, author of the latter article, wrote: "What a disappointing weekend for this country which is forever searching for its identity, which treats itself to a royal celebration, and which is still waiting for its real spring." Other commentators spoke bluntly of "failure": "We missed the boat," Lysiane Gagnon, *La Presse*, April 19, 1982; "The day after a botched celebration," Marcel Pépin, *Le Soleil*, April 17, 1982. Jean-Louis Roy noted in *Le Devoir* of April 17, 1982 at p. 10: "A veritable guerilla war characterized by mistrust, insecurity, over-reaction, threats and unilateralism could only produce insignificant results. In a sense, the objectives pursued were essentially political; they were only incidentally constitutional. It was more a question of controlling an adversary, even of setting a trap for it, and of eliminating its pretentions to hegemony. Each side perceived the actions of the other as a strategy of destabilization. . . . In such a context, negotiation never took place; aggression and provocation took up all the room."

7. In an interview with journalist Richard Daignault, the prime minister recalled it rather bluntly: "The only promise I made was to ensure that Canadians would have the means to amend their own constitution, with respect to the preservation of its basic elements. . . . I went into federal politics to prevent the federal government from being devoured by the provinces. . . . One would have had to be naive to think that I considered the Canadian government weakened after the referendum, to the contrary, . . . that would have been a pure delusion." *Le Soleil*, April 17, 1982.

8. The Liberal MP Louis Duclos, the Conservative MP Roch Lasalle.

9. In his reply to an article by Maurice Duverger (*Le Monde*, February 7, 1982, reprinted in *Le Devoir*, February 16, 1982), he stated: "Unfortunately, Mr. Lévesque exchanged the veto for a hill of beans by signing an agreement with seven other provinces in April 1981, providing for an amending formula without special consideration for Quebec." *Le Devoir*, March 31, 1982, p. 7.

Using this type of argument is on the same level as the interpretation that had been given earlier of the Quebec proposition respecting "reciprocal agreements" between the provinces on the language question.

10. See Claude Morin's letter to his counterparts from the provinces in the "gang of eight" (*Le Devoir*, November 17, 1981, p. 16); Roy J. Romanow's reply (*Le Devoir*, January 21, 1982, p. 7); Claude Morin's reply (*Le Devoir*, February 20, 1982, p. 15); an unpublished letter from Roy Romanow to Claude Morin, dated March 9, 1982; and especially Claude Morin, "Le Québec seul dans son coin," *Policy Options*, vol. 3, no. 4, July-August, 1982, pp. 10-17.

11. Gérard Bergeron, *Le Devoir*, December 11, 1981, p. 10.

12. Perhaps this is a good time to recall the scandalous non-application of section 133 of the BNA Act in Ontario, which is regarded in Quebec as being an unequivocally harmful omission.

13. Bill 62, recently passed by the Assemblée nationale, is aimed at a general and complete extension of the celebrated "notwithstanding" clause.

14. *La Presse*, December 15, 1981, p. A2. According to Lise Payette, former PQ government minister, Trudeau and Lévesque are "like an old couple whose confrontations are something of a spectacle. Cheered by Quebecers as saviours of the nation, both men will drive us, with bravado and gallant last stands, to the emptiest dead end in our history." *Le Pouvoir?* (Montreal: Québec-Amérique, 1982), p. 138.

Chapter 4/A Dangerous Deed: The Constitution Act, 1982

Donald Smiley

As the First Ministers' Conference ended on November 5, 1981 Prime Minister Trudeau and the premiers of all the provinces except Quebec preened before the television cameras in mutual congratulation. This paper is an attempt to evaluate whether other Canadians have reason to be grateful for what these self-proclaimed great and good men have done for them.

The Constitutional Developments of 1980-82:
The Third National Policy and National Unity

The constitutional actions of the government of Canada that culminated in the Constitution Act were an integral part of a coherent set of initiatives undertaken by the federal Liberal Party after it returned to power in 1980. Bruce Doern has detailed the five elements of this strategy, which emerged in 1980-81: constitutional change, the National Energy Policy, a new and more rationalized approach to economic development, western economic development and new measures to improve relations with the West, and the re-structuring of fiscal relations with the provinces in both their equalization and social program dimensions.[1] These new directions had a coherence in the general assertion of the federal government that the power of the provinces, and the perceived disposition of Canadians to emphasize their provincial rather than national allegiances, "has increased, is increasing, and ought to be diminished." The original National Policy gave direction and a measure of legitimacy to the central government in the period between its adoption and the accomplishment of its major objectives by the beginning of the First World War. During and immediately after the Second World War, the federal government committed the country to a broad set of goals which I have elsewhere designated as the "New National Policy": Ottawa's responsibility for full employment and relative price stability, the development under federal leadership of a Canadian welfare state, and Canadian efforts towards the establishment of a new international economic order on liberal principles.[2] The initiative of 1980-81 can reasonably be viewed as our Third National Policy.

The relations of Quebec with the wider Canadian political community were, of course, the central influences in the constitutional developments which culminated in the Constitution Act, 1982, and it is reasonable to evaluate these developments largely in terms of their probable impact on present and future Quebec-Canada relations. Prior to the 1960s there was an underlying consensus in Canada that the constitution itself did not stand in the way of any legitimate purposes that individuals and groups might want to pursue. Much of the constitutional debate centred around one version or another of the compact theory of Confederation, on the underlying conservative premise that the original constitutional settlement possessed a continuing legitimacy. Even those who rejected the compact theory, particularly in the vigorous debates of the 1930s, asserted the ongoing legitimacy of the Confederation settlement as embodied in the British North America Act of 1867 and turned their criticism of the constitutional order not on the constitution itself, but on its interpretation by the Judicial Committee of the Privy Council. Thus the increasing disposition of Canadians towards explicit constitutional reform is a relatively new development, with few roots in our earlier history.[3] The late Daniel Johnson of Quebec may reasonably be regarded as the father of this development. The election of the Union Nationale in the provincial election of 1966, along with the increasing influence of the "new guard" federal Liberals from Quebec over the policies of the Pearson government, apparently encouraged Premier Robarts of Ontario to convene the Confederation of Tomorrow Conference in November 1967, and this initiative developed into the federal-provincial constitutional negotiations which culminated in the Victoria Charter of 1971. While in opposition, Johnson had published a short book, *Egalité ou Indépendance*, which asserted the urgency of early and radical constitutional reform on a bi-national basis—a decisive rejection of both the equivocations of the Lesage Liberals about the necessity of explicit constitutional change and the traditional Quebec conservatism in constitutional matters articulated in the compact theory of Confederation.

The more immediate context of the constitutional developments of 1980–82 was the Quebec referendum of May 1980. In the referendum campaign, Prime Minister Trudeau and his federal Liberal colleagues made highly generalized commitments to the Quebec electorate that if a "no" verdict were returned, something unprecisely designated as "renewed federalism" would be effected. Very shortly after the referendum, there was a series of intensive intergovernmental meetings on constitutional reform, culminating in the abortive First Ministers' Conference of September 1980.

Within the framework of constitutional debate in Quebec over the preceding two decades, what could the pledge of "renewed federalism" reasonably be taken to mean? The pressures of both government and opposition parties in Quebec provincial politics from 1960 onward has been for an enhanced range of autonomy for the authorities of that province and corresponding restrictions on the powers of the federal government over Quebecers. The Constitution Act, 1982 *restricts* the powers of the Legislature and government of Quebec and was brought into being by a procedure which *was opposed* by that Legislature and government. Furthermore, the constitutional reform which was effected in the spring of 1982 was an integral part of a general initiative from Ottawa towards a more highly centralized federal system. The pledges of constitutional reform made to the Quebec electorate by the federal Liberal leaders have *not* been honoured, and it is not too much to say that this electorate has been betrayed.

One must squarely face the question whether the conventions of the Canadian constitution required Quebec assent to a request of the Parliament of Canada for an amendment altering the powers of the provinces. My conclusion is that such consent *was* required.

The late Sir Ivor Jennings in his *Law of the Constitution* crisply summarized the tests by which a constitutional convention can be distinguished: "We have to ask ourselves these questions: First, what are the precedents; secondly, did the actors in the precedents believe that they were bound by a rule; and thirdly, is there a reason for the rule?"[4] The majority of the Supreme Court of Canada, in the decision of September 28, 1981 which declared that convention would be breached by the Parliament of Canada acting on the proposed constitutional Resolution in the face of the opposition of eight provinces, quoted Jennings' three-fold test as authoritative.

The relevant precedents in the circumstances under discussion would appear to be those past amendments explicitly altering the constitutional distribution of federal and provincial powers: the amendments of 1930, 1931, 1940, 1951 and 1964.[5] Such amendments were effected after the consent of all the provinces had been secured, except in the case of the 1930 amendment, where the consent of only the prairie provinces, which were the only ones directly affected, was obtained. Yet this, of course, does not lead directly to a convention requiring Quebec assent, especially in the light of the majority decision of the Supreme Court on September 28. It asserted that not unanimity, but a substantial measure of provincial consent was required by convention for such amendments.

Jennings' second rule involves the major political actors giving some indication that adherence to the rule is obligatory. In his statement to the House of Commons on the 1940 Resolution transferring legislative jurisdiction over unemployment insurance to the Dominion, Prime Minister King said that his government had avoided raising the issue of whether unanimous provincial consent for such an amendment was required by having obtained the prior agreement of all the provinces. The last sentence of the statement of the 1965 White Paper on the fourth "principle" (note that the word "convention" was not used here) governing amendments to the constitution is equivocal:

> the Canadian Parliament will not request an amendment directly affecting federal-provincial relationships without prior consultation and agreement with the provinces. This principle did not emerge as early as the others but since 1907, and particularly since 1930, has gained increasing recognition and acceptance. *The nature and the degree of provincial participation in the amending process, however, have not lent themselves to easy definition.*[6]

The more relevant circumstances in my view are those surrounding the Victoria Charter of 1971.[7] The Charter *did* propose significant changes in the federal-provincial distribution of powers and was agreed to by the federal government and the governments of the provinces other than Quebec. After the Quebec government had given notice of its dissent from those changes, there was no serious discussion to the effect that the Charter should be embodied in a Resolution of the Parliament of Canada requesting Westminster to amend the Canadian constitution in these terms. In this situation, which I believe has a direct relevance to the events of 1980–82, the major political actors showed at least tacit acceptance of the principle that Quebec assent to amendments altering federal-provincial powers was by convention required.

Jennings' third criterion relates to the reason for the rule. To put it another way, conventions must have a rationale in the essential nature of the political and constitutional order. How does the test apply here? Such an application almost inevitably involves judgements about the fundamental nature of the political community upon which competent and disinterested observers will differ. In my view, the first-line protection of the rights of the francophone community of Quebec is and has been since Confederation among the powers of the Legislature and government of that province, and on this basis Canadian constitutional convention dictates that these powers should not be restricted without Quebec's assent. The historical record is clear that the Dominion of Canada emerged as a federal political community, albeit one with certain quasi-unitary features, only because the francophone leaders of lower Canada would not have it otherwise,[8] and several important terms of the BNA Act of 1867 gave explicit recognition to Quebec's particularity—most crucially, perhaps, section 94, which envisaged a very different distribution of legislative powers between the Dominion and Quebec than the one prevailing in the common-law provinces. One is not required to accept a thorough-going two-nations view of Canada to believe that *some* considerable constitutional recognition of cultural duality is essential to the continuing stability, if not the existence, of Confederation, and that the most crucial elements of such recognition will be embodied in safeguards for the powers of the provincial authorities of Quebec.

The short-run political impact on Quebec of the constitutional developments between the "consensus" of November 5 and the proclamation of the Constitution Act on April 17 has been to compromise national unity. The November agreement between Ottawa and the other nine provinces led the Parti Québécois decisively to turn its back on *étapisme*. According to PQ policy, the next provincial election is to be fought on sovereignty; if the party receives a majority of the popular votes, it will regard this as a mandate to take immediate steps towards sovereignty, and economic association with Canada is not to be a pre-condition of independence. The previous policy, as accepted in 1974, divorced the sovereignty issue from that of the PQ's electoral fortunes. Following this distinction, the party won decisive electoral victories in 1976 and 1981 on campaigns where sovereignty was down-played, and sustained an equally decisive defeat in the sovereignty-association referendum of 1980. If the commitment to *étapisme* had continued, and in my view it was in the interests of those committed to Confederation that it should, it was at least possible that the PQ government's conduct would increasingly have been motivated by the objective of remaining in power, and there is ample evidence that its commitment to Quebec independence was the party's major electoral liability. Furthermore, and this is equally significant, the November "consensus" denied the Ryan Liberals a defensible constitutional position on which to stand. In my view, the party's Beige paper of 1980 was constructive both in spirit and substance, and would have been a useful starting point for constitutional discussions leading to a genuinely "renewed federalism." Yet in the current context this general thrust towards reform has been completely frustrated.[9]

The legitimacy of the Constitution Act is thus denied not only by the government of Quebec, but also by a significant body of Quebec opinion which has not accepted the sovereignty option. The National Assembly has passed legislation which provides for a maximum use of the *non obstante* clause of section 33 of the Charter of Rights and Freedoms by Quebec, and asserts that the Quebec human rights charter is to be regarded as having primacy over the Constitution Act. While the *raison-d'être* of the PQ is to remove Quebec from Confederation, the Constitution Act and the process by which it was put in place gives the separatist government an opportunity it did not have before to make a fundamental challenge to the *existing* constitutional order of which Quebec remains a part.

In general, then, an exercise in constitutional review and reform whose alleged objectives were to create more harmonious relations between Quebec and the wider Canadian community has involved a betrayal of the Quebec electorate, a breach of fundamental constitutional convention, a recrudescence of Quebec nationalism, and an even more serious Quebec challenge than before to the legitimacy of the Canadian constitutional order.

There is, of course, a contrary argument to the one I have advanced. Its general assertion is that because of the commitment of the Parti Québécois to Quebec independence, the government of the province could not reasonably be expected to participate in any but an obstructive way in efforts to reform the federal system. Certainly it appears to have become the consensus that Premier Lévesque could not be brought into agreement on any significant matters of reform acceptable to the other governments. One may also conjecture that any hesitations which the premiers of the provinces who signed the consensus may have had about the PQ's dissent were in large part overcome because the major actors in the federal government were themselves québécois.

This line of argument has something to it. The West Germans speak of the "spirit of constitutional comity." Certainly in a political order based as largely as the Canadian is on convention, one might reasonably question the legitimacy of constitutional actors who explicitly challenge the basic elements of that order, and whose *raison d'être* is to destroy it. However, to proceed on this assumption in the Canadian context of November 1981 is in the highest degree dangerous. Certainly it is indefensible to argue, as does the PQ, that Quebec members of Parliament are not legitimate representatives of the will of Quebec. Yet it is equally indefensible to assert that these persons are the *only* representatives of that community. Premier Blakeney of Saskatchewan lucidly stated the essentials of federalism in his closing statement to the First Ministers' Conference of September 1980:

> I do not believe that the national interest is represented by a consensus of all provincial governments. The federal government has a role to play. It is not a creature of the provinces. This is not a confederation. Nor, however, do I believe that the national interest is to ascertain [sic] by the majority will of Canadians. This is something more than a collection of citizens and, accordingly, the national interest cannot be stated by the majority view in the House of Commons. That is the view of a unitary state and under these circumstances one does not really need a constitution. One can deal with the national interest and identify it from time to time. . . . The essence of Canada is therefore that on major matters we need a double majority. We need the majority of citizens as expressed by the popular will in the House of Commons and we need the majority, however defined, of the regional will. That is the essence of federalism.[10]

The Quebec community, alone of the provinces, did not participate in the double majority of the November consensus. It is distressing for non-Quebecers at least that both protagonists of the two extreme options— Quebec independence, and the highly centralized version of Canadian federalism embodied in the Third National Policy—have decisive mandates from the Quebec electorate. Yet it is both constitutionally inappropriate and politically dangerous for non-Quebecers to attempt to resolve this impasse by acting as if one or the other of these contending Quebec factions were the sole authentic representative of the Quebec community.[11]

National unity in the contemporary Canadian context involves much more than relations between Quebec and the wider Canadian community. In a perceptive paper delivered in 1978, Alan Cairns turned his attention away from the preoccupation with French-English relations to what he designated as "the other crisis of Canadian federalism."[12] He described this as,

> the crisis of a political system with a declining capacity for the effective use of the authority of government for the attainment of public goals. This . . . is a constitutional crisis in the sense that the working constitution of Canadian federalism can no longer control and channel the

activities of governments in order to minimize their self-defeating
competition with each other. Far from existing in splendid policy-
making isolation from each other, these governments jostle and compete
in an ever-more destructive struggle which reduces the beneficial public
impact of the massive public sector produced by their conflicting, overlapping and discordant ambitions.[13]

The Constitution Act, 1982 does nothing to resolve Cairns' "other
crisis." The "consensus" of November 5 was quickly succeeded by the
February First Ministers' Conference on the economy, which ranged all the
provinces against the federal government in criticism of Ottawa's economic
policy, and about six weeks later by the imposition by the federal government of a new federal-provincial fiscal regime with less provincial agreement than had been attained in any such settlement since the Second World
War. To the extent that national unity requires explicit changes in the
federal dimensions of the constitutional order—either by way of changes
in the distribution of legislative powers, or of "intrastate" changes to make
the central government structures more representative of and responsive to
provincial/regional interests—the reform of 1982 is at best irrelevant.
Among the governments there appears to be, for the time being at least, a
feeling of constitutional exhaustion. Furthermore, the pervasive centralizing thrust of the Third National Policy makes it improbable that any
significant degree of agreement can be reached in the short-term future on
reforming the federal dimensions of the constitutional system.
　　There is a counter-argument to my negative assessment of the impact
of recent constitutional changes on these elements of national unity other
than Canada-Quebec relations. It has been asserted that the very act of
patriation—"bringing the constitution home"—has been a profoundly
nationalizing experience for Canadians. More fundamentally, the Charter
of Rights and Freedoms—the so-called "people's package"—has been
viewed by the federal authorities as a potentially nationalizing device,
weaning Canadians away from their provincialism by causing them to
define themselves as possessors of certain nation-wide rights guaranteed in
the final analysis by a national Supreme Court.
　　One must be very tentative in assessing the future consequences of the
Charter of Rights and Freedoms on the political culture, and in particular
the impact of the Charter on national unity. The legal philosopher Ronald
Dworkin wrote in 1970, "The language of rights now dominates political
debate in the United States. . . . It is not surprising that these questions are
now prominent. The concept of rights, and particularly the concept of
rights against the Government, has its most natural use when a political
society is divided, and appeals to co-operation or a common goal are
pointless."[14] From this perspective, the Charter is inherently a fragmenting
rather than unifying measure; while one may make some rhetorical
mileage by asserting that the Charter binds Canadians together in their

common possession of certain rights, the defence of rights centres on conflict rather than co-operation. Furthermore, the process by which the Charter was contrived after the introduction into Parliament of the government Resolution in October 1980 centred on the claims of special interest groups. Most of the witnesses heard by the Special Joint Committee represented such interests—women, ethnic groups, religious denominations, native peoples and so on—and the action on the constitutional front between the end of the First Ministers' Conference in November 1981 and the passage of the Resolution in its final form by Parliament the next month centred on the mobilization of groups representing the claims of women and native peoples. In the concluding chapter of his recent *Memoirs*, J.A. Corry expresses a sombre view of the prospects of liberal democracy on these terms:

> The busier governments are in granting or denying special claims, the more their credit sinks. However reasonable, even inescapable, a claim for special treatment may be, granting it leads governments into ignoring an important requirement of democracy. One of the basic demands of the early democrats was for equality before the law and the wiping out of privileges maintained by law under royal or aristocratic regimes for particular persons or special classes.... The concentration of politicians, legislatures and public debate on the rival claims of diverse interests keeps our attention riveted on matters much more likely to divide us than to draw us together.[15]

Unfortunately, I think, the debate on the Charter emphasized special claims rather than those rights possessed by all Canadians, and in particular there was relatively little debate on what the Charter itself designates as "fundamental freedoms." The Charter and the procedure by which it was evolved appear to me to have limited capacities for furthering national unity. Certainly the exaggerated claims made for entrenchment by some of its supporters, including Prime Minister Trudeau, will almost inevitably lead to disillusionment as individuals and groups discover that rights cannot be guaranteed in any such sure and absolute way.

The more extensive entrenchment of language rights has been a central aspect of the federal Liberals' constitutional strategy since the first federal-provincial conference on the constitution in 1968. A document issued under Prime Minister Trudeau's signature in 1977 lucidly elaborated the rationale for the strategy:

> The federal government rejects the concepts of a Canada divided into two mutually exclusive unilingual separate countries or two mutually exclusive unilingual regions within one country. While these two options have a superficial appearance of dissimilarity, they amount in practice to the same thing, a province or state of Quebec that is unilingual French speaking and the rest of Canada, or a truncated Canada, that is unilingual English speaking. The government rejects

these concepts above all because they entail a denial of the existence of the official language minority groups of Canada.[16]

The protection of the rights of the official-language minorities has been central both to Ottawa's constitutional initiatives and to the Trudeau government's version of national unity. In a speech to the Quebec Chamber of Commerce on October 22, 1980 the prime minister referred to linguistic rights in terms that suggested that these were the crucial arms of the government's constitutional goals. Encapsulating their rights in a broader Charter made the protection of English and French more palatable to English-speaking Canadians and fended off the charge that constitutional reform was an exercise of "French power." Because of the crucial role of the protection of language rights in the Trudeauvian constitutional strategy, it is reasonable to evaluate the Constitution Act, 1982 in these terms, whether or not one shares the federal government's perspective.

There are undoubted gains for official-language minorities in the Charter. In effect, the Official Languages Acts of Canada and of New Brunswick are given constitutional entrenchment. Perhaps more significantly, the nine provinces with English-language majorities accepted the entrenchment of the educational rights of the francophone minorities on a where-numbers-warrant basis. Yet by Ottawa's own tests, the Charter is seriously deficient in the protection of the rights of official-language minorities. The two largest minorities receive limited protection. As a part of the bargain that Ontario would support Ottawa's constitutional initiative, it was agreed that the Charter would not provide for the constitutional entrenchment of the equality of the two languages in the Legislature and courts of that province. Thus, so far as provincial and local services are concerned, Ontario francophones receive no additional protection from the Charter except for the constitutional protection of educational rights. Similarly, such protection for the English-speaking minorities of Quebec is also somewhat restricted, although it will remain for the courts to determine fully what, if any, elements of existing Quebec language legislation are incompatible with the Charter. Section 59 of the Constitution Act provides that section 23(1)(a) shall come into effect in Quebec only when authorized by the government or Legislative Assembly of that province. This seems to mean that until that time only Canadian citizens residing in Quebec who have had their primary education in Canada in English will have the right to have their children educated in that language. That right appears to be denied to other parents who are Canadian citizens, but who had English-language primary education outside Canada. If this interpretation of section 59 is accurate, there is a clear, and to me indefensible, discrimination among citizens on the basis of national origins. Section 20(1)(a), relating to services from federal agencies apart from their respective head offices, and section 23(3), governing education in the minority official language in particular provinces, provide much more limited protection than was suggested by the 1967 Report of the Royal Commission on Bilingualism and Biculturalism. The report recommended that after each biennial census, bilingual districts be drawn up in which 10 percent of the population or more had the minority official language of the province as its mother tongue, and that within such districts all public services be provided in both languages.[17] The Charter provides a more limited protection, and in effect charges the courts with establishing standards on a piecemeal basis for minority language access to education and federal services.

One's view of the relation between the position of official-language minorities and national unity is derived from fundamental assumptions about the nature of the Canadian Confederation. On the basis of Ottawa's premises about the primacy of this relation, the Charter is seriously deficient.

My judgements about the implications for national unity of the Constitution Act and the procedures by which it was effected are on the whole adverse. Yet it is necessary to be quite clear about the perspectives from which the critique is made. The perspective asserts that the resources of the Canadian political system for conciliation, compromise and persuasion have not been exhausted. In pursuing the Third National Policy the federal government has clearly been willing to make compromises, and in particular, significant compromises were made by Ottawa in forging the consensus of November 5, 1981. Yet the allegedly hard-nosed view of the provinces taken by the federal government since the Liberal restoration of 1980 appears to be based on the premise that such compromises should be entered into only on the face of overwhelming pressure, and that conflict rather than conciliation is the normal condition of federal-provincial relations.[18] In an address delivered to the Law Society of Upper Canada in 1978, J.A. Corry gave a wiser counsel in conducting our common offices, based on "a meticulous constitutional morality, a mutual comity which never overlooks advance notice and consultation, always strives for accommodation." He added, "In the constitutional law of a federal state, particularly where the interests and sensitivities of minorities are involved, only in the rarest circumstances should nation-wide majorities insist on getting everything the constitution makes possible."[19] Unfortunately, this prudent advice was not taken.

Another premise of the Third National Policy is that the attachment of citizens to their respective provinces and to Canada are competing rather than complementary allegiances, and that steps must urgently be taken to strengthen national loyalties. David Elkins and Richard Simeon have presented the findings of recent survey research to the effect that, "citizens generally see no need to 'choose sides'—to renounce either their federal and provincial loyalties and identities," and go on to suggest, "We have urged that political leaders weigh carefully any actions or policies which might lead people to feel that a choice was being forced on them—a dilemma posed in terms of 'he who is not for me is against me.' We believe firmly that no such final choice is necessary or desirable.''[20] The Third National Policy, of which the Constitution Act is a central element, rejects this temperate stance.

The Substance of the Canada Act

We now turn to a brief critical assessment of the two most important elements of the Constitution Act—the new amending formula and the Canadian Charter of Rights and Freedoms. Part VI of the Act, dealing with provincial powers over non-renewable natural resources, will not be discussed. It was added to the federal Resolution presented to Parliament in October 1980, in what proved to be an unsuccessful attempt to get the support of the Saskatchewan government for Ottawa's constitutional initiative.

Ottawa's justification for its constitutional policies from October 1980 onward was based on the urgency of breaking the constitutional impasse of 54 years.[21] The alleged immediacy about patriation and a wholly domestic amending formula badly needs to be put in perspective. Prior to December 1981, Canada had not requested an amendment from the Parliament of the United Kingdom since 1964, and there is not the slightest doubt that Westminster would have enacted any such a request in a *pro forma* way if the prior consent of all the provinces had been secured. Despite federal talk about the "unanimity trap," there was no projected amendment on the constitutional horizon which was likely to be opposed by only one or two of the smaller provinces, and I have already argued that it would have been inappropriate to proceed with any amendment re-defining provincial powers without the consent of Quebec. If anyone was seriously interested in the reality as opposed to the symbolism of Canadian autonomy, he would have been more concerned with the continuous influence of the U.S. Federal Reserve Board over Canadian interest rates than the infrequent involvement of the United Kingdom Parliament in the amending process.

Despite what has been written above, the patriation/amending formula situation had become profoundly unsatisfactory. Although one may believe that public urgency about this issue was somewhat contrived, a large number of Canadians had come to regard it as a sign of national humiliation, and it is arrogant to ignore these feelings as being without much substance. The real as opposed to the symbolic difficulty in 1980–81 was in a circumstance where a constitutional amendment would be requested by the Parliament of Canada in the face of opposition from one or more provinces, and where the British authorities would have no alternative to choosing sides between the Canadian disputants.

In my view, successive federal governments since the Victoria Conference of 1971 could be faulted for not taking decisive action to break the patriation/amending formula deadlock. The solution provided for in the Victoria Charter was a useful starting point, and Quebec's rejection of the Charter did not involve opposition to the proposed amending procedure. In late 1974 the federal government attempted to re-activate the process of constitutional review, which had lapsed since Victoria, by suggesting that the new constitutional agenda be confined to the resolution of the patriation/amending formula issue. The provinces responded by demanding that it be linked to discussion of the distribution of legislative powers. I believe that Ottawa should have pushed forward to enact a patriation/ amending formula with whatever degree of provincial support that could be secured. Such a course of action could have been defended on the grounds that resolution of this deadlock was a necessary preliminary to future substantive reforms, and that such reforms could not be fully legitimized if enacted by the Parliament of the United Kingdom. Furthermore, there was a precedent for such action by Ottawa in the 1949 amendment, which put in place the amending procedure that was in effect until the enactment of the Canada Act, 1982. Although the British North America Act (No. 2) of 1949 left unchanged the procedure by which parts of the constitution relating to the division of legislative powers and minority rights could be amended, the distinction between these matters and those where Parliament could act alone was made unilaterally by the federal government without the advice or consent of the provinces. It is likely that there would have been some degree of provincial opposition to the course I have suggested, particularly from Alberta and possibly from British Columbia. Because the Victoria formula gave Quebec a permanent veto over the most crucial of amendments, it would have been difficult to mount any plausible objection from that province. Also, it seems unlikely that the dissenting provinces could have found significant support in the United Kingdom.

There was remarkably little debate about the proposed amending formula among governments or the informed public during 1980–81. The proceedings of the Joint Committee of the Senate and House of Commons were almost completely monopolized by discussions of the Charter, to the neglect of the other major element of the government's constitutional Resolution. The eight-province Accord of April 1981, which formed the basis for the amending procedure embodied in the Constitution Act, was widely interpreted at the time, and perhaps even by some of the participating provinces themselves, as a strategic ploy and was not subjected to much critical examination. Thus we now have an amending formula which has received little scrutiny. Such scrutiny could have proceeded by examining either the likely fate of projected amendments under the formula or what might have happened to past amendments had this formula been in effect.

In light of the failure of governments from 1927 onward to agree on a domestic amending formula, the federal and provincial administrations in 1981 were surprisingly willing to compromise on this matter. By signing the April Accord, the Lévesque government turned its back on the traditional Quebec demand for a veto over amendments and on the position that discussions of a new amending formula must take place only within the context of a review of the distribution of powers. British Columbia, as another member of the "gang of eight," put aside its claim, advanced from 1978 onwards, to be recognized as one of Canada's five regions with its own veto over future amendments. At the beginning of the November conference, Premier Davis of Ontario also expressed his willingness to accept a formula that did not contain an Ontario veto.

The flexibility of the federal government is even more notable. Throughout the 1970s the Trudeau administration clearly favoured the Victoria formula, with possible minor modifications related to the Western and/or Atlantic provinces. After the introduction of the 1980 Resolution, Ottawa appeared to put a high value on some sort of procedure for popular referenda to resolve federal-provincial differences about proposed amendments. As late as the opening day of the November conference, Mr. Trudeau and his colleagues were harshly critical of the "Vancouver formula" on the general grounds that this might involve the "checkerboarding" of human rights. In accepting the basic elements of this formula three days later, the government put aside its long-standing objections to any procedure which might result in some provinces having greater legislative powers than others.

The Constitution Act divides the constitution into several parts, with a differing amending procedure applied to each. Some elements of the categorization follow previous Canadian law and practice—for example the provisions that amendments affecting one or more but not all the provinces are to be made with the consent of Parliament and of the province(s) concerned, and that Parliament may unilaterally amend the aspects of the constitution related to the federal executive and the House of Commons. However, the rationale of other provisions is less evident: (1) Under section 42(f), new provinces can be established only with the consent of Parliament and the Legislatures of two-thirds of the provinces with 50 percent of the Canadian population. This is a marked and potentially significant departure from past law and practice under which the federal authorities exercised the unilateral power to establish new provinces so long as the boundaries of pre-existing provinces were not affected. (2) Apart from the rights of the English and French languages, the Charter of Rights and Freedoms may be amended by the Vancouver formula procedure. Despite the alleged urgency of securely entrenching rights, the major elements of the Charter are not subject to the requirement of unanimous provincial consent. (3) Section 41(w) enacts that unanimous provincial consent is needed for amendments related to "the office of the Queen, the Governor

General and the Lieutenant Governor of a province." Any future disposi-
tions of Canadians to modify or abolish the monarchical forms will be very
difficult to effect. (4) Section 41(d) requires unanimous provincial consent
for amendments relating to the "composition of the Supreme Court of
Canada." This provision is somewhat puzzling as the existing constitution
does not specify this composition, and section 41(d) can only be taken to
mean that a future amendment related to this matter can come into the
constitution only by the unanimous consent procedure and is subject to
subsequent amendment by that procedure. (5) Section 41(e) enacts that an
amendment to the amending procedure itself requires unanimous provincial assent. Section 49 provides that the prime minister of Canada is to
convene a First Ministers' Conference within 15 years to renew the provisions of the amending formula, but with the rigidities under section 41(e) it
could seem unlikely that the formula will be changed even if it had considerable support.

The most critical and contentious issues in devising a Canadian
amending formula have been the extent of provincial consent required for
amendments to the distribution of powers. In such discussions four considerations are relevant: (1) the number of provinces consenting; (2) the
combined population of consenting provinces; (3) the special position of
Quebec in Confederation; (4) the way of grouping of the Western and
Atlantic provinces. The Victoria Charter of 1971 took into the account all
these considerations by its provision that:

> Amendments to the Constitution of Canada may from time to time be
> made by proclamation issued by the Governor General under the Great
> Seal of Canada when so authorized by resolutions of the Senate and
> House of Commons and of the Legislative Assemblies of at least a
> majority of the provinces that includes:
>   (1) every province that at any time before the issue of such proclama-
> tions had, according to any previous general census, a population of at
> least twenty-five per cent of the population of Canada.
>   (2) at least two of the Atlantic provinces;
>   (3) at least two of the Western provinces that have, according to the
> latest general census, combined populations of at least fifty per cent of the
> population of all the Western provinces.

The corresponding procedure in the Constitution Act does not take into
account the last two of these four factors, i.e. Quebec is given no special
status (as it had permanently under the 25-percent-of-the-population
provision of the Victoria Charter), and there is no account taken of regional
groupings of the Atlantic and Western provinces.

It is significant that the amending formula of the Act differs from the
eight-province April Accord in not providing for the interdelegation by
mutual consent of legislative powers between Parliament and the provinces.

Before 1960 there was some discussion of this device as a way of overcoming the inflexibility of a division of legislative powers which was hard to change through formal amendment and evolving patterns of judicial review. The Fulton-Favreau formula of 1964 attempted to temper the rigidities of a procedure requiring unanimous provincial consent for the most crucial of amendments by a provision allowing the delegation of some provincial powers to Parliament and of all federal legislative powers to the provinces so long as at least four provinces consented. There was almost no discussion of delegation in the review procedure begun in 1967–68 until the Beige paper of the Quebec Liberal Party in 1980 recommended that delegation be permitted if approved by the projected Federal Council, with the proviso that the delegating government(s) should retain continuing financial responsibility for such programs. The eight-province Accord of April 1981 contained a procedure permitting federal-provincial delegation in certain areas on the condition that the delegating government(s) would provide the other(s) with "reasonable compensation . . . taking into account the per capita costs to exercise that jurisdiction." The public record does not contain any mention that delegation was discussed at the November 1981 meeting of first ministers.

The first ministers did agree to permit as many as three provinces to opt out of certain amendments as an alternative device. Section 38(3) of the Constitution Act says in respect of amendments effected under the procedures requiring the consent of two-thirds of the provinces with half the Canadian population:

> An amendment referred to in subsection (2) shall not have effect in a province the legislative assembly of which has expressed its dissent thereto by resolution supported by a majority of its members prior to the issue of the proclamation to which the amendment relates unless that legislative assembly, subsequently, by resolution supported by a majority of its members, revokes its dissent and authorizes the amendment.

Section 40 says that when such amendments transfer,

> provincial legislative powers relating to education and other cultural matters from provincial legislatures to Parliament, Canada shall provide reasonable compensation to any province to which the amendment does not apply.

If conflicts should arise under section 40, the courts will be faced with the difficult decisions of defining "reasonable compensation" and/or "education or other cultural matters." Part of the Quebec objection to the Act has been that compensation should be extended to all matters on which provinces opt out. However, provisions for compensation are significant only where costly public services are involved, and would have little meaning in situations relating to economic regulation or to most aspects of the Charter.

One can only speculate about the future impact of the new formula on Canadian constitutional development. It is significant that the federal authorities have the discretion to determine whether an amendment altering the division of powers will be effected without a *larger* extent of provincial consent than that of two-thirds of the provinces with half the Canadian population. Gordon Robertson suggests that Ontario may in effect have retained its veto on the assumption that Quebec is most likely to oppose amendments desired by Ottawa and most of the other provinces, and in such circumstances Ontario will have the power either to frustrate or to facilitate such amendments.[22] The regional character of previous amendment proposals is weakened, since changes could be made against the opposition of three of either the Western or the Atlantic provinces, although if the amendments derogated from the rights or powers of such provinces they could, of course, opt out.

The other major element of the Constitution Act is the Charter of Rights and Freedoms. There was no necessary or logical connection between the resolution of the patriation/amending formula issue and the Charter, and it was unfortunate that the federal government chose to link them. In the debates during 1980–81, Prime Minister Trudeau challenged the Progressive Conservatives on the grounds that since they supported the general principle of entrenchment of rights, it was illogical to oppose the only way in which such entrenchment could come about. However, it is not altogether improbable that the required amount of provincial consent for a Charter could have been quickly found using the new amending formula, if Ottawa had been willing to wait. Since the end of the Second World War, elite and mass opinion had come to support entrenchment,[23] and by 1980–81 all three federal parties had accepted the position. Subsequently, the two premiers who had been the strongest opponents of entrenchment, Lyon of Manitoba and Blakeney of Saskatchewan, went down to electoral defeat in November 1981 and April 1982 respectively. In general, then, those who in principle oppose the further entrenchment of rights have been rendered a minority. From a symbolic point of view the Charter of Rights and Freedoms, the embodiment of the highest ideals of the Canadian political community, was put in place not by the Canadian authorities, but by the Parliament of the United Kingdom.

The Canadian Charter of Rights and Freedoms is the most radical break ever made with a constitutional and legal order hitherto characterized by continuity and incremental development. The Charter also imposes on the courts—the institutions of the governmental system most attuned towards incrementalism—the major responsibility for effecting this rupture with the past. Since April 17, 1982 Canadian law in the field of human rights has been in disarray. It will take decades, or even longer, for the courts to give authoritative meaning to the general phrases of the Charter. It is honey-combed with terms new to jurisprudence in Canada or elsewhere: "such reasonable limits prescribed by law as can be demonstrably justified in a free and democratic society," "the amelioration of the conditions of disadvantaged individuals or groups," "significant demands for communications with and services from that office in such minority official language," the "where-numbers-warrant" provisions in respect of education in the minority official languages, "proceedings which would bring the administration of justice into disrepute," "the principles of fundamental justice," "mental or physical disability," etc. Besides giving authoritative meanings to such terms, the courts must define standards of governmental conduct concerning, for example, legal rights and fundamental freedoms where hitherto Parliament and the premiers acting within their own sphere of legislative jurisdiction were supreme. It has been accurately said that the Charter will be a gold-mine for lawyers.

Lawyers are most active when the law is most uncertain, and this new source of profitable work is profoundly to be deplored by the rest of us. A defensible regime of human rights must embody not only substantive freedom and equity, but also a reasonable certainty in the definition of such rights as are protected by law. The situation vested on Canadians by the Charter demonstrably fails this second test. Admittedly, the Charter removes some of the former ambiguities in the division of powers over particular kinds of rights between Parliament and the Legislatures. Yet on balance, the Charter brings more uncertainty than it removes. In his *Quebec and the Constitution 1960-1978*, Edward McWhinney posits "digestibility" as one of his five "axioms of constitution-making."[24] Unfortunately, perhaps, Canadian decision-makers chose not to follow his prudent advice.

Both the supporters and the opponents of the Charter made regrettably weak cases for their respective positions. It was, for example, indefensible to argue, as did Premier Lyon, that constitutional entrenchment of rights would be in itself a renunciation of our monarchical and parliamentary traditions. The 1982 reforms do not constitute any change in Canada's adherence to the monarchy, and as we have seen, unanimous provincial consent is required for any amendment affecting "the office of the Queen, the Governor General and the Lieutenant Governor of a province." Several other countries which have retained the Westminster model have entrenched bills of rights. Furthermore, the British North America Act of 1867 contained a limited entrenchment of the rights of denominational minorities in education under section 93(2), and of the English and French languages in section 133.

Neither is it much of an argument to suggest that entrenchment is to be avoided by Canadians because it is an acceptance of American ways. Whatever one thinks of the general view that the devices of the United States are to be eschewed, the American constitutional traditions and circumstances in respect of human rights are so different from the Canadian that there is little correspondence between the two countries even after the

Charter has come into effect: the United States Bill of Rights protects a much more limited number of claims; there is a long tradition of civil rights jurisprudence in the United States; the courts have played and continue to play a much different role in the governmental system; the American constitutional tradition is as inextricably linked with natural right and natural law assumptions as ours is not.

Also, I find unpersuasive the view that the entrenchment of rights is undemocratic because it removes final decisions about the definition and ranking of rights from elected Legislatures to appointed courts.[25] Martin Shapiro, in his spirited defence of judicial activism in the protection of First Amendment rights of free speech, argues that American opinion that judicial review is undemocratic proceeds on a very hard-nosed view of the judicial process, but that same opinion accepts a highly inaccurate and mythologized account of how Legislatures do in fact make decisions. He says "Congressional policy is today largely made in the crosscurrents of clashing committee jurisdictions, not by an orderly implementation by the will of any Congressional majorities."[26] While the Canadian parliamentary system is more closely attuned to parliamentary majorities acting in response to popular opinion, it is indefensible to argue that elected officials act almost by definition in response to such opinion. Furthermore, it is probable that the major impact of the Charter will not be on Parliament and the provincial Legislatures, but on various executive agencies, such as police forces and administrative tribunals, operating under some considerable degree of independence.

Supporters of the Charter also made a weak case. It was argued that rights could be safeguarded in an absolute fashion, but section 1 of the Charter reads, "The Canadian Charter of Rights and Freedoms guarantees the rights and freedoms set out in it subject only to such reasonable limits prescribed by law as can be demonstrably justified in a free and democratic society." No prudent consumer would buy a refrigerator with a "guarantee" subject to such imprecise qualifications. The Charter would have been more honestly and accurately entitled "A Constitutional Enactment for the Better Protection of Certain Rights and Freedoms in Canada." The problem is not, after all, the "guaranteeing" of rights, but rather the procedures by which governmental actors are permitted by law to define, rank, modify and override certain claims of individuals and groups. If the primary objective of the Charter was the more effective protection of the rights and freedoms that this document purports to "enhance," we would have proceeded by disaggregation. It is unlikely that the procedures most efficacious in relation to, say, the protection of freedom of expression would be the same as those devised to support the claims of native peoples or the physically handicapped.

A persuasive case can be made for the entrenchment of legal rights as defined in the Charter: Canadians do have a persistent and regrettable disposition to defer to policemen; there have been many recent examples of excesses in the exercise of police powers; law enforcement and correctional officials characteristically carry out their activities largely outside public scrutiny and the control of elected officials. Because of their traditions and experience, judges may be assumed to have some capacity for wisdom in ranking the competing claims of individual freedom and effective law enforcement. There is less reason to believe that judicial procedures will be effective means of resolving intricate questions of social policy involving, for example, "equality rights," the native peoples, and the official-language provisions. The fault of the process by which the Charter came into effect was not that it resulted in entrenchment *per se*, but rather the indiscriminate entrenchment of a large number of individual and group claims without sufficient discussion of the expected impact of constitutional recognition on particular kinds of rights or on the political culture more broadly.

It is trite to point out that the draftsmanship of constitutional provisions is crucial because it is subject to subsequent change only by the inflexible process of amendment. I have no credentials to judge the Constitution Act from this point of view, and at any rate whatever ambiguities, anomalies and contradictions it contains will become evident only through future judicial interpretation. However, because of the conditions under which the Act was contrived, Canadians will be almost unbelievably fortunate if the quality of draftsmanship proves to be high. Some of the clauses of the Charter evolved in the activities of the Special Joint Committee of the Senate and House of Commons. As Edward McWhinney says:

> The Special Joint Committee . . . perhaps yielded too easily to the temptation of acting as a legislative drafting committee before the public television cameras. The Special Joint Committee's numbers—25 members—were too large to perform a technical legal drafting function easily or usefully, and though some of the Committee members were lawyers by training, their specialized expertise in legislative drafting was not always apparent.[27]

Other changes related to the Constitution Act were made late at night, just before the "consensus" of November 5. While the kitchenette in the conference centre on which Chrétien, McMurtry and Romanow bargained out the "historic compromise" has been already elevated by the mythologizers to a place in Canadian memorabilia akin to that of Laura Secord's cow, the Last Spike and the rope by which Riel was hanged, the result signed by the first ministers was a broad statement of principles not expressed in legal form. As the text of the Resolution subsequently evolved through telex and telephone exchanges between Ottawa and the provincial capitals, changes were being made up until hours before the final adoption of the measure by Parliament. Only the future will reveal the difficulties brought about by the process, but certain unresolved difficulties may be mentioned: (1) Section 28, which women's groups pressed to have included in the Charter, was regarded as a major victory for women: "Notwithstanding anything in this Charter, the rights and freedoms referred to in it are guaranteed equally to male and female persons." Yet, as Dan Soberman has pointed out, the courts might possibly interpret section 28 to preclude affirmative action programs for women otherwise authorized under section 15(2). (2) Certain rights protected by the Charter are conferred only on Canadian citizens, including the right to vote and hold elective office, mobility rights, and educational rights relating to education of one's children in French or English. Yet the Charter appears not to restrict Parliament's power to define who may be a citizen apart from the equality rights provisions of section 15(1). On this basis, the federal authorities might limit certain important rights by making the conditions of citizenship more restrictive. (3) Qualified lawyers have informed me privately that it remains uncertain whether certain protections in the Charter are related only to individuals, or may be extended to corporations. If this crucial matter was unresolved by the draftsmen, they surely can be faulted. (4) Section 40 of the Act specifies compensation for provinces dissenting from amendments transferring powers over "education and other cultural matters" from provincial Legislatures to Parliament. "Culture" is one of the most imprecise terms in our vocabulary. Conflicting claims and counterclaims have been and are being made in Canada in terms of culture; and after prolonged and earnest deliberation, the Royal Commission on Bilingualism and Biculturalism was unable to make any sense of "biculturalism" in its terms of reference. One would have expected careful constitutional draftsmen to avoid the term like the plague.

Conclusion

There is little cause for national self-congratulation in the Constitution Act, 1982 and the procedures by which it became a part of the constitution. There have been some gains of course—we have a wholly domestic amending process, the procedures of constitutional amendment are now in the realm of law rather than convention, there is a more secure protection of legal and democratic rights. Yet on balance, the damage done to our legal, political and constitutional order outweighs the gains. The act of changing the elements of the constitution embodying the powers of the provinces was a betrayal of the commitments made to the Quebec electorate in 1980 and created new hazards in the relations between Quebec and the wider Canadian community. The Charter imposes on the judiciary a set of responsibilities the courts are institutionally ill-equipped to deal with. And by embodying in the constitution important provisions which were hastily drafted, we have done what has been done in an inexpert and unsophisticated way.

Notes

1. "Liberal Priorities 1982: The Limits of Scheming Virtuously," in G. Bruce Doern, ed., *How Ottawa Spends Your Tax Dollars: National Policy and Economic Development, 1982* (Toronto: James Lorimer & Co., 1982), pp. 1-2.
2. *Constitutional Adaptation and Canadian Federalism since 1945*, Documents of the Royal Commission on Bilingualism and Biculturalism (Ottawa: Queen's Printer, 1970), Chapter II.
3. I can find only two major and important sets of suggestions for basic constitutional change prior to the 1960s: the report emanating from the interprovincial conference of 1887, and the highly centralist thrust of the proposals of the League for Social Reconstruction in 1935.
4. Fifth ed. (London: University of London Press, 1959), p. 134.
5. Those are the amendments believed relevant by the Supreme Court majority in their September 28 decision to the effect that convention required a substantial measure of provincial consent for amendments affecting provincial powers. The minority regarded as relevant all of what might reasonably be considered as amendments, and come to a contrary conclusion. I agree with Peter Russell's argument in this volume about the relevant precedents.
6. Canada, Department of Justice, *The Amendment of the Constitution of Canada* (Ottawa: Queen's Printer, 1965), p. 15. (Emphasis added).
7. Some might argue that the actions of Ottawa and the other provinces in not pressing ahead with the Fulton-Favreau formula of the mid-1960s in the face of Quebec dissent is also a relevant precedent. However, this proposed measure related to the amending procedure alone and did not impinge directly on the federal-provincial distribution of legislative powers.
8. The recent book of A.I. Silver emphasizes the importance of Quebec autonomy in the thought and actions of the pro-Confederation forces in Quebec in the 1860s. See *The French-Canadian Idea of Confederation of 1864-1900* (Toronto: University of Toronto Press, 1982), Chapters II and III. This is in marked contrast with the view of Peter Waite, in his *Life and Times of Confederation, 1864-1867* (Toronto: University of Toronto Press, 1962), where the argument is made that the French-Canadian leaders of the time saw the chief defence for their community within the institutions of the central government. See particularly Chapter 5.
9. See the analysis by Claude Ryan "La dualité canadienne," 3 *Policy Options* (July/August 1982), pp. 17-23.
10. *Memo* document from Premier's Office, Saskatchewan.
11. It is equally indefensible to view the separatists as the only authentic voice of Quebec, as was the tendency among members of the English-Canadian left prior to the referendum of 1980.
12. "The Other Crisis of Canadian Federalism," *Canadian Public Administration*, Vol. 22 (Summer 1979), pp. 175-95.
13. *Ibid.*, pp. 175-176.
14. Ronald Dworkin, *Taking Rights Seriously* (Cambridge, Mass.: Harvard University Press, 1977), p. 184.
15. *My Life and Work, A Happy Partnership* (Kingston: Queen's University Press, 1981), pp. 228-29.
16. *Canada: A National Understanding* (Ottawa: Supply and Services Canada, 1977), p. 41.

17. (Ottawa: Queen's Printer, 1967).

18. This view is expressed in its most extreme form in the Kirby Memorandum of 1980. There is no way of knowing how close the views of that document were and are to that of the prime minister and his Cabinet colleagues, although successful courtiers seldom get out of touch with the predilections of their patrons. One is left to conclude that war-gaming federal-provincial relations are an exercise for precocious juveniles.

19. "The Uses of a Constitution," in *Law Society of Upper Canada, Special Lectures*, 1978 (Toronto: Richard de Boo, 1978), p. 3.

20. David J. Elkins and Richard Simeon, eds., *Small Worlds: Provinces and Parties in Canadian Political Life* (Toronto: Methuen, 1980), p. 308.

21. It was, of course, indefensible to link this with the Charter; the impasse related only to patriation and a wholly domestic amending formula.

22. "The Amending Formula," 3 *Policy Options* (January/February, 1982), p. 13.

23. For an account of the background to the bill of rights movement, see Walter S. Tarnopolsky, *The Canadian Bill of Rights* Second Revised Edition (Toronto: McClelland and Stewart, 1975).

24. (Toronto: University of Toronto Press, 1979), p. 147.

25. There has been a long debate in the United States about whether judicial review of the constitution is inherently undemocratic. For an admirably balanced account of the controversy, see Leonard W. Levy's *Judgements: Essays on American Constitutional History* (Chicago: Quadrangle Books, 1972), pp. 24-63.

26. *Freedom of Speech, The Supreme Court and Judicial Review*, (Englewood Cliffs, N.J.: Prentice-Hall, 1966), p. 18.

27. "The How, When and Why of Constitution-Making: The Machinery for Developing a New Constitution," in Edmond Orban, Gérard Bergeron, Edward McWhinney et Gerald-A. Beaudoin, *Mécanismes pour une nouvelle constitution*, (Ottawa: Editions de l'Université d'Ottawa, 1981), p. 87.

Chapter 5/The Constitutional Misfire Of 1982*

Daniel Latouche

The federal-provincial mountain has given birth to a constitutional mouse. The emperor is indeed naked. For twenty years, Canadians and Québécois were engaged in a challenging political dialogue, their first such encounter. Throughout the process, the exasperation always ran high: "What does Québec want?" "What is English Canada?" But already we remember these questions with nostalgia. To have come so far, and to get so close! There is indeed no God for constitution-makers.

Now we know. There will be no "New Canada." Perhaps it was doomed to failure from the start. At last we are told, we can invest our replenished energies and collective imagination in solving the so-called "real" problems we neglected for so long: unemployment, inflation, re-industrialization. But when one looks at the results achieved in the constitutional realm, maybe we should leave these problems well enough alone.

What happened? Since by now Canadians and Québécois are left with only this constitutional failure in common, it is worth examining in more detail. We might learn something about ourselves.

Spitting in the Wind

The affair had begun ever so simply, and ever so promisingly. In July 1960, only weeks after being elected, the Quebec government agreed to participate in a federal-provincial conference devoted to a round-table discussion of the state of the Canadian federation. Before attentive listeners the new Quebec premier, Jean Lesage, proposed a six-point constitutional reform program:[1] (1) the immediate resumption of discussions on patriation and the amending formula in order to eliminate this vestige of colonialism; (2) the inclusion in the "patriated" constitution of a Charter of Basic Rights, particularly to ensure the language and education rights of French-speaking minorities outside Quebec; (3) the creation of a constitutional court distinct from the Supreme Court and more impartial than the latter; (4) the establishment of a permanent federal-provincial secretariat to oversee and expedite the proposed reform; (5) the convening of a permanent provincial premiers' conference to harmonize policies and adopt common positions in negotiations with Ottawa; (6) an end to conditional subsidization policies and joint programs through which Ottawa had repeatedly intervened in areas outside its jurisdiction.

---

*Translated from the French by Terrance Hughes. Special thanks to Daniel Drache, Ken McRoberts, Richard Simeon and Donald Smiley for their pertinent comments.

These demands were met twenty years later. The Parti Québécois government, supported by the Quebec Liberal Party, nonetheless considers the new constitutional agreement a veritable catastrophe. Some even admit to the worst political defeat in Quebec's history. The six objectives outlined in 1960 have become as many nightmares: (1) at the November 1981 constitutional conference, the prime minister and all the provincial premiers except René Lévesque agreed not only on the principle for patriating and amending the constitution, but on practical details and procedures as well; (2) agreement was also reached on the inclusion of a Charter of Rights in the constitution; (3) no agreement has yet been reached on the establishment of a constitutional court; however, the intensive discussions held since 1978 suggest that agreement is imminent, not on the creation of another tribunal, but on a reform of the Supreme Court as such; (4) a permanent federal-provincial conference secretariat has been in place for several years, and the Federal-Provincial Relations Office was responsible for elaborating Ottawa's policies and negotiating positions. This department was to a large extent responsible for the tactical defeat of Quebec's negotiators; (5) the annual interprovincial conference is now a part of Canada's political landscape, and it certainly contributed to the establishment of the common front of the nine English-speaking provinces at the last constitutional conference; (6) following abortive negotiations, the federal government drastically reduced its funding of joint programs, which particularly affects Quebec.

This assuredly is not what Premier Lesage had in mind in 1960. How can this constitutional hijacking be explained? Our hypothesis is that serious constitutional negotiations never really took place, nor was there any process of constitutional reform. Consequently, there was and will be no new constitution. Of course, a constitutional debate took place, constitutional conferences were convened, and agreement was reached on the amending formula and a Charter of Rights and Freedoms. However, one must not confuse negotiations with debate, process with conferences, and supplementary constitutional provisions with a new constitution.

English Canada never bothered to come to the negotiating table. If any negotiations ever took place, they were limited to an exchange of views between Pierre Trudeau and the premiers of the rest of Canada as to how far they would go along with *his* agenda and *his* way of doing things, including putting the Quebec separatists in place. And he won, in part by claiming he was "negotiating" on behalf of Quebec. He was not, and nobody really believed he was. But the premiers liked so much what he was saying that they chose to bypass the Quebec political reality.

Can we talk of negotiation when one partner acts in bad faith and the other is not sure of its objectives? The negotiation of a new constitutional order could never take place for want of a meeting between the two partners. Since 1960, Quebec has shown itself to be interested in negotiating with

English Canada, but not necessarily in reaching agreement on revising the constitution. As for English Canada, it took an interest in constitutional reform at a late stage, but there was never any question of really negotiating with Quebec. One partner wanted to negotiate without necessarily reaching agreement, while the other would have liked to reach an agreement without negotiating. One could not have hoped for greater ambiguity, which brought great satisfaction to both parties.

This hypothesis, which has somewhat the aura of a confession, may seem surprising coming from someone who has literally lived, intellectually, politically and professionally, what is commonly called "the constitutional question." But one's intellectual livelihood is like the Boy Scouts: an extraordinary experience as long as you can get out of it.

This chapter discusses the history of this ambiguity as seen from a Quebec viewpoint. As will soon be evident, the vision is painful enough. There is no need to increase the pain by also taking into account English Canada and its attitude towards Quebec and constitutional change. If Quebec negotiators can be accused of naiveté and ambivalence, what can we say about the treachery and pettiness of their Canadian counterparts.

However one looks at it, the Quebec approach to constitutional change has failed. The easy way out is to put all the blame on the rest of the country, or on some intrinsic defect of the federalist formula itself. But if Canada and federalism were the major culprits, then Quebec's error becomes one of foresight and planning. If nothing else than treachery was to be expected from English Canada, why did successive Quebec negotiators fail to take this expectation into account while elaborating their own strategy?

The same critical thinking should also be applied to the often-heard argument that English Canada had to drop Quebec from the final agreement because the present Parti Québécois government would never have accepted any constitutional package. Under a pretense of *realpolitik*, this charge is nothing but a sectarian attack against all Quebecers, since it postulates that repeated official statements by a democratically elected government are not to be believed because that government presumably does not truly represent Quebec. One is left speechless at such a vision, especially when it is put forward by the same people who were so quick to repudiate their own signatures under the pretext that "it was just a bargaining position." But this has more to do with the English-Canadian side of our joint failure.

Humble Beginnings (1960–1962)
In 1960, the Quebec Liberal Party decided to include proposals aimed at changing Canadian federalism in its electoral program. As will be seen later, this was neither an upheaval nor a calling into question of the principle of federalism, but simply a request for practical adjustments.

Formulated at the height of the election campaign, these proposals had the tactical objective of silencing critics in the rival Union Nationale, who had always skillfully argued in favour of the defence of Quebec's interests, and who cast doubt on the Liberal Party's sincerity in this respect.

Indeed, there was little reason for the Quebec Liberal Party to take a serious interest in the Canadian constitution. At that time, the party was still only a provincial branch of the Liberal Party of Canada; they shared structures, contributors, members and ideologies.[2] Jean Lesage, the new leader, a former Cabinet minister in the federal Liberal government of Louis Saint-Laurent, had participated in numerous attempts by the federal government to increase its areas of responsibility at the expense of the provinces. Even more paradoxically, he had been federal minister of natural resources, a field that the 1867 constitution had placed under the exclusive jurisdiction of the provinces.

The other members of the Liberal team, including René Lévesque, were also better known for their social, economic or international preoccupations than their nationalist ones, the only exception being Paul Gérin-Lajoie, author of a highly technical study on the question of the amending formula. All had been opposed to the régime of Maurice Duplessis; to varying degrees they were convinced that traditional nationalism had hindered the emergence of a modern, secular, progressive Quebec society.[3] None of the nationalist leaders of the 1930s was to be found in their ranks.

As for Quebec voters, they were unaware even of the existence of a constitutional debate, and the first political survey ever carried out in Quebec revealed that federal-provincial relations came far behind unemployment, morality, strikes and purchasing power among their preoccupations.[4] Moreover, the same survey also revealed that those questioned considered the Union Nationale more credible than the Liberal Party on all of these issues. Even after the death of Maurice Duplessis, it was still thought that his party continued to put forward the best candidates, the best program, and the best defence of Quebec's interests.

This diagnosis obviously does not conform with the image of an oppressed, paralyzed Quebec waiting for a Quiet Revolution which would throw open the doors of progress. It must be remembered that in 1960 a majority of Quebecers were generally satisfied with their system of Church-run schools, their health services, the discreet role played by the government in economic development, and Quebec's complete lack of international outlook. The electorate did not support the Liberal Party because it judged the Union Nationale government a disaster. Rather, and more prosaically, it felt that the Liberals must also be given a chance. Pierre Trudeau has provided a good description of this concept of democracy, a concept in which democracy becomes a see-saw between alternative sets of politicians of which little is expected and who generate little deception when the "new beginning" fails to materialize.[5]

In 1959, the majority (72 percent) of Quebecers was unaware of the financial scandals that had been denounced with considerable indignation by the elites, the mass media and the Liberals. This ignorance is understandable when one bears in mind that 70 percent of the electorate admitted to never reading about current political affairs in the newspapers. The phenomenon which came to be known as *"la prise de la parole"* had yet to take place. At the time, political platforms were found only in the editorials of *Le Devoir*, at the annual conference of the Canadian Institute for Public Education, and in the columns of *Cité Libre*. Much the same situation then prevailed in English Canada, where, except for the lone voice of *The Canadian Forum*, nothing was being said and much less done about the dependent state of the Canadian cultural, economic and political sphere.

The results of the election in 1960 itself can hardly be depicted as a sweep or a clear mandate: with 51.3 percent of the popular vote, the Liberal Party obtained 53.7 percent of the seats; in relation to the election in 1956, the Union Nationale lost only 5.4 percent of its support; overall, 65 percent of the seats were won with majorities of less than 10 percent, and 36 percent with majorities of less than 5 percent; in his riding, René Lévesque was elected with 47.8 percent of the vote, as opposed to 47.7 percent for his Union Nationale opponent. A very modest beginning indeed! This detour into Quebec electoral sociology suggests that the so-called Quiet Revolution was not inaugurated under the aegis of a mass movement which a progressive political party would have succeeded in channeling.[6] In 1960, the Quebec Liberal Party also received contributions from big companies and certain interest groups. Its main complaint with respect to this perversion of the democratic system was that it received less than the Union Nationale.

The constitutional question was quite simply absent from internal political debate. In 1957, there had been a debate on grants the federal government proposed to give to Quebec universities, although they did not fall under Ottawa's jurisdiction. The episode was brief and without great impact. Almost by definition, a discussion of university finances is only of interest to those directly concerned. Moreover, Maurice Sauvé, who succeeded Premier Duplessis, was quick to accept the grants discreetly, which immediately put an end to discussions. The brief debate confirmed that conflicts of a nationalist character had become outmoded and necessarily led to incongruous situations. For example, it was on this occasion that Pierre Trudeau, who had been banned from the Université de Montréal by Maurice Duplessis, agreed with the latter in denouncing the grants, as they undermined the spirit and the letter of Canadian federalism.

It was against this electoral background that Premier Lesage made his first pronouncement, in the summer of 1960, on the matter of federal-provincial relations:

> Federalism in Canada, I wish to repeat, rests on the sovereignty of the Federal Parliament and of the Provincial Legislatures in their respective

fields of jurisdiction. . . . For its part, the Province of Quebec intends to safeguard the rights and powers given it by the Constitution . . . [and] use them fully in order to promote the welfare of our population in all matters under provincial jurisdiction. . . . In the cultural field our principal objective is to work vigorously towards the continuing development of French Canadian culture. . . .[7]

Not content to confirm Quebec's right to cultural sovereignty, Premier Lesage also indicated the political dimension of this sovereignty:

> We also take in the political field, within the framework of Canadian federalism, the same position that we take in the cultural field. Provincial sovereignty must not be a negative concept incompatible with progress; it must be a truly living reality, a principle that is put in concrete form in institutions and by legislative measures. . . .
>
> In short, the government of the Province of Quebec intends to exercise its full sovereignty in the fields which are within its jurisdiction while recognizing the fact that all the governments in our country are inescapably interdependent.[8]

The almost accidental nature of Quebec's first demands in this domain was parallelled in the reactions of the other provinces and the federal government. In 1961–62, no one had the impression that a general re-negotiation was being called for, much less a discussion between two nations. Quebec's initiative was perceived as quite in keeping with the Canadian way of doing things: adjustments, settling outmoded problems (such as patriation), a warning to the federal government, which reacted affably, agreement on the necessity of holding another conference. Upon closer examination, Quebec's position, in spite of its singularity, remained entirely in keeping with similar pronouncements made by Maurice Duplessis: attachment to Canada, priority given to the culture and language, the necessity of respecting the spirit and the letter of the 1867 agreement, and so on. It would take a vivid imagination to conclude that in 1960 the Quebec government was adding the principle of a complete constitutional reform to its political agenda. At the time no one, either within the Liberal Party or outside it, would have dared to suggest that the Canadian constitution was an obstacle to Quebec's socio-economic transformation.

Immediately following the July conference, a procedure for consultation was established, without haste, but without undue slowness either. Four meetings were held between November 1960 and November 1961 to settle the question of patriation and the amending formula. Agreement was almost reached on a formula which provided for the unanimous consent of the provinces on any change to the constitution affecting their areas of jurisdiction. In the end, it was rejected by Saskatchewan because it granted a veto to each province. At most, Saskatchewan was willing to accept the right of veto with respect to questions relating to civil law in Quebec. Quebec subsequently objected to this formula too, but its objection was of a secondary nature. It objected to postponing consideration of the federal government's power to modify the constitution in areas under its own jurisdiction. Quebec's refusal was above all tactical, one of a number of means of re-opening discussions on tax-sharing arrangements, the only question of real interest to it.

Little importance was attached to Saskatchewan's refusal at the time. Anyone who would have considered this refusal as a rejection of Quebec by the whole of English Canada would have been subject to considerable ridicule. Even in Quebec it was acknowledged that Canada had survived without an amending formula up until then, and it could very well go on doing so. However, this refusal set the tone for what was to follow: (1) by recognizing Saskatchewan's veto, all the participants implicitly accepted the rule of unanimity in order to establish a new amending formula, whether or not such a formula recognized that unanimity would be necessary in the future; (2) henceforth, negotiations on the constitution would have to be regarded as an undertaking involving ten partners, not just two (English Canada/Quebec) or three (English Canada/Quebec/federal government); (3) constitutional conferences, with their mixture of public and private sessions, were to be the focal point of the constitutional debate; (4) politicians alone would be responsible for the reform and its outcome; there was no question of organizing a constituent assembly or a referendum; (5) "muddling through" would be the order of the day, without deadlines, schedules or agenda.

Saskatchewan's refusal in January 1962, and the new framework it created for constitutional discussions, would not have had significant consequences without the changes that occurred in Quebec's internal political situation. Suddenly, English Canada, which until then had only existed as *"Les Anglais"* in the collective mind of Quebecers, was provided with a collective soul of its own, at least in the minds of the new, emerging political elites of Quebec. As is often the case with a minority's vision of the majority, the "others" were characterized by total unanimity of views and uniformity of visions. There had to be an English Canada because there was now a French Quebec in the making.

Between the elections of June 1960 and November 1962 only thirty months had elapsed, but they were decisive months for subsequent Canadian constitutional history. Three events should be mentioned: (1) the Rassemblement pour l'indépendance nationale was founded on September 10, 1960. For the first time, a movement which rapidly became a political party proposed the hitherto unheard of option of political independence; (2) in October 1961, English Canada was "horrified" to discover the first "illegal" acts committed by separatists: a few graffiti on public monuments. Another debate began: "What does Quebec want?" (3) the first major public debate on the double theme of federalism and independence was held at Université Laval in November 1961. Public debate under the watchful eye of the news media had begun.[9]

In less than a year the national question, which had been secondary in

1960, became the object of tumultuous debates, complete with contradictory options, heroic participants and special forums, all of which was noted by André Laurendeau in a famous editorial in 1961. He publicly recognized the symbolic appeal of separatism, which "openly expresses an idea kept secret for a long time, an unconfessed potential habit, a tendency almost always repressed by many French Canadians."[10]

If ideas were changing, political practice in Quebec was changing all the more. In the course of several months it seemed to get carried away with what some have called a "moment of folly"—one of those periods when everything seems possible, and the usual constraints suddenly seem less imposing. The main manifestations of this enthusiasm are well known: new government departments (cultural affairs, natural resources, federal-provincial relations) were created, the government opened an office in Paris, the *Société générale de financement* and the *Conseil d'orientation économique* were established, educational reform was set in motion, and the mores of politicians and civil servants were rehabilitated.

However, the most important event during this time was undoubtedly the Quebec election of 1962. Consideration of the importance of this election is usually limited to its immediate consequences: the nationalization of electricity and the coming to power within the Liberal Party of its most progressive elements. But the event had an equally important impact on relations between Quebec and Canada, for its theme of economic liberation consummated a still shaky marriage between nationalism and socio-economic development. For the main participants, the demonstration was conclusive.

While surveys revealed that public opinion in Quebec had scarcely changed since June 1960,[11] it now became profitable for political parties to change their way of thinking. The lesson of his electoral defeat was not wasted on Daniel Johnson, the new leader of the Union Nationale. He began to study the constitutional question resolutely, while attempting to elaborate a position different from that of the Liberals and the *indépendantistes*.[12] To Pierre Trudeau and a group of progressive intellectuals involved in *Cité Libre*, the 1962 election marked a break with a nationalism that was considered as ethnocentric as that of Maurice Duplessis. Major realignments were already underway.

Notwithstanding the verbal inflation surrounding any election campaign, certain aspects of the 1962 Liberal program, including its central message, were surprising:

> The people of Quebec are confident, just as all young nations which have decided one day to assert themselves are confident. For the first time in their history, the people of Quebec can become masters in their own house. The era of economic colonialism has come to an end. We are marching toward liberation! Now or never: MASTERS IN OUR OWN HOUSE![13]

But as for the constitution, the Liberal program was even less elaborate than that of 1960, and only contained one sentence: "Assert Quebec's role in Confederation."

In terms of rhetoric, the Liberal program was a veritable hodgepodge of words, ideas and problematics. By August 1962, Premier Lesage's tone at the provincial premiers' conference had altered considerably. For the first time, he linked the question of French Canada to that of Quebec. For the first time as well, he spoke of the daily aggravations faced by French Canadians and of the anxiety of a growing number of Quebecers about the course being taken by the Canadian government:

> The answer that will be given to this question—the answer that all Canadians will have to give to it—is of such vital importance to the French-Canadian people of Quebec that they cannot remain indifferent to the solutions which may be put forward or to the propositions which may be made to them. In some ways, this includes the survival of the French Canadians as an ethnic group, and in this second half of the 20th century, almost one hundred years after the establishment of a federal system of government in our country, the concrete facts of which they are becoming aware every day oblige them to look around and ask themselves in what direction the political, economic and social development of our country is leading them. And a good proportion of the citizens of Quebec are uneasy, and justly so, because of the tendencies which they perceive in the development of the federal system.[14]

This entire speech is placed under the dominant theme of the "question," a sort of existential interrogation that the Quebec premier put to his astounded colleagues. It marked the beginning of a Quebec tradition of addressing itself to English Canada as if the latter were a distinct cultural and political entity. The lack of a reply was not interpreted as proof of the non-existence of its interlocutor, but as an encouragement to repeat and increase its demands. Who in Quebec in 1962 could pretend to have the slightest knowledge of this English Canada which was being continually questioned. The long struggle against *duplessisme*, the Diefenbaker years, and the excitement of the Quiet Revolution had contributed more to dividing the two cultures than had linguistic barriers. Were not these years characterized by a "primitive anti-Canadianism," with its jokes about Toronto, and its nascent scorn for a culture which one delighted in regarding as a by-product of America?

Having just discovered all the electoral advantages to be derived from nationalist rhetoric, Quebec's elites had scarcely any time to devote to English Canada, and even less energy to lose in the formulation of a common negotiating position on the constitution. Having just discovered the joys arising from interrogating an English Canada which was unable to reply, there was no question of bringing this little game to an end and sitting down at the constitutional negotiating table. Clearly, the belief that

Quebec has been eagerly pressing English Canada for constitutional change since 1960 is as ill-founded as that other belief that Canadians have been desperately trying to find an amending formula for half a century. Canadians and Québécois have nothing to learn from Soviet historians in reconstructing recent events.

The Pleasures of Constitutional Guerilla Warfare (1962–1966)

Between 1962 and 1966, the socio-economic initiatives of the Liberal government proliferated, as did confrontations with the federal government. Quebec's international relations, pension plans, the financing of so-called joint programs, fiscal agreements and responsibility for policies respecting the family were all the subject of repeated controversy. But strictly speaking, there were still no negotiations on the constitution during the Liberal government's second term of office.

In 1963, the tone of voice rose again. This time, the Quebec premier announced that it was essential to call into question the very foundations of Canadian federalism:

> In order to reach this objective of a true federalism, or of a cooperative federalism as it is sometimes called, it is the whole Canadian federal system and its present workings that need to be thought out anew. . . . We shall even be called upon to transform it, for the realities around us will inevitably lead us to question the system; it will perhaps be necessary to modify certain of its elements, even those which have appeared to be its most stable ones.[15]

Four months later, this same appeal was accompanied by an acknowledgment of failure with respect to Quebec's demands. Mr. Lesage announced that "except for a few points, our legitimate demands [have come up against] almost total refusal,"[16] without elaborating further. It is this official version of the facts that has gone down in history, at least in Quebec: on the one hand, a federal government and an English Canada insensitive to Quebec's demands; on the other, a Quebec government borne by the dynamism of an entire society and hindered in its attempts to make English Canada understand that nothing would ever be the same again. But is this really what transpired?

Throughout this second period, the only concrete initiative undertaken was that of the federal government which, with the consent of all the provinces, tried to revive its amending formula. The new formula was more explicit and provided for various amending mechanisms according to the areas of jurisdiction. The Quebec government initially accepted it, but subsequently reversed its position when the official opposition, always on the lookout for a "national" angle with which to attack the government, immediately raised a storm. Jacques-Yvan Morin, the spiritual leader of this circumstantial nationalist opposition, summarized the reasons for it in this way:

> The amending formula proposed very effectively protects areas under the jurisdiction of Quebec, as well as the use of French in Parliament, but it offers the disadvantage of protecting them too well. We are no longer living at a time when it might be feared that French would disappear from the House of Commons, or that the federal government would encroach upon domains under provincial jurisdiction. . . . The greatest difficulties will arise when Quebec seeks to have more extensive powers recognized and have the structure or the method of nomination of federal institutions changed. . . . Quebec will then come up against the two-thirds majority rule, and the practical impossibility of modifying the Constitution on essential points.[17]

Unfortunately, Quebec was hardly in a hurry to formulate concrete propositions in order to sustain a constitutional reform it claimed to want very much. In March 1963, the Legislative Assembly created a parliamentary committee on the constitution, but its first actual working session did not took place until June 1964. At that time, the committee decided to receive briefs and have a number of technical studies carried out. Although an *États Généraux du Canada français* had been mentioned unofficially since 1961, it was only in March 1966 that the *Fédération des Sociétés Saint-Jean-Baptiste* convened a meeting of some twenty organizations to ascertain whether they were still interested in the idea. The first meeting did not take place until 1967.

Not only was Quebec in no hurry, but on no question, not even that of constitutional reform, was there a consensus. Three events illustrated this situation: (1) In 1965, the Royal Commission on Bilingualism and Biculturalism submitted its preliminary report which stated that Canada was going through the worst crisis in its history. We have got into the habit of glorifying this report with the passage of time. At the time, however, it was hardly received enthusiastically by the nationalist elite or the socialist counter-elite. Reviews such as *Parti Pris* and *Révolution Québécoise et Socialisme* scarcely mentioned it, or did so only to make fun of it as a collection of platitudes. Marc Lalonde, and the *Comité pour une politique fonctionnelle*, writing in *Cité Libre*, denounced the "bizarre algebra" which added to ideas already in circulation "corrosive, badly developed, unjustified" principles, including that of the equality of the two founding peoples.[18] (2) In November 1967, the two thousand one hundred and six delegates to the *Assises nationales des États Généraux* met for their first working session. In a preliminary resolution, they voted overwhelmingly in favour of three principles that must guide all subsequent deliberations: (a) French Canadians constitute a nation; (b) Quebec is the national territory of this nation; (c) this nation possesses the right to self-determination. Supported by 98 percent of Quebec's delegates, this resolution, which was hardly restrictive, as it spoke not of the Quebec nation, but the French-Canadian nation, was ultimately supported by only 52 percent of Acadian delegates, 35 percent of those from Ontario, and 30 percent of those from Western Canada. There was no consensus on this question either.[19] (3) The *Comité parlementaire de la Constitution* inaugurated its public hearings, during the course of which it would hear thirty-eight briefs, on June 5, 1964. While the committee was assigned the task of synthesizing the various proposals then under discussion and setting out a constitutional policy likely to rally all parties in the search for a common denominator, its activities rapidly degenerated into partisan battles, the settling of accounts using constitutional options, and even internal dissension within the parties, particularly the Liberal Party. The first phase of the committee's work reached a dead end in the fall of 1966, without a summary report, a single recommendation, or a plan for continuing its work.

These events marked three breaks, which were to degenerate into a sort of constitutional stagnation that renewed itself more quickly than federalism. The first break was between various factions of Quebec's intelligentsia which, as early as 1965, was divided among a nationalist-and-socialist wing, a nationalist-above-all wing, a socialist-before-nationalist wing, and a Marxist-Leninist wing. The second occurred between Quebec nationalists and the French-Canadian minorities outside Quebec. The third took place between the federalist and autonomist factions of the major political parties, both of which nonetheless allowed the constitutional question to become an instrument of election battles.

To these three breaks must be added Premier Lesage's trip to Western Canada in the fall of 1963, which had the effect of a cold shower. It was a resounding failure, which should have confirmed to the premier the cultural and political non-existence of the English Canada to which he had tried to address himself. Greeted with hostility, and even occasional insults, Premier Lesage had nonetheless limited himself to generalities concerning the necessity of re-thinking Confederation. The absence of firm proposals was the hallmark of all his appearances outside Quebec. His only concrete demands concerned the status of both official languages and the treatment of French-speaking minorities. On the other hand, the hostility displayed was very concrete.[20] An anecdote illustrates this point about the elusiveness of an English-Canadian collectivity. Allegedly, on his return, Lesage stopped in Toronto to visit with Premier John Robarts. Upon meeting him, Lesage explained: "You had better go out West too. They hate you even more than they hate me." Some things never change.

All those concerned, and above all the Quebec government, took advantage of every occasion to remind English Canada of the urgency of the situation, although a feeling of urgency seemed scarcely to affect them. The government confined itself to ongoing constitutional guerilla warfare without concern for medium- and long-range objectives. It was aware that even among the most impatient elements of the population, it could never obtain a consensus on the various political formulae then circulating (associated states, special status, two nations). This ambiguity resulted in increasingly public divisions within the Liberal Party. Electorally, it was also proving to be profitable for the Union Nationale which managed to erase the anti-nationalist image it had in 1962.

The arrival of Pierre Trudeau in Ottawa and the electoral defeat of the *"Equipe du tonnerre"* in 1966 took away from Quebec the two most valuable resources it needed in order to arrive at a constitutional consensus: time and initiative. Between 1962 and 1965, there was not enough time to harness the large reservoir of political initiative of which Quebec had an exclusive monopoly; too many things to do and too few good people. By 1966, there was no time left, and the initiative was gone. Having been deprived of the spoils of the anti-Duplessis struggle, and seeing itself bypassed on every side, a fraction of the French-Canadian elite chose to make a career in Ottawa out of their capacity to tell English Canada what Quebecers really wanted. The fact that both English Canada and Quebec so avidly bought this offer only testifies to how little they had to say to one another. Both sides agreed to sell the show to this interpreter.

Talk and Do Nothing (1966–1968)

For the Union Nationale, the battle against the Fulton-Favreau formula was undoubtedly nothing more than a fortuitous diversion which enabled it to make the voters forget that it had no real socio-economic program. Of course, there was a desire to fraternize with the nationalist elements of the Quebec intelligentsia, but throughout the struggle the leader of the opposition, Daniel Johnson, took great care to stay away from any specific proposal.

While accusing the Liberal government of betraying the nation, Daniel Johnson seized every opportunity to attack each of the reforms undertaken during the Quiet Revolution, resorting without hesitation to accusations of communism, atheism and Marxism. With respect to the constitution, his attitude was characterized by opportunism and a wait-and-see policy. In an otherwise laudatory biography, P. Godin describes Johnson's style thus:

> For Daniel Johnson, there were two types of problems: those which solved themselves with time—no point in intervening—and those which had not yet fully matured, and for which a wait-and-see policy was the most appropriate.[21]

Occasionally, the wait-and-see policy was even accompanied by instant ideological reversals. *Égalité ou indépendance,* his pre-election manifesto, proposed re-structuring the country on the basis of legal and political equality between the country's two founding nations. Such equality would only make sense with a new constitution which,

> instituted at the top, for the country as a whole, a truly binational organ, where representatives of both cultural communities would be able to work together, on an equal footing, in managing common interests.[22]

To achieve this end, it proposed convening a binational constituent assembly, followed by a referendum to ratify the new political structure called upon to sit "above the central and provincial organs."

Daniel Johnson never again mentioned political equality between both nations, or a constituent assembly, a referendum or new political structures. Today, it is considered in poor taste to cast doubt on the quality of his constitutional performance; he rapidly became a "statesman," thanks to a process of "political transubstantiation" which would not have fooled even him. Nonetheless, the facts are there: (1) In order not to be over-taken by the left or the right, Daniel Johnson suspended the work of the *Comité parlementaire de la Constitution*, which finally disappeared in 1968, having waited seventeen months for the government to reconvene it. (2) It was Ontario Premier John Robarts who took the initiative to convene the "Confederation of Tomorrow Conference" in Toronto in November 1967. (3) Ontario was also the first province to put forward an articulate vision of Canadian federalism, through the Ontario Advisory Committee on Confederation. (4) It was the federal government, absent from the Toronto conference, which took the initiative by convening a Constitutional Conference in February 1968, which would continue to meet under its direction until June 1971. (5) At the federal-provincial conference on tax-sharing arrangements held in Ottawa in the fall of 1966, the new Quebec premier, Daniel Johnson, received a blunt refusal from Mitchell Sharp, federal minister of finance, who felt no need to await the arrival of Pierre Trudeau before putting Johnson in his place.

As for the premier's style and strategy in constitutional negotiations, they must be qualified as a totally unconvincing theatrical improvisation. Here is how Pierre Godin describes Daniel Johnson's strategy (we have added the headings):

> *Improvisation*
> Johnson entrusted the elaboration of Quebec's strategy to a working group composed of technocrats Claude Morin [and] Jacques Pari-zeau.... The task was arduous for the technocrats. To Morin, who asked for clarification of the situation, Johnson replied: "Read my book, *Egalité ou Indépendance*, and you'll understand where I'm headed." The former took his advice, but was still perplexed. The attentive, repeated reading of the gospel according to Saint Daniel did not enable him to clearly understand the constitutional position of his boss.[23]

Theatre

Johnson negotiated like a union leader. He began by making threats and asking for the moon. He had understood for a long time that the idea of separation frightened English-speaking Canadians, and he didn't shy away from brandishing it. . . . Once at the negotiating table, far from his nationalist public, the tiger turned into a nice little pussy-cat. . . . The other provincial premiers, accustomed to Lesage's storms, were delighted to discover that tiger Johnson's teeth were made of paper.[24]

Confused hesitation

[Following the failure of the fiscal conference in 1966] But first, he had to defuse the independence bomb in order to reassure English Canada. Johnson maintained that journalists had been hasty in concluding that he was speaking of independence . . . as he was leaving the plane. "I was seeking the equality or the independence of the French-Canadian nation, not Quebec, which is not the same thing. . . . One hundred percent of direct taxes is one thing; equality is another. Independence is something else again. Some people have come up with the following equation: one hundred percent equals equality and without one hundred percent, it's independence. In fact, there are three separate things."[25]

Permeability

[During his convalescence in Hawaii] During these long moments of idleness, Paul Desmarais succeeded in persuading the premier to effect a strategic retreat in order to restore confidence among Anglo-American businessmen toward Quebec. . . . Johnson finally gave in to Paul Desmarais' request. Before doing so, he wanted to make one last check. From his cabana, he reached Paul Dozois, who once again confirmed the hysterical reaction in the business community. . . . However, he neglected to request information from the *Caisse de dépôts*, where Jacques Parizeau had not noted any unusual transactions with respect to Quebec government bonds. Now, these bonds would normally be the most threatened of all. . . . Unfortunately for him, Johnson did not know how to make the most of the *Caisse de dépôts*.[26]

The Johnson government did not attempt to consolidate a common position which it could have defended at the negotiation table, while making gestures which would have compelled the debate to move forward. It was more preoccupied with what René Lévesque and his *Mouvement Souveraineté-Association* were preparing, and with the government's symbolic battles with the federal government.

In 1967, the Quebec government was still in a strong bargaining position, although less so than in 1965. English Canada was still in a state of shock. Everything coming from Quebec was surprising. The FLQ, the Créditistes, De Gaulle—these things all contributed to a plethora of questions. Since 1963, Lester B. Pearson had been prime minister; he wanted to understand Quebec, although he remained at the level of clichés and was guided by a philosophy of negotiation at any price. It was still not clear if Pierre Trudeau would become another Ernest Lapointe. All of Quebec's elites, the official opposition, the news media and student associations were demanding a new constitutional status for Quebec. In this respect, the control of "official" public opinion was total.

During the crucial years 1966 and 1967, Quebec limited itself to skillful pronouncements which were a mixture of calls for change, threats, and diagnoses of failure. While governments are credited with an overly large capacity for reflection, it is tempting to conclude that during those years the Quebec government was obsessed with obtaining the strongest possible negotiating position by not missing an opportunity to discredit its adversary and by imposing *de facto* situations that placed it on the defensive. It forgot that real political power can only be measured when it can be exercised. It is in this light that Quebec's refusal to accept the amending formula proposed in 1965 must be interpreted. It was necessary to avoid, at all costs, being put in a straitjacket which would later prevent Quebec from obtaining what it wanted.[27] This was an elegant—perhaps excessively so—fashion of avoiding negotiation.

Daniel Johnson was a master of the theatrical, and if politics is but a theatre, he could have succeeded. After all, he had come to power through a manipulation of the constitutional and national issues. He would have had no difficulty in maintaining himself in office through perseverance in the same direction. Time again proved the elusive resource.

The Quiet Capitulation (1968-1981)

When the first meeting of the Constitutional Conference was held in February 1968 in Ottawa, it was already apparent that Quebec would not emerge a winner. Only the extent and the speed of the failure remained to be determined. It materialized thirteen years later, and was total. In this respect, the failure of the Constitutional Conference in November 1981 is not primarily attributable to the mistakes made by the Parti Québécois government, although its conduct of the final round of negotiations cannot be ignored. If one is adamant about attributing blame for this failure, responsibility must be shared equally by the Lesage, Johnson, Bertrand, Bourassa and Lévesque governments, with an honourable mention divided among the nationalist elites in Quebec and English Canada. Rarely have so many participants contributed as equally to a defeat.

Until 1967, it was the Quebec government and all the Quebec participants, including groups, associations and individuals, who took the initiative. It is in this light that the affirmation that "without Quebec there would never have been a constitutional crisis" must be understood. This was true until 1967; it was already less so beginning in 1968 and with the "arrival" of Pierre Trudeau. It was no longer the case at all beginning in 1973, with Alberta's entry. Indeed, this entire period is characterized by Quebec's being slowly relegated to the sidelines; for a number of reasons, some fortuitous, some more of a structural nature, it ceased to be the main actor.

Beginning in 1968, the federal government decided to devote money and energy to the constitutional debate. It initially did so without enthusiasm, convinced that the problem was more symbolic than real. But the results of the 1968 election made the government aware of the debate's usefulness in an election campaign. (It forgot it in 1972, and remembered again in 1974.) Success was not long in coming. Since 1968, the federal government has effectively controlled the agenda, the progress and the timing of constitutional discussions. It has monopolized the "how" and the "why" of such discussions.

At no time was this monopoly more evident than at the Victoria Conference. Quebec had entered the 1968 negotiation round with one objective in mind: to increase both its legislative powers, especially over social affairs, and its fiscal autonomy. By June 1971, nothing had been gained on these two fronts. In the hope of making gains on these issues, and as a way to show its good faith, the Quebec government had agreed to a discussion of the bill of rights and amending questions. Having already shown its hand and made its only possible compromise, Quebec was left with no bargaining chips when Ottawa refused to reciprocate. Having manipulated the agenda, and basking in the glory of the October crisis, the federal government had no difficulty in pushing Quebec into the no-win situation of refusing the Victoria Charter.

One has to be impressed with the negotiating skill of the federal government, which succeeded both in 1971 and in 1981 in rallying the other provinces by offering Quebec precisely the contrary of what it was asking for. At Victoria, Quebec was offered a veto right over constitutional changes that would affect its legislative powers, as long as it contained 25 percent of the Canadian population. It was suggested at the time that this veto power would be useful only if Quebec dropped below the 25 percent mark, which was precisely the level where the veto would not apply. But in 1971, Quebec was not concerned with its veto or that of the other provinces, since such vetoes could block any constitutional reform. In 1981, Quebec was refused such a veto when it had become a necessity, since the Ottawa-English-Canada Holy Alliance threatened to impose upon it changes it found unacceptable.

Quebec has always sought political equality with English Canada, and the constitutional debate was a means of attaining that equality. But at various times it has also been used for internal political ends, and in establishing a "new" Quebec society. By 1975, however, the constitutional battle no longer played a part in either the electoral game or the Quiet Revolution. Were it not for the surprise victory of the Parti Québécois in the fall of 1976, the events of 1981 would have taken place then. Premier Bourassa was fully aware that the rest of the country was ready to get down to business in order to bring an end to what it considered to be a pointless discussion. The 1976 election result simply pushed back the deadline and momentarily clouded the issue.

The victory of the Parti Québécois also shifted the dynamics of the debate. Constitutional reform became the principal tool of the federal government in its attempts to eliminate the PQ. In effect, the federal Liberal Party became more interested in the tactics than the content of the reform, just as the Quebec government had been between 1960 and 1966. The referendum was to have enabled Quebec once again to take the initiative in the debate; its aftermath is well known. Quebec would have to pay the price of its admission of weakness. Only when this weakness had clearly been established did the rest of the country proceed with its solution to the constitutional question.

From 1968 to 1981, it would appear that all the parties involved in the constitutional debate chose to maintain a constant ambiguity. For the minority (Quebec), this ambiguity served to hide the unpleasant reality of an English Canada not the least interested in re-modeling Canada along the lines of political equality. For the majority (English Canada), it was a civilized way not to have to say "no" to its minority. Over the years, this ambiguity became self-perpetuating, enabling mistrust and suspicion to grow to such an extent that the participants finally found themselves prisoners of their own strategies and images.

As Edward McWhinney has pointed out, all of the following elements are essential to the success of any constitutional negotiations: (1) a desire by all concerned to reach a solution within a reasonable length of time, based on a recognition of the fact that the cost of failure is much higher than that of an agreement; (2) even a vague, imprecise notion of the nature of a possible solution; (3) agreement on the definition of the main problem, and the identification of the main obstacles to be overcome; (4) a minimum of mutual confidence, or at least of healthy political respect; (5) an appropriate forum for the carrying out of negotiations; (6) opinions that are sufficiently coherent that it is possible at least to identify clearly the positions of the parties concerned and the support they enjoy from the public. At the negotiating table, overlapping opinions are more often a hindrance than a help.[28] Because of the political situation, they were never all present in 1981.

Nothing indicates that these conditions will suddenly appear in the immediate future. The 1980 referendum—the only attempt to shed some light on the situation, to sever the accumulation of knots, each one more Gordian than the others—settled nothing at all. As it was the Quebec government that had the most to win if the referendum succeeded, it also had the most to lose in case of defeat. While one may deplore the fact, it must be noted that Quebec's relegation to the fringe had already begun in 1968. It clearly indicates that there is nothing paradoxical about the

Canadian political game; it is governed by the same relationships and mechanisms as those in other nation-states.

The (Not Very Royal) Road to the Future

Now that the ambiguity has been dispelled, Quebec federalists and *indépendantistes* have only to abandon their dreams. There will be no renewed federalism any more than there will be sovereignty-association. In both cases it takes two to succeed, and the "other" has not kept the appointment.

Quebecers have only two avenues open to them to obtain the recognition of the political duality, which for them constitutes a vital minimum: total co-operation, or total independence.

The second solution is easier to define, and the Parti Québécois is already moving in that direction. The December 1981 PQ congress, which had to reconvene a few months later to disavow some of its more extremist earlier language, is an indication that this move towards radicalization will not be achieved without some pain. Nor will this new, purified version of *indépendantisme* be easy to sell to an electorate. The Liberal Party under a new, more federalist leader, and the *indépendantistes* themselves, will see to it that all possible obstacles are raised. Moreover, one must not think that Quebec voters will automatically adopt the extreme solution of independence simply because it is less ambiguous than sovereignty-association, and because renewed federalism has been rejected by the rest of the country. Confronted with a choice fraught with consequence, voters do not necessarily choose through a process of elimination or out of gratitude. Having refused sovereignty-association, and with renewed federalism no longer open to them, they will not necessarily rush to embrace a more radical solution. The electorate rarely rewards a political party promoting a radical solution, even if it is less ambiguous.

It is often said that Quebecers refused to give their government a mandate to negotiate sovereignty-association because it had: (a) chosen a roundabout way of selling them independence; (b) neglected to explain what sovereignty entailed; (c) allowed the federal government to impose its own conception of renewed federalism; (d) let the debate shift to the choice between the dream of an independent Quebec and the secure reality of Canada; (e) let the rest of the country declare to all and sundry that Canada would never negotiate sovereignty-association. If such is the case, one would have to be extremely naive to think that an election based on the theme of Quebec's independence would be easier to win, under the pretext that the government would act openly this time and only talk about the wonderful world of independence. That would be too easy. Doses of enlightenment do not win elections, especially in times of economic difficulty.

The path of full co-operation between Quebec and Ottawa that a Quebec Liberal government might choose to implement is as radical in its own way as that of full independence. Never, except for the 1940–44 interval when Premier Adélard Godbout let go major legislative powers, has a Quebec government accepted the role of a branch-plant of the federal government, letting Ottawa make the important decisions in return for the privileged treatment that comes with being the staunchest ally of centralization. This strategy has worked well for Ontario. It could work for Quebec.

Or could it? It is one thing to replace Claude Ryan, but it is another to purge the party of the "Quebec First" members who have joined since 1978. The costs could be very high. Furthermore, even if the unconditional federalists succeeded in gaining control of the party, they would still have to face the electorate one day. During the 1981 election, the voters were not very kind to the Liberal Party, over which the suspicion of collusion with the Liberal Party of Pierre Trudeau hung. In the event of open complicity, the result could be disastrous. Furthermore, even if it did win power, this new pro-Ottawa Liberal government could well find itself with no one in Ottawa to talk to. The days of Pierre Trudeau and of the "French Mafia" are numbered. A Quebec government might want to sell the shop to Ottawa, but will there be anyone willing to buy?

One fact remains: Quebec's demographic importance within the Canadian federation continues to decline constantly. This is not the fault of the federalists, or the separatists, and certainly not that of the constitution, but the fact remains. This decline in importance and in political power has created a zero-sum situation between French-Canadian political representatives sitting in Ottawa and those in Quebec City. From 1960 to 1976, each group had sufficient manoeuvring room not to get on the other's nerves. In Ottawa they were working at conquering Canada and transforming it into a bilingual, bicultural state. In Quebec City there was all manner of catching up to be done. Each group of representatives could work at its task without interfering with the other.

Since 1976, the two projects have become incompatible; the turning point has become known as the air traffic controllers crisis. For the first time since Riel and the Conscription Crisis of 1944, a purely "federal" event could be manipulated by Quebec provincial politicians into great electoral successes. If the Quebec government was allowed to speak for all French Canadians across the country, then the federal Liberal Party would lose its electoral magic as the great conciliator. In addition, the danger of an alliance of disenchanted federal MPs and ministers with a nationalist Quebec government had to be avoided at all costs. A seat in the Senate for Jean Marchand and a seat in Cabinet for Serge Joyal was a small price to pay to ensure that Quebec and Ottawa remained on a collision course.

The Parti Québécois is currently considering entering the federal arena in order to carry the battle into the enemy camp. The strategic intention is interesting; should it succeed, it would considerably alter the Canadian political game. For the first time, a group of MPs would sit in the

House of Commons, not as *representatives* from Quebec, but as *delegates* of the Quebec government. The nuance is important. It will be remembered that on the question of direct involvement by Quebec's delegates in federal institutions, the White Paper on sovereignty-association and the Quebec Liberal Party's Beige paper on renewed federalism defended the same position.

Another advantage of this strategy is that it no longer forces Quebec to wait for English Canada to sit down at the negotiating table. It can now be taken for granted that English Canada does not exist as a distinct political entity. At best, it might represent a branch of real political power that is exercised in Ottawa. Why waste time talking to the branch office when it is possible to move into the very heart of the beast. Federalism as it has evolved in Canada is now threatening the very economic and social survival of the country. Other provincial premiers have learned to play the anti-Ottawa game as skillfully as successive Quebec governments. With the Quebec issue out of the way, the emptiness of Canadian projects is only more apparent, as now mirrored in the balkanized stand-off in which provincial and federal state-builders have locked themselves. The country could afford constitutional conferences-of-the-last-chance, which repeatedly failed only to be reconvened. Can it afford a similar merry-go-round for economic decisions?

Quebec has failed in its attempt at a political reconstruction of federal Canada. Perhaps it could share in its economic downfall. In July 1981, the Canadian dollar slipped below the level where so-called experts had assumed the Quebec dollar would have stabilized after independence. The question then becomes, can Canada afford federalism and can Quebec afford Canada and its Rocky Mountains?

Notes

1. See Jean-Louis Roy, *Le Choix d'un pays: 1e débat constitutionnel Québec-Canada, 1960-1976* (Montréal: Leméac, 1978), and Edward McWhinney, *Quebec and the Constitution 1960-1978* (Toronto: University of Toronto Press, 1979), for a discussion of the evolution of the constitutional debate. The contrast between these studies clearly illustrates the difficulty experienced by Canadians and Quebecers in achieving an identical vision of political reality. While Jean-Louis Roy (now director of *Le Devoir*) does not openly embrace all the tenets of the sovereignty thesis, he does display considerable sympathy for this option. On the other hand, Edward McWhinney (who has the distinction of being the only English-Canadian constitutional expert ever consulted by a Quebec government), regardless of how understanding he may be with respect to Quebec's arguments, remains nonetheless firmly entrenched in an essentially pro-federalist and pan-Canadian outlook.

2. Officially, the rupture between the parties only took place in 1965. Even now, while the break may be complete with respect to structures and financing, it still has not occurred with regard to local officials and party members. The

problems of internal unity experienced by the party result from this overlapping. In a recent article, Yvan Allaire, secretary of the strategy committee of the Quebec Liberal Party, suggested that about 70% of voters in the provincial Liberal Party actually supported the federal party's constitutional position, which Claude Ryan, then leader of the QLP, had fought against. See "Being Liberal: paradoxes and dilemmas," *Le Devoir*, January 16, 1982. On the Quebec Liberal Party, see P.-A. Comeau, "La transformation du Parti Libéral Québécois," *Canadian Journal of Economics and Political Science*, Vol. 31, No. 3 (1965), pp. 358-67, and particularly the following works of Vincent Lemieux: *Le Quotient politique vrai* (Québec: les Presses de l'Université Laval, 1973), and *La fête continue* (Montréal: Boréal express, 1979).

3. In 1960, observers did not consider French-Canadian nationalism of much import. No one foresaw that it would succeed in adapting itself, and even become a driving force in the Quiet Revolution. The change of viewpoints is well illustrated in two articles by political scientist Léon Dion, "Le nationalisme pessimiste: sa source, sa signification, sa validité," *Cité Libre*, No. 18 (1957), pp. 3-18; and "Genèse et caractéristiques du nationalisme de croissance," in Congress on Canadian Affairs, *Les nouveaux Québécois* (Québec: les Presses de l'Université Laval, 1964), pp. 59-77.

4. *Les électeurs québécois; attitudes et opinions à le veille de l'élection de 1960; un rapport*, (Montréal: Groupe de recherches sociales, 1960).

5. Pierre Trudeau, "Some Obstacles to Democracy in Quebec," in Mason Wade, ed., *Canadian Dualism* (Toronto: University of Toronto Press, 1960), pp. 241-59; "La démocratie est-elle viable au Canada français," *L'Action nationale*, Vol. 44, No. 3 (1954), pp. 190-200.

6. In 1960, the electoral program of the Liberal Party was written in two days in a hotel room by Georges-Emile Lapalme, a former leader of the party, without his seeking any consultation. His memoirs provide a slightly more realistic view of the arrival of the Quiet Revolution (*Mémoires*, 3 vol. (Montréal: Leméac, 1964, 1970, 1973)). With respect to the 1960 election campaign, he mentions the very effective use which was made of religion by the Liberal team; each candidate in turn had to reveal the number of priests and nuns in his family. At the same time, Fathers O'Neil and G. Dion were denouncing the use of religion for electoral ends. See Gérard Dion, *Le chrétien et les élections* (Montréal: Éditions de l'Homme, 1960).

7. Canada, *Dominion-Provincial Conference 1960* (Ottawa: Queen's Printer, 1960), Appendix A, p. 125.

8. *Ibid.*, pp. 125-26.

9. It resulted in the publication of Congrès des affaires Canadiennes, *Le Canada: expérience ratée ou réussie* (Québec: les Presses de l'Université Laval, 1961). A new industry was born.

10. André Laurendeau, "A ciel ouvert," *Le Devoir*, October 28, 1961, p. 4.

11. Another survey carried out by the *Groupe de recherches sociales* on the eve of the election shows that the attitudes of Quebecers had not changed since 1960. Evidently, voters were unaware that they were in the midst of a Quiet Revolution. Maurice Pinard has also shown that the nationalization of electricity in 1962 did not play a decisive role in influencing the voters. See M. Pinard, "La rationalité de l'électorat," in V. Lemieux, ed., *Quatre élections provinciales au Québec* (Québec: les Presses de l'Université Laval, 1969).

12. Daniel Johnson, *Egalité ou Indépendance* (Montréal: Editions de l'Homme, 1965). Daniel Johnson, a skilled political practitioner, had realized, following his defeat in 1962, that the Union Nationale must at all costs eliminate three handicaps if it were seriously to hope to take power: the negative image of its leader, the reactionary image of the party, and its anti-nationalism.
13. Quoted by Jean-Louis Roy in *Les programmes électoraux du Québec*, Vol. 2 (Montréal: Leméac, 1970-71), p. 395.
14. Jean Lesage, "Quebec in Canadian Confederation," Banquet—Interprovincial Conference, Victoria, August 7, 1962, pp. 1-2. This and other quotations in this essay are taken from Jean-Louis Roy, *Le choix d'un pays*.
15. Quebec, *Statement by the Honourable Jean Lesage*, Federal-Provincial Conference, Ottawa, November 25, 1963, pp. 1-2.
16. Quebec, *Statement by the Honourable Jean Lesage*, Federal-Provincial Conference, Quebec, March 31, 1964.
17. Jacques-Yvan Morin, "Le rapatriement de la Constitution," *Cité Libre*, No. 72 (1964), pp. 11-12. The author of that article has come a long way since.
18. A. Breton *et al.*, "Bizarre algèbre!" *Cité Libre*, No. 82 (1965), pp. 13-20.
19. These figures are taken from Roy, *op. cit.*, p. 123. See also *Les Etats généraux du Canada français*; Assises nationales (Montréal: Editions de l'Action Nationale, 1969).
20. See R. Daignault, *Lesage* (Montréal: Libre expression, 1981), pp. 161-74.
21. P. Godin, *Daniel Johnson*, Vol. 2 (Montréal: Editions de l'Homme, 1980), p. 366.
22. D. Johnson, *Egalité ou indépendance* (Montréal: Editions de l'Homme, 1965), p. 109.
23. Godin, *op. cit.*, Vol. 2, p. 302.
24. *Ibid.*, pp. 303-304.
25. *Ibid.*, pp. 305-307.
26. *Ibid.*, pp. 269-70.
27. This is the main argument of Jacques-Yvan Morin.
28. *Constitution-Making: Principles, Process, Practice* (Toronto: University of Toronto Press, 1981).

Chapter 6/Constitutional Politics and the West

Roger Gibbins

> ". . . Canadians are more attached to their problems than to any
> man or woman who might suggest solutions. We cherish our
> problems so much that we have even enshrined them in our new
> Constitution so that our children may inherit them intact."
> —Solange Chaput-Rolland[1]

Now that the Constitution Act is in place and the arduous constitutional
negotiations are behind us, we can consider the likely impact of the Act on
the broader political and social orders. Of particular concern here is its
impact, and the impact of the constitutional process, on regional politics.
Admittedly, any such assessment must be tentative, for in many ways the
Act and the constitutional process leading up to it are analogous to large
stones tossed into what had been the relatively placid pool of Canadian
political life. At the time of writing, the resulting pattern of concentric
waves has only begun to ripple out through the political order. Yet, while
the long-term effect must remain a matter of speculation, the splash itself
can be examined in some detail.

The newness of the Constitution Act forces one to examine it within
some pre-existing interpretive framework. My own such framework, one
that can neither be examined in detail nor adequately defended here, rests
on the assertion that Canadians face an intensifying institutional crisis that
threatens to dismember the Canadian federal state. More specifically,
national political institutions have not only failed to provide an outlet,
much less a remedy, for territorial conflict within the body politic, but have
perpetuated, and indeed exacerbated such conflict. This viewpoint, it
should be emphasized, is not entirely idiosyncratic, for it draws heavily
upon fifteen years of institutional analysis by Alan Cairns, Richard
Simeon, Donald Smiley and Garth Stevenson, among many others. It is,
moreover, an intrinsically nationalist viewpoint that looks with alarm on
the erosion of federal institutions and political authority, and on the
growing strength of provincial governments and identifications. It is also a
viewpoint from which the Constitution Act must be seen as a lost
opportunity, perhaps tragically so, to re-vitalize national institutions and
political life in Canada.

Constitution-Making in the West

To assess the impact of the Constitution Act on regional politics, one must
begin with an examination of the constitutional process in western
Canada. The reasons for doing so go beyond matters of personal preference
and competence, although these are significant. Just as Quebec has been at

the centre of the bicultural conflict that has done so much to shape the character of the Canadian federal state, it is the West that historically has provided the engine for regional conflict in Canada. It is also in the West that regional conflict has been most inflamed during the past decade, and it is the economic muscle, the provincial government strength, and the deep-set alienation of the West that will shape the major thrust of regional conflict in the decade to come. Admittedly, the West is only one, or four, of Canada's peripheries and is by no means the only stage for vitriolic regional conflict; one would hesitate to label the rhetoric of Newfoundland's Premier Brian Peckford as moderate or restrained. Yet the Newfoundland government, Hibernia's potential wealth notwithstanding, lacks leverage on the national political system equivalent to that provided by the resources, population and land mass of the West. The stridency of the Newfoundland government, moreover, is dampened somewhat by the relative acquiescence of the other three Atlantic provinces in the existing political order. It is, then, in western Canada that the future dynamics of regional conflict will unfold.

Traditionally, constitutional reform has not been a major concern among western Canadians, even though it can be argued that they have had more cause for concern than Canadians living elsewhere. This is not to suggest that western Canadians have been satisfied with the political status quo; the multitude of protest movements that rocked the national and provincial party systems provide ample evidence to the contrary. Western discontent, however, never crystallized into an alternative constitutional vision. Protest was directed more against party discipline, the electoral weight of the East, and the control of national parties by eastern financial interests than against the constitutional underpinnings of the Canadian federal state. Only rarely was it recognized that problems such as rigid party discipline were essential features, rather than corruptions, of parliamentary institutions. These institutions were generally, and indeed enthusiastically, supported despite the demonstrable fact that they failed to provide effective outlets for the regional interests of the sparsely populated West. Parliamentary institutions failed to provide a sense of full regional participation in the national government and national political life, and failed to address adequately long-standing regional economic grievances relating to the production, transportation and marketing of western Canadian natural resources.

Despite the influence of American political reform movements in the early Canadian West, few Westerners saw the congressional system as a preferred alternative to parliamentary institutions. Seldom were American constitutional principles such as fixed elections, the separation of powers, and territorial representation through an elected Senate advanced as solutions to western Canadian problems of political representation. While Senate reform has lately edged onto the constitutional agenda, it has received lukewarm support from provincial politicians (the British Columbia government was an exception), who quite correctly see elected senators as potent rivals to their own influence within the Canadian federal system. Senate reforms that have received the most support have been those that would provide an Ottawa stage for provincial *governments*; direct and elected Senate representation of the *people* of western Canada is viewed as an undue intrusion into the provincial governments' jealously-guarded role as regional spokesmen in national affairs. Public support for Senate reform, however, is far from negligible. In a survey conducted in the early fall of 1981, 34 percent of 647 respondents interviewed across the West felt that the Senate should be reformed, 21 percent felt that it should be abolished, and only 28 percent felt that it should be left as currently constituted.[2] When asked to indicate what type of reform they would support, 2 percent favoured the current system of appointment by the federal government, 3 percent favoured appointment by provincial governments, 22 percent favoured joint appointments, and 61 percent favoured direct popular election. However, this opinion has yet to be mobilized into public pressure for Senate reform, and it has not been a significant factor in the constitutional calculus of the provincial or federal governments.

Throughout the history of western political protest, little attention has been paid to the federal-provincial division of legislative powers, even though the national government's handling of transportation, banking and international trade has been a common bone of contention. The major exception was the struggle by Manitoba, Alberta and Saskatchewan for provincial ownership of natural resources. When the provinces were created in 1870 and 1905, natural resource ownership remained in Ottawa's hands in order to facilitate national settlement, railway and economic development policies. The 1931 transfer of resource ownership to the provinces, an event described by Premier Lougheed as second in importance only to Alberta's birth as a province, was certainly a milestone, but one that marked the full integration of the West into the existing federal system rather than any reform of that system. More recently, there has been both governmental and public support for a greater devolution of power within the federal system, but this mood is by no means restricted to the West; it does not spring from problems unique to the West or from a uniquely western critique of the federal system.[3] Western political protest has always been more concerned with the way in which Ottawa has carried out its constitutional responsibilities than with the scope of those responsibilities.

In short, one of the more puzzling aspects of the rich and protracted history of western political protest has been the failure to generate an alternative constitutional vision. Despite the manifest regional failures of parliamentary institutions and their accompanying party structures, western Canadians have been hesitant to embrace institutional alternatives.

Indeed, some of the principal spokesmen for western discontent, including John Diefenbaker in particular, and to a lesser extent Joe Clark, have been among the most vociferous defenders of parliamentary institutions, their British roots, and their attendant British symbols. The inherent conflict between the majoritarian norms of parliamentary institutions and the federal needs of the sparsely-populated Western provinces has not been recognized or, when it has been recognized, has not been married to a coherent platform of institutional and constitutional reform.

As a consequence, western Canadians were ill-equipped for the constitutional bargaining of the past several years. In the absence of a coordinated, forceful and carefully articulated western argument, the reform of national political institutions slipped off the constitutional agenda. In its stead, mere refinements of the existing federal order, designed to safeguard provincial powers, came to the fore, refinements such as provincially-controlled constitutional limitations on Ottawa's declaratory, emergency and spending powers. Lacking an alternative constitutional vision, western provincial governments fell into a largely defensive posture, protecting an institutional status quo that should not have been defended, not in its present form, and not by the West.

In the end, the constitutional Accord failed to address, much less solve, the chronic problems of regional representation that have fostered western alienation and eroded the bond between western Canadians and their national government. The opportunity to fulfill the long-standing desire of western Canadians to be full partners in Confederation was lost when institutional reform was abandoned, and the blame must be shared by both levels of government. While western provincial governments successfully protected their own status and jurisdictional interests, they failed to advance the *national interests* of their constituents. Although the institutional status quo may have been acceptable to western provincial governments, it should never have been acceptable to the people of the West. If western Canadians are to feel a part of the national political community, they must have a direct voice in Ottawa quite apart from that provided by their provincial premiers in the closed councils of executive federalism.

Constitution-making can have considerable nation-building potential; that was demonstrated by the 1789 Philadelphia convention, which gave birth to the American constitution. In that case, the convention format—participation by a relatively broad spectrum of the nascent American society, the spirited articulation of constitutional principles, and the constitution capstone itself—all made important contributions to a growing national bond, mythology and political culture. In Canada, the constitutional process stretching from 1980 to 1982 had few, if any, of these attributes. Indeed, it can be argued—and not only with respect to regional politics in the West—that the constitutional process further strained an already fragile national political fabric and crippled whatever integrative potential the new Constitution Act might have had.

To understand western reactions, the constitutional process must be viewed against the abrasive and deeply suspicious political context of the times. The stage was set by the 1980 general election, in which the short-lived Conservative government, led by Albertan Joe Clark and enjoying strong electoral support across the West, was swept from power by the Trudeau Liberals, whose victory brought them but two seats in western Canada. The election results inflamed western alienation, illustrating the apparent political impotence of the West. In a survey of 1370 western Canadian residents conducted by the Canada West Foundation in October 1980, 84 percent agreed with the statement that "the West usually gets ignored in national politics because the political parties depend upon Quebec and Ontario for most of their votes," 60 percent agreed that "the West has sufficient resources and industry to survive without the rest of Canada," and an ominous 28 percent agreed that "western Canadians get so few benefits from being part of Canada that they might as well go it on their own."[4] By March 1981, the situation had deteriorated further; a survey of 652 western Canadian respondents showed 36 percent agreeing with the statement that "western Canadians get so few benefits from being part of Canada that they might as well go it on their own."[5] In Alberta the proportion rose from 30 percent in October 1980 to 49 percent, while in British Columbia the increase was from 29 percent to 37 percent. Agreement among Saskatchewan and Manitoba respondents declined slightly from 25 percent in October 1980 to 23 percent in March 1981.

The 1980 election results also touched off a vitriolic western separatist movement, spearheaded initially by Doug Christie's Western Canada Concept and Elmer Knudson's West Fed. More importantly for the constitutional process in the short term, the election meant that Ottawa's constitutional initiatives were put forward by a government all but devoid of elected western representatives. Consequently, they were viewed with distrust bordering on paranoia; many western Canadians were prepared for the worst and were difficult to convince that the worst was not exactly what they were getting. Westerners were ripe for extremist conspiratorial interpretations of federal motives. Separatist speakers, particularly in Alberta, were quick to take the absence of property rights in the constitutional proposals as proof positive that Ottawa intended to strip Canadians not only of their property rights, but also, under the new constitutional regime, of their property itself. The disturbing mood of the times could be picked up in multitudinous public meetings in which apparently reasonable people accepted with grim resignation separatist claims that Ottawa intended to move Calgarians out of their homes and replace them with unemployed miners from northern Ontario, that Ottawa was buying land in northern Alberta for concentration camps, that once the Constitution Act was in place the federal government would never have to call another election, and that an import ban on grenade launchers struck at the basic personal freedom of all Canadians.

Ottawa's constitutional initiatives not only came from a government with miniscule western Canadian representation, but they also came hand-in-glove with the National Energy Program. At least in Alberta, the immensely unpopular NEP and the constitutional proposals were commonly seen as a single package. Public meetings held to discuss the constitutional proposals focused almost entirely on the NEP, and the NEP became the layman's interpretive guide to the constitution debate. The Constitution Act proposals were seen as a means to constitutionally entrench the NEP, while the NEP was seen to foreshadow the dangers ahead should the Constitution Act become the law of the land. Thus the details of Ottawa's constitutional proposals were examined from a very narrow perspective; what would be their impact on the resource base of the western Canadian economy? And here the proposals were found to be extremely suspect; the protection given to provincial ownership of natural resources was seen to be weak, Ottawa's feared and generally misunderstood declaratory power was unimpaired, natural resources were not shielded from the federal government's emergency powers, and the proposed amending formula seemed to open up the spectre of some future, Ottawa-orchestrated gang-rape of the natural resource wealth of individual Western provinces.

In concert, then, the lack of elected representation in the national government, intensified western alienation, the National Energy Program, and other factors such as the federal budget muddled and distorted the constitutional debate in western Canada. Important substantive issues such as the debate over the legislative protection versus the constitutional protection of human rights, the concerns of native Canadians, and the constitutional status of Canadian women were all but ignored; there was simply too much background noise from the NEP *et al.* for such issues to be heard.

In addition, the defensive posture of the western premiers obscured both the influence they exerted in the constitutional process and the very real gains they achieved; it was the concessions made by the premiers, no matter how few, that came to the fore, rather than the concessions they were able to wring from Ottawa and the other provinces. The gains were seen as little more than fingers in the dike restraining an aggrandizing, centralist and regionally unbalanced national government, the cutting edge of whose ambition had been starkly revealed by the NEP, while any concessions to Ottawa were seen as a sellout of regional interests. (In a similar manner, the 1981 energy pact between Alberta and Ottawa has been increasingly portrayed by separatist sympathizers in Alberta as a sellout to the federal government, a perception that is not shared by Ottawa, the Alberta government, or Canadians living outside Alberta.) While in an objective sense it is difficult to see the constitutional process as demonstrating western political impotence, this perception has gained strength over time in the West. The participating premiers stand to become the scapegoats for any shortcomings in the Constitution Act, for any failure to nail down western interests or special interests, such as property rights and the right to bear arms, that have gained particular prominence in the West.

The constitutional process dramatized the virtual exclusion of the West from a succession of national Liberal governments, and in so doing elevated and inflated the role of provincial premiers. As they hunkered down to protect regional interests from the "outside threat" of federal constitutional initiatives, the premiers increasingly monopolized the articulation of regional interests in the national political system. This development is an important one for at least four reasons. First, it plays to the long-standing tenet of western alienation that the West lacks any effective power within national institutions, and therefore the policies flowing from those institutions must be viewed with suspicion. Second, it strengthens the very governments which have been prone to fan the flames of western alienation in order to promote their own status, power and electoral survival. Third, it undercuts the stature of western Canadian MPs, who are increasingly seen as incidental to the major regional conflicts fought out between Ottawa and the provincial premiers. Fourth, it further erodes the general political authority of the national government in the West, weakens the bond between western Canadians and national political institutions, and reduces Ottawa to a government that does things to but not for western Canadians.

To summarize, the constitutional process was damaging to the regional fabric of Canada, particularly in the West. Political conditions ensured that any constitutional proposals forthcoming from Ottawa would be viewed with grave suspicion in the West; only with the most determined effort could the federal government have been able to use the constitutional process to strengthen its hold on the hearts, minds or political loyalties of western Canadians. Yet not even a modest effort was made. Ottawa's initial constitutional proposals contained nothing to appeal to western Canadians *as western Canadians.* There was no rhetorical appeal to western visions of the national community, no attempt to address western resource and transportation concerns or western fears surrounding the declaratory, emergency, reservation and spending powers of the federal government. There was no implicit constitutional log-rolling, no regional trade-off of constitutional costs and benefits. In the West, as a consequence, constitution-making was not an exercise in nation-building; Ottawa's proposals were seen by far too many western Canadians as the regionally-insensitive product of one government, one party, and one man. However, the damage done by the constitutional process would have been tolerable if the final constitutional product had addressed the institutional underpinnings of regional conflict in the Canadian federal state. Unfortunately, the Constitution Act did not do so; regional conflict was entrenched within rather than mitigated by the new constitution.

The Constitution Act

The constitutional process leading up to the Constitution Act grew out of a wide array of strains within the body politic, including but by no means restricted to the unsettled place of Quebec within Confederation. Other pressures included the intensifying regional conflict, particularly in the West; the lack of a formal amending formula; the perceived need for constitutionally-entrenched language rights; the desire to remove the colonial vestiges from Canada's relationship with Great Britain; growing intergovernmental conflict and the related uncertainty about the federal division of powers; an interest in shielding the rights of individuals from the powers of government; and a plethora of special interests that could be addressed through or attached to the constitutional process, including aboriginal rights, property rights, and the rights of women, the handicapped and the unborn. The point to be made is that the constitutional *process* engaged a much wider array of issues than were finally addressed by the Constitution Act itself. A great many fell by the wayside, and among the casualties was intensifying regional conflict and its roots deep within parliamentary institutions. Somewhere between Bill C-60 and the November 1981 constitutional Accord, the failure of national institutions to reflect the "territorial particularisms" identified by Donald Smiley fell from the constitutional agenda.[6]

The Constitution Act has three essential components: patriation, the Charter of Rights and Freedoms, and the amending formula. The first of these is unlikely to have any detectable impact on regional conflict. If patriation had been accompanied by an outpouring of nationalist sentiment, federal politicians might have been able to tap that sentiment to the benefit of national institutions; regional conflict might have been muted as Canadians re-affirmed their commitment to the national political community. Clearly, this did not happen. While the patriation ceremonies may have struck a responsive and enthusiastic chord in Ottawa, they were received with general indifference outside the capital, and with public protest in Quebec. April 17 is unlikely to occupy a place in the Canadian political culture comparable to that of May Day, Bastille Day or the fourth of July. Although there is no doubt that patriation was supported by the vast majority of Canadians, including those in the West, it is unlikely by itself to alter significantly the issues, tone or intensity of regional conflict.

The second component of the Constitution Act—the Charter—may strengthen the national political community over the long run, and in so doing may dampen regional conflict. The Charter should raise the profile of the Supreme Court, as Canadians turn increasingly to this national institution for the protection and definition of their basic rights and freedoms. In time, the Charter may come to have the same nationalizing influence within the Canadian political system as the Bill of Rights has had within the American system. And yet there is little in the Charter that directly touches upon the major underpinnings of regional conflict; one can only hope that as the Charter elevates the position of the Supreme Court in the Canadian political system, there will be some halo effect on other national institutions. Significant short-term effects, however, are not to be anticipated. The "day of mourning" declared on May 20, 1982 by the Newfoundland government in response to Ottawa's decision to send the off-shore resources dispute to the Supreme Court demonstrates the limited leverage of the court on issues of regional conflict.

It is with the amending formula that a regional analysis of the Constitution Act begins to take on more substance. We should note at the outset, however, that formal procedures of constitutional amendment such as those embodied in the Constitution Act are seldom of great practical importance. In the United States, for example, the formal amendment procedure is rarely used, much greater reliance being placed upon judicial re-interpretation. In Canada, the lack of a patriated amending procedure did not prevent Canadian governments from turning the original constitutional document virtually inside-out in the 115 years since 1867. The importance of the formal amending formula comes from its symbolic content rather than from its practical utility, from what it says or can be interpreted to say about the fundamental structure of political power within the society.

From this perspective, the amending formula in the Constitution Act makes a number of important statements: (1) that Quebec is a province like any other; (2) that, in violation of the political equality of individuals, the provinces are equal in the amending process. Governments are equalized, not people, although the numerically large provinces are more equal than others because of the requirement that the seven or more provincial governments supporting constitutional change must represent more than 50 percent of the national population; (3) that the constitution is the property and prerogative of governments rather than the people governments represent; (4) that there can be no constitutional appeal to popular sovereignty; when governments clash, the people cannot serve as a court of last resort. From the perspective of regional politics in western Canada, the amending procedure reinforces the claim of provincial governments that they alone speak for their provincial electorates *in national affairs.* Ottawa cannot appeal directly to the people of the West over, under or around their provincial governments. In a region where the political authority of Ottawa has already been dangerously eroded, the absence of any claim to popular sovereignty on the part of the national government may be critical.

A number of aspects of the amending formula should serve as palliatives for western Canadian political discontent. The principle of provincial equality, for instance, has been an important constitutional goal for provincial governments in the West. Furthermore, its application to Quebec addresess a long-standing component of western alienation—the irritating belief that Quebec enjoys disproportionate power, influence and rights within the Canadian political system. While antipathy towards Quebec appears to be a diminishing feature of western alienation, it is still present. There is little doubt that the reception of the Constitution Act in the West would have been much more contentious had the Act provided a special place for Quebec in Confederation; whether the gains made in the West will offset the damage done within Quebec remains very much an open question. Parenthetically, it is worth noting that neither Quebec's exclusion from the November 1981 Accord nor the continued opposition of the Quebec government to the Act have evoked much concern in the West. There appears to be a growing indifference to Quebec that is by no means restricted to the West, and that does not augur well for the ability of English Canadians to handle the future challenges to national unity that will inevitably emerge from Quebec.

The Constitution Act addresses another western Canadian bugbear by re-affirming provincial ownership of natural resources. Part VI of the Constitution Act amends and elaborates section 92 of the British North America Act with respect to natural resources, although it should be stressed that the Constitution Act by no means precludes a vigorous federal presence in the resource field. The opting-out provision in the amending formula is also seen in the West as a safeguard for provincial resource ownership; in the constitutional negotiations, the Alberta government was particularly concerned that without such a provision its energy wealth would be open to constitutional plunder.

The problem is that the ownership and control of natural resources are such key issues in the West, and of such symbolic importance, that any constitutional guarantees are likely to be seen as falling short of the mark. Westerners can argue, for example, that as long as federal legislation such as the National Energy Program is permitted under the Constitution Act, the resource base of the West is insecure. For western critics of the Constitution Act's resource provisions, the NEP provides ample ammunition. The problem here extends to the logical foundations of the Canadian federal state. As long as Ottawa enjoys paramountcy in international and interprovincial trade, something that seems inescapable if the country remains united, and as long as Ottawa is active in the corporate tax field, the West's *control* of natural resources will be compromised even though its *ownership* of those resources may be constitutionally guaranteed. But absolute provincial control over the production, pricing and marketing of natural resources is incompatible with the continued existence of a federal state.

While the Constitution Act addresses a number of western concerns, it leaves others untouched. Perhaps the least serious of these are issues such as the constitutional entrenchment of property rights, where western extremists are at odds with their provincial governments, or the "inalienable right to bear arms," where the same extremists are at odds with majority public opinion both within the West and across the country. More serious are some of the existing provisions of the British North America Act which have been carried forward by the new Constitution Act. The peace, order and good government clause, the national declaratory power, Ottawa's ability to disallow provincial legislation, and the federal government's emergency powers are often poorly understood in the West; their constitutional evolution over time and the conventional restrictions on their use by Ottawa are little appreciated. As a consequence, they have become the warp and woof of conspiracy theories that abound in the region. The following statement by Prime Minister Trudeau, made shortly after the constitutional Accord, has received great play in separatist publications:

> We've got all the aces, we've got the right of disallowance, declaratory power, expropriatory power under Peace, Order and Good Government. And we've got the entrenchment of both official languages, which can never be removed. We've got French in the educational system of every English province.

From the western Canadian perspective, it was hardly a sales job for the new constitution. If these powers had been clarified in the Constitution Act, if the conventional restrictions on their use had been articulated, it is possible that the more extreme conspiratorial interpretations of the Canadian federal system could have been undercut, although probably not driven completely from the field.

Unquestionably the most serious shortcoming of the Constitution Act for western Canadians is its failure to address the longstanding problem of regional representation within national institutions. The argument has been made here that the Act, both in its content and in the political process leading up to it, strengthened the position of western Canadian provincial governments. In itself this would not be a problem if at the same time the Act had addressed regional representation within national institutions. This the Constitution Act does not do. Fundamental institutional reforms, including those of the Senate and electoral system, are not tackled and may in fact be impeded by the Act in the future. Nothing has been done to enhance the effectiveness of MPs as regional representatives, to undercut the premiers' monopoly as regional spokesmen in national politics, to encourage provincial champions and firebrands to pursue national office, to weaken the restrictive bonds of party discipline, to ensure that national institutions will be more sensitive to regional interests. This in turn is indicative of a broader failure of the Act; it does not address the majority of strains within the body politic that launched the process of constitutional reform in the first place, and in particular it does nothing to strengthen the position of the West or Quebec within Confederation. Nor does it moderate the acrimonious climate of intergovernmental conflict that has come to characterize the Canadian federal system. By so failing, the Constitution

Act both sustains and exacerbates fundamental institutional weaknesses within the Canadian political system.

In the past, western Canadians have had a strong national vision. They, after all, were the Canadian nation-builders; they were the people from foreign lands who merged with and fostered a new Canadian nationality, who broke the prairie sod and pushed back the resource frontier, who participated enthusiastically in the two world wars that did so much to define Canadian nationhood. Admittedly, the western national vision was not always well-suited to broader political realities; John Diefenbaker's "one Canada" had little appeal to the nation's francophones, and western support for Canada's war efforts was tinged with hostility towards Quebec. Nevertheless, there was in the West a truly *national* vision, which today has begun to falter and fade. The "national interest" is spoken of with derisive cynicism, and for many the "national" government is not only remote from, but apart from the West. The Constitution Act, with its understandable, if regrettable lack of rhetorical flourishes, does nothing to revive the national vision in the West. There is no emotional linkage to the strong sense of Canadian nationalism that used to be so prevalent in the region. What, then, lies ahead?

Regional Politics in the Wake of the Constitution Act

If the process of constitutional reform heightened regional and intergovernmental conflict, and if the content of the Constitution Act fails to address such conflict, what does the future hold? While any crystal ball is flawed, I would argue that some of the events that occurred between the November 1981 constitutional Accord and the proclamation of the new Act on April 17, 1982 provide instructive signposts: (1) in the April Newfoundland election, Ottawa-bashing was elevated to new heights as Brian Peckford evoked treason in his campaign against opponents of his stand on offshore resources: "They're traitors, traitors to Newfoundland's ever having a fair chance at the future";[7] (2) in a speech to the annual convention of the Alberta Progressive Conservative party, Premier Lougheed said to tumultuous applause: "We moved them [Ottawa] from the living room to the porch, and I'm beginning to think we should move them off the property;" (3) in conversation with the author, a moderate and left-of-centre Alberta MLA expressed his deep concern that the federal government owned property within the province; all federal holdings, he argued, be they office space or the national parks, should be on a short-term lease arrangement that would be subject to yearly renewal by the provincial government; (4) in Alberta, and to a lesser extent in the other three Western provinces, the Western Canada Concept acquired a measure of popular support on the basis of a separatist and stridently right-wing political platform; in a by-election in the Alberta provincial riding of Olds-Didsbury, a separatist candidate was elected for the first time in western Canada, though he held his seat only until the provincial election of the fall of 1982; (5) across the West and across the country, intergovernmental conflict remains at a boil. In the jurisdictional battle over pay TV, to give but one example, Quebec labelled Ottawa's policy as "a declaration of war," Alberta announced that it would develop its own regulations and ignore those of the federal government, and B.C. warned television networks that a federal licence issued by the CRTC would not be honoured by the province.[8] In short, little happened to suggest an abatement in regional or intergovernmental conflict.

To be sure, none of the prevailing regional conflicts may deliver a knockout punch to the Canadian state; not even the long-standing Quebec separatist movement, firmly in control of the Quebec provincial government, has been able to deliver such a punch. But each conflict nonetheless delivers a damaging blow to the body politic, and to the continued vitality, effectiveness and political authority of national institutions. When premiers threaten to move Ottawa off the property, label Ottawa as the enemy, depict national attachments as potentially treasonous, or brand the prime minister as an arsonist, as Premier Bill Bennett did during the constitutional negotiations, the national political community is diminished. The legitimacy of the national government, already weakened in the West by gross regional imbalances in political representation, is further eroded.

From the perspective of regional politics, the Constitution Act can best be seen as a tragic lost opportunity. In the early stages of the decade-long constitutional process, two things were possible. The first was the reform and re-vitalization of national parliamentary institutions so as to provide for the effective representation of regional interests *within national institutions by national politicians.* The second was the constitutional enshrinement of popular sovereignty which might, at least at the margins, have strengthened the attachment of individual Canadians to the national political community and thereby dampened intergovernmental conflict. Through both, regional conflict could have been moderated, although not eliminated. Neither, however, was achieved. The institutional conflict between the majoritarian norms of parliamentary democracy and the federal protection of minority interests was not resolved, the attractiveness of national office for provincial politicians was not enhanced, neither the effectiveness nor the visibility of regional representation in the House of Commons was improved, the Senate was not reformed, and the electoral system was not revamped so as to yield more-regionally-balanced parliamentary parties.

Admittedly, the Constitution Act could not have accomplished all of these things, nor perhaps are all necessary. However, it could have but did not set in motion the institutional reform of the Canadian political system, and here it failed the West. While the Act cannot be said to work against the interests of the West, it does nothing to advance those interests through much-overdue institutional reform. At the end of a long and bitter constitutional process, western Canadians are left with a strengthened provincial vision and a weakened national vision of the Canadian federation, neither of which will serve them well. They are left with a political system that fails to capture the national aspirations that once flourished in the West.

It can be argued, of course, that institutional reform is still possible, that a second round in the constitutional process lies ahead. Yet continued economic malaise, the acrimony that surrounded the first round of constitutional negotiations, and the accompanying public weariness make it unlikely that governments will move further constitutional reform to the top of the political agenda. Thus we face an unsettled future locked into parliamentary institutions that fail to mitigate regional conflict and, in that limited but important sense, fail to provide the Canadian people with the government they deserve.

Writing in 1960, the American political scientist E.E. Schattschneider made the following observation:

> All forms of political organization have a bias in favor of the exploitation of some kinds of conflict and the suppression of others because organization is the mobilization of bias. Some issues are organized into politics while others are organized out.[9]

There is little doubt that in the past the Canadian political system organized regionalism into Canadian politics, and virulent regional conflict was the price. In the Constitution Act, we missed the opportunity to organize regional conflict out of the political system, or at least to reorder our institutional life so that regional conflict could be moderated and contained. Instead, the Constitution Act takes a troubled political past and casts it in constitutional cement for an uncertain future.

Notes

1. "A Federalist No More," *Today Magazine*, July 10, 1982, p. 8.
2. Canada West Foundation *Opinion Update*, Report No. 11, January 4, 1982.
3. In October 1980, the Canada West Foundation posed the following question to a random sample of 1370 western Canadian respondents: "In a reformed constitution, which of the following would you prefer to see—more power to the federal government, more power to the provincial governments, or should the powers remain about as they are now?" Across the West, 53% opted for "remaining the same," 32% for more provincial power, and 9% for more power to the federal government. Canada West Foundation *Opinion Update*, Report No. 6, November 1980.
4. Canada West Foundation *Opinion Update*, Report No. 9, May 1981.
5. *Ibid.*
6. *Canada in Question: Federalism in the Seventies*, Second Edition (Toronto: McGraw-Hill Ryerson, 1976), p. 211.
7. *Calgary Herald*, April 3, 1982, p. B28.
8. *Calgary Herald*, May 22, 1982, p. A2.
9. *The Semisovereign People* (New York: Holt, Rinehart and Winston, 1960), p. 71.

Chapter 7/Quebec, the Economy and the Constitution

Raymond Hudon

On November 5, 1981, eighteen months after the Quebec referendum on sovereignty-association, Canadian political leaders announced a constitutional agreement to which Quebec alone was not a party. The terms of the Accord made it clear that the commitments made to Quebecers during the referendum were not going to be fully respected; and the rhetoric of the ensuing months symbolically demonstrated the growing political marginalization of Quebecers and their government. The very day that the final version of the constitutional document was adopted by Parliament with an overwhelming majority, federal Minister of Justice Jean Chrétien claimed that the Resolution was supported by "nine and a half provinces!" In the literature it distributed in Quebec to celebrate the royal proclamation of the new constitution, the federal government chose to sum up the events of November 5, 1981 in these terms: *"A la suite de nouvelles discussions, le premier ministre fédéral et les premiers ministres provinciaux signent, le 5 novembre, un accord qui met fin à l'impasse constitutionnelle."*[1] The English version appeared closer to the truth: "After further discussions in early November, the Prime Minister and *nine provincial premiers* signed an accord on November 5 that breaks the impasse."[2] The two versions appeared in the same brochure!

The results of May 20, 1980 and November 5, 1981 did not in any way resolve the conflict between Quebec and Ottawa. However, only the complete eradication of Quebec's desire to make further claims, it seemed, would relieve federal peevishness. Henceforth the political recognition of Quebec would be linked to its degree of subservience. The old question "to be or not to be" seemed to be reduced to "how not to be!" Having dared to encourage Liberal MNAs to deplore Quebec's absence from the constitutional agreement of November 5, 1981, Claude Ryan was made to realize that his position as leader had become unbearable in the summer of 1982. His resignation was the price to be paid for not having totally assumed that narrow option of "how not to be." The Toronto magazine, *Maclean's*, captured part of the spirit prevalent during the royal proclamation of the "new" constitution in April 1982. The cover page of its April 26, 1982 issue announced the "Rebirth of a Nation." Against a background picture of the Queen signing the proclamation, followed the captions: "the historic moment," "the new era" and "the angry losers."[3] Losers, as everyone knows, are ultimately condemned to resignation so that history may all the more easily consign them to oblivion.

But it would be a mistake to assume that history suddenly came to an end in 1982. Such a conclusion would simply duplicate the error of those who have assumed for too long that Quebec history only begins in 1960. In both cases, it is presumed that the Canadian constitutional conflict has arisen solely as a result of the "difficulties of intergovernmental relations in a federal system," and that it in no way constitutes a "crisis undermining the social and economic order of Canadian society."[4] In fact, however, the constitution is the product of a "confrontation of diverging interests,"[5] interests rooted in significant measure in the economic structure of the country.

Any serious attempt to advance the constitutional debate inevitably involved dealing with the Quebec question. We contend, however, that the results of the May 20, 1980 referendum eliminated many of the obstacles which until then had prevented the clarification of certain federal ideas. Secondly, we will show how the structure of the Canadian economy has become increasingly one of the fundamental stakes in constitutional revision. We then discuss important elements of the Canadian and Quebec economic policies which enable us to put the conflict between Quebec and Canada in a wider or larger perspective. Finally, we examine the thesis of the confrontation of two nationalisms[6] in order to identify more clearly those interests involved in the "conflicting conceptions of Canada" that underlie, in the perception of Pierre Elliott Trudeau, the opposition between the federal government and the majority of the provinces.

The Constitution and Quebec

Once more isolated after November 5, 1981, Quebec found itself again in a position similar to the one it had been in fifteen years before, when it was the only province asking for a revision of the constitution.[7] In the interim, however, a fundamental change had occurred. The basic issues had shifted towards economic concerns, a shift that can be seen in the evolving tension between the constitution and Quebec.

In the middle sixties, Quebec spokesmen could successfully argue the specificity of the Quebec collectivity within the Canadian ensemble, and gain acknowledgment of the crucial nature of the problems that it posed for Canadian federalism. In spite of considerable resistance, the Laurendeau-Dunton commission helped to legitimize many of Quebec's demands. Ontario leaders, for instance, deemed it appropriate to call an interprovincial conference on the "Confederation of Tomorrow." Prime Minister Lester B. Pearson summed up the spirit of the time by asserting explicitly the existence in Canada of *two* societies.[8] It was all the more significant that he chose to address this particular topic at a conference dealing more specifically with the economic dimensions of Canadian unity. One week later, at a meeting of Quebec Liberals in Montreal, he repeated the same idea: "I believe in one sovereign Canadian Confederation composed of two founding nations, one English-speaking, the other French-speaking."[9] The Progressive Conservative Party considered the "two nations" theme popular enough to make it a central issue in its electoral campaign of 1968.

However, their decision benefited Pierre Elliott Trudeau, who advocated the equality of the two main linguistic groups in Canada in order to maintain the existence of *one* Canadian nation.

To this prospect of a chance to resolve the thorny Quebec question, the reaction was simply infatuation. Trudeaumania took over. Canada was declared officially bilingual. But Anglophones soon realized that bilingualism at the national level did not check the rising tide of Quebec nationalism. In its first election, the Parti Québécois obtained 23 percent of the vote. The new Liberal government led by Robert Bourassa was soon rocked by the 1970 October crisis, and a year after its election, it felt obliged to reject the agreement reached by the other participants at the constitutional conference held in Victoria. From Quebec's point of view, patriation of the BNA Act with a new amending formula would only be acceptable if it were accompanied by guarantees for the French language and culture linked to a new division of powers. Quebec's demands thus went far beyond the changes introduced by the *Official Languages Act*. The following year, the PQ increased its electoral support from 23 percent to 30 percent. Although the Quebec Liberal Party won an unprecedented number of seats in the National Assembly, having benefited from a temporary polarization over the national question,[10] the Bourassa government was nevertheless prompted to emphasize the theme of *souveraineté culturelle*, or cultural sovereignty, during this second mandate.

Bourassa had called the election before his mandate of 1973 had expired on the pretext that he needed a new one to counter the attack planned by the prime minister. The federal initiative finally came in 1976, when the prime minister sent a letter to eight provincial premiers, excluding the premiers of Quebec and British Columbia, to remind them that a year earlier they had agreed not to consider for the time being "any fundamental change in the BNA Act, for to pursue that issue, as the discussions between 1968 and 1971 had shown, would be to preclude any immediate progress."[11] The federal strategy was clear. Patriation was to be the only real priority.

However, the federal approach was blocked. On October 14, 1976, the Alberta premier, on behalf of his provincial colleagues, gave the "final" answer of the provinces to Prime Minister Trudeau:

> All provinces agreed with the objective of patriation. They also agreed that patriation should not be undertaken without a consensus being developed on an expansion of the role of the provinces and/or jurisdiction in the following areas: culture, communications, Supreme Court of Canada, spending power, Senate representation and regional disparities.[12]

Thus a conflict between the provinces and the federal government seemed to be taking shape, a conflict which *could have* replaced the widely recognized tensions between Quebec and the rest of the country. But one month later, the PQ was elected. There was a renewed sense of urgency, and for the time being the attention of the rest of the country was focussed once again on the "Quebec problem."

The rest of the provinces behaved as though they found it quite accept-able that the response to the secessionist threat be orchestrated by Ottawa. The federal government, however, clearly had no intention of deviating from its previous course. In his reply of January 19, 1977 to Premier Lougheed, the prime minister declared that the federal government was "prepared to see if agreement could be achieved" with the provinces "so that patriation could be effected as soon as possible." But he expressly suggested that discussions "not enter in any way into the distributions of powers. The federal government is quite ready to go into that problem but it is both complex and difficult."[13]

Persuaded to take into account the position of the provinces, the federal government was eventually to retreat on this point. At the same time, it was still important to resolve the Quebec question. Considering any break-up of the country as a "crime against humanism," Prime Minister Trudeau continued to speak of *one* Canadian nation, which he referred to before the American Congress in terms of a "pluralistic dream" and a "cultural mosaic."[14] Two months later, at the annual meeting of Canadian broadcasters, he undertook to explain that the election of the PQ was simply due to Quebecers' conviction that they "are not sharing fully in Canadian society, nor sharing fully in its benefits," but his only practical conclusion was to affirm "the vital importance of language equality."[15]

Obviously, it was necessary to promise Quebecers a *change*, without, however, indicating the substance or extent of this change, to induce them to reject the *souverainiste* option put before them in the referendum of May 20, 1980. Only after the referendum did the prime minister clarify his promises. In his opinion, the new constitution should recognize "even more clearly the existence of the country's two main linguistic and cultural communities, the French-speaking one having its origins and its centre of gravity in Quebec although it extended out into all of Canada." However, those who were tempted to link the existence of these *two communities* to the possible existence of *two nations* were simply invited to return to their sociology class.

> On the other hand, I object to the two nations theory, for it has lost all cultural and political relevance. Barely valid historically because it fails to take into account the American Indians and the Inuit, it certainly no longer reflects the sociological reality of the country.
>
> The Canada of today is infinitely richer and more diverse than it was in the beginning, and if one were to re-think the country in terms of "nations," one would have to increase the number of nations far beyond what the *péquistes* would themselves be prepared to accept.[16]

As Prime Minister Trudeau said himself at a press conference on the same day this letter appeared, it did not contain "anything new."[17] It clarified, however, his interpretation of the results of the referendum. By their majority decision to remain within Canada, Quebecers had allowed any vague *souverainiste* impulse or simply any claim to the distinctive nature of Quebec society to be decreed henceforth non-existent. The political representatives of the other parts of the country, along with their federal counterparts, agreed all the same to continue to impose section 133 of the BNA Act on Quebec although Ontario managed to argue successfully its claim to a continued exemption. Although Quebec was denied its right to special status, it nonetheless deserved "special" treatment!

In the last analysis, the result of the Quebec referendum was apparently to exorcize the rest of Canada; Quebecers had determined their fate themselves. On April 13, 1981 they even carried the paradox so far as to re-elect with an increased majority the party whose major platform they had rejected less than a year earlier and grant it a mandate to negotiate a renewed federalism, which was the very position of its parliamentary opposition, led by Claude Ryan. Of course, one made a show of being concerned with Quebec's fate. At a speech given at the Carnegie Foundation in New York soon after the setback of September 1980, the premier of New Brunswick—the only province, along with Ontario, to support at the time the constitutional proposals of the federal government, and the only province eventually to entrench its bilingual status in the Canadian Charter of Rights and Freedoms—undertook to explain the reaction of Quebecers: "Quebecers are extremely disappointed. They feel that they were deceived at the time of the referendum, and I believe that they were, particularly by Ontario whose only wish is to maintain the status quo."[18] However, such paternalism only opened the way to contempt; Quebecers were in effect to be told later that their electoral caprices were the main obstacle to constitutional progress. In practice, that meant that Quebecers should elect a government which would be prepared to sell them minor concessions presented as major changes!

By choosing to put Quebec in its place, Quebecers helped increase the room for manoeuvre of the federal government, for whom constitutional revision was not restricted to a re-evaluation of Quebec's place within the Canadian whole:

> After the referendum of May 1980, Prime Minister Trudeau took advantage of the euphoria created by the federalist victory to attack a serious problem of the Canadian economy, one that had lately grown more acute. This was the gradual balkanization of the national economy, mainly under the impact of provincial laws and regulations. The transfer from the British to the Canadian Parliament of authority over the constitution was to be the occasion for a more precise definition of the nature and the extent of the powers of the central government.[19]

The old dynamics of the constitutional debate were reversed, as Quebec negotiators stressed during the summer of 1980:

It is no longer a question, as it has been until now, of limiting Ottawa's interventions based on resort to the major powers it enjoys under the existing constitution. On the contrary, the provinces are now the ones which, in the federal view, have excessive economic powers and whose freedom of action should, therefore, be limited.[20]

After May 20, 1980, federal authorities laid their cards on the table. However, it had already been evident for some time that the economy and the constitution could not be dissociated, despite statements to the contrary by numerous people who demanded a rapid end to the constitutional debate in order that the more serious economic problems of the country finally be solved.

The Constitution and the Economy

Given its late inclusion on the agenda of the constitutional discussions of the summer of 1980, the federal position on federal and provincial economic powers appeared to be somewhat improvised. The question was officially added to the agenda on June 9, 1980, during the first ministers' meeting in Ottawa. However, the detailed position of the federal government was only submitted on July 17, a delay which seemed to indicate a certain lack of preparedness. The federal government proposed three types of techniques "for securing in the Constitution of Canada the basic operational rules of our economic union and for ensuring that both orders of government abide by these rules."[21] Set out in rather general terms to facilitate any necessary adjustments, and especially to prevent them from being "circumvented," the "complementary techniques" proposed were:

   (i) entrenching in the Constitution the mobility rights of citizens, as well as their right to gain a livelihood and acquire property in any province, regardless of their province of residence or previous residence, subject to laws of general application;
  (ii) placing limitations upon the ability of governments to use their legislative and executive powers to impede economic mobility by way of general provisions through the revision and expansion of Section 121 of the BNA Act;
 (iii) broadening federal powers so that they may encompass all matters which are necessary for economic integration, thus ensuring that the relevant laws and regulations will apply uniformly throughout Canada, or that the "test" of the public interest will be brought to bear upon derogations from uniformity.[22]

It should be noted that these proposals had been formulated almost word for word by A.E. Safarian as early as 1974 in a study sponsored by the Privy Council Office of the Government of Canada.[23] The intention was clear: to increase the economic powers of the central government.

In fact, only the first paragraph of the federal proposal was actually adopted, appearing as section 6 of the Canadian Charter of Rights and

Freedoms. Given the demands that had been formulated in previous years by a large majority of the provinces, it was undoubtedly impossible to include all the federal proposals on economic powers in the agreement reached on November 5, 1981. Indeed, for a few years several provinces resembled Quebec, the province customarily described as "not like the others." In the terms used in 1978 by Frank Moores, then premier of Newfoundland, the provinces complained of not being masters of their "own economic destiny."[24] Such was also the position of Saskatchewan's representatives at the constitutional conference of September 1980, who expressed their conviction that the federal proposals "would result in a significant shift of jurisdiction from the provinces to the federal government and would seriously impair provincial capacity to deal with local economic, social and cultural matters."[25]

Warned in *A Time for Action* that they were not in any event to contemplate a "massive shift of powers from the federal government to the provinces,"[26] the provinces had also been reminded that too much decentralization would render the central government "incapable of managing efficiently the economy, of controlling fluctuations in this sector and of continuing to improve the standard of living of the population."[27] This constituted a complete reversal of the federal position as expressed in the Molgat-MacGuigan report, where it was deemed that "the cost of centralization would be much too high in Canada."[28] The new federal orientation was confirmed unequivocally in the report of the Task Force on Canadian Unity. With regards to the development of an "industrial strategy, the main weapon for economic adjustment," the task force felt there seemed to be "no substitute for further concentration of power in the central government, a solution which runs counter to the realities of dualism and regionalism."[29] These latter problems identified by the task force were considered to all intents and purposes secondary:

> Indeed, it seems to us that reform of the constitution and political institutions would be justified even if our sole purpose was to improve the ability of the Canadian public and private sectors to address themselves to the economic policy requirements of the future.[30]

Such comments show clearly that the Quebec question was no longer as central an issue in the constitutional debate. Ultimately, it had become more than anything a pretext for introducing more important points. In practice, as long as the results of the pre-referendum debate remained unknown, it was risky to turn openly to these other issues. The Quebec delegates to the post-referendum negotiations held in the summer of 1980 reproached the federal government for having unilaterally transferred "powers over the economy" to the list of first priorities. At the opening of the September 1980 conference, Prime Minister Trudeau retorted caustically:

Now, this item concerning economic powers was on the second list, the one which has been approved by the Committee of Ministers and we have simply added it to the first list. I do not think that either the Quebec government nor Quebecers will object to that because what we are asking, in sum, under the item, powers relating to the economy, is . . . the re-establishment . . . of a Canadian common market, the sort of association about which the Parti Québécois has talked a lot, where goods, people, merchandise and services would travel freely across the country.[31]

This statement by the prime minister has proven to be rich in "information." The references to the *péquiste* objectives reveal a certain triumphant exultation, an attitude which reflected all the same his new position of strength after the federalist victory in the Quebec referendum. On that basis, it seemed possible to move the problem of the distribution of powers relating to the political management of the economy from the second to the first list of priorities. Furthermore, the terms used by the prime minister and the insistence with which he explicitly related the discussion of this question to the positions defended by Quebec spokesmen demonstrated clearly that despite an apparent detour into economic matters, the constitutional debate was not diverted to the point where the Quebec question could be ignored.

At the beginning of the talks held in the summer of 1980, federal negotiators presented a framework for the discussion of the "powers over the economy" by identifying the issues which should be addressed first:

For purposes of constitutional review, it might be useful to divide the item "Powers over the economy" into five broad categories. These are first the maintenance of an economic union in Canada, second the redistribution of incomes among persons and regions, third the promotion and influencing of economic development, fourth the stabilization of the economy as a whole, and fifth the conduct of international economic relations. For the current stage of the Constitutional review, it has been suggested that the maintenance of the Canadian economic union should be the focus of attention.[32]

At first glance, except for the last category the main concern appeared to be with the internal dimensions of economic policy. However, it must be understood that it was the "prevailing trends in the world economy" which served to underscore the urgency of "safeguarding and strengthening our economic union:"

Technological developments, the internationalization of factors of production, the need to get the benefits of greater economies of scale and specialization of production facilities, have generated considerable pressure for larger markets. There has been continuing liberalization of market access among the main industrialized countries through major tariff reductions. A number of countries have combined their market power through the creation of free trade areas or common markets. These and other developments in the world market place, including the constant emergence of new exporters, have made unavoidable structural adjustments of numerous individual sectors and lines of production within the Canadian economy. These adjustments run the risk of being less effective and costlier if we are unable to exploit fully the potential strength of our national market.[33]

In short, "maintenance of an economic union in Canada" appeared to be a pre-condition for the "conduct of international economic relations" and at least concomitant with the "promotion and influencing of economic development." Furthermore, these objectives could not be pursued without consideration of the eventual repercussions on the "redistribution of incomes among persons and regions." To "focus attention" on the "maintenance of an economic union in Canada" could thus hardly imply the abandonment of the other "categories" which the federal government made a point of identifying in connection with "powers over the economy."

In the last analysis, there was an obvious overlap between the constitutional debate and the establishment of the economic options of the country. Given the importance of the stakes involved in the supposedly more limited discussions proposed by the federal government, it is easy to understand why its intentions met with such resistance from eight provinces. This resistance demonstrated quite clearly that the constitutional debate following the Quebec referendum would inevitably lead to a confrontation between the industrialized centre and the more resource-dependent periphery.[34] In this context, the reasons for Ontario's ardent support for federal proposals become clear.

Ontario explicitly stated its determination to strengthen the Canadian economic union: "Canada is one country and it should have one economy, not ten."[35] In 1977, the Ontario premier had expressed the opinion that such an approach was in the interests of all Canadians: "At a time when great trading and other blocs are forming for economic reasons, the decentralization of economic power could prejudice the economic rights of all Canadians considerably."[36] The representatives of the other provinces, however, seemed more convinced that centralization could only protect further the "economic rights" of Ontarians. The extent of regional disparity in Canada lent considerable credence to that belief.

Provincial opposition to the federal government's constitutional package led to an appreciable reduction in its scope. After final compromises on both sides, an agreement was reached, and the ephemeral alliance with Quebec was shattered. Quebec refused to come around, a refusal due to a great extent to the very terms of the economic policies developed in Ottawa and Quebec to re-deploy the Canadian and Quebec economies. More concurrent than differently defined, these policies led to and continue to lead to a confrontation which can only be resolved through a continued political struggle.

Canadian and Quebec Economic Policies

For a long time, Quebec economic aspirations were limited essentially to ensuring the continued survival and protection of its religion and language, and could be adequately summed up by Jean-Charles Falardeau as follows:

> Many French-Canadians were associated with the industrial development of our natural resources, but they were not businessmen. They were provincial cabinet ministers invited by American capitalists to sit on their board of directors. The Quebec government, especially after S.-N. Parent, adopted a policy of forestry, hydro and mineral concessions which favoured "foreign" investors, especially Americans. The story of our welcome and their takeover of our geographical heritage is sadly familiar. Rather than "masters in our own house," as Bouchette proposed, we became once more strangers in our own home. The arrival of American capitalism and new forms of industrial concentration led to the takeover or the disappearance of several French-Canadian companies.[37]

The Committee for an Independent Canada and, to some extent, the New Democratic Party evaluated the situation of the whole of Canada in similar terms. At the end of the sixties and the beginning of the seventies, they called for a new direction in Canadian economic policy, based on similar grounds to the *Maîtres chez nous* policy whose merits had been expounded upon to Quebecers by the Liberals under Jean Lesage as early as 1962.

This desire to take charge once more of Quebec's economic development led initially to a re-evaluation of those government practices described by Falardeau and pushed to paroxysmal proportions under Duplessis, who visited "his" province *at the invitation* of the "big American capitalists."[38] In concrete terms, it was reflected in a remarkable increase in state intervention in the Quebec economy, especially through the creation of numerous state-owned companies:

> The creation and development of a network of public companies has been without a doubt one of the cornerstones of the economic policy of Quebec governments since the sixties. In spite of relatively limited means, the Quebec government has intervened directly in a great number of economic sectors (electricity, steel, mining, forestry, financial management and petroleum) through state-owned companies.[39]

The limited means were at the very heart of the new demands made by Quebec leaders on the federal government. After a series of extremely strained discussions, the Quebec government set up the *Régie des rentes du Québec* and the *Caisse de dépôt et de placement du Québec*. The demand for a new division of the tax base led to interminable discussions on the transfer to Quebec of tax points, which according to current estimates were rarely granted in sufficient quantity. Finally, the realization of these new

Quebec aspirations required the granting of new constitutional powers to the Quebec state within the Canadian federation. Even before the advent of the Parti Québécois, this position had already been clearly formulated in 1967 by the constitutional affairs committee of the political commission of the Quebec Liberal Party:

> The responsibilities which the State of Quebec has assumed and will assume require that it possess wider powers for directing its economic development. The influence of the latter on state activity and the whole development of the collectivity is such, and the degree to which it is conditioned by education, manpower, labour, social security, fiscal policy and public investment is such, that it is inconceivable that Quebec should have no role in monetary, credit or tariff matters. This does not mean that Quebec should have its own currency and its own Customs, but it should, of necessity, participate directly in the development of monetary and tariff policy. This policy is too important a tool for collective development for Quebec to be deprived of a say in it.[40]

Strong support for these positions, along with the practical impossibility of their realization within the Canadian political context, led to a more radical view of Quebec's place within or outside of the Canadian federation. This gap in the political landscape was filled in 1969 by the creation of the Parti Québécois. Provincial Liberals then had no other option than to seek a new electoral stance, and under Bourassa they returned to a more orthodox form of federalism, and particularly to more traditional economic policies.

Once again, foreign capital was sought in order to ensure the economic development of the province. In September 1975, Minister for Industry and Commerce Guy Saint-Pierre affirmed in New York that he saw "no difference between foreign and local capital."[41] Premier Bourassa showed no reticence whatsoever in confirming the new policy a few weeks later during a trip to Frankfurt designed to dispel any remaining fears: "Quebec needs foreign capital and will continue to encourage it by maintaining its open policy and developing programs to attract new investments."[42]

However, Liberal adoption of softer constitutional positions did not eliminate all the sources of tension between Quebec and Ottawa. For instance, the Bourassa government gave a poor welcome to federal controls on foreign investment. For Bourassa, "any measure to control foreign investment enforced before the structure of the Quebec economy has been transformed to enable it to assume efficiently the role previously played by foreign initiative, could result in a real loss for Quebec."[43] This statement was clarified in a brief submitted to the House of Commons Standing Committee on Finance, Trade and Economic Affairs, which examined the Foreign Investment Review Act: "In practice, given the present state of Quebec's economy, if it has to count on foreign investment for the immediate future, at least to obtain certain types of technology, the Quebec government feels it is its privilege to make its own decisions in this respect according to its own needs and priorities."[44] When a year later, in 1973, the federal government introduced a new version of the bill, which introduced controls on investments in new foreign-controlled companies, the Quebec government did not hesitate to invoke the constitutional argument. In its view, the federal government was intervening in "a jurisdiction which has been exclusively provincial until now and for which the provinces consider they have greater constitutional responsibilities."[45]

Basically, the *péquiste* government did not carry this policy much further, although it adopted as its own the suggestions for sector control of foreign investment formulated in the Tetley report. It criticized the screening process set up in 1974 by the federal government in similar terms:

> Instead of this pretence of foreign investment controls, the Government of Quebec suggests a sectoral approach whereby foreign investors would know in advance which sectors were open to them and from which ones they were completely or partially excluded. This kind of control, as shown elsewhere, would encourage numerous indigenous initiatives and allow for the planned and methodical development of key sectors in the Quebec economy. Needless to say, such a policy will only be effectively applied when the Government of Quebec controls the means necessary for its implementation.[46]

If one leaves aside the political conclusion—the need for sovereignty in order to control foreign investment—the concerns of the *péquiste* government were really not much different from those of its predecessors. Every policy involving intervention, as opposed to more or less complete *laissez faire*, would be defined in terms of a necessary re-structuring of the Quebec economy.

The Parti Québécois undoubtedly attached more importance to the role of Quebecers in the economic development of Quebec. However, it must be remembered that it was Liberal Minister of Finance Raymond Garneau who insisted that it was necessary to *negotiate* with investors so that Quebec assistance programs be conditional upon the "use of Quebec suppliers and the hiring of French-speaking executives."[47] The Tetley report went much further:

> With respect to the structural weakness of the Quebec economy, the action taken by the Department of Industry and Commerce must give greater consideration to the problem of the underrepresentation of indigenous firms (in the manufacturing industry for instance) and the necessity for drawing greater benefit from the foreign presence in Quebec through further integration of the operations of enterprises with the economy and society of Quebec.[48]

As Pierre Fournier remarked, Quebec economic policy under different governments since the sixties has been based on two main objectives: "the transformation of Quebec industrial structure"[49] and "the development of indigenous executive personnel and indigenous companies."[50] To achieve these goals, governments opted for greater intervention in the economy. It was therefore not surprising, to quote Fournier again,

> [that] the economic role of the Quebec State has increased spectacularly since 1960. Government spending increased from 15% of the GNP to more than 33% in 1976, compared to an increase of only 2% between 1940 and 1960. In 1977, public investment, including Hydro-Quebec and the James Bay projects, amounted to $2.7 billion and represented 42% of all investment, compared to 26% in Ontario. In fact, most of the key economic development projects were financed by the Quebec government.[51]

These statistics demonstrate quite forcibly the extent of Quebec government intervention in Quebec economic development. They also show to some degree the lack of private initiative. This important deficiency led the government to intervene through protection or assistance programs which favour or discriminate against companies according to the sector involved, their competitive capacity, and the location of their control. It was precisely in order to eliminate this type of intervention leading to the fragmentation of the Canadian market that the federal government gave priority, in the constitutional discussions of 1980, to the adoption of mechanisms aimed at maintaining and consolidating the Canadian economic union.

As we have seen, this concern with the Canadian economic union sprung explicitly from worries about the new relationship between the Canadian and world economies. The economic policy which thus emerged took a variety of forms, but was never presented in a clear and comprehensive way. Its main points can nevertheless be retraced and identified easily enough. Basically, the desire to diversify the country's economic relations arose from a new appreciation of Canada's position within the world economy; dependency on the United States no longer constituted the surest or the only way to achieve Canadian economic growth. The economic hegemony of the United States in the post-war period was obviously losing its lustre. As could be foreseen in *A Foreign Policy for Canadians*,[52] Canada was to adopt new directions which would allow it to carve a new place for itself within the world economy.

Such diversification could not be restricted to trade alone. The internationalization of Canadian capital was also considered necessary for the adjustments required by the changing state of the international division of labour. Accordingly, early in 1981, Secretary of State for External Affairs Mark MacGuigan stressed how important it was for Canada "to begin thinking of foreign countries as sources of investment, skilled labour, technology, energy and strategic natural resources" and to benefit to the utmost from the opportunities provided by these countries for "Canadian investors and entrepreneurs."[53]

This policy of diversification and internationalization required first of all a greater concentration of Canadian capital. The Economic Council of Canada had stated as early as 1969 that "Canadian competition policy should aim primarily at bringing about more efficient performance by the economy as a whole."[54] Such efficiency, it should be noted, was no longer measured at the national level alone. Competition policy, along with the economy, had become international. As the Bryce commission was to stress later, despite a very high level of capital concentration in Canada, "over the last 15 or 20 years, many of Canada's largest corporations have declined in size relative to those operating in the same industries in other countries."[55] The government, for its part, felt that "competition legislation cannot of itself actively encourage rationalization," but it added that "it should not, however, block mergers where economic advantages are demonstrable."[56]

For this policy of diversification and internationalization to be achieved, it was also necessary that Canadian production become specialized. This meant, as the Economic Council of Canada had recommended, a shift in Canada's "industrial structure away from highly protected, labour-intensive, and standard-technology activities in which comparative advantage clearly lies with the third world countries."[57] Federal spokesmen such as the minister of state for small business also began to express this theme openly: "We should accept that some of our production sectors be gradually transferred to the developing countries in order that we keep in Canada the sectors which are the most dynamic and productive for us."[58]

In short, the economic policy of the federal government was aimed at ensuring the re-deployment of the Canadian economy through the diversification of Canada's economic relations within the world economic order and the internationalization of Canadian capital. On the domestic level, these objectives were to be achieved through a global policy of rationalization and specialization of Canadian production. As the importance of this policy was likely to vary greatly from one region to another, given the territorial nature of the Canadian industrial structure, it was essential, in the minds of federal leaders, that an appropriate form of political organization be adopted to further these economic goals. Accordingly, the recognition of federal ascendancy in all related matters became imperative. This was refused by the provinces, especially Quebec.

These elements of federal economic policy explain Quebec's fierce opposition to the constitutional proposals put forth openly after the Quebec referendum. For the Quebec government, it was "inconceivable for the moment, given the extent of unemployment and the under-utilization of productive capacity" to abandon the textile, clothing, hosiery and footwear sectors to their fate.[59] The fact that the textile industry, for instance, provided "22 percent of total employment in Quebec's manufacturing sector" in 1976 makes it easy to understand why the federal proposals for this sector were not welcomed with enthusiasm by Quebec which "accounted for 59 percent of total employment" in the textile industry in Canada.[60] An examination of the size and nature of Quebec manufacturing[61] provides ample explanation of Quebec's strong resistance to a global economic program based primarily on the most concentrated and the most technologically advanced sectors of Canadian industry.

Despite undeniable progress in the economic rise of francophones, the situation was far from being completely redressed. Above all, the industrial structure of the Quebec economy still showed serious weakness in spite of all the efforts aimed at re-deployment. In the view of the *Office de planification et de développement du Québec*, federal policies had undoubtedly not been the most beneficial to Quebec:

> In the present state of affairs, Quebec finds itself in an unenviable position. Rather than real economic development policies, it too often inherits social assistance from Ottawa. Deprived of the major tools to control the economy, it cannot ensure the necessary changes in direction itself; historical factors and recent years have shown that they are not likely to come from Ottawa either. The situation is very serious. The potential economic costs for Quebec of integration into the Canadian economy in its present form could be considerable in the long term.[62]

Given such a view of the situation, it is understandable that Quebec would oppose a federal constitutional approach aimed specifically at increasing the degree of integration of the Canadian economy.

Nationalism and the Economy

The signing of the federal government's modified constitutional package, with the support of nine provinces, can undoubtedly appear to have little *direct* impact on the pursuit by Ottawa and Quebec of their respective economic policies. It must, however, be noted that the political prestige that Ottawa now enjoys in its relations with the provinces increases appreciably its chances for "success" in the establishment of a "National Policy" which has been compared by some to the policy developed a century ago by Sir John A. Macdonald.[63] In the present context of global crisis, this success seems extremely mitigated. At the same time, the "National Policy" conceived and gradually implemented since the end of the sixties has become, in the aftermath of the latest constitutional developments, the increasingly exclusive prerogative of the federal government even if its dominance has not been stated explicitly in the text of the new constitution.

In such conditions, the struggle between Quebec and the Canadian government is not likely to disappear. It has become customary to state, as Pierre Fortin has done, that "several elements of francophone dissatisfaction are shared to various degrees by other segments of the Canadian population," stressing at the same time that "what makes this problem so much more acute in Quebec than in the rest of the country is the intensity of its socio-cultural dimension and political expression."[64] This explains why it is necessary to distinguish regional from *national* stakes.

Clearly, the taking in hand of the national question in Quebec cannot be attributed to the Parti Québécois alone. Nevertheless, of the Quebec political parties in existence since 1960, the PQ is the one that has attempted to capture fully the aspirations which started to take shape during the Quiet Revolution. One can begin to understand the significance of its program, which gives "priority to general restructuring of the Quebec economy, that is to say to modernization and specialization with a view to a new form of interdependence with the North American economy and a true emancipation of Quebec capital."[65] In practical terms, this could only place the PQ in direct conflict with the federal government, whose policy was and still is based on similar goals.

Before the referendum, the *péquiste* government had found it politically useful to present itself as a rampart against federal designs needed to counteract, or at least mitigate, the adverse effects of the latter on the Quebec economy. The referendum strategy failed. The "final" decision on the national question was to be postponed. What could already be perceived in 1979 in *Bâtir le Québec* became quite explicit in *Le virage technologique*,[66] published by the Quebec government in the spring of 1982. Indeed, the change of direction in technology was to be accompanied by an important political re-orientation:

> During its first mandate, the Parti Québécois government paid particular attention to traditional sectors: pulp and paper, textiles, clothing, hosiery, furniture, footwear, etc. These industries, whose importance in Quebec in terms of jobs and local benefits is well known, were experiencing difficulties at the time, which in certain cases threatened their very existence. . . . These traditional sectors are still very important for the Quebec economy, and the government continues to give them special attention. Programs aimed at restructuring these industries have been set up and will be continued. However, it must be recognized that growth in these sectors cannot generate new jobs in the future. It is essential to define Quebec's industrial priorities in terms of changes in domestic demand and foreign markets, and especially with respect to proven strengths, to factors of production and comparative advantages.[67]

It was no longer a question of *waiting* for a sovereign Quebec. The time had come for immediate action. It was no longer enough to repeat time and again that Quebec did not possess the means necessary to re-direct its economy. Furthermore, in 1982 the role of the Quebec state was not considered as crucial as it had been thought to be in previous years. Of course, the *péquiste* government made it clear that it "in no way intended to call into question the principle of direct state intervention."[68] At the same time, however, it defined more specifically the direction of its future efforts:

> The responsibility for ensuring sufficient and continued development falls first of all on the private sector, because a large majority of companies are found in this sector. The Government of Quebec is primarily concerned with creating and maintaining conditions favourable for the development and the dynamism of private initiative. It believes

that the market economy should generally be preserved as the system most able to ensure the efficient allocation of resources.[69]

This explicit change of direction should not be interpreted as a conversion from interventionism to non-interventionism, and even less from socialism to capitalism. The previous options only became more obvious. What did change significantly, however, were the elements which were to be favoured within the private sector. If the Quebec of the PQ could be presented only a few years ago as the "champion of small business" by the president of the Canadian Federation of Independent Business,[70] this was no longer necessarily to be the case, even with a *péquiste* government:

> Small- and middle-sized Quebec businesses often play a part in that market structure as suppliers to wholesalers and subcontractors to heavy equipment suppliers, or as suppliers of special light machinery! This dependency is reflected in the foreseeable distribution of the economic spin-off. The regrouping, merger or association of interests will be necessary to ensure a better adjustment to technological challenges, to increase the profitability and competitive capacity of businesses and thus to encourage the strengthening of Quebec's industrial structure.[71]

Clearly, the *Parti Québécois* government knew that the economic re-direction of Quebec had to be undertaken before the political re-orientation, which it had proposed and continues to propose to Quebecers, could be achieved. It therefore had to make peace with the business community, which had opposed it mercilessly up until the referendum. However, this adjustment of *péquiste* policy may not bring about an equivalent peace in its relations with the rest of Canada, especially if it continues to consider it "imperative for the development of the Quebec economy that a greater number of companies controlled by Quebecers become sufficiently large to influence, at least within their own market, the evolution of the industry in which they are involved" and to postulate that "it is virtually indispensable for a company to control a sizeable part of the domestic market in order to establish itself in foreign markets."[72]

In such conditions, one can foresee the continuation of a ruthless struggle, with little chance that the constitutional agreement of November 5, 1981 will lead to a permanent "peace treaty"[73] between Quebec and the rest of Canada. At the very least, it must be taken into account that any attempt at achieving a valid understanding between Quebecers and Canadians could only with difficulty be based on the recognition of minority linguistic and cultural rights alone. The exercise will be even more dangerous if the federal government persists in interpreting the facts differently according to whether it is speaking to French Quebecers or to other Canadians.*

---

*The appointment of a Royal Commission on Economic Union and Development Prospects for Canada, chaired by the Hon. Donald Macdonald, provides additional support for the basic argument in this chapter.

Notes

1. Canada, *Notes sur la Constitution* (Ottawa: Supply and Services Canada, 1982), p. 33. Emphasis added.
2. Canada, *The Constitution and You* (Ottawa: Supply and Services Canada, 1982), p. 31. Emphasis added.
3. *Maclean's*, April 26, 1982.
4. See Jeff Evenson and Richard Simeon, "The Roots of Discontent," in Queen's University, Institute of Intergovernmental Relations/Economic Council of Canada, *Workshop on the Political Economy of Confederation, Proceedings*, Kingston, November 8–10, 1978 (Hull: Supply and Services Canada, 1979), pp. 165-196.
5. Alfred Dubuc, "Les fondements historiques de la crise des sociétés canadienne et québécoise," in Pierre Fournier, ed., *Le capitalisme au Québec* (Montréal: Les Éditions coopératives Albert Saint-Martin, 1978), p. 53. Our translation.
6. For a precise formulation and an application of this thesis, see Robert Gilpin, "Les investissements directs américains et les deux nationalismes canadiens," in *Études Internationales*, vol. 1, no. 1 (March 1971), pp. 44-57.
7. Richard Simeon, *Federal-Provincial Diplomacy. The Making of Recent Policy in Canada* (Toronto: University of Toronto Press, 1972), p. 89.
8. Lester B. Pearson, Speech given at "The Conference on the Economics of Canadian Unity," Banff, October 15, 1967, reproduced in *Journal of Canadian Studies*, vol. 11, no. 4 (November 1967), p. 56.
9. Lester B. Pearson, "L'unité canadienne, tâche commune des partis et des citoyens," Speech given before members of the Liberal Party of Canada (Quebec), Montreal, October 22, 1967, reproduced in *Le Devoir*, October 26, 1967, p. 5. Our translation.
10. For a brief discussion of this point, one can refer to my article, "Political Parties and the Polarization of Quebec Politics," in Hugh G. Thorburn, editor, *Party Politics in Canada*, Fourth ed. (Scarborough: Prentice-Hall of Canada, 1979), pp. 228-42.
11. Letter from Pierre Elliott Trudeau to the provincial premiers (excluding the premiers of Quebec and British Columbia) dated March 31, 1976. Reproduced in Québec, Ministère des Affaires intergouvernementales, *Dossier sur les discussions constitutionnelles 1978–1979* (Quebec: Gouvernement du Québec, 1979), Annexe b. Our translation.
12. Letter from Peter Lougheed to Pierre Elliott Trudeau, dated October 14, 1976, reproduced in *Proposals on the Constitution 1971–1978* (Ottawa: Canadian Intergovernmental Conference Secretariat, 1978), p. 10.
13. Letter from Pierre Elliott Trudeau to Peter Lougheed, dated January 19, 1977, reproduced in *ibid.*, p. 15.
14. Pierre Elliott Trudeau, "Unity in Canada Won't Be Fractured," Speech given before the two Chambers of the American Congress, Washington, February 22, 1977, excerpts reproduced in The *Toronto Globe and Mail*, February 23, 1977, p. 7.
15. Pierre Elliott Trudeau, "Chance for West to Get a Better Deal," Speech given before the annual meeting of Canadian broadcasters, Winnipeg, April 18, 1977, excerpts reproduced in The *Toronto Globe and Mail*, April 19, 1977, p. 6.
16. Pierre Elliott Trudeau, "Lettre ouverte aux Québécois," reproduced in the

Quebec French-speaking press, including *Le Soleil,* July 15, 1980, p. A7. Our translation.

17. See extracts published in *Le Devoir,* July 17, 1980, p. 12. Our translation.
18. *Le Devoir,* October 21, 1980, p. 1. Our translation.
19. Dominique Clift, *Quebec Nationalism in Crisis* (Kingston: McGill-Queen's University Press, 1982), p. 138.
20. Quebec, *Comments of Quebec on Federal Positions Regarding Powers over the Economy* (Secretariat translation), Vancouver, July 22-24, 1980, p. 3.
21. Canada, *Powers over the Economy: Securing the Canadian Economic Union in the Constitution.* Discussion paper submitted by the Government of Canada to the Meeting of the Continuing Committee of Ministers on the Constitution, July 9, 1980, p. 24.
22. *Ibid.,* pp. 24-25.
23. A.E. Safarian, *Canadian Federalism and Economic Integration.* Constitutional study prepared for the Privy Council Office (Ottawa: Information Canada, 1974).
24. Frank D. Moores, *Opening Statement,* Federal-Provincial Conference of First Ministers on the Constitution, Ottawa, February 13-15, 1978, p. 2.
25. Saskatchewan, *Powers over the Economy: An Analysis of Federal Proposals,* Federal-Provincial Conference of First Ministers on the Constitution, Ottawa, September 8-13, 1980, p. 13.
26. Pierre Elliott Trudeau, *A Time for Action. Toward the Renewal of the Canadian Federation* (Ottawa: Supply and Services Canada, 1978), p. 22.
27. Canada, Conseil Privé, Centre d'information sur l'unité canadienne, *Certains aspects de la souplesse du fédéralisme canadien* (Ottawa: Centre d'information sur l'unité Canadienne, 1978), pp. 26-27. Our translation.
28. Canada, Parliament, Senate and House of Commons, Special Joint Committee of the Senate and the House of Commons of the Constitution of Canada, *Final Report* (Ottawa: Queen's Printer, 1972), p. 82.
29. Canada, Task Force on Canadian Unity, *A Future Together. Observations and Recommendations* (Hull: Supply and Services Canada, 1979), p. 74.
30. *Ibid.,* p. 67.
31. Pierre Elliott Trudeau, *Opening Remarks at the Federal-Provincial Conference of First Ministers on the Constitution,* (Transcript), Ottawa, September 8-13, 1980, pp. 10-11. Our translation.
32. Canada, *Powers over the Economy, a Framework for Discussion,* Continuing Committee of Ministers on the Constitution, Montreal, July 4, 1980, p. 1.
33. Canada, *Powers over the Economy: Securing the Canadian Economic Union in the Constitution, op. cit.,* pp. 3-4.
34. This is also the thesis defended by Barbara Hodgins, *Where the Economy and the Constitution Meet in Canada* (Montreal: C.D. Howe Research Institute, 1981), p. iii.
35. "La position constitutionnelle du gouvernement de l'Ontario," Toronto, August 5, 1980, translated by and reproduced in *Le Devoir,* August 11, 1980, p. 13. Our translation.
36. Address to the Canadian Club, Montreal; extracts published in the *Toronto Globe and Mail,* March 22, 1977, p. 7.
37. "L'origine et l'ascension des hommes d'affaires dans la société canadienne-

française," in *Recherches sociographiques*, vol. VI, no. 1 (January-April 1965), p. 39. Our translation.

38. Robert Rumilly recounts such events whose unlikelihood only equals the candour of his narration. See *Maurice Duplessis et son temps*, Tome II: (1944-1959) (Montreal: Coll. Vies canadiennes, Éditions Fides, 1973), especially pp. 233-35. Our translation.

39. Pierre Fournier, *Les sociétés d'État et les objectifs économiques du Québec: une évaluation préliminaire*, Coll. Etudes et dossiers. Office de planification et de développement du Québec (Québec: Éditeur officiel du Québec, 1979), p. 9. Our translation.

40. Parti libéral du Québec, "Rapport du Comité des affaires constitutionnelles de la Commission politique de la Fédération libérale du Québec," Submitted to the Annual Convention of the Party, October 1967, reproduced in *Journal of Canadian Studies*, vol. 11, no. 4 (November 1967), p. 45. Our translation.

41. See *Le Devoir*, September 10, 1975, p. 1. Our translation.

42. See *Le Devoir*, October 21, 1975, p. 17. Our translation.

43. Letter from the Quebec minister for financial institutions, companies and cooperatives, William Tetley, to the federal minister of revenue, Herb Gray, dated June 14, 1972. Reproduced in Québec, Interdepartmental Task Force on Foreign Investment, *A Québec Policy on Foreign Investment* (Québec: Éditeur officiel du Québec, 1974), Appendix 1, p. 175.

44. Quebec, Brief submitted to the Senate Standing Committee on Banking, Trade and Commerce and to the House of Commons Committee entrusted with studying Bill C-132, "The Foreign Investment Review Act," July 19, 1973. Reproduced in *ibid.*, Appendix 2, p. 188.

45. Letter from the Quebec minister of financial institutions, companies and cooperatives, William Tetley, to the federal minister of industry, trade and commerce, Alastair Gillespie, dated March 15, 1973. Reproduced in *ibid.*, Appendix 1, p. 178.

46. Quebec, Ministère d'Etat au Développement économique, *Bâtir le Québec. Enoncé de politique économique* (Québec: Editeur officiel du Québec, 1979), p. 119.

47. Raymond Garneau, Speech given at a colloquium on "Les investissements étrangers au Canada," organized by the Chambre de commerce France-Canada and the Chambre de commerce française au Canada, Quebec, October 5, 1974 (Québec: Editeur officiel du Québec), p. 7. Our translation.

48. Interdepartmental Task Force on Foreign Investment, *A Québec Policy on Foreign Investment*, op. cit., p. 74.

49. Pierre Fournier, *Les sociétés d'Etat et les objectifs économiques du Québec, op. cit.*, p. 49. Our translation.

50. *Ibid.*, p. 14. Our translation.

51. Pierre Fournier, "Les nouveaux paramètres de la bourgeoisie québécoise," in Pierre Fournier, editeur, *Le capitalisme au Québec, op. cit.*, pp. 152-53. Our translation.

52. The white paper on foreign policy published in 1970 by the Canadian government.

53. Mark MacGuigan, *A Bilateral Approach to Canadian Foreign Policy*, (Speech to the Empire Club of Canada, Toronto, January 22, 1981), *Statements and Speeches*, External Affairs Canada, Ottawa, No. 81/2, p. 2.

54. Economic Council of Canada, *Interim Report on Competition Policy* (Ottawa: Queen's Printer, 1969), p. 9.

55. Canada, Royal Commission on Corporate Concentration, *Report* (Hull: Supply and Services Canada, 1978), p. 405.

56. Canada, Board of Economic Development Ministers, *Action for Industrial Growth. Continuing the Dialogue* (Ottawa: Government of Canada, 1979), p. 47.

57. Economic Council of Canada, *For a Common Future. A Study of Canada's Relations with Developing Countries* (Ottawa: Economic Council of Canada, 1978), p. 60.

58. Quoted in *Le Devoir*, November 21, 1980, p. 15. Our translation.

59. Québec, Ministère d'Etat au Développement économique, *Bâtir le Québec, op. cit.*, p. 519.

60. Canada, Privy Council, Canadian Unity Information Office, *The Textile Industry—A Canadian Challenge*, Understanding Canada Series (Ottawa: Canadian Unity Information Office, 1979), p. 3.

61. See André Raynauld, *La propriété des entreprises au Québec. Les années 60* (Montréal: Les Presses de l'Université de Montréal, 1974).

62. Québec, Office de planification et de développement du Québec, *Politiques fédérales et économie du Québec*, 2e éd., Rapport préparé pour le ministre d'État au Développement économique, Coll. Dossiers (Québec: Éditeur officiel du Québec, 1979), p. 62. Our translation.

63. See for example, James Laxer, *Canada's Economic Strategy* (Toronto: McClelland and Stewart, 1981), p. 202.

64. Pierre Fortin, "La dimension économique de la crise politique canadienne," in *Canadian Public Policy*, vol. IV, no. 3 (Summer 1978), p. 320. Our translation.

65. Pierre Fournier, Yves Bélanger and Claude Painchaud, "L'enjeu économique et la question nationale au Québec," in Pierre Fournier, éditeur, *Capitalisme et politique au Québec* (Montreal: Coll. Recherches et documents, Éditions coopératives Albert Saint-Martin, 1981), p. 71. Our translation.

66. Québec, Ministère d'Etat au Développement économique, *Le virage technologique, Bâtir le Québec—Phase 2. Programme d'action économique 1982–1986* (Québec: Éditeur officiel du Québec, 1981).

67. *Ibid.*, p. 24. Our translation.

68. *Ibid.*, p. 22. Our translation.

69. *Ibid.*, p. 21. Our translation.

70. See *Le Soleil*, July 14, 1980, p. A13. Our translation.

71. Québec, Ministère d'État du Développement économique, *Le Virage technologique, op. cit.*, p. 33. Our translation.

72. *Ibid.*, p. 24. Our translation.

73. It is in these terms that Alfred Dubuc proposes to view the constitution of a country. See "Les fondements historiques de la crise des sociétés canadienne et québécoise," *loc. cit.*, p. 53. Our translation.

Chapter 8/The Future of Quebec Nationalism

Pierre Fournier

Given the desire of the Parti Québécois to put the question of sovereignty back on the political agenda in Quebec, and the federal government's determination to crush nationalism in Quebec, the constitutional question will undoubtedly continue to occupy an important position in this province's politics. Despite the referendum defeat of April 1980, many factors point to a potential resurgence of nationalism in Quebec. The uncompromising attitude of the federal government in the post-referendum period, including the adoption of the constitution without Quebec's approval, has contributed to a rally of nationalist forces in the province. Moreover, the "new" Canadian constitution has failed to meet even traditional Quebec positions, and weakens the province.

The coming decade is likely to bring about an unprecedented struggle for legitimacy between the federal and provincial governments in Quebec. The outcome will be closely tied to the continuing economic crisis and to the ability of the Parti Québécois on the one hand, and of French power in Ottawa on the other, to convince Quebecers that their respective political and constitutional solutions provide real gains in economic terms. At this level, there is a clear contradiction between a Quebec-centred economic strategy and an Ottawa-centred one. The PQ's probable participation in the next federal election, as well as a provincial general election on sovereignty, are likely to provide the next battlegrounds for nationalist and federalist forces in Quebec.

The Future of Quebec Nationalism and the Constitution Act

There is no question that the referendum defeat, coupled with Trudeau's patriation of the Canadian constitution, deals a severe blow, at least in the short run, to Quebec's hopes of nation-building. Outside Quebec, and sometimes within the province, the dominant interpretation has been that nationalism, in the broad sense of moving from more autonomy towards outright independence, has peaked in Quebec, and that its ultimate defeat as a political objective is only a matter of time.

While the crippling effects of the economic crisis have done much to take some of the limelight away from national issues in Quebec, many trends are working in the opposite direction. In fact, however, these simplistic interpretations seriously underestimate the depth of national sentiment in Quebec and the potential for an eventual Quebec majority behind sovereignty. First, the actual *rapport de force* over sovereignty, while clearly favourable to the federal option, is more fragile than it appears to be. Second, the root problems which have spurred the development of nationalism in Quebec have not been seriously dealt with or resolved. Third, the federal response in the aftermath of the referendum has been so inadequate and uncompromising as to breathe new life into the national movement in Quebec. Let us examine these factors in turn.

As regards the *rapport de force*, polls and other research indicate quite clearly that neither sovereignty nor centralized federalism represents a majority option in Quebec at the present time. The hard-core nationalists and the "unconditional" federalists each represent roughly 40 percent of the Quebec electorate. The key to the future lies in the "soft" 20 percent or so that remains. Survey research indicates that this group is made up mainly of "moderate" nationalist francophones who advocate a "Quebec first" approach and more powers to the provinces. The attachment of this group to the federal system derives above all from economic insecurity.

Equally important, sovereignty has continued to obtain overwhelming support from the upwardly mobile "dynamic" elements in Quebec society, including the young, the educated, the professionals, and the skilled and organized segment of the work force. The youngest age group, while less "political" and vocal than the sixties generation, remains committed to sovereignty. There is evidence to suggest that the continuity of support for sovereignty is quite high, and that very few supporters change their minds, contrary to the popular myth that nationalist sentiment wanes as the separatists grow older and wiser. This continuing strength reflects the fact that the various linguistic, cultural, demographic and economic factors which underlie the development of Quebec nationalism remain unaltered.

The heart of the nationalist view is the need for a strong Quebec state with substantial powers in many areas, including language, culture, social policy and, increasingly, economic policy in order to protect the high concentration of francophones in the province. A strong Quebec can be the only secure and viable bastion for francophones in North America. Sovereignty is needed as protection against the vagaries of federal government policies.

In the long term, the central issue is the declining political influence of francophones within Canada, given the projected decline in the demographic weight of francophones in the country as a whole as well as the decline of Quebec's population relative to other provinces. By the end of the century, Quebec will only represent 20 percent of the total Canadian population, down from 27 percent in 1980. The last constitutional conference has already given some insight into how easily Quebec can be dumped off the cart, even by a federal government that rides on the myth of French power.

Quebec nationalists are also convinced that the successive governments in the province have been much more effective in dealing with the key problems facing Quebec than has any federal government. In the area of language, for example, the federal government, rather than attempting to promote the use of French within Quebec, has more often than not sought to reduce the impact of Quebec laws, as witnessed by its attacks on Bill 101. Instead of helping Quebec achieve its goals, the federal government has concentrated its efforts on promoting Canada-wide bilingualism and pumping artificial life into the dying French minorities outside Quebec. The provision of government services in French as well as the support of some French schools and cultural groups has largely amounted to window-dressing in an attempt to give Quebecers the impression that the federal government is concerned with the development of francophone minorities, and also in order to convince them the French fact went beyond the borders of Quebec.

Yet even a superficial look at federal government statistics shows that assimilation will eventually do away with most, if not all francophone clusters outside Quebec, with the possible exception of the Acadians in New Brunswick. Given that the only francophones who have had some success in resisting assimilation have tended to be isolated from the mainstream of the economic and social life of their province, the future appears bleak indeed. The present federal government has rendered Canadians a disservice by making them believe that coast-to-coast bilingualism was the key to the Quebec problem. For an overwhelming majority of francophones in Quebec, bilingual government services in Vancouver are a cruel farce when the long-term survival and development of francophones within Quebec remain in jeopardy.

Within Quebec, the federal government's major ideological victory has been its ability to convince a majority of Quebecers that sovereignty would be followed by an economic doomsday. Contrary to the "national" campaign, which put forward more principled ideals, the federal strategy at the grass-roots level during the 1980 referendum was built around crude manifestations of economic blackmail. Old-age pensioners and the unemployed, among others, were led to believe that their cheques would no longer be forthcoming in the event of a "yes" vote.

When the balance sheet of "French power" in Ottawa during the seventies is finally drawn up, it will show that remarkably little was done to improve Quebec's position within Canada. More than anything, French power has been a highly successful public relations effort to increase francophone "visibility," but with no fundamental impact on the real distribution of power within Canada.

Even though it affects Quebec only indirectly and would only have been symbolic, the refusal of the federal government to impose official bilingualism on Ontario provides a crushing indictment of the ephemeral nature of French power in Ottawa and of the prime minister's underlying motives as regards patriation. Once again, it is obvious that the federal Liberals have worried about and condescended to their volatile Ontario constituency at the expense of Quebec. For Pierre Trudeau, the judgement of history will be devastating. He chose to forge ahead against a common front of all provincial political parties in Quebec while at the same time refusing to impose even a bare minimum on Ontario, thus consciously betraying his own constituency and humiliating his people.

There is little doubt that the referendum victory put the federal government back in the driver's seat, a position it had not been in since the election of the Parti Québécois in 1976. In many ways, however, the referendum was costly to the federal government. Under pressure, spokesmen for the "no" side made and repeated promises that federalism would be renewed substantially, implicitly rejecting the status quo. While specific commitments were rare, "renewed federalism" was understood to mean, at the very least, a major decentralization of federal powers in favour of the provinces. Hundreds of statements by various federalist spokesmen confirm that the increase in Quebec provincial powers was at the heart of the proposed "new deal."

Yet when the constitutional proposals were brought down a few months after the referendum, there was never any question of reinforcing or re-defining some Quebec powers in order to make that province more secure within Confederation. On the contrary, the package set out permanently to strengthen the hand of the federal government. Other recent measures, including the unilateral reduction of payments to the provinces and a clear statement of intent to get involved in setting the priorities of higher education through more stringent conditional subsidies to the provinces, demonstrate unequivocally the will of the federal government to cast aside not only "co-operative federalism," as Trudeau has stated, but also federalism as it has evolved in Canada over the past two decades. If the present trends continue, especially with respect to fiscal arrangements, the provinces will slowly become mere administrative regions in a highly centralized state rather than areas of genuine, if limited, sovereignty.

Given that the most insistent demands for constitutional change in recent years have come from Quebec, it is a paradox that the province should come out the clear loser from the latest "negotiations." Superficially and in the short run, the impact of the Constitution Act will not be devastating, and this partly explains why the Parti Québécois has not attempted to mobilize mass opposition to it. Many aspects of the new constitution will have to be interpreted by the courts, and several restrictive clauses could be invoked, so the Quebec losses could be more potential than real.

Nonetheless, the judgement by Jules Deschênes of the Quebec Superior Court in September 1982 dealt a severe blow to Bill 101, Quebec's main language law. Section 23(1)(b) of the Charter of Rights and Freedoms, which substantially opens up the access to English schools in Quebec, was said to prevail over Bill 101's "Quebec clause."[1] Whatever the respective merits of the Quebec and federal positions, the judgement makes it clear that even in the field of language and education, Quebec prerogatives have been scaled down. And nothing would prevent the federal government along with the provinces from attacking Quebec's position even further. Given that many federalist spokesmen have used Quebec's "autonomy" in the cultural field as one of the main arguments against outright independence, the court decision and the Charter of Rights more generally will certainly provide ammunition for Quebec nationalists in the years to come.

Several observers, including federal government spokesmen, have suggested that Quebec alone is responsible for the loss of its power to veto constitutional amendment, having agreed to give it up as part of the "gang of eight" compromise of April 1980. While the soundness of the Lévesque government's strategy at the talks is open to question, and while the Parti Québécois was particularly naive in its assessment of the political forces at work in Canada, Quebec cannot be blamed for the loss of the veto power. The agreement of the eight provinces was a package. Quebec agreed to forgo its veto *in exchange for other major concessions*, including an opting out clause with full financial compensation. Since the concessions were never obtained,[2] and since the package was thus rejected, Quebec's offer has to be considered null and void.

Here it should be stressed that the prime minister's claim that Quebec would never have agreed to any constitutional change because it is committed to separatism makes no sense. It is too easily forgotten that the provincial Liberals as well as the PQ rejected the proposals. Moreover, it was not Quebec that backed down from the eight-province agreement, but the other provinces. Quebec's isolation was not of its own making. And, of course, in the event of an uncompromising PQ position, nothing would have prevented the federal government from imposing unilaterally an agreement more favourable to the interests of Quebec.

But the effect of Quebec's losses in the latest constitutional agreements on its position within the federation can be more fully measured in the long-run perspective. Quebec's minimum position ever since 1960 has always been that patriation should be accompanied by a clear definition of provincial powers in such areas as communications, education and social affairs. To round out the package, it was felt that a rigid amending formula coupled with the Quebec veto power would add to the province's long-term security.

The loss of the veto power thus constitutes a major blow to the Quebec position. While not included in the BNA Act, this power had been validated by constitutional custom. It was invoked for the last time in 1971 in Victoria, when the Bourassa government refused to endorse constitutional changes judged detrimental to Quebec. Most of the major proposals for constitutional reform in the last decades have recommended that the Quebec veto be formalized. The loss of the veto power is closely related to another major setback for Quebec in the new constitution: the refusal to recognize the binational character of the country or, at the very least, the province's special role as the homeland of one of Canada's founding nations. When coupled with the fact that Quebec's agreement will no longer be necessary for changes affecting even its own powers over education, language and culture, this represents a serious defeat, as it flies in the face of the minimum demands put forward in the last several decades.

In more general terms, one of the key consequences of the constitutional changes is to establish the precedent of the federal government's ability, in alliance with the provinces, to exact fundamental changes without Quebec's agreement. Through this precedent, the federal government holds all major trump cards for future negotiations. It can continue to act unilaterally in many areas. It also has its own veto over any future constitutional change.

Another time bomb for Quebec stems from the Charter of Rights and Freedoms, which will inevitably leave wide powers to the Supreme Court. With the often vague wording of the Charter, the judges will be called upon to play a substantial legislative role in addition to a judicial one, which does not augur well for the future of democracy in Canada. In addition, the Charter, which will be interpreted by federally-appointed judges, is likely to have a profound impact on many Quebec laws, particularly in the areas of language and economic policy.

On a more moralistic note, Pierre Trudeau's refusal to obtain an electoral mandate for his constitution or to submit it to a national referendum constitutes a violation of fundamental democratic principles, as would have been a unilateral declaration of independence by the Parti Québécois after the 1976 or 1981 provincial elections. Quite a contradiction for a man who, in his early writings, heaped scorn on the people of Quebec for their lack of a democratic tradition.[3]

More than two years after the referendum, the federal proposals offered nothing that even vaguely approximated "renewed federalism." The prime minister admitted that under the new constitution, Quebec emerged with considerably less than what it was offered in Victoria, stating that "those who were too greedy in 1971 now have much less."[4] And all indications are that constitutional reform of any significance is now over. The federal government has gambled that a severe weakening of the province at the constitutional level will put an end to the growth of nationalist sentiment. However, the winner-take-all attitude may backfire; in the next Quebec election or referendum over sovereignty, broken promises and unfulfilled expectations may well come back to haunt. The real question for the future of Quebec nationalism is the long-term reaction of the people of Quebec.

While, paradoxically, it may have served the federal government well in the short run, the re-election of the Parti Québécois in 1981 represents the first concrete manifestation of the constitutional backlash in Quebec. Until the introduction of the constitutional package, the provincial Liberals had led the polls by a wide margin. Both *péquistes* and Liberals agree that the latter began fading and eventually lost the election as a result of the constitutional coup. The majority of Quebecers chose to elect a party dedicated to sovereignty, a party whose basic option had been soundly defeated in the referendum, rather than a federalist party that could not be trusted to defend Quebec's basic rights.

By reacting hastily and uncompromisingly in the aftermath of the referendum, the federal government may have overplayed its hand. Precisely as the PQ had been predicting, the referendum results weakened the province's position, as the rest of Canada now considered that the Quebec problem had been solved. There is no question that before the referendum, the federal government would not have dared to impose a new Canadian constitution without Quebec's agreement. A moderate federal reaction could have pulled the rug from underneath the PQ, at least for a time. Trudeau chose instead to re-fuel nationalist sentiment by undermining the nationalist "moderates," including the Ryan wing of the provincial Liberal party. While the constitutional coup represents a setback for the outmanoeuvred PQ leadership, it is at least as severe a defeat for the partisans of "renewed federalism." More than anything else, the cynical and short-sighted response of the federal government and English-Canada to the referendum has provided the PQ with a base from which to launch a new offensive. The undermining of Bill 101, the expropriation of Quebec land for Newfoundland hydro lines, the reduction of transfer payments and, of course, the new constitution have restored the legitimacy of the PQ and given a new sense of urgency to sovereignty.

The future of Quebec nationalism, then, will likely continue to be influenced by the actions of the federal government, including Supreme Court decisions and federal policies. The struggle for legitimacy between the Canadian and Quebec governments will dominate the Quebec political scene for the foreseeable future, and its outcome will obviously be crucial to the issue of Quebec sovereignty. The outcome in turn will be determined in large part by each government's ability to lay the blame on the other for the economic crisis, and on the evolution of the economic, social and cultural position of francophones within Quebec.

The Federal Liberals: The Myth and Reality of French Power
One of the most important factors to influence the evolution of Quebec nationalism in the coming years will be the ability of francophones in the Canadian state to fill the vacuum created by the denial of greater autonomy for Quebec. French power will have to prove convincingly that it is capable of fulfilling Quebec's cultural, economic and social aspirations in the Canadian context.

Thus far, the influence of French power in Ottawa has been more artificial than real, characterized by visibility rather than effectiveness. As has been the case throughout most of Canadian political history since Confederation, Ontario has continued to be the main beneficiary of federal political and economic activity because of its sheer demographic and economic weight. In the last few decades, Ontario has also benefited from its favourable electoral position. Unlike the western provinces and Quebec, which have for all practical purposes been one-party systems at the federal level and which have cancelled each other out in partisan terms, Ontario has shifted its support between the two major parties, effectively giving it the ability to choose the government.

As a result, it is not surprising that the need to win swing ridings in Ontario has mobilized most of the political energies of the federal Cabinet. More often than not, it is there that the federal booty is distributed for the next election. Journalist Patricia Dumas spoke of a "contract" between the Trudeau government and the people of Ontario, who brought it to power. She argues that this contract, the essence of which is the continued economic and political supremacy of Ontario within Canada, is much more serious than a simple agreement with that province's government. Quebec, on the other hand, is considered safe territory and therefore not the subject of any special attention. Consequently, federal officials did not have to take Quebec opposition to the constitutional package very seriously, or impose official bilingualism on Ontario. From their viewpoint, "Quebec is in the bag."

Unlike the political representatives, and even some civil servants, from Ontario and the West, francophone Quebecers in Ottawa define their role in Canada-wide terms and are much less prone to defend the interests of their province. More often than not, they can be convinced to accept policies clearly detrimental to Quebec on the grounds of an overriding and ephemeral "national interest." Often they are the only Canadians in Ottawa. Moreover, French power defines itself *against* rather than for Quebec. Members of the political staff of Cabinet ministers from Quebec, as well as francophone civil servants, privately suggest that the main objective of French power in Ottawa, and therefore one of the conditions for political and administrative promotion in Ottawa, is to short-circuit the Quebec government and win political victories against it.

This behaviour contrasts sharply with that of Ontario political representatives and civil servants on the federal scene. Their efforts are concentrated on bettering the economic conditions of their region—by attracting new industry, influencing the orientation of federal economic policy and obtaining governmental contracts for Ontario-based industry. Their loyalty and effectiveness in serving the interests of their province are crucial to their political and administrative careers.

The attitude of "French power" towards the economic development of Quebec has been, to say the least, ambivalent. More often than not, the province has found little support in Ottawa for its industrial strategy or projects. In April 1982, when the Parti Québécois government asked for federal assistance to re-structure Quebec industry according to the terms laid out in its blueprint, *Bâtir le Québec II*, federal MPs answered that it was not up to them to help a separatist government, as if the central government was attempting to undermine the PQ by forcing Quebec into bankruptcy. It should be noted, however, that this attitude towards Quebec largely predates the election of the PQ.

A speech by Minister of State Serge Joyal given to a group of investors in New York in May 1982 is typical of the federal approach. Joyal not only attacked the PQ, but denounced the language legislation and the social and economic climate of the province.[5] This kind of attack in a foreign country is highly detrimental to Quebec's credit rating and investment climate. It would be clearly unthinkable for a federal Cabinet minister from Ontario to attack the Davis government in this way, despite their political differences.

According to André Maltais, Liberal MP for Manicouagan, the problem with the Quebec delegation in Ottawa is that it has been in power too long, has little economic knowledge, enjoys too much security, and therefore has had little motivation to fight.[6] This unusually candid statement is supported by several staff members of the economic departments in Ottawa. According to them, Ontario MPs are much more aggressive and effective than their Quebec colleagues. One political staff member explained: "Ontario MPs will call us repeatedly to get action on a dossier (a subsidy or a loan); Quebec MPs, on the other hand, will give you a token phone call and you will not hear from them again, to say nothing of the guys who have been there for more than ten years and don't even know who to talk to when economic development is involved." This kind of attitude has already caused irreparable damage to the Quebec economy.

The PQ threat to move into the federal arena may have injected some new life into the Quebec federal caucus. There may be some hope that, in the near future, Quebec MPs will at least attempt to give the impression that they are fighting for the economic development of their province. One way or another, the political pressure on French power to show more concrete economic results in the province is bound to increase in the next few years.

Political and Social Forces in Quebec in the Eighties

Many forces within Quebec are likely to have an impact, direct or indirect, on the national question. The most important elements for our purposes, however, are the major political parties at the provincial level—the Parti Québécois and the Liberals—as well the English community in Quebec and the possible development of an organized opposition on the left of the PQ.

The Parti Québécois: The Parti Québécois' perception of the Quebec electorate is that the "soft 20 percent" mentioned earlier is already won to the ideal of Quebec nationhood, at least in the emotional sense. Thus, it feels, future gains for the cause of sovereignty can only come about through attempts to convince this group that federalism is not essential to the Quebec economy, and that independence will bring about no hardships. In these difficult economic times, one of the key challenges to the PQ position is to show that the constitution and the economy are linked, and that federal policies and the distribution of powers between the two levels of government are responsible at least in part for the province's economic problems. In concrete terms, this has meant an almost daily war of attrition against federal policies in Quebec. The PQ has apparently decided to push on with this strategy, even though it met with quite limited success during the referendum. In fact, the major defeat of the party during the referendum was its inability to go beyond its "hard base" in selling sovereignty-association.

The increasing criticism from the grass-roots membership of the Parti Québécois is partly the result of this soft-sell approach to sovereignty. The more radical elements in the party have even claimed that the PQ has killed the struggle for sovereignty by reducing the ideal of independence to some sort of administrative re-arrangement between Quebec and the rest of Canada. They have also argued that the PQ is moving towards an "autonomist" position, defending traditional provincial rights rather than independence. The critics point to the 1981 provincial election, when the PQ refused to make sovereignty the main issue, and to the constitutional conference, when Quebec joined other provinces in a common front to prevent the scaling down of provincial powers. They also stress the PQ's refusal to mobilize on a mass scale after the federal government's constitutional coup.

While much of the criticism is justified, it is too easy to forget that the Parti Québécois is not and has never been dedicated to outright independence. Ever since the creation of the *Mouvement Souveraineté-Association* in 1968, Lévesque and the PQ leadership have put forward as a negotiating position a common market arrangement with many common institutions.

The "low key" approach to sovereignty is a double-edged sword. It is ideally suited to winning the support of the undecided. But if the PQ wants the support of the younger generation and its militants throughout the eighties, sovereignty as a political ideal will have to be made more meaningful, and will have to correspond to significant political change. It will have to be presented and perceived as a first step towards a more progressive society, not simply as a new administrative arrangement. Within the party, the battle between the *autonomistes* and *indépendantistes* is ongoing, and the outcome is difficult to predict. There is little doubt, however, that as long as the PQ remains in power with René Lévesque as its leader, the moderate option will continue to be dominant.

Even though the precise means of intervention have not yet been finalized, it seems more and more likely that the PQ will present its own slate of candidates in the next federal election. The minimum objectives are the defeat of Trudeau and French power in Ottawa in order to remove one of the perceived obstacles to sovereignty, and the creation of a new platform from which to criticize and "expose" the negative impact of federal policies on Quebec. Assuming that the PQ invests substantial energy and money in this adventure, and assuming that it is prepared to field "name" candidates, it stands a good chance of achieving its minimum objectives. There are, however, some potential hazards. The PQ's presence in the federal arena could help the federal Liberals fight another election on national unity, a real bargain given the state of the economy. They could possibly compensate for the Quebec losses in other areas of the country. There is also the "danger" that federalism could in fact work better for Quebec with a group of *péquistes* in Parliament. One way or the other, a federal PQ would be trapped between the need to denounce federal policies and the need to be effective by winning a better deal for Quebec and for the constituents of individual members, all of which could lead to substantial problems between the provincial and federal wings of the party. And finally, the PQ would, of course, suffer many of the electoral handicaps common to third parties. It would have to convince the electorate to vote for a party that does not have even an outside chance of gaining power.

The Quebec Liberal Party: Paradoxically, the effectiveness of Claude Ryan and the Quebec Liberal Party during the referendum campaign prompted their electoral defeat in 1981. The lopsided referendum victory was interpreted by Trudeau as a mandate for a frontal attack on all manifestations of Quebec nationalism, making no distinction between *péquistes* and nationalist moderates within the QLP, including Claude Ryan. As a result of the constitutional coup, a large number of nationalist moderates abandoned the federalist camp and contributed to re-electing the Parti Québécois.

Still in a state of shock after the last provincial election, the "unconditional federalists" in the provincial and federal wings of the party succeeded in forcing Claude Ryan's resignation. Insisting that the leader's lack of charisma was the source of the party's problems, this group refused to consider the possibility that party policies did not correspond to the aspirations of the majority in Quebec. At the social level, the reformist appeal that the party had in the sixties seems definitely lost. Given the Parti Québécois' shift to the right, including dramatic cuts in social programs and a tough attitude towards unions, the QLP seems to have little room to manoeuvre. Ryan himself was the leader closest to a social democrat in the party. Given its conservative image and its inability to generate credible policy alternatives, it is not entirely surprising that the party is faced with severe recruitment problems. It seems unable to attract the more dynamic elements of the young generation. At the present time, a protest vote and the crippling effects of the economic crisis are hopeful signs for the Liberals. They may yet prove to be sufficient.

On the national question, the Liberals are having more and more difficulty appealing to the moderates. The unconditional federalists, which include the anglophone minority and francophone "Trudeauites," now represent a clear majority within the party. Ryan understood full well that his party could not gather a majority in Quebec on the basis of the Trudeau position and must avoid alienating nationalists even further. This, in part, is why he supported the Lévesque government's position on the Trudeau package in the National Assembly. By putting his leadership on the line, Ryan managed to rally a majority of MNAs from his party. But the move put fatal strains on his leadership; the dominant forces within the party were clearly unwilling to compromise on the national issue.

The English Community in Quebec: Fear of the French majority in Quebec has prompted English Quebecers to become Canada's most ardent Canadians. As a result of their refusal to integrate within Quebec society to any significant extent, anglophones have always been firm supporters of a strong central state and of a correspondingly weak Quebec state.

During the referendum campaign, however, the main spokesmen for the English community went on record as supporting a new flexible, decentralized form of federalism where everything would be negotiable. Logically, this should have led the community to oppose the Constitution Act. Yet most English Quebecers have been unconditional and enthusiastic supporters of the latest moves towards a stronger central state. Apart from being cynical and dishonest with respect to the promises made during the referendum period, this attitude constitutes a major political mistake. When sovereignty-association is put back on the table in Quebec, English Quebecers and other anti-sovereignty forces will have a tremendous handicap to overcome.

Despite some abrasive bureaucratic moves by the PQ government, including legislation for French-only signs, the overall position of anglophones within Quebec remains excellent. In the economic field, their average income and their control over business institutions indicate clearly that the anglophones are not an oppressed minority. In cultural and linguistic terms, Quebec anglophones not only enjoy a substantial degree of institutional autonomy in areas such as schools and hospitals, but are also part of the North American majority, which provides economic and cultural security.

The English community can certainly be faulted for its inertia in the face of rapid developments in the province during the sixties and seventies. Efforts to learn French on a mass scale only began seriously as a response to the development of nationalism in Quebec, which indicates the community's begrudging attitude towards change. The same rigidity has been evident in the refusal to accept even the moderate position of former Liberal leader Claude Ryan. At times, it seems, the anglophones yearn for the good old days of Maurice Duplessis.

Quebec anglophones also have failed to play a role in attempting to improve relations between Quebec francophones and the rest of Canada. On the contrary, through dramatic, personalized, and often wildly exaggerated accounts of "oppression" in Quebec (the latest example being the victims of Bill 101), they have earned greater resentment from French Quebecers. The English press outside Quebec has tended to play up these stories, and one of the consequences has been the destabilizing of the investment climate in Quebec. By not defending a "renewed federalism" more closely in line with Quebec aspirations, by attacking Claude Ryan with a vengeance after he failed to support Trudeau's constitutional package, and by contributing so substantially to the destruction of Quebec's image within Canada, the English community has missed an historic opportunity to restore its credibility within Quebec and to strike a new deal with the francophone majority.

The Left in Quebec: The evolution of the left in Quebec is another factor to consider in the social and constitutional development of the province in the eighties. The restraint policies adopted by the Parti Québécois as a result of the economic conditions as well as a perceived watering down of the concept of sovereignty as a political goal has gone a long way towards alienating the progressive elements within the union movement and in the PQ itself. While the union movement is likely to remain committed to an independent Quebec, its support for the PQ will undoubtedly dwindle. What remains to be seen is the extent to which the left can adopt and carry through independent political objectives and make serious inroads in the popular support of the two existing parties.

When the PQ was created in the late sixties, most Quebec social democrats and socialists either joined or tacitly supported the party in the hope that the question of socialism could be dealt with more easily after independence. However, as a result of the PQ's social and economic policies and the referendum defeat, disillusionment has set in, and many social democrats have either left the party or have been relegated to its fringes. In terms of the national question, the progressive wing, which in large majority favours outright independence, suffered a major defeat in the March 1982 party congress. At the December 1981 congress, they had succeeded in dropping the question of "association" from the PQ program. Lévesque then called a referendum within the party, threatened to resign, and succeeded in reversing the decision. After that, several PQ party members left the party and rallied behind political movements calling for socialism and independence.

It is too early to predict what impact the *Mouvement Socialiste* (MS) and the *Regroupement pour le Socialisme,* both of which were created in 1981, will have on the Quebec political scene. They seem, however, to be developing rapidly. The MS, for one, has attracted substantial support from the union leadership; for example, Marcel Pépin, former head of the Confederation of National Trade Unions and of the World Labour Congress, became president of the movement. The bulk of the membership, however, is made up of intellectuals. On paper, the MS defends a hard-line socialist approach, advocating a complete break with the capitalist system and the socialization of the means of production. But in practice, it is more likely that the MS will evolve towards a social-democratic position, perhaps comparable to François Mitterand's socialist party in France.

In general terms, the progressive movements in Quebec, including women's groups, ecological groups, cultural movements as well as the more doctrinaire Marxist-Leninist parties, are showing substantial organizational and ideological vitality. The rapid development of a quality "alternative press" provides evidence of this trend.

In the aftermath of the referendum, the eventual unity of the Canadian and Quebec left seems as unattainable as ever. The Canadian left, including the New Democratic Party and the Canadian Labour Congress, supported the "no" option during the referendum and participated in the renewed federalism hoax as much as anyone else. Given that most Quebec social democrats support if not outright independence, then at least a decentralized form of federalism, the potential for joint action seems limited indeed.

The Quebec Economy and Constitutional Change

In a federal system, constitutional change and the distribution of powers between levels of government have important economic implications. Similarly, economic factors are often crucial in federal-provincial relations. We will examine here some of the trends that are likely to have a key influence in the eighties from Quebec's point of view. Given that the chapter in this volume by Raymond Hudon has dealt with many of the broad issues underlying the economic strategy of the federal government and the development of regionalism in the provinces, we will concentrate mainly on the implications of these trends for constitutional change.

Federal Economic Objectives and Centralization: In the last few years, the federal government has chosen to play a much more active and aggressive role in the economic field, assuming principal responsibility for the restructuring of the Canadian economy. This occurred in a context of declining American investments in Canada, the deterioration of the relative economic position of the United States among industrial countries, and the increasingly obvious problems of Canadian over-dependence on its southern neighbour. The new policy of economic nationalism implied, among other things, Canadian government support for the development of

Canadian-owned corporations at home and abroad, the participation of the government in the takeover of foreign firms, and the creation of an important network of Crown corporations. Particular emphasis was placed upon the resource and energy sectors.

In terms of the federal system in Canada, these policies have obvious implications. As Philip Resnick has argued, "the trend to centralization will increase in the 1980s, buoyed up by the need to restructure Canadian capitalism the better to compete in the new international order."[7] As such policies are costly, the federal government will have to find ways of increasing substantially its financial resources. The tough negotiations with the oil-producing provinces and the cuts in transfer payments to provinces are clear indications of what is to come. The central government is also looking for a clearer definition and a substantial increase in its economic powers. Its goal in this quest is to strengthen the relative position of the federal state and of Canadian, mainly Ontario-based, capital against provincial states and regional capital, which have developed very rapidly as semi-autonomous centres of economic decision-making power. Quebec and Alberta are seen as the main targets at this level.

The objective of re-establishing the federal government's hegemony over the provinces is clearly incompatible with the "co-operative federalism" of the sixties. In this light, the Constitution Act, along with the National Energy Program and the unilateral cuts in transfer payments, constitute elements in a calculated attempt to modify the Canadian political equilibrium in favour of the central government. At the constitutional and economic level, the new "opting out" clause in the amending formula, which provides financial compensation in only a limited number of cases, is a major loss for the provinces. It will be difficult for the provinces to reject federal social and economic programs, which their taxpayers will help to finance anyway.

In the Quebec case, the federal government has found additional motivation and impetus to forge ahead with increased centralization. Ottawa is convinced not only that unchecked regional economic development is incompatible with a national industrial strategy, but also that an attempt to stop nationalism and the Parti Québécois must imply a reduction of the economic power base of the Quebec state. Political and economic autonomy are seen as closely linked, and the aftermath of the Quebec referendum provided a favourable context for this kind of counter-offensive.

The federal government is walking a tightrope in attempting to reconcile several potentially contradictory objectives. It is not only seeking to weaken the provincial state, but also striving to lay the blame on the Quebec government for the economic crisis and to convince Quebecers that the federal system is best for the Quebec economy in the long run. The continuing economic crisis may well topple both the PQ and the federal

Liberals, but its effect on nationalism and federalism in the province is difficult to predict. The result will largely depend on each level of government's ability to lay the blame for the economic crisis on the other.

Quebec's Economic Strategy: The substantial increase in the economic activities of the Quebec state in the sixties and seventies, as well as the rapid development of local capital, has been documented at length elsewhere.[8] In the early sixties, the Lesage government launched a concerted effort to boost economic development in the province and to improve Quebec's position within the Canadian economy. Some attempts were made to induce foreign capital to increase the local benefits of their economic activity, through sub-contracting, for example, but it soon became apparent that a strengthening of local capital and local control over the economy was a more realistic solution. Successive Quebec governments put forward two main types of policy: the creation of an important network of state corporations (Hydro, Sidbec, the Quebec Deposit and Investment Fund, the General Investment Corp.), and state support for Quebec-based companies and co-operatives through subsidies, contracts and preferential buying.

The net result of these policies has been the relative improvement of the conditions of middle class or *petit bourgeois* francophones and a shift in power in favour of Quebec-based private and state corporations. It should be noted, however, that the strengthening of local capital was often done at the expense of national "Canadian" companies, and included several takeovers and nationalizations. Sectors such as banking, insurance, food processing and distribution, pulp and paper, and the production of electricity, which can all be considered "intermediate" in technological terms and which are mainly controlled by Canadian companies, were prime targets for Quebec government moves. In addition, this strengthening of Quebec regional capital tended to occur in sectors where the provincial government had the constitutional power to intervene (natural resources and energy, for example). Thus, in economic terms, sovereignty-association can be seen as an attempt to seize greater financial resources and power from the federal government in order to go further along the same road.

In many ways, Quebec learned the art of economic planning and economic nationalism a decade or so before the central government, and for much the same reasons. Historically, Canadian firms have behaved in Quebec in much the same way as American capital in Canada, and with the same negative results for the Quebec economy. They have drained savings and profits generated in the province and have invested them elsewhere; they have concentrated their research and managerial activities closer to "home," more often than not in Toronto; and, other things being equal, they have chosen to invest outside the province. All of those trends have, of course, become more pronounced as Quebec's desire for a larger part of the economic pie has become more vocal.

Thus the provincial governments in Quebec in the sixties and seventies decided that the impetus for economic development must come from within. But there was also another reason for the province to adopt nationalist policies in the economic field. It was found that even stringent legislation was insufficient to guarantee a minimal use of French in the workplace. The ownership and control by francophones of an increasing number of business concerns was found to be a much more effective tool for promoting the use of French.

French Power and the Quebec Economy: The federal government has contributed relatively little to the economic development of Quebec. If francophones in the province have improved their relative position in terms of income and power, it is primarily as a result of the policies of the Quebec state. While the federal government has pumped in large amounts of "social" money through programs such as unemployment insurance and old-age pensions, and has subsidized the construction of infrastructure such as Mirabel Airport, industrial parks and the port of Montreal, the "solid" economic investments, which lead to new industrial plants, have more often come from the Quebec government.

As mentioned earlier, the general attitude of francophone MPs and Cabinet ministers in Ottawa, especially since the referendum, has been to block the regional development initiatives of the Quebec state rather than to promote new federal initiatives that would help the provincial economy. This is true for both general economic policies and specific economic "*dossiers.*" As regards federal economic policy, French power has been unable to put across the case either for supporting financially Quebec's small- and medium-sized corporations, which have been hit hard by high interest rates, or for lowering those rates. As a result of the tighter operating margins, business failures in Quebec have been higher in the last two years than anywhere else in North America.

The federal government has also adopted a general strategy of refusing to support any new investments that come into competition with existing Canadian firms. This argument was invoked by Pierre De Bané, then minister of regional economic expansion, when the federal government refused to subsidize the development of a salt mine at Iles de la Madeleine. Another example was Air Canada's refusal to sell Nordair to Québecair, despite repeated earlier promises to the contrary. The federal government apparently feared that a Quebec-based regional carrier might compete effectively with Air Canada.

On the surface, this may seem to be rational economic policy. The problem, however, is that given the long-term recession, such an approach perpetuates the industrial status quo. Except in a very limited number of sectors, Quebec cannot possibly hope to improve its position if the federal government refuses to finance any project that enters into competition with Ontario or other Canadian firms. In the summer of 1982, the federal government did offer substantial financial support to Bombardier in its efforts to win a major contract in New York. This was one of the first cases where the Liberal caucus from Quebec held its ground. It should be noted, however, that no Ontario competition was involved.

One of the best examples of French power's ineptitude in defending the economic interests of Quebec revolves around the decision by the federal government to purchase F-18 fighter planes, the largest contract ever awarded by a Canadian government. The aeronautical construction field is one of the few sectors of heavy industry where Quebec is in a better position than Ontario. Fifty percent of the industry is located in the province, compared to 40 percent in Ontario. The choice of the F-18 over the F-16 involved much more than the choice of an airplane. The F-18 is built by McDonnell Douglas, which has important plants in Ontario; the F-16, on the other hand, is produced by General Dynamics, and its main Canadian subsidiary is Pratt and Whitney of Montreal. It was obvious from the start that the government's choice would be crucial to the evolution of the industry in the two provinces.

The federal government eventually chose the F-18, claiming that it was better suited to Canadian military purposes. The "experts" were divided on the question, and even Quebec MPs were unconvinced. For example, P.A. Massé, MP for St-Jean, complained publicly that he had been taken for a ride, and that the caucus had been given almost no information on the contract despite repeated pleas.[9] To add insult to injury, it now appears that the F-18 contracts in Quebec will amount to less than half of the $1.8 billion promised by the company and federal politicians. Ontario, on the other hand, is well on its way to obtaining the full amount anticipated in the contracts.[10]

In general, then, the federal government has given top priority to the economic development of Ontario. Quebec initiatives, whether state or private, that threaten to compete with Ontario interests have been discouraged. Despite increasing francophone representation in key Cabinet posts and the civil service, the concrete impact of the federal system in Quebec provides real constraints in economic terms.

Conclusion

What, then, can we expect in the next few years on the political front in Quebec?

First, while it is never easy to predict the future, it would be premature and politically foolish to bury the national question in Quebec, irrespective of the electoral fortunes of the Parti Québécois. The problems and questions which prompted the development of a pro-independence movement in Quebec remain unresolved. While much of the emotion surrounding the national debate has subsided, the new generation and the rising forces of Quebec society continue to support nationalism. The federal government, on the other hand, has moved quickly to fill the vacuum provided by their referendum victory, but may have created the conditions for an even more serious challenge to the federal system.

Second, one can expect a long and arduous struggle for legitimacy between the federal and provincial governments in Quebec. It is likely that economic issues, including the concrete impact of federal policies in Quebec, will come to occupy centre-stage. Both governments will be hard pressed to demonstrate that their constitutional option, be it centralization, decentralization or sovereignty, will provide maximum short- and long-term economic benefits. This debate should be heightened if the Parti Québécois participates in the next federal election.

Third, the outcome of the struggle between the federal government and Quebec will largely be determined by the perceived effectiveness of "French power" in Ottawa. Sooner or later, francophones in Ottawa and in the federal system will be judged on the concrete economic benefits they bring to Quebec. Unsubstantiated claims that separation will bring about an economic doomsday will no longer suffice.

Finally, one can only hope that English Canada will develop its own response to the problem of Quebec. In this respect, the monopoly exercised by "French power" in Ottawa, even though it has been effective in the short run, must be broken. Enlightened political leadership is needed if a reconciliation or "new deal" is to be struck with Quebec. No matter what constitutional solution Quebecers choose in the next decade, English Canada will have to think again on the Quebec issue and do better than give tacit approval to the actions of its federal government.

Notes

1. Bill 101's "Quebec clause" provides access to English schools only for a child whose mother or father was educated in English in Quebec. Section 23 of the Charter of Rights and Freedoms, on the other hand, opens up English schools in Quebec to children whose parents received schooling anywhere in Canada in the English language. The Charter also provides for access to English schools in the case where a brother or sister has attended a primary or secondary school in English anywhere in Canada.
2. With the exception of fiscal compensation on cultural issues.
3. In *Federalism and the French Canadians* (Toronto: Macmillan, 1968), pp. 110 and 111, Pierre Trudeau underscored the "complete lack of a democratic frame of reference for French-Canadian political thinking" and "French-Canadian lack of concern for the liberties and traditions of Parliament."
4. *La Presse*, April 14, 1982, p. A10.
5. *La Presse*, May 22, 1982, p. A10.
6. *La Presse*, May 8, 1982, p. B2.
7. Philip Resnick, "The Maturing of Canadian Capitalism," unpublished paper presented to Canadian Political Science Association, Ottawa, June 1982, p. 23.
8. See my article, "The New Parameters of the Québec bourgeoisie," *Studies in Political Economy*, vol. 3 (Spring 1980), pp. 67-92.
9. *La Presse*, April 12, 1980, p. A14.
10. François Roberge, "F-18-A: les retombées ne pleuvent plus," *Finance*, May 17, 1982.

Part III/The Courts in the Constitutional Process

Chapter 9/The Supreme Court of Canada and Basic Constitutional Amendment

W.R. Lederman

After September 28, 1981, events moved with considerable speed towards the resolution of Canada's urgent problems of major constitutional reform. On that date, the nine justices of the Supreme Court of Canada rendered their landmark decision on the nature of the amending process necessary to accomplish fundamental constitutional changes directly affecting the essentials of the Canadian federal union. The decision had been preceded by many months of political and legal deadlock in the country on the issues, with eight provincial governments arrayed against the federal government and the two remaining provincial governments. In the winter of 1980–81, the controversy was taken to three provincial Courts of Appeal, those of Manitoba, Newfoundland and Quebec. When these courts had spoken, with mixed results,[1] their respective decisions were in effect consolidated for the purposes of a single appeal to the Supreme Court of Canada. Argument was heard there at the end of April 1981, and the decision of the court was given about five months later, on September 28.[2] The issues were as complex as they were basic, so the Supreme Court certainly moved with quite remarkable speed in the circumstances, as had the provincial Courts of Appeal earlier in the year.

It soon became apparent after September 28 that while the Supreme Court had not by any means settled all the constitutional issues confronting Canadians, it had nevertheless moved us much closer to their resolution by settling some important questions of method concerning the right way of doing things in the realm of basic constitutional change, as only the court of final authority for Canada could have done.[3] Look at what happened after the judgement. On November 5, at a federal-provincial conference, nine provincial governments and the federal government agreed on a domestic amending formula for basic change that would accomplish patriation of the Canadian constitution. They also agreed on a wide-ranging Canadian Charter of Rights and Freedoms to be entrenched in the constitution as part of the patriation process. Certainly these would be fundamental changes to the federal union. Sadly, however, it must be added that the provincial government of Quebec was not a party to this consensus. As a political fact, this is a matter of general regret and continuing anxiety among Canadians, including Quebecers. Nevertheless, the near unanimity of the political consensus was quite remarkable and was deemed constitutionally sufficient to enable Parliament to proceed. It seems clear that all governments in Canada, except for that of Quebec, construed the critical Supreme Court majority judgements of September 28 as having been to this effect.

After making a few changes in the Charter, with the Quebec government maintaining its general dissent, all-party support for the joint address to the Queen was obtained in both Houses of Parliament, and the address was sent to Westminster in early December 1981. The British parliamentarians also regretted the absence of the Quebec government from the otherwise complete Canadian consensus, but in their turn they took the view that this was not a constitutional impediment for the British Parliament. In due course, the legislation requested in the joint address from Canada was passed without change by both Houses of the British Parliament and became law on receiving Royal assent on March 29, 1982. Thus the British Parliament discharged its traditional function in this respect for the last time. The legislation itself provided that it was to come into force on a day to be fixed by a proclamation issued by the Queen or the Governor-General under the Great Seal of Canada.[4] This was done by the Queen as Queen of Canada in Ottawa on April 17, 1982, with effect on that day.

Nevertheless, the Quebec government continues its objections, and it had earlier gone back to the Quebec Court of Appeal claiming that the lack of Quebec government consent would invalidate these changes, if not as a matter of constitutional law, at least as a matter of constitutional convention. On April 7, 1982, the Quebec Court of Appeal gave judgement unanimously rejecting this claim to a veto power.[5] The Quebec government appealed against this verdict to the Supreme Court of Canada; but on December 6, 1982, the latter unanimously affirmed the Quebec Court of Appeal.

In any event, the decision of the Supreme Court of Canada rendered on September 28, 1981 had a great and continuing effect on the subsequent developments, and it is therefore proper to attempt a short critical analysis of the reasons of the judges to explain this influence. Because the reasons referred to occupy well over 100 pages in the law reports, composing a short commentary is indeed a formidable task. But the nine judges do fall into four groups according to the positions taken by them on the issues, and if one keeps to the main thrust and emphasis of these four positions, reasonable accuracy may be combined with some brevity. In any event, this is what I will attempt to do.

The constitutional issues to which the Supreme Court of Canada addressed itself arose out of the historical fact that while the British North America Act of 1867, an Act of the British Parliament, provided Canada with a federal constitution, it did not provide any domestic process for amending the basics of that constitution in Canada by some adequate measure of domestic agreement between the provinces and the central government. Accordingly, it has been necessary during the past 114 years to obtain such amendments to the BNA Act by an appropriate request to the Parliament of Britain from Canada. Over the years, as Canada grew to independent nationhood, certain principles or customs developed inform-

ally concerning what was an appropriate request. The two principles
involved in the issues before the Court were as follows: (1) the British
Parliament would not enact any basic amendments to the Canadian constitution except at the request of both Houses of the Parliament; and (2) the
Canadian Parliament would "not request an amendment directly affecting
federal-provincial relations without prior consultation and agreement
with the provinces."[6]

Accordingly, the questions for determination by the Court concerned
primarily the constitutional status, if any, of the second principle or
custom. Was it a law of the constitution binding on all parties, or if not, was
it at least a convention of the constitution having objective obligatory
character? If it was neither of these, then it was a mere precept of desirable
political behaviour in some circumstances, having no objective binding
force for the governments concerned? The government of Prime Minister
Trudeau had taken this latter position and had decided it was free to
proceed unilaterally, without provincial agreement, to request that the
British Parliament enact the basic constitutional changes it proposed. In
early October 1980, with this intention, the government introduced the
necessary parliamentary Resolution for an address to the Queen. For
several months prior to this, it had tried without success to obtain provincial agreement.

Political objection to this unilateralism developed quickly in Parliament, primarily on the part of the Progressive Conservative Party. Furthermore, the six dissenting provinces that took the federal government to court
alleged that the unilateral procedure being followed was unconstitutional
in the legal or conventional sense. By the time the three provincial Supreme
Court judgements reached the Supreme Court of Canada on appeal, eight
provinces were supporting this position against the federal government.
Also, by this time, largely owing to the efforts of the official opposition, the
constitutional Resolution had been tabled in Parliament to await the
decision of the Supreme Court, and the federal government had agreed to
abide by the decision when it came.

Let us turn then to the positions taken by the judges and their reasons
for those positions. The problems they had to deal with are both basic and
complex, so it is not surprising that two majority positions and two
minority positions emerged in the form of joint opinions by the various
judges in agreement on each of the four positions. I will speak hereafter of
the majority and minority judgements number I (on strict constitutional
law), seven judges to two; and of the majority and minority judgements
number II (on established constitutional conventions), six judges to three.
Majority Judgement I was given by Chief Justice Laskin, and Justices
Dickson, Beetz, Estey, McIntyre, Chouinard and Lamer;[7] Justices Martland
and Ritchie dissented in Minority Judgement I.[8] Majority Judgement II
was given by Justices Martland, Ritchie, Dickson, Beetz, Chouinard and

Lamer;[9] Chief Justice Laskin and Justices Estey and McIntyre dissented in Minority Judgement II.[10]

The judges forming Majority I ruled that as a matter of law, there was no requirement for any provincial consent to be obtained before the Parliament of Canada could properly request amendments directly affecting federal-provincial relationships from the British Parliament. A unilateral request to Westminster by the government and Parliament of Canada was legal. Justices Martland and Ritchie, forming Minority I, dissented, taking the view that in these circumstances, the strict law of the constitution required provincial consent. The unilateral address planned was, in their view, illegal. They left open the question whether, in their opinion, the consent of all the provinces had to be obtained, or whether some lesser but still substantial measure of provincial consent would suffice as a matter of law.

The judges forming Majority II ruled that as a matter of established constitutional convention apart from law, the Canadian constitution had come to require that the Canadian Parliament not request an amendment directly affecting federal-provincial relationships without prior consultation and agreement with the provinces. Moreover, they ruled that a substantial measure of provincial consent would suffice to satisfy the convention, thus holding that the unanimous consent of all the provinces was not required by the terms of the convention. Chief Justice Laskin and Justices Estey and McIntyre, forming Minority II, dissented. They concluded that an established convention had not developed requiring provincial consent in the circumstances, so that conventionally as well as legally, the planned unilateralism of the federal government and the Parliament of Canada was constitutional.

It will have been noticed that four of the judges are common to Majority I on law and Majority II on convention. They are Justices Dickson, Beetz, Chouinard and Lamer. If one analyzes carefully what accounts for this, one can largely explain not only the different positions taken by the two majority groups, but also those taken by the two minority groups. My thesis is that the judges in each of the four groups were responding to three primary constitutional questions which had to be faced one way or another for them to dispose of the case. Their responses differed in critical ways; nevertheless, the majority view that did emerge enabled the Canadian political actors to make the remarkable progress toward the Accord of November 1981.

The three primary themes or questions I have in mind are as follows: (1) Given that the constitution is a combination of laws and conventions, what is the nature of law itself, what is the nature of convention itself, what is the relation between the two, and from what sources do they respectively originate? (2) Given that the constitution is a federal constitution of some sort, what kind of a federal constitution is it? In other words, what is the nature of Canadian federalism? (3) What is the proper function of the traditional courts, especially of the Supreme Court of Canada, as the final guardians of compliance with the constitution as a matter of law or convention or both? In other words, what basic constitutional issues are justiciable? What is the extent of the power of judicial review?

Let us now examine how the four groups of judges—the two majorities and the two minorities—divided and combined on these questions.

In Majority Judgement I, the seven judges take a rather narrowly positivist and historically static view of the nature of Canadian constitutional law—at least at the primary level in question, that of the basic amending process. They assert that legal rules at this level must be directly expressed in formal authoritative documentary sources such as relevant British statutes, or judicial decisions either British or Canadian.[11] They hold that no such source can be found giving a legal amending process for Canada that requires a measure of provincial consent, or any provincial consent at all, in relation to the legal power of the Parliament of Canada to ask what it pleases of the British Parliament by way of joint address. And especially, there is no legal requirement that limits the old imperial supremacy of the British Parliament to do whatsoever it pleases about requested amendments from Canada.[12]

I have characterized this view of law as narrowly positivist because it treats certain authoritative formal sources of law as unique and exclusive of the operation of any other source of law. I have characterized it as historically static because Canadian federalism and independence are both undoubted and long-standing historical facts in the modern world. Yet neither fact is accommodated in this conception of the strict law of the constitution. This seems to take us back not just to 1867, but to 1866. I respectfully submit that there is something wrong with a conception of basic constitutional law that is so unreal. Nevertheless, the result of Majority Judgement I was that as a matter of law, we needed one last British statute that gave us a domestic constitutional amending process of a suitable federal type before we had such a legal Canadian amending process at all. Until then, they said, there was simply a large gap in our constitutional law; quite simply, it was drastically incomplete.

Finally, we should notice that this strict and narrow definition of law permitted all seven judges in Majority I to avoid issues concerning the nature of Canadian federalism. It is only because they agreed on a narrow definition of law that they could join in Majority Judgement I, which was strictly confined to the legal issue. As we shall see, Chief Justice Laskin and Justices Estey and McIntyre on the one hand (Minority Judgement II), and Justices Dickson, Beetz, Chouinard and Lamer on the other hand (in Majority Judgement II), have quite different conceptions of the nature of Canadian federalism. The minute that issue is raised, the seven judges who agreed in Majority Judgement I split into the groups of three and four just mentioned.

But before pursuing that point, we should look at the significance of Minority Judgement I, the dissent on strict law of Justices Martland and Ritchie. In Edwards v. Attorney General for Canada in 1930,[13] Lord Sankey said: "The British North America Act planted in Canada a living tree capable of growth and expansion." Justices Martland and Ritchie took this broader sociological and organic view of Canadian constitutional law as it relates to basic amendment processes. They considered constitutional law to have been growing to completeness in the federal sense, and to independence from Britain, in the 114 years since Confederation. They inferred a requirement for provincial consent in a typically federal amending process as a matter of law by necessary implication from formal legal sources—the BNA Act itself, the Statute of Westminster of 1931, and a number of important judicial decisions in the Judicial Committee of the Privy Council and the Supreme Court of Canada distributed through the whole period since Confederation. They considered the formal sources in the light of the full facts of Canadian political and constitutional history, including the political facts about how amendments were secured from the British Parliament throughout the period.[14] This use of the full historical context for the formal sources in aid of legal inferences manifests a very different conception of what basic constitutional law is and where it comes from than what we found in the majority judgement on the legal issue. The legal result reached by Justices Martland and Ritchie is realistic, but it *is* a minority judgement, and therefore however great its theoretical validity, it did not directly influence subsequent events.

Turning to Majority Judgement II, however, we find that Justices Dickson, Beetz, Chouinard and Lamer recognized that the narrow conception of law in which they had concurred when they were part of Majority I was so incomplete that it had nothing at all to say about a basic amending process appropriate for Canadian federalism. They were nonetheless willing to complete the constitution as a *federal* constitution in this respect by rules arising from constitutional conventions that had been established over the years since Confederation. They found that there was indeed a conventional rule requiring a substantial measure of provincial consent for basic amendments affecting the federal union. Moreover, they held that such constitutional conventions could be identified, defined and authoritatively declared as obligatory rules by the court, even though they were not legal rules and the court could do nothing to enforce them if there were not willing compliance by the political actors concerned. The tests they used to identify and define the relevant convention arising from the custom and usage of the official political actors over the 114 years since Confederation were those stated by Sir Ivor Jennings:

We have to ask ourselves three questions: first, what are the precedents; secondly, did the actors in the precedents believe that they were bound by a rule; and thirdly, is there a reason for the rule? A single precedent with a good reason may be enough to establish the rule. A whole string of precedents without such a reason will be of no avail, unless it is perfectly certain that the persons concerned regarded them as bound by it.[15]

We can see that Justices Dickson, Beetz, Chouinard and Lamer arrived at virtually the same conclusion respecting the present basic amending process as a matter of convention as that reached by Justices Martland and Ritchie as a matter of law. Moreover, this was done in each case by virtue of the same reading of the obligatory significance of the historical evidence. It was natural and proper, then, that Justices Martland and Ritchie should join with the other four judges just named to give Majority Judgement II on convention, the judgement that really counted, as we shall see later. For Justices Martland and Ritchie, a rose by any other name still smelled as sweet. Finally, it should be emphasized that the unifying factor for the six judges in Majority II was not just a common view of the nature and function of established constitutional conventions; it was also a common view of the nature of Canadian federalism. All six judges in Majority II viewed the total Canadian constitution (by virtue of convention) as essentially in harmony with the classic federal model insofar as the requirement of provincial consent for basic amendments was concerned. According to the classic model, federalism is an equal partnership between the provincial governments and Legislatures on the one hand, and the government and Parliament of Canada on the other. Those who read Canadian constitutional history and jurisprudence as manifesting classic, balanced federalism would naturally infer that there was always a requirement for at least substantial provincial consent, along with that of the Parliament of Canada, for amendments directly affecting the federal union. As we have seen, for Justices Martland and Ritchie this inference was both legal and conventional, whereas for Justices Dickson, Beetz, Chouinard and Lamer it was conventional only, albeit very real at that level. In terms of the Jennings tests, the classic character of Canadian federalism was the reason for the convention requiring provincial consent.

The contrasting view of the nature of Canadian federalism is found at full strength only in the dissenting opinion on convention of Chief Justice Laskin and Justices Estey and McIntyre (Minority Judgement II). In their view, Canadian constitutional history and jurisprudence manifest only a partial and incomplete federalism at the level of basic amendments directly affecting the federal union of the country, whether one is talking of law or convention. Indeed, they deny that there is any one "classic" model of federalism in political science or constitutional jurisprudence. In any event, they conclude that the Canadian constitution is only partially federal and has included from the beginning some elements of a unitary state that give certain overriding powers to the Parliament of Canada. They conclude that these are inconsistent with a finding, legal or conventional, that Canada is or was intended to be a classic balanced-partnership federalism, at least where the basic amending process is concerned and in certain other respects as well. What are these overriding, formal legal powers that give the Parliament of Canada superior status? Minority II emphasizes the potentially extensive overriding character of the legislative power of the Parliament of Canada under the "Peace, Order and Good Government" clause of the BNA Act,[16] the paramountcy of Parliament in concurrent legislative fields, the power of Parliament to take over regulation of provincial works by declaring them to be works for the general advantage of Canada,[17] and the power of the federal Cabinet to disallow provincial legislation by order-in-council.[18]

It is no doubt clear to readers by now that I favour the classic version of the nature of Canadian federalism, though no constitution is absolutely pure in compliance with a given model. I agree in principle with both Minority Judgement I and Majority Judgement II, and this has been my position for many years. Nevertheless, I am bound to admit that the rather centralized and partial version of the nature of Canadian federalism given in Minority Judgement II has been until quite recently the prevailing version among professors of constitutional law and political science in English Canada. By contrast, the prevailing view among these groups in French Canada has been and still is the classic version. They see the special central powers pointed to in Minority Judgement II as anomalies. And it should be added that the courts have definitely set close limits to the potentially sweeping character of the "Peace, Order and Good Government" clause.[19]

In any event, to come back to the judgements of September 28, 1981, I am suggesting that the differing beliefs of the respective judges about the nature of Canadian federalism had a significant steering effect on the results they came to in three of the four groups into which they formed themselves—Minority I (law), Majority II (convention) and Minority II (convention). I admit that to attempt to detect a "steering effect" is something of a chicken-and-egg problem. But after all, the three groups were reading the same constitutional history and court judgements. So how else does one explain that one group of judges went one way and the other two groups the opposite way on the issue of a present constitutional requirement for provincial consent to basic amendments? How else does one explain that the same fact of history or jurisprudence is the "usual thing" to one person, but "anomalous" to another person? To carry the point a little further, what accumulation and selection of historical facts provides evidence of a dominant type or pattern for Canadian federalism?[20]

We come now to the third basic question or theme concerning which all the judges recognized that a response was necessary: What is the proper function and authority of the traditional superior courts, especially the Supreme Court of Canada, as guardians of compliance with the constitution? Whether basic constitutional law is defined narrowly as by Majority I, or more broadly as by Minority I, all the judges in the case presumably agreed that the Supreme Court had final authority to declare, define and enforce the law according to whatever a majority of the court found to be the law in any given case. Since 1867, to go no further back, it has been accepted that the superior courts do have the legal power of judicial review respecting the legal limitations on the powers of provincial Legislatures and the Parliament of Canada that obtain, for example, by virtue of the BNA Act. But there is no specific text that literally spells this out in any formal fundamental legal document. I believe the power to be legal, and no doubt it could be implied from formal sources *if full context historical interpretation were used,* as it was in the case under discussion by Justices Martland and Ritchie in Minority Judgement I. Or one can say that custom and usage for such judicial review have so long been consistently and widely accepted that they have crystallized into law. I suggest that these two ways of putting it come to the same thing. Either way, something legal has been *added* to what could be derived only by direct literal interpretation of what is contained in formal documentary sources.

Be that as it may, the open differences between the judges on the power of judicial review relate to the justiciability of established conventions, accepting the sharp dichotomy between law as narrowly defined by Majority I and convention as defined by Majority II. Chief Justice Laskin and Justices Estey and McIntyre doubted that established conventions were justiciable at all, and they only addressed themselves to the existence and terms of a relevant convention because they were, so to speak, pressured into doing so by Majority II, who held that conventional issues were justiciable, except for judicial enforcement measures. The six judges of Majority II found that the Court had both the power and the duty to look for relevant constitutional conventions, and if they found one to be established by the Jennings tests, to declare it authoritatively and to define its terms. They admitted they could do nothing to enforce compliance if the political actors would not willingly comply. Nevertheless, this goes a long way beyond the preferred position of Chief Justice Laskin and Justices Estey and McIntyre that conventions were not justiciable at all. So, by a majority of six to three, we have a precedent that serious allegations concerning established constitutional conventions are justiciable to the extent explained.

As a final observation on such justiciability, I suggest that the non-enforceability of conventions by the court is of only marginal importance, at least in most situations. The power authoritatively to identify and declare the terms of established constitutional conventions will usually be sufficient to exact voluntary compliance from the political actors. At the end of the day, if the prestige of the Supreme Court of Canada and the legitimacy of its power of judicial review in our federal country are widely accepted by the official political actors and by the people at large, the judicial declaration will induce willing compliance. If there is no such official and general acceptance of the role of the court, what effective enforcement measures would be possible anyway? Fortunately, it appears that we do have this kind of acceptance in Canada. Is this not what explains in large part the Accord of November 1981?

More specifically, I am asserting that it was the terms of Majority Judgement II by Justices Martland, Ritchie, Dickson, Beetz, Chouinard and Lamer that impelled the Canadian political actors to accomplish the political agreement on constitutional issues. In conclusion then, we should look in more detail at what these judges said.

A summary of their position can be given in six points: (1) The sum total of rules and principles making up the Constitution of Canada fall into two parts: "Constitutional conventions plus constitutional law equal the total constitution of the country." (2) Constitutional law consists of statutes, including relevant British statutes such as the BNA Act, and common-law rules. The parentage of the latter is that they have been originated by the courts as judge-made law. The courts decide issues arising in these areas and make appropriate enforcing orders. (3) Constitutional conventions are rules or principles of the constitution that govern the conduct of the public affairs of the country. They evolved through custom, usage and precedent developed by important political leaders in office, and were accepted by the electorate over the years. Such conventions have never been enforced by the courts and cannot be. Nevertheless, in appropriate cases the courts may authoritatively declare that a particular convention has been established and likewise declare what its terms are. This reference case, the group of six says, is one of those appropriate occasions. (4) Established conventions are full-fledged obligatory rules of the constitution. They are binding and ought to be obeyed by all concerned, even though there are no specific judicial processes available to enforce them. (5) Conventional constitutional rules are frequently of very great importance. Often their purpose is to limit the use of legal powers and discretions which are very wide or extensive. In spite of the letter of the law, conventions prescribe that such legal powers should be used only in a certain limited manner, if at all. To a vital degree, democracy itself in our country rests on conventions—in this case the conventions of responsible government. For example, in law, the Queen is the all-powerful head of state. By convention she can only exercise those powers according to the advice of ministers who have the confidence of the majority of the members of the popularly elected House of the parliamentary body concerned. Likewise, in the vital realm of basic constitutional amendment, Canadian federalism itself rests upon, and is defined by, the convention for provincial consent in addition to the consent of the Parliament of Canada. (6) Legally, the Parliament of Canada can pass any Resolution it pleases on any subject whatever and address it to any person in the world. But as a matter of constitutional convention, it would clearly be unconstitutional for it to pass a joint address intended to procure amendments from the British Parliament "directly affecting federal-provincial relationships without prior consultation and agreement with the provinces."

The six judges in Majority II dealt also with the quantification of provincial consent called for by the terms of the convention just quoted. They said the unanimous consent of all the provinces was not required, and then continued:

> It would not be appropriate for the Court to devise in the abstract a specific formula which would indicate in positive terms what measure of provincial agreement is required for the convention to be complied with. Conventions by their nature develop in the political field and it will be for the political actors, not this Court, to determine the degree of provincial consent required.
>
> It is sufficient for the Court *to decide that at least a substantial measure of provincial consent is required* and to decide further whether the situation before the Court meets with this requirement. The situation is one where Ontario and New Brunswick agree with the proposed amendments, whereas the eight other provinces oppose it. By no conceivable standard could this situation be thought to pass muster. It clearly does not disclose a sufficient measure of provincial agreement.[21]

This substitution of a substantial measure of consent as the requirement, rather than unanimous provincial consent, was an essential element of the decision of Majority II impelling the political actors to reach the federal-provincial political Accord of November 1981.[22]

Finally, by way of overview, I wish to say two things. First, fundamental theoretical issues about the proper definition of law have been around for a long time, and they will continue to occur in our constitutional jurisprudence. I do not think the sharp dichotomy between law, narrowly defined, and established conventions—a dichotomy favoured by seven of the nine judges in the case under discussion—will last very long. Its historical legitimacy is doubtful, and even the seven judges of Majority I admit that custom and usage do make international law. Nevertheless, it must be conceded that this sharp dichotomy is standard English constitutional doctrine. What many forget is that it developed in England to meet the needs of a unitary state. Secondly, the major contrasting views of the nature of Canadian federalism discussed earlier have been with us for 114 years, and the tension between them will continue as an influence, one way or another, in our constitutional jurisprudence. There is much more to be said on both these matters, but it cannot be said here.

What should be said here is a word or two in praise of the Supreme Court of Canada. All nine judges identified the three fundamental theoretical issues that had to be faced as a matter of constitutional jurisprudence. They differed in critical ways on the right answers concerning those issues, but when they discovered in their private conference room that this was so, they then grouped themselves very effectively into two majorities and two minorities. The resulting four judgements explored the basic themes thoroughly from all angles with great professional skill and distinguished scholarship. Choices had to be made, and they were made. The judges faced the music, so to speak, and Majority Judgement II on convention emerged. I think authoritative judicial review is alive and well and living in Canada.

Notes

1. *Reference Re Amendment of the Constitution of Canada* (1981), 117 D.L.R. (3d) 1 (Man. C.A.); *Reference re Amendment of the Constitution of Canada (No. 2)* (1981), 118 D.L.R. (3d) 1 (Nfld. C.A.); *Reference re Amendment of the Constitution of Canada (No. 3)* (1981), 120 D.L.R. (3d) 385 (Que. C.A.).
2. *Reference Re Amendment of the Constitution of Canada (Nos. 1, 2 and 3)* (1981) 125 D.L.R. 1.
3. *Attorney General for Ontario v. Attorney General for Canada*, [1947] A.C. 127. See also Lederman, "Amendment and Patriation" (1981), 19 *Alberta Law Review* 372.
4. Constitution Act, 1982, s. 58.
5. *Re Attorney General of Quebec and Attorney General of Canada* (1982), 134 D.L.R. (3d) 719.
6. Canada, Department of Justice, *The Amendment of the Constitution of Canada* (Ottawa: Queen's Printer, 1965), p. 15.
7. *Reference re Amendment of the Constitution of Canada (Nos. 1, 2 and 3), loc. cit.*, p. 12.
8. *Ibid.*, p. 49.
9. *Ibid.*, p. 79.
10. *Ibid.*, p. 107.
11. *Ibid.*, p. 29.
12. *Ibid.*, p. 47.
13. [1930] A.C. 124 at 136 (P.C.).
14. *Reference re Amendment of the Constitution of Canada (Nos. 1, 2 and 3), loc. cit.*, pp. 73, 78-79.
15. *The Law and the Constitution*, Fifth ed. (London: University of London Press, 1959), p. 136.
16. The British North America Act, 1867 U.K., c. 3, s. 91.
17. *Ibid.*, s. 92(10).
18. *Reference re Amendment of the Constitution of Canada (Nos. 1, 2 and 3), loc. cit.*, pp. 125-26. The judges forming Minority II said: "The *B.N.A. Act* has not created a perfect or ideal federal State. Its provisions have accorded a measure of paramountcy to the federal Parliament. Certainly this has been done in a more marked degree in Canada than in many other federal States. For example, one need only look to the power of reservation and disallowance of provincial enactments; the power to declare works in a Province to be for the benefit of all Canada and to place them under federal regulatory control; the wide powers to legislate generally for the peace, order and good government of Canada as a whole; the power to enact the criminal law of the entire country; the power to create and admit Provinces out of existing territories and, as well, the para-

mountcy accorded federal legislation. It is this special nature of Canadian federalism which deprives the federalism argument described above of its force. This is particularly true when it involves the final settlement of Canadian constitutional affairs with an external government, the federal authority being the sole conduit for communication between Canada and the Sovereign and Canada alone having the power to deal in external matters. We therefore reject the argument that the preservation of the principles of Canadian federalism requires the recognition of the convention asserted before us."

19. See *Reference re Anti-Inflation Act*, [1976] 2 S.C.R. 373.

20. Between January 30, 1981 and January 18, 1982, the all-party Foreign Affairs Committee of the British House of Commons (the Kershaw committee) published three unanimous reports on the British North America Acts and the constitutional position in relation to their amendment by the British Parliament. As a matter of constitutional convention binding the British Parliament, the committee, guided by the research assistance and testimony of outstanding British constitutional experts, found in effect that Canada followed the classic federal model. Hence they said that the British Parliament should respond only to "the clearly expressed wishes of Canada as a federally structured whole." See United Kingdom, Parliament, House of Commons, Foreign Affairs Committee, *The British North America Acts: The Role of Parliament*, First Report, January 30, 1981; Second Report, April 15, 1981; Third Report, January 18, 1982.

21. *Reference re Amendment of the Constitution of Canada (Nos. 1, 2 and 3), loc. cit.*, p. 103 [emphasis added].

22. Substantial consent rather than unanimity had not been argued before the provincial Courts of Appeal. However, it was carefully put to the Supreme Court of Canada in late April 1981 by counsel for the province of Saskatchewan in both written and oral argument. (The province of Saskatchewan had intervened against the Trudeau government's unilateralism only at the Supreme Court level.) No other province made this argument. It may well be, however, that the judges of Majority II already had the point in mind. The Foreign Affairs Committee of the British House of Commons (the Kershaw committee) in their First Report published on January 30, 1981 had concluded, for purposes of advising the British Parliament of its constitutional position, that some substantial measure of provincial consent rather than unanimity was what constitutional convention required, at least so far as the British Parliament was concerned. This report and the two that soon followed are very distinguished documents, fully researched and thoroughly argued. Obviously, the reports owe much to the guidance of leading British experts in constitutional matters who either were part of the staff of the committee or gave testimony to it. I do not believe that the First Report was formally brought to the attention of the Supreme Court of Canada by counsel, but I strongly suspect that the judges were familiar with it anyway.

Chapter 10/Legality, Legitimacy and the Supreme Court*
Gil Rémillard

By declaring the federal government's constitutional Resolution legal but unconstitutional in the conventional sense, the Supreme Court of Canada introduced for the first time in Canadian law the distinction between legality and constitutionality. This distinction is not new in itself; it is a potential part of any judicial system. But a strict link must exist between the politico-socio-economic implication of the exercise of power and its theoretical scope. Nonetheless, the temptation is very much present in any judicial system to draw an arbitrary line between the theory of law and its practice in relation to the exercise of power.

The Supreme Court's recent constitutional decisions confront us with a difficult situation; the possible consequences of this new perception of legality and legitimacy for the evolution of our constitutional law cannot be stressed too strongly. The purpose of this essay is to situate the concepts of legality and legitimacy in this new perspective and to elucidate their possible consequences with respect to the evolution of Canadian constitutional law.

Legality
The concept of legality has been frequently defined in judicial literature. Essentially, it may be said that legality is conformity with the rule of law. The English publicist, Dicey, was the first to place this "fundamental" legal concept in its true perspective. His study, written in the nineteenth century, is still relevant today, at least in its basic elements. According to Dicey, the "rule of law" is essentially based on the sovereignty of Parliament, which has law as its primordial expression. Hence, legality in English and Canadian law means sanctioning the supremacy of law. No one is above the law; it applies to ordinary citizens just as it does to all the constituent parts of the state.

In its judgement on the federal government's constitutional Resolution, the Supreme Court noted:

> The "rule of law" is a highly textured expression, importing many things which are beyond the need of these reasons to explore but conveying, for example, a sense of orderliness, of subjection to known legal rules and of executive accountability to legal authority.[1]

This definition of the rule of law is probably the most comprehensive to be found in our jurisprudence. It briefly but clearly articulates the

---

*Translated from the French by Terrance Hughes.

concept of legality, both in relation to the state and subjects of the law. Orderliness, discipline and authority are part of our democracy and are made concrete, in a way, by the rule of law. They are acceptable insofar as they refer to the desire of a society to share a common goal and to ensure that the power which it has institutionalized through a constitution is exercised in compliance with its wishes.

The conformity of the exercise of power with the constitution is the first guarantee a citizen has against arbitrariness,[2] and of the respect of democracy. Power is natural. It is found not only in human societies, but among animals, or even plants. Indeed, all living things are naturally inclined, whether consciously or unconsciously, first to survive, then to improve their conditions of existence.

The quest for survival and growth inevitably creates conflicts in which there is a loser and a winner, whose power will increase as a result.[3] The search for and exercise of power are, in this way, linked to the instinct of all living things. The instinctive notion of power includes an equally instinctive corollary: the abuse of power, the utilization of power which is both disproportionate to the needs of the person exercising it and detrimental to anyone subjected to it. Thus all living beings are instinctively inclined not only to exercise their power but, as Montesquieu stated so aptly in 1748 in his *Esprit des lois,* to amplify it, and even possibly to misuse it.

Among human beings, the notion of power must, in addition to its instinctive aspect, be conceived according to the analytic possibilities that their reason gives them. Man should thus consider power in an organized fashion on the basis of a more or less conscious social perception. He and others like him will form a society identified with a common good, which will be attained by a social order—a moral and material discipline that will foster the cohesiveness necessary for any collective action.

A society forms according to social goals corresponding to a common good, an improved condition one seeks through community life. The common good cannot be defined once and for all; it will be what society decides it will be during the course of its evolution. However, the common good will encompass the same search for a social order and a justice corresponding to social reality in any free, democratic society. The social order will be based on the fact that by consenting to live in society, man implicitly agrees to renounce absolute individual liberty in favour of a certain social autonomy based on the respect of other individuals living with him in society, and respect of the common good.

Community life necessarily implies notions of order, discipline and sanction. By agreeing to live in society, man must accept the idea of social order. However, it must then be asked what social order and what rules of discipline are acceptable. It is for this reason that a socio-politico-economic reality must correspond to this notion of social order. It is then that the concept of justice takes on its full meaning, and the necessity of substituting the idea of law for that of social order appears, for it is the role of justice to ensure that the idea of social order and the socio-politico-economic reality of that order conform.

Justice, the *suum cuique tribuere* of the ancients, acts in a way as a barrier against the arbitrary, the abusive exercise of power in relation to the common good. In this regard, one cannot deny justice a definite political implication which confirms and protects the bonds of interdependence that the members of a society have accepted. Aristotle did not hesitate to link justice and law; according to the philosopher, "there is a political justice which qualifies any action likely to contribute to the establishment or the maintenance of the happiness of the political community."[4] Thus, justice is an integral part of the common good and of the popular consensus on which it must rest.

The idea of law derives from the social order and justice, which the common good underlies. It will formalize both the social aspirations of a society and the conditions in which power is exercised. Its first formulation will be found in the constitution.[5] From the notion of law glimpsed in the constitution will appear the legality of the concrete achievements both of the state and subjects of the law. Thus, it is the "subjection to known legal rules" that guarantees respect for the social idea which, in our society, is founded on the democratic principle.

This is what Jean-Jacques Rousseau called the social contract.[6] Although this expression may be somewhat naive, it remains basically true. If, as Rousseau has written, the idea of justice is innate in man, it is nonetheless more by necessity than by nature. When such necessity disappears, in the context of the exercise of power, for example, it may well be that man is less interested in the idea of justice and the democracy that must result from it. However, as Jennings has so aptly written, the veritable source of democracy and the liberty which it underlies are not laws or institutions, but the spirit of liberty which may be found in a people.[7] In a way, the Supreme Court returns to this idea when it states in its judgement on the constitution:

> the constitutional value which is the pivot of the conventions stated above and relating to responsible government is the democratic principle: the powers of the State must be exercised in accordance with the wishes of the electorate.[8]

This idea in itself is certainly not new. For as long as the concept of democracy has existed, it has been associated with the will of the governed, and therefore with the idea of liberty. However, this is the first time that the democratic principle has been so clearly stated in a Canadian legal decision. It is also the first time that it has been situated not exclusively in relation to the sovereign authority of Parliament or the state, but directly in relation to the people.[9] This new approach to the notion of democracy, which was more or less hidden until now under the rule of the "sovereignty of Parliament," rests on a concept which hitherto has been little discussed in our constitutional law: legitimacy.

Legitimacy

The relation of power to the idea of law, which is found in any democratic community, is the first condition of popular consensus. This power, both in terms of its existence and its exercise, must first of all be granted, thus making it not only legal, but above all legitimate.

Formal legitimacy and material legitimacy: Legitimacy is a complex concept which has been, and often still is used in a demagogic manner. Following the Supreme Court's September 28, 1981 decision respecting the constitution, one might argue that an authority acts legitimately when it is qualified to do so. It is usually accepted that the first criterion for this qualification resides essentially in the convergence of the aspirations of a society and the objectives of power in relation to the common good. Thus there must be a close relation between legality and legitimacy, as both concepts are postulates of the common good and its democratic foundation. When such a congruence does not exist, there is a conflict between legality and legitimacy, between the theory of law and its practice with respect to the exercise of power. Legality defines the limits of power; legitimacy defines the limits of its exercise. The Supreme Court judgement offers an eloquent example of this duality, indeed of the gulf that may exist between the rule of law and the exercise of power.

On the one hand, the Supreme Court confirms the essential role of constitutional conventions in relation to the respecting of legitimacy; on the other hand, it confines itself to a doctrinal conception of law which ignores them, basing itself exclusively on positive law—legislative rules and of common law. The consequences of such a distinction between the theory and the practice of law may be very serious in the evolution of our constitutional law. Any exercise of the state's power must be subordinate to its respect of a higher rule. If this rule is not complied with, the exercise of power becomes illegitimate, and its legal value is cancelled. As in any democratic society, the higher rule in our law is the constitution, which the Supreme Court of Canada defines by the equation: "... constitutional conventions plus constitutional law equal the total Constitution of the country."[10] However, the Supreme Court divides this constitution into two parts: (a) constitutional law, which "... designates the parts of the Canadian Constitution which are composed of legislative rules and common law rules;" and (b) constitutional conventions such as Dicey defined them in 1885 in the first edition of *Law of the Constitution*, whose principal object is "... to ensure that the legal framework of the

Constitution will be operated in accordance with the prevailing constitutional values or principles of the period."[11]

This division of the higher rule (the constitution) into law and practice leads the Supreme Court to conclude, following the jurisprudential and doctrinal tradition of the United Kingdom, that only law can be sanctioned by the courts, given that conventions exist only in relation to political, not legal, precedents. In doing so, for the first time in our constitutional history the court expressly erects an impenetrable barrier between law and its practice, between legality and legitimacy.

This distinction between two concepts so fundamental in any society claiming to be democratic calls into question the celebrated problem of the foundation of the state's authority, which has been discussed since the time of Aristotle. A constitution is the expression of a nation's intention to define the exercise of power in relation to the rule of law. One of the first consequences of the constitution is that governors are made servants of the law. It is the constitution which determines the source, nature, conditions, purposes and limits of their power. According to the French constitutionalist, Georges Burdeau,

> the governors' authority derives from the constitutional regularity of their investiture; its nature is that defined by the type of regime adopted by the constitution; its purposes are those prescribed by the notion of law which it implicitly recognizes; its limits result from the organization of their function within the constitution."[12]

In fact, these answers are not answers at all. They are only the channel markers of a formal legitimacy based essentially on the constitution. It is to this legitimacy that the Supreme Court of Canada initially refers when it declares the federal patriation resolution unconstitutional because it is at odds with constitutional conventions.

The Supreme Court, having established that conventions ". . . are not administered by the courts," because they have political, not legal, origins, asks itself if it must reply all the same to the second question put to it by the provinces, whether it should determine if there exists a convention requiring the Canadian Parliament to proceed only with the assent of the provinces in amending an element of the constitution affecting federal-provincial relationships. The court, which is the ultimate interpreter of Canada's constitution, concluded that it must determine if a convention exists even if its sanction does not come under its jurisdiction, because "question 2 is not confined to an issue of pure legality but it has to do with a fundamental issue of constitutionality and legitimacy." [13] The court's reasoning could not be clearer: (a) conventions ". . . form an integral part of the constitution and the constitutional regime . . ." and are ". . . directly concerned with a fundamental point of constitutionality and legitimacy;" (b) the federal government's Resolution goes against the constitutional convention which obliges the Canadian Parliament to proceed with an appreciable degree of agreement from the provinces in order to amend the aspects of the constitution affecting federal-provincial relationships; (c) "... the passing of this Resolution without such agreement would be unconstitutional in the conventional sense"[14] and consequently, illegitimate.

However, the court subsequently completed this formal conception of legitimacy based exclusively on the constitution with a more material approach which referred to the people, the first component of any democracy. The exercise of power must not only be carried out in compliance with the constitution, comprising positive law and conventions, but it must also comply with the wishes of the electorate.[15]

Thus we must conclude that the Supreme Court considers legitimacy as the exercise of power in compliance with "... the prevailing constitutional values or principles of the period" and "the wishes of the electorate." This is the best definition of legitimacy. Democracy, just like its corollary, liberty, requires legitimacy for both its formal and its material sense. This power is legitimate when it is exercised in compliance with the constitution, and when the latter responds to the wishes of the electorate. If we accept this concept of legitimacy, it must be understood that governors who impose a constitution by force cannot legitimately exercise their power, even if they comply with the constitution and the notion of law arising from it. Conforming to the law does not mean respecting legitimacy. A government is not legitimate for all time because it has been legally invested with power. On the contrary, legitimacy is a daily challenge for an authority invested with the power of the state. Of course, as much can be said of legality; however, if legitimacy and legality are relative concepts, it is obviously easier to verify legality than legitimacy.

The vast majority of legal writers agree in stating that legality can be appreciated in relation to the rules of positive law. This is the reasoning followed by the Supreme Court in its judgement respecting the patriation of the constitution. It is more difficult to delineate the fundamental norm which would guarantee respect for legitimacy. Strictly speaking, there are no objective criteria for legitimacy, which has as many forms as there are political ideas. Each political philosophy sustains a certain idea of legitimacy. For example, monarchical legitimacy is not the same as democratic legitimacy. Sometimes related to the idea of divinity, legitimacy may alternatively be considered in relation to the legislative assembly, or even to society. It is not easy to define legitimacy; it is probably best not to attempt to do so in order to avoid shackling oneself with the yoke of political ideas which may well be clear and logical, but which do not correspond to the fundamental reality of legitimacy, which is essentially the conformity of the exercise of power with the socio-politico-economic reality of a society. Instead of defining legitimacy, it would be better to situate it, as the Supreme Court has done so well in its constitutional decisions, by using both the democratic principle based on the wishes of the electorate and the constitution, including positive law and conventions, as references.

Based on this assessment of legitimacy, the Supreme Court concluded that the Trudeau government's Resolution respecting the patriation of the constitution of Canada was not legitimate because it did not conform to the constitutional conventions which are the basis of our federalism. This impeccably logical conclusion is fraught with political, if not legal consequence. The respect of conventions is not a legal but a moral issue. Acting against constitutional conventions is a question of morality, given that "this portion of constitutional law may, for the sake of distinction, be termed the 'conventions of the constitution,' or constitutional morality."[16]

By deciding that the federal government's Resolution was unconstitutional because it did not respect constitutional conventions, the Supreme Court judged it severely, qualifying it as illegitimate, if not immoral on the constitutional level. However, another cause of illegitimacy might also have been discussed by the Supreme Court if one of the questions had been oriented in that direction. Starting with the democratic principle that the exercise of power must conform with the wishes of the electorate, a fundamental question with regard to the legitimacy of the federal government's Resolution respecting patriation of the constitution would be: can the government and Parliament make fundamental changes to the constitution without an explicit mandate from the electorate to do so? This is a difficult question that challenges the very essence of our parliamentary regime and the notion of democracy underlying it.

Legitimacy and parliamentarianism: The preamble of the British North America Act situates Canada's parliamentary regime in the British tradition; therefore, it refers to the basic rules of British parliamentarianism. The history of parliamentary institutions, both in the United Kingdom and in Canada, is closely linked to the evolution of the democratic principle and to the concept of sovereignty, which served as a cornerstone in their constitutional evolution. The constitutional monarchy is a compromise which was achieved gradually. It preserves the monarch as legal holder of sovereignty in the exercise of the state's powers, while confirming through practices, customs and conventions that it is exercised by Parliament.

Thus, according to the letter of our constitution, executive power is held by the Queen, who is also the head of the armed forces. Sections 9 and 15 of the BNA Act stipulate that: "The Executive Government and Authority of and over Canada is hereby declared to continue and be vested in the Queen;" and "The Command-in-Chief of the Land and Naval Militia, and of all Naval and Military Forces, of and in Canada, is hereby declared to continue and be vested in the Queen."

However, as customs and conventions have shown, the Queen reigns but does not govern. Both on the federal and provincial levels, the head of the government is usually the leader of the political party that has won a majority of seats during a general election. The prime minister chooses his ministers, who are appointed by the Crown on his recommendation when he forms or shuffles his Cabinet. The government stays in power as long as it enjoys the confidence of the elected chamber.[17] Indeed, most of the sovereign's powers that exist by virtue of the constitution or common law are exercised on the advice of the prime minister or the Cabinet.

However, just like the vast majority of the rules of our parliamentary system, this relationship between the Crown and the government is purely conventional. Thus, the Supreme Court notes:

> But many Canadians would perhaps be surprised to learn that important parts of the Constitution of Canada, with which they are the most familiar because they are directly involved when they exercise their right to vote at federal and provincial elections, are nowhere to be found in the law of the Constitution. For instance, it is a fundamental requirement of the Constitution that if the Opposition obtains the majority at the polls, the Government must tender its resignation forthwith. But fundamental as it is, this requirement of the Constitution does not form part of the law of the Constitution.[18]

Our constitutional monarchy is, therefore, a compromise based on practices, customs and conventions whose existence depends upon the fair play of those to whom they are addressed.

The composition of the British Parliament also results from a compromise, as it consists of a first chamber (House of Commons) composed of representatives of the people, and of a second, non-elected chamber (House of Lords), representing the elite of society, such as the nobility and the bourgeoisie. Such compromises were not achieved painlessly; their evolution was influenced by various events, by politicians and sovereigns, by changes in practices, customs and constitutional conventions, always in the context of celebrated British fair play.

Canadian parliamentarianism, both on the provincial and federal levels, followed a similar course from the arrival of responsible government in the middle of the nineteenth century to the loss, in practice, of the effective powers of the Senate a little more than a century later.[19] In other words, the exercise of power belongs without a doubt, by our practices, customs and conventions, to Parliament, whence flows the fundamental principle of English and Canadian constitutional law to the effect that Parliament is sovereign and may, therefore, do as it pleases in compliance with the rule of law. However, the sovereign authority of Parliament in the English constitutional tradition comes from the Crown and not from the people, as is the case in other modern democracies. As Senator Eugene Forsey has so aptly noted: "Governments, under the British system, derive their authority not only in law but in constitutional fact, solely from the Crown and could derive it from no other source.''[20]

While the American and French Revolutions erupted in the name of equality, liberty and democracy based on the sovereignty of the people, English parliamentarianism asserted itself gradually, being limited to an institutional sovereignty. Professor Jean-Maurice Arbour has clearly described this difference in perception of the idea of democracy and sovereignty thus:

> It is an historical fact that the builders of liberal democracy first freed themselves from a power which had become despotic and arbitrary, before taking power themselves. ... The principle of the separation of powers, as well as the constitutional idea and its corollary, the control of the constitutionality of laws, then appeared to be the two ideal instruments apt to ensure a regime of liberty, at least in France and the United States. England followed a different route, but achieved the same results.[21]

The distinction is important, as the notion of sovereignty is the basic concept of any dialectics in public law. The creation of a state is contingent upon the presence of three essential elements: a people (the human element); a territory (the material element); and sovereignty (the juridical element). For a state to exist, it is essential that the people accept that its behaviour be regulated by a higher authority responsible for ensuring the respect of public interest. Sovereignty is the judicial expression of this power situated above individual interests.[22] Thus sovereignty calls upon the notion of will. Dean Duguit has elaborated on this notion:

> sovereignty is a will which, alone, is characterized by only being determined by itself. The only motive that can impel sovereign will to act is a motive which it draws from itself. A sovereign will can never be induced to act by this motive unless another will wishes it to act in such and such a way.[23]

The remarks of the French constitutionalist place him in the same school of thought as German writers, for whom sovereignty is a will which has "the competence of its competence." This is certainly the most acceptable definition of the idea of sovereignty. It is an absolute, an ultimate authority which expresses itself in a total dimension of the state's power. R. Carré de Malberg defines the notion of the state thus:

> each state *in concreto* [is] a community of men, settled in its own territory and possessing an organization which, for the group in question, results in a higher power for action, authority and coercion among its members.[24]

This sovereign authority has always given rise to numerous reflections concerning its relationship to the citizen. Jean-Jacques Rousseau vividly underscored this dilemma in his social contract when he wrote that people must "call themselves individually *citizens,* in so far as they share in the sovereign power, and *subjects,* in so far as they put themselves under the laws of the State.[25] Without discussing the absolutism which the French philosopher's reflection may engender, it still situates sovereignty very well within the society. In a way, the social contract is the expression of sovereignty in that it leads to the creation of the state's authority and the power to make laws.[26] In fact, Rousseau wrote of the social contract to establish a new legitimacy based essentially on the sovereignty of the people. "Any legitimate government is republican," he wrote. It is this principle which served as a basis for the United States constitution of 1787, and which influenced the establishment of all modern democracies.[27]

It is also important to note that the notion of the state does not really exist in English public law. The Crown personifies the state; therefore, sovereignty is invested not in the state, but in the Crown.

In English law, sovereignty belongs to the Sovereign,[28] contrary to French constitutional law, for example, in which sovereignty belongs to the people.[29] The advent of constitutional monarchy in England did not change this judicial conception of sovereignty. The speech from the throne, during which the Sovereign enumerates the government's projects while employing the expression "my government," and the Sovereign's power to convene or dissolve the Houses even if it is the prime minister's responsibility to do so are vivid examples. In the English regime, the Crown is the fountainhead of all powers, whether they be legislative, executive or judicial.[30]

Of course, the results of these two distinct perceptions of sovereignty are very similar in terms of the respect of the democratic principle. However, one difference, which may prove to be fraught with consequence, remains with respect to the difficult question of the mandate of parliamentarians. In our parliamentary regime, senators and members of Parliament have a representative mandate; contrary to the imperative mandate, once they are elected or appointed, they are responsible to no one for the carrying out of their mandate. They are not accountable for their opinions any more than they are obliged to honour their electoral promises. Professors Brun and Tremblay have noted that "having been elected, [they] represent the entire State for a certain time. In designating a representative, society divests itself of its sovereignty during this time."[31]

Members of Parliament, like those of the provincial Legislative Assemblies, are elected or appointed to legislate in the name of "peace, order and good government." This theory of the implicit power of the members of Legislative Assemblies corresponds clearly to the context of the perception of sovereignty in English law. However, we must ask ourselves if it can be envisaged in this way in relation to Canadian constitutional law. The United Kingdom does not have a written constitution. Its constitution is a collection of common-law rules, important constitutional texts and

basic laws.[32] Canada's constitution is essentially a written one; the BNA Act
of 1867 remains its cornerstone. English parliamentarians may amend their
constitution by going against or completing constitutional rules because it
does not formally exist in a written text. The constitution is created
according to the wishes of Parliament. In Canada, we have a written
constitution, or what might be called a social contract, which guarantees
order and justice.

Can it then be said that Parliament alone is able to amend this social
contract as though it were a simple law, without an explicit mandate from
the electorate to do so? If one adopts the theory of the implicit mandate,
the answer is yes. If one accepts the definition of the democratic principle
given by the Supreme Court in its judgement respecting patriation of the
constitution on September 28, 1981—the conformity of the exercise of
power with the wishes of the electorate—then the answer may be no. A
democratic government cannot pretend to act democratically by changing
the terms of the social contract of a society without the latter's express
consent. To state the contrary is to admit that there may be a very slight
difference between parliamentarianism and totalitarianism. If, in the
United Kingdom, parliamentarianism in its purest form based on absolute
sovereignty may be envisaged without endangering the democratic principle, it is because it refers to a mentality based on fair play, the implications of which are respected by virtue of an ancestral tradition which,
moreover, is part of the very mentality of a people. The Supreme Court
touched lightly on the problem when it stated that:

> The Attorney General of Canada was pushed to the extreme by being
> forced to answer affirmatively the theoretical question whether in law the
> federal Government could procure an amendment to the *British North
> America Act* that could turn Canada into a unitary state. That is not what
> the present Resolution envisages because the essential federal character of
> the country is preserved under the enactments proposed by the Resolu-
> tion.[33]

The Supreme Court does not answer the question which was put to the
Attorney General of Canada. However, the answer is obviously yes strictly
in law, as nothing prior to the patriation of the constitution prevented it
from doing so, given that Parliament, which is controlled by the government, is sovereign.

On the basis of the democratic principle defined by the Supreme Court
in its judgement on the constitution, we can conclude that the patriation of
the constitution of Canada and the constitutional amendments it includes
were made illegitimately, not only because they go against convention, but
above all, because they do not expressly comply with the wishes of the
electorate. Following the Supreme Court's decision, new discussions took
place; nine out of ten provinces reached a compromise with the federal

government. This compromise was subsequently voted on in the form of a Resolution by the Parliament of Canada, and in the form of a law by the Parliament of the United Kingdom, thus becoming constitutional law. One observation must be made about this process: at no time were the Canadian people consulted with respect to the important changes made in its constitution. Moreover, the Canadian government not only did not consult the population, either through elections or a referendum, but it also never requested a mandate from Canadians in order to make the constitutional amendments. A referendum could have been the best way to test the will of the Canadian population. According to two of the most important features of Canadian federalism, regionalism and dualism, before proceeding with patriation the results of such a referendum would have had to have been positive in the four Canadian regions: Western provinces, Maritime provinces, Ontario, Quebec.

With respect to the provinces, the situation is very similar, as no premier had a specific mandate from the electorate to accept the November 5 compromise; none of them considered it necessary to have the compromise ratified by the provincial Legislatures. The Quebec government was the only one to manifest its disagreement by having the National Assembly vote on a resolution denouncing the agreement reached by the nine other provinces following negotiations from which Quebec was absent.

As a result of the Supreme Court's judgement respecting patriation, the legality of the patriation and the constitutional amendments it contains can no longer be doubted. However, its legitimacy may be open to considerable criticism, as it is impossible to confirm that it was carried out according to the wishes of the electorate, that is, in compliance with the democratic principle which is the foundation of our society. The question of legitimacy arises especially for Quebec, whose government and National Assembly dissociated themselves from the federal-provincial compromise which led to patriation. Moreover, the Supreme Court's recent decision establishing that Quebec has never in the history of Canadian federalism had a right of veto does not completely settle the question of the 1982 Constitution Act's legitimacy.[34]

By agreeing to render an opinion on the existence of a right of veto, which is a purely political question, the Supreme Court established an important precedent in the history of Canadian jurisprudence. Neither the Judicial Committee of the Privy Council in its time, nor the Supreme Court, has ever, to the best of my knowledge, expressed an opinion on a strictly political question, dealing only with the existence of a constitutional convention. By refusing to conclude that there exists a constitutional convention which confirms Quebec's right of a veto, the Supreme Court thus indicated that patriation was carried out in accordance with convention. The question of the legitimacy of patriation in relation to the respecting of convention is therefore settled. However, it should not be concluded that the matter of the 1982 Constitution Act's legitimacy is settled once and for all in Quebec.

Indeed, only a referendum could permanently settle the question of its legitimacy. Of course, the scope of the democratic principle must not be exaggerated to the point of demanding of a government that it govern by a series of elections or referenda.[35] The democratic principle does not mean government by the people, but government for the people according to the common good and the idea of law which it has freely defined for itself. However, the amendment of the constitution cannot be considered a simple procedure of good government which, like any other legislative or administrative measure, serves as a criterion for the electorate, which may re-elect the government for a second term or choose new leaders. It is difficult to pretend that the next federal and provincial elections will be able to guarantee the legitimacy of patriation and the amendments included in it. Indeed, how can one pretend to proceed "according to the wishes of the electorate" when the voters are faced with a *fait accompli*, placed in a social, political and economic context which, in fact, leaves them no choice. Even if the Trudeau government were defeated in the next election, the patriation would still be legal. Moreover, how might one discern the public's verdict on patriation if that were only one among many issues debated during the election? A referendum would be the most appropriate means of establishing the legitimacy of the Constitution Act of 1982.

Were Quebecers to indicate through a referendum that they agreed with the Constitution Act, then the question of its legitimacy would be settled. Not only would patriation have been carried out in accordance with constitutional conventions, but also according to the wishes of the electorate. However, if Quebecers clearly indicated that they did not approve of the Act, we would then be faced with a situation which would be hard to explain according to our law and democracy: patriation would have been carried out legally but illegitimately because it was done without Quebec's consent. This would mean that Quebecers would have an illegitimate constitution.

It is obvious that such a situation is hardly tolerable in a state which considers itself democratic, as Canada does. There are four possible solutions: (1) a federal-provincial conference could be convened in order to find a compromise which would satisfy Quebec; (2) the Quebec government could call a special election on the question, requesting a clear mandate from the voters with a view to carrying out constitutional negotiations on a number of specific points; (3) Quebec voters could wait for the next federal elections, vote out the government responsible for patriation and elect one more likely to rectify the flaws in the 1982 Constitution Act. However, doing so would in no way guarantee that the Act would be amended according to their demands. It must be remembered that the unanimous consent of all the provinces and Ottawa is necessary to change the amending formula and other provisions in the Act; (4) the last solution is what Saint Thomas Aquinas prudently and wisely called disobedience to authority when power is unjust.[36] St. Thomas discusses the injustice of laws according to two criteria: those which are contrary to divine law and those which are contrary to human good. The first criterion suggests, for example, that it would be evil to be obliged to obey the law of a tyrant who established idolatry. But while this criterion was meaningful at the time of St. Thomas, it provides less clear guidance in modern societies. The second criterion is more relevant, yet there are problems here as well. We have already pointed out the great difficulty of establishing the common good in an objective fashion. This inherent subjectivity makes it very difficult to adopt St. Thomas' fundamental criterion for civil disobedience—the certainty of the grave injustice of the law.[37]

Moreover, the evolution of the democratic principle since the time of St. Thomas has appreciably altered the context in which civil disobedience is applicable. As Esmein has stated, ". . . the first duty of a citizen is to respect the laws of his country, especially in a free country where there is always the hope of overcoming political opinion in order to obtain the abrogation or the modification of laws which offend you."[38] In the same vein, Georges Del Vecchio adds that ". . . anyone who rashly breaks the law disturbs the very bases of civic life, and strikes a blow at the conditions on which the individual's respectability depends."[39]

Therefore, the possibility of engaging in civil disobedience must be considered very carefully. One of the few cases which might be considered in our democratic system would be during the actual usurpation of power. In its decision respecting the constitution, the Supreme Court gives an interesting example of this:

> Another example of the conflict between law and convention is provided by a fundamental convention already stated above: if after a general election where the Opposition obtained the majority at the polls the Government refused to resign and clung to office, it would thereby commit a fundamental breach of conventions, one so serious indeed that it could be regarded as tantamount to a *coup d'état*. The remedy in this case would lie with the Governor General or the Lieutenant-Governor as the case might be who would be justified in dismissing the Ministry and in calling on the Opposition to form the Government. But should the Crown be slow in taking this course, there is nothing the courts could do about it except at the risk of creating a state of legal discontinuity, that is a form of revolution.[40]

Without explicitly mentioning the possibility of civil disobedience in such an instance, the Court nonetheless leaves this option open by evoking the revolutionary situation which would be created by such a usurpation of power. It is also interesting to note that the ultimate interpreter of the constitution of Canada seems to consider the Governor-General and the

Lieutenant-Governors the guardians of legitimacy through the respect of convention, at least in this case. Thus, civil disobedience would hardly be acceptable with respect to the legitimacy of the patriation, except if there were a flagrant usurpation of power.

The question of the legitimacy of the patriation will probably never really be discussed. We are faced with a *fait accompli*, and its conformity with the wishes of the electorate can no longer be verified. The people's consent should have been requested before the address was sent to Westminster.

Canada's leaders in 1981 made the same mistake as Sir John A. Macdonald and Sir Georges-Étienne Cartier who, in 1865, called upon the sovereignty of Parliament in order to avoid consulting the people on the 72 Resolutions, which were the foundation of the British North America Act of 1867. This period was marked by the conflict between ultramontanism and liberalism. According to the first ideology, sovereignty belongs to God, who delegates it to a human authority who employs it under the surveillance of the church. The second is based on the notion that sovereignty resides in the people, who, within the limits of the constitution, entrust its application to a political authority. Thus the position of the Fathers of Confederation was in keeping with the logic of the ultramontanism of the time. However, how can one still defend such a position in the context of today's democracy?

Beyond these considerations, which are both judicial and political in character, it seems urgent that we ask ourselves what meaning we are to give to our parliamentarianism in light of the Supreme Court's judgement. From an open power whose imperatives are dictated by the popular will, we are rapidly evolving toward a closed power, which is subservient to the authorities that be. The exercise of the state's power in a parliamentary regime must be carried out through a series of checks and balances which limit the risks of the abuse of power. This fundamental brake on the temptation to resort to totalitarianism, which is ever-present in a parliamentary regime, can only be effectively applied insofar as it is accepted that man does not serve institutions, but that institutions serve man. As the constitutionalist Georges Burdeau has aptly stated, "closed power shuts itself like armour on the absolutism of its truth."[41]

Conclusion

The Supreme Court's judgement respecting patriation of the constitution is unquestionably the most important judicial decision ever rendered in the history of Canadian constitutional law. Its importance with respect to the future orientation of our law, parliamentarianism and federalism cannot be overestimated.[42]

It was obvious since the case was heard in April 1981 that the court was divided between the defenders of the legalistic argument and the supporters of the evolutionary thesis. According to the former, a convention cannot have a legal value; the latter claim that the constitutional compromise in relation to the intentions of the Fathers of Confederation gives these conventions the force of law through what has been called the process of crystallization. The Court was confronted with complex considerations which forced it to play the role of impartial referee with respect both to the population and to Parliament and the legislators. As Robert Décary has pointed out, this meant "that it could not adopt the federal government's point of view unanimously and without the slightest criticism. . . ."[43] The decision was made in relation to these judicial and political contingencies; in this respect, it is essentially a compromise which contains all the elements of King Solomon's judgement.

The court settled the question in favour of the legalistic argument, distinguishing for the first time in the history of Canadian constitutional law between legality and constitutionality. However, the court was not content just to establish this distinction. On the contrary, it elaborated at some length its conception of constitutional conventions and their role in relation to the respect of the principle of Canadian federalism. As is the case with many compromises, it is difficult to see the logic of such a procedure.[44] On the one hand, the court firmly established that constitutional conventions are outside its jurisdiction; on the other, it established the existence of such conventions, then strongly denounced the failure of the government's Resolution on patriation to respect them. Does this mean that the part of the judgement concerning the existence of a convention (the answer to question 2), is *obiter dictum*? Logically, one might think so. In this respect, Professor Peter Russell has written that "convention is *entirely* political and in no sense legal, in strict logic the Court should not have answered the question about the content of convention."[45]

It does seem that the Supreme Court clearly understood that by shackling itself with a strictly judicial yoke, it risked ignoring reality. That is why the court could not avoid analyzing this reality, even though it qualified it as political. Under the circumstances, this was a wise thing to do. Rarely, if at all, in the history of Canadian federalism has the court so directly condemned a political action. By creating this precedent, the court facilitated a return to the negotiating table and the compromise which led to the 1982 constitutional law, although without Quebec's participation.

If this decision may be considered wise on a political level, it appears that we must moderate our viewpoint in legal terms. One can only deplore the fact that the court referred so arbitrarily to the jurisprudence of the United Kingdom and refused to make the necessary allowances in order to apply it to our federal regime, based essentially on the shared exercise of state sovereignty. As dissenting judges Martland and Ritchie clearly pointed out, the federal Parliament does not have complete control over Canadian sovereignty; it is only with considerable reservation that one may refer to the writers who have discussed Westminster's powers and privileges.[46]

Moreover, in some respects the Supreme Court's decision contradicts a number of very important decisions made by the Judicial Committee of the Privy Council, which established the federalist foundations of the BNA Act of 1867, and recent decisions made by the court itself. By considering theories on the 1867 pact as "theories belonging to the realm of politics, to the study of political sciences," the Court is going against its unanimous judgements in the Senate case,[47] and the Blaikie[48] and Forest cases.[49]

In these various cases, the court referred extensively to the intentions of the Fathers of Confederation. It is difficult to understand the court's reluctance to do so in the case of patriation, as it recognizes that the theories of the pact might be discussed when "they could have some peripheral relevance to actual provisions of the *British North America Act* and its interpretation and application."[50] The case of patriation certainly called into question the interpretation that might be given to sections 92(1) and 91(1) of the BNA Act respecting the powers of the two levels of government to amend their own constitution, which occurred in the Senate case, and the Blaikie and Forest cases. In an historical context, section 91(1) might have added an interesting dimension to the question, beginning with the principle that it was an amendment and, consequently, that the Fathers of Confederation did not give the Canadian Parliament the power to amend the Canadian constitution, then elaborating on the definition of "Canadian constitution." On the last point, the court's decision thus conflicts with the Senate case, in which the Supreme Court decided that the Canadian constitution "does not mean the whole of the *British North America Act*, but means the constitution of the federal government, as distinct from the provincial governments."[51] With this fundamental decision, the court went against that of Chief Justice Laskin in the Jones case,[52] which at least gave the impression that "'the Constitution of Canada' . . . certainly includes the *British North America Act*, 1867 and its amendments."

The ambiguities of the Supreme Court's judgement are no longer important, as section 52 of the 1982 Constitution Act clearly stipulates what the constitution of Canada is. The procedure for amending the constitution in Part V clarifies the possible scope of section 91(1), now abolished, and that of section 92(1). However, one ambiguity remains, and its importance cannot be overestimated in relation to the implications of the duality the court has created by distinguishing between constitutionality in the legal sense and constitutionality in the conventional sense. This distinction, which can bring legality and legitimacy into conflict, leads us to ask a question which may well have enormous consequences: in our democratic regime, how can we accept that a law be legal but illegitimate, that is, immoral in political terms? By employing objective elements for verifying legitimacy, such as the respect of constitutional conventions and the wishes of the electorate, the Supreme Court's judgement opens the door to important political conflicts which it can hardly refuse to arbitrate. The question of Quebec's veto is the first example. This brings to mind the following poem of the late constitutionalist of Laval University, Jean-Charles Bonenfant, written in 1977:[53]

> Dans leur coquet édifice de la rue Wellington,
> les juges de la Cour suprême
> Peuvent briller par leur science et leur dialectique,
> mais quand même
> Du gouvernement par de bon juges,
> délivrez-nous Seigneur!
> Pour cela donnez le goût d'agir et l'esprit
> de compromis aux législateurs
> Faites surtout qu'ils modernisent et utilisent
> les institutions!
> Ce sera peut-être un des moyens de garder
> le Québec dans la Fédération.*

---

*In their cozy building on Wellington Street, / the Supreme Court justices / May shine through their knowledge and dialectics, / All the same, / God save us from government / by good judges! / Give the legislators the will to act / and a spirit of compromise / Above all, make them modernize and utilize / our institutions! / This will perhaps be one way of keeping / Quebec in Confederation. /

Notes

1. *Reference re Amendment of the Constitution of Canada (Nos. 1, 2 and 3)* (1981), 125 D.L.R. (3d) 1 at p. 46.
2. In the nineteenth century, Dicey defined the arbitrary especially in relation to the discretionary, which he limited to a very rigid framework for action. However, the principles he enunciated still apply: (1) the exercise of a discretionary power must be derived from the law; (2) the field in which it is exercised must be limited; (3) it must be sufficiently advertised so that the ordinary individual is not taken by surprise.
3. For a discussion of the preservation instinct as a guide for social ideas, see Mihaïl Manoïlesco, *Le siècle du corporatisme* (Paris: Librairie Félix Alcan, 1938), p. 22.
4. Quoted in J. Darbeltay, *L'objectivité du droit*, Mélanges J. Dabin, 1963, p. 61.
5. Louis Le Fur wrote: "... the idea of law finds its most dynamic expression in the political forces which tend to carry it out." *La théorie du droit naturel depuis le XVIIe siècle et la doctrine moderne* (Paris: Hachette, 1928), p. 266.
6. Jean-Jacques Rousseau, *The Social Contract* (tr. by Maurice Cranston) (Harmondsworth: Penguin Books, 1981).
7. W.I. Jennings, *The British Constitution*, Fifth ed., (Cambridge: Cambridge University Press, 1966), p. 203.
8. *Reference re Amendment of the Constitution of Canada (Nos. 1, 2 and 3), loc. cit.*, p. 84.
9. In *Attorney General of Nova Scotia v. Attorney General of Canada*, [1951] S.C.R. 31 at p. 34, Chief Justice Rinfret wrote: "The constitution of Canada does not belong either to Parliament, or to the Legislatures; it belongs to the country. . . ."
10. *Reference re Amendment of the Constitution of Canada (Nos. 1, 2 and 3), loc. cit.*, p. 87.
11. *Ibid.*, p. 84.
12. Georges Burdeau, *Traité de science politique*, (Paris: Librairie générale de droit et de jurisprudence, 1967), tome IV, p. 144.
13. *Reference re Amendment of the Constitution of Canada (Nos. 1, 2 and 3), loc. cit.*, p. 88.
14. *Ibid.*, p. 107.
15. *Ibid.*, p. 84.
16. A.V. Dicey, *Introduction to the Study of the Law of the Constitution*, Tenth ed. (London: Macmillan and Co., 1961), p. 24.
17. The provincial Legislatures do not have a second chamber. A vote of non-confidence in the federal Senate does not, in itself, have any effect on the government. Obviously, when a bill is defeated in the Senate the government is not defeated, but the legislation cannot be passed.
18. *Reference re Amendment of the Constitution of Canada (Nos. 1, 2 and 3), loc. cit.*, p. 82.
19. See Henri Brun, *La formation des institutions parlementaires québécoises 1791–1838* (Québec: les Presses de l'Université Laval, 1970).
20. Eugene Forsey, "The Crown and the Cabinet: a note on Mr. Ilsley's Statement" (1945), 25 *Canadian Bar Review* p. 187.
21. Jean-Maurice Arbour, "Axiomatique constitutionelle et pratique politique: un décalage troublant" (1979), 20 *Cahiers de droit* 113 at p. 117.

22. See Paul Isoart, "Souveraineté italique et relations internationales," in *La souveraineté au XXe siècle* (Paris: Armand Colin, 1971), p. 14.
23. Léon Duguit, *Souveraineté et Liberté* (Paris: Librairie Félix Alcan, 1922), p. 75.
24. R. Carré de Malberg, *Contribution à la théorie générale de l'État* (Paris: Lib. du recueil Sirey, 1920, 1963), tome I, p. 7.
25. *Op. cit.*, Book I, chapter 6, p. 62.
26. It is not our intention to pursue the analysis of this very interesting passage from Rousseau's works. In doing so, it would be necessary to discuss the divergence between the German doctrine, which establishes the absolute power of the state, and the classic French thesis, which merges the state's power and national sovereignty. Professor Burdeau has opted for " . . . the existence of a state power resting directly on the idea of law embodied by Power instituted in the State." *Op. cit.*, tome II, 2e édition, p. 321.
27. Some thirty years later, the French revolutionaries benefited from it in their own way.
28. See A.V. Dicey, *Introduction to the Study of the Law of the Constitution*, ninth ed. (London: Macmillan and Co., 1939), p. 59.
29. Section 3 of the current French constitution states that "national sovereignty belongs to the people, who exercise it through their representatives and through referendums."
30. Professor Dawson defines the Crown as "that institution which is possessed of the sum total of executive rights and powers, exercised by the sovereign, by the individual or collective action of his or her ministers, or by subordinate officials." R.M. Dawson, *The Government of Canada*, 4th ed. Rev. by Norman Ward (Toronto: University of Toronto Press, 1963), p. 156. According to other writers, the Crown is the fountainhead of all power, and the government derives its authority from the Crown. In *Institutions politiques et droit constitutionnel*, 7e éd. (Paris: P.U.F., 1963), p. 283, Maurice Duverger states that the Crown is a group of powers. An abundant jurisprudence associates the Crown with the government. See *McArthur v. Le Roy* (1943), R.C. de l'E. 77; *Wardle v. Manitoba Farm Loan Association*, [1953] 9 W.W.R. 529; *City of Quebec v. The Queen* (1894), 24 S.C.R. 420; *Formea Chemicals Ltd. v. Polymer Corporation Ltd.*, [1967] 1 O.R. 546; *Demers v. R.*, (1898), 7 B.R. 433; *Municipal Council of Sydney v. The Commonwealth* (1904), 1 C.L.R. 208; *The Commonwealth v. State of New South Wales* (1906), 3 C.L.R. 818.
31. Henri Brun and Guy Tremblay, *Droit public fondamental* (Québec: Les Presses de l'Université Laval, 1972), p. 106.
32. Jennings has written: "There are thus four kinds of rules in England which would be inserted in a written constitution. They are: (1) Legislation; (2) Case law or law deduced from judicial decisions; (3) "The law and custom of Parliament"; (4) Constitutional conventions." Sir Ivor Jennings, *The Law and the Constitution*, Fifth ed. (London: University of London Press, 1959), pp. 65-66.
33. *Reference re Amendment of the Constitution of Canada (Nos. 1, 2 and 3), loc. cit.*, p. 47.
34. The decision was brought down on December 6, 1982, but at the time of writing had not yet been published.
35. See Karl Delwaide, "La législature québécoise peut-elle implanter un système complet d'initiative et de référendum" (1971), 22 *Cahiers de droit* 695.

36. See Jacques Zeiler, *L'idée de l'État dans saint Thomas d'Aquin* (Paris: Félix Alcan, 1910), p. 22.
37. See P.B. Mignault, *La Résistance aux lois injustes et la doctrine catholique* (Ottawa: Bibliothèque de l'Action Française, 1920), p. 55.
38. A. Esmein, *Éléments de droit constitutionnel français et comparé*, 7e éd. (Paris: Sirey, 1921), tome II, p. 534.
39. Georges Del Vecchio, *La Justice et la Vérité* (Paris: Dalloz, 1955), p. 132.
40. *Reference re Amendment of the Constitution of Canada (Nos. 1, 2 and 3), loc. cit.*, p. 86.
41. Georges Burdeau, *op. cit.*, tome I, p. 488.
42. See Professor William Lederman's interesting article, "The Supreme Court of Canada and Basic Constitutional Amendment" in this volume.
43. Robert Décary, "Le pouvoir judiciaire face au jeu politique," in Peter Russell *et al. The Court and the Constitution* (Kingston: Institute of Intergovernmental Relations, 1982), p. 33.
44. See Nicole Duplé, "Le rapatriement de la constitution" (1981), 22 *Cahiers de droit* 619 at p. 645.
45. Peter Russell, "Bold Statescraft, Questionable Jurisprudence" in this volume, p. 234.
46. The dissenting judges base their opinion on section 7(3) of the Statute of Westminster which, according to them, confirms the division of the exercise of sovereignty resulting from the sharing of legislative powers. See Noel Lyon, "Constitutional Theory and the Martland-Ritchie Dissent" in Peter Russell *et al., op. cit.*, pp. 57-60.
47. *Reference re Legislative Authority of Parliament of Canada in Relation to Upper House*, [1980] 1 S.C.R. 54.
48. *Attorney General of Quebec v. Blaikie*, [1979] 2 S.C.R. 1016.
49. *Attorney General of Manitoba v. Forest*, [1979] 2 S.C.R. 1032.
50. *Reference re Amendment of the Constitution of Canada (Nos. 1, 2 and 3), loc. cit.*, p. 45.
51. *Reference re Legislative Authority of Parliament of Canada in Relation to Upper House, loc. cit.*, p. 56.
52. Jones v. Attorney General of New Brunswick, [1975] 2 S.C.R. 182 at p. 196.
53. Jean-Charles Bonenfant, "L'étanchéité de l'A.A.N.B. est-elle menacée?" (1977), 18 *Cahiers de droit*, p. 396.

Chapter 11/Bold Statescraft, Questionable Jurisprudence

Peter Russell

On September 28, 1981 the Supreme Court of Canada released its decision in what is surely the most momentous case in the court's history. Never before has Canada awaited so expectantly for a decision from its highest court. Indeed, even if we look south of the border to the democracy in whose history Supreme Court decisions have played such a dramatic role, it is difficult to find a similar occasion when the main stream of national political life flowed so relentlessly up to a Supreme Court decision. Perhaps the Dred Scott case is a parallel.

The political consequences of the decision now appear to be essentially positive. The Supreme Court's decision was the decisive event in paving the way for a federal-provincial accommodation that enabled the Canadian constitution to be patriated in a manner acceptable to the federal government and nine provinces. The split nature of the court's verdict gave both Ottawa and the provinces a strong incentive to return to the bargaining table they had abandoned a year earlier. While the decision gave Ottawa a legal green light to proceed unilaterally with its constitutional plans, it cast a heavy mantle of political illegitimacy over the constitutional changes that would result from such a procedure. On the other hand, while the decision confirmed the provinces' claim that their participation in fundamental constitutional change was a constitutional requirement, it warned the provinces that if they failed to work out an agreement with Ottawa, Ottawa could go ahead without them and the courts would do nothing to enforce the provinces' right of participation. When the federal and provincial leaders assembled at the Ottawa Conference Centre on November 2, their opening statements testified to the efficacy of the Supreme Court's decision in restoring their interest in reaching an accommodation on the constitution.

But the risk to Canada inherent in the court's decision was also apparent as one contemplated the possibility that an accommodation might not have been reached and the federal government might then have exercised its legal option of proceeding unilaterally. If that had occurred, the country would have experienced the worst possible consequences of the court's decision. Patriation with an amending formula and a Charter of Rights would have been achieved, but in a manner which our highest court considered to be unconstitutional. One could scarcely think of a worse way for Canada finally to take charge of her own constitutional affairs and inaugurate a new regime of entrenched rights and freedoms.

The risk I have described was not entirely dissipated by the November 5 Accord. The Lévesque government's rejection of that agreement raised the question of whether, as a matter of constitutional convention, Quebec's consent was required for a change in the constitution affecting Quebec's powers. Quebec referred this question to the Quebec Court of Appeal in December, 1981.[1] A positive answer would have meant that patriation was being achieved in an unconstitutional manner. The courts, however, have managed to avoid reaching such a politically troublesome conclusion. On April 7, 1982, Quebec's Court of Appeal unanimously found that Quebec's consent was not required, and this decision has now been upheld by the Supreme Court of Canada.[2]

In the meantime the Parti Québécois government has turned to other means of attacking the new constitutional arrangements. In June 1982, a bill was passed by Quebec's National Assembly to take advantage of the legislative override clause in the new Canadian Charter of Rights and Freedoms by declaring that every Quebec law enacted before the Charter came into effect on April 17, 1982 will operate notwithstanding the Charter. This notwithstanding clause, however, cannot be used to protect Quebec's laws restricting access to English schools from the Charter. Here, while Quebec is committed to fighting court actions based on its view that restrictions on minority language rights are reasonable, it is significant that the Lévesque government has not threatened a program of non-compliance amounting to civil disobedience against the requirements of the "new" constitution.

Criteria for Assessing the Decision

Given the decision's weighty political consequences it is tempting to assess the decision solely on the basis of its political results rather than on the quality of the judges' reasoning. Certainly the key political actors in the constitutional struggle do not appear to have been greatly influenced by the arguments the Supreme Court judges advanced for their holdings. Federal and provincial politicians were making public statements about the decision within hours of its release. These political leaders looked for what they could use in the decision to enhance their cause—the provincial premiers (at least the eight who opposed the federal initiative) emphasizing the majority's conclusion that the federal government's unilateral approach was unconstitutional in a conventional sense; federal leaders emphasizing a different majority's finding that there was no legal bar to the federal government's proceeding in this unconstitutional fashion. For the media and the public, whose opinion is shaped by the media, the justices' reasoning was of little consequence. The mass media cannot communicate information about as complex a matter as the reasons for a judicial decision. They can only report the "bottom line"—the bare results. Given that the decision had, in effect, two "bottom lines" with no clear winner, the public probably found the decision confusing. Any damage this may have done to the Supreme Court's public reputation was likely offset by the fact that the split nature of the court's verdict immunized the court from attack by either group of contending politicians and re-kindled interest in seeking a broad Canadian consensus.

Even if short-run political reactions are not influenced by the court's reasons, it is to be hoped that in the longer run the reasons advanced by the judges as the grounds for their decision will figure more prominently in Canadians' assessments of the merits of the decision. For adjudicative decisions, unlike the decisions of the political branches of government, "the quality of rationality . . . is a prerequisite for their moral force."[3] Judges, especially those who serve on our highest court of appeal, are required to persuade us by their reasons that their findings are based on a wise and accurate reading of our constitutional and legal experience. But while the nature of the judicial process obliges us to examine the soundness of the reasoning on which the judges' conclusions rest, we may well find that the rationality of a decision of this kind might have to be tested on two planes—one more narrowly jurisprudential and related to the internal logic of the decision, and the other more politically prudential and related to the exigencies of the national crisis.

Having emphasized the importance of assessing the judges' reasons, I must acknowledge that the central issue in this case is such as to reduce the long-run importance of the majority and dissenting opinions. Normally, judicial opinions can have a developmental effect on the law by leaving certain aspects of a question somewhat open and by providing ideas and arguments that might be used by counsel in subsequent cases to persuade judges to revise or further refine legal doctrines. However, aside from the response to Quebec's court challenge, there will not likely be an occasion for future judicial decision-making on the main point at issue in the case at hand—namely, whether some or all of the Canadian provinces must consent to constitutional amendments affecting their powers. Now that the Canadian constitution has been patriated with a comprehensive amending formula, this particular question will henceforth be governed by the written constitutional text.

There is, however, a broader constitutional issue at the very core of this case which will be of enduring importance and is not capable of being definitively resolved by amendments to our written constitution. That issue is the nature of constitutional convention and its relationship to law. If the Supreme Court's decision in this case is read fifty years from now for more than its "bottom line," I suspect that it will be because of what the judges said on the general question of law and convention. Accordingly, my own comments on the decision will give priority to the court's treatment of that question.

Should the Court Have Answered the Questions?
Before considering the Supreme Court's decision on the substantial issues, a threshold question must be raised. Were the questions appropriate for a

court to answer? The federal government's position throughout was that the rules and principles concerning Canadian requests to the United Kingdom Parliament for amendments to the BNA Act were entirely in the realm of convention, not law, and as such were not appropriate for judicial determination.[4] This is one of the reasons for the federal government's refusal to exercise its option of referring questions concerning the validity of its unilateral approach directly to the Supreme Court of Canada. The court's holding on the nature of convention may seem to vindicate the federal government. The court held that conventions, although part of the constitution, are distinct from the law of the constitution and that the remedy for breach of convention must be obtained in the political arena, not from the courts. If in the court's view constitutional conventions are entirely political and not at all legal in nature, what, it might be asked, was a court of law doing rendering a decision on a non-legal subject?

It is no answer to say that the Supreme Court had no choice but to answer the questions put to the provincial Courts of Appeal and appealed to the Supreme Court. Although provincial and federal legislation establishing the reference case procedure appear to put virtually no limits on the questions which governments can submit to courts, Canadian judges have refused to answer questions considered to be inappropriate for judicial determination. As recently as the Senate Reference of 1980, the Supreme Court had refused to answer several questions about Parliament's power to make certain changes in the Senate because these questions were too vague and indeterminate.[5] Also, a majority on the Manitoba Court of Appeal had refused to answer the first question at issue in this case—whether the contents of the constitutional Resolution before the court, if enacted, would affect federal-provincial relations or provincial powers—because, at the time, the Resolution was still being debated in Parliament and there was no telling how it might be amended before it was finally adopted. This objection to the indeterminate nature of the first question had, however, been overcome when the case went on appeal to the Supreme Court by virtue of an all-party agreement in the House of Commons that no further amendments would be made to the Resolution submitted to the Supreme Court in April 1981.

Still, the issue remains whether the Supreme Court should have answered the question about the existence of a convention—a question which, in its own view, was not a legal question. This, it should be noted, is to pose the issue of justiciability in narrower terms than the federal government's claim that there was no justiciable question concerning its unilateral procedure. That broad claim was surely untenable. There were a number of important arguments based, *inter alia*, on an interpretation of the Statute of Westminster to the effect that there was a legal requirement of provincial consent. These arguments clearly raised issues appropriate for judicial determination. Furthermore, the relationship of constitutional convention to law is itself a legal question.

When disputes arise about a person's or a government's rights, obligations or powers, it is the function of courts to provide authoritative rulings on these disputed questions of law. That is the *raison d'être* of the judiciary in our system of government. Thus, the Supreme Court had no difficulty in determining, without dissent, that the questions whether provincial consent was a constitutional requirement in a legal sense (one dimension of the third question in the Manitoba and Newfoundland appeals) or whether Parliament was authorized by statute to proceed with certain amendments without provincial consent (one dimension of the second Quebec question) were justiciable.[6]

But the court could not give the same justification for its decision to treat the question about constitutional convention as justiciable. Here, I think, the Court was "hoist with its own petard." Because it separated convention from law so completely, it had difficulty explaining what business it had as a court of law answering a non-legal question. Personally, I am not persuaded by the court that there is such a complete gulf between law and convention. I will advance my arguments on this point later in this chapter. Here I wish only to draw attention to a lack of intellectual coherence in the court's overall handling of the convention question.

The three dissenting judges on the convention question (Chief Justice Laskin, Justices Estey and McIntyre) were clearly troubled by the justiciability issue. At the beginning of their opinion, they explain that because in their view (and the view of the majority) convention is not law, questions concerning the existence of convention normally ought not to be answered as "it is not the function of the Court to go beyond legal determinations." Still, they were willing to answer these questions—"notwithstanding their extra-legal nature"—"because of the unusual nature of these References and because the issues raised in the questions now before us were argued at some length before the Court and have been the subject of the reasons of the majority."[7] The majority appear less conscience-stricken about justiciability. They adopt the opinion of Chief Justice Freedman of the Manitoba Court of Appeal that even if the existence of a convention is not a question of law, it is nevertheless a question which is "constitutional in character." Furthermore, they point out that in answering the question, they are not enforcing a constitutional convention, but simply recognizing its existence—something which courts have often done in the past when conventions have been used as an aid to constitutional or statutory construction.[8]

I can accept the latter argument because, in my view, it is the courts' very use of conventions and the principles upon which they are based in interpreting legal rights and duties that makes it wrong to divorce convention completely from law. But on this point, of course, the court's view is different from mine. In the Supreme Court's view convention is in no sense part of constitutional law. So I remain unconvinced by the court's or Justice Freedman's reasons that, given their views on the nature of convention, they should have answered this part of the reference questions.

To understand why the Supreme Court judges answered the questions concerning convention we have to look beyond the internal logic of their arguments to their sense of the necessities of judicial statescraft. This is hinted at in the dissenting judges' vague reference to "the unusual nature of these References." The circumstances surrounding these References certainly were unusual. The country was caught in a very difficult constitutional impasse. There was a widely shared assumption by the people and the politicians that a Supreme Court decision was the next essential step in resolving the crisis. A refusal to deal with a major dimension of the reference questions might reasonably have been regarded as threatening greater damage to the constitutional fabric of the country than would stretching the notion of justiciability to embrace what the court regarded as a constitutional question of a non-legal kind.

Partisans of the federal government might contest the view that a judicial decision was needed. Mr. Chrétien, the federal justice minister, is reported to have opposed suspending the federal initiative to await a court decision on the grounds that,

> such a delay would set a dangerous precedent, whereby any citizen or group could challenge the legality of Government action before it was taken and thus suspend the ability of Parliament to pass legislation.[9]

Such an argument is not sound. Among other things, it ignores the fact that the reference procedure can only be initiated by governments, and that it has been used many times by both levels of government to obtain advisory opinions on legislative proposals.[10]

No doubt court references are often used by a province or by the federal government partly to obtain some tactical advantage in federal-provincial bargaining. In this case, clearly it was the provinces that felt they had most to gain by referring the matter to the courts. At the very least the court cases would slow down the federal initiative. A number of provincially-initiated references would entail even more delay than a federal reference directly to the Supreme Court and increase the probability of obtaining a judicial ruling favourable to the provincial position. The federal government's decision not to pre-empt the provinces and initiate its own reference gave the provinces the additional advantage of being able to frame questions in a manner best calculated to elicit answers favourable to their position.

The fact that reference cases may be tactical manoeuvres in federal-provincial controversies does not negate their value in Canada's constitutional system. While they entail the risk of enabling politicians to plunge our higher appeal courts into the thick of the hottest federal-provincial controversies, they have the advantage of making it possible to remove constitutional doubts before implementing major changes in legislation or the constitution. Imagine the situation which would have occurred had Parliament forged ahead in 1979 and replaced the Senate with a House of the Federation only to have the constitutional amendment effecting this change subsequently challenged in the courts. Assuming the Supreme Court would have decided such a case in the same way it decided the 1980 reference, Canada would have had an unconstitutional House of Parliament.

In the case at hand, where the very foundation of Canada's constitution and a major change in its system of government—a constitutional Charter of Rights—were at issue, it was in the country's interest to resolve doubts about the constitutionality of these changes before rather than after they were made. Having said this, it must be admitted that the court's decision was such as to retain the possibility that the changes might still be made in a manner not only alleged by provincial politicians to be unconstitutional, but also held by a majority of the Supreme Court to be unconstitutional. This was surely the great risk inherent in the court's decision: that Canada might find itself in the predicament of having an unconstitutional constitution.

The Nature of Convention

For Canada, and indeed for all democracies whose constitutions combine "unwritten" conventions with "written" constitutional instruments, a court's holdings on the nature of constitutional conventions have enduring implications. And in the case of the Supreme Court of Canada's decision, the intellectual coherence of the court's conclusion that provincial consent for amendments affecting provincial powers, while a constitutional requirement, was not a legally enforceable right, depends on the validity of the way in which the court drew the line between law and convention.

It was clear from the opening moments of the hearing before the court that this would be a crucial, if not the crucial, issue in the case, Mr. Twaddle, the lead counsel for Manitoba, had just begun to develop the provincial case when Chief Justice Laskin leaned across his desk and asked, "Mr. Twaddle, are you talking about law or convention?"[11] Clearly, in the Chief Justice's view, law and convention belonged to different realms. As it turned out, all of his brethren shared this point of view.

In examining the court's position on this issue, it is useful to begin by setting out what the majority of six (Justices Martland, Ritchie, Dickson, Beetz, Chouinard and Lamer) say about convention that is relatively uncontentious, at least in the sense that it is generally consistent with the writings of English and Canadian constitutional scholars. The three judges who dissent on the question of convention agree with much of the majority opinion on the general nature of convention, although they clearly disagree on a few points.

Both the Supreme Court judges and constitutional writers take the discussion of constitutional conventions in A.V. Dicey's *Introduction to the Study of the Law of the Constitution* as their starting point.[12] This is to be expected, for it was largely through the influence of Dicey that the concept of constitutional convention came into use. Dicey used the term to refer to precepts or rules of political conduct (to use his own language, "a body of constitutional or political ethics")[13] concerning the proper use of legal powers. He wrote primarily about the conventions relating to Cabinet government, the Crown's prerogatives and the relationships between the three branches of government.

The following passage from the majority opinion captures the essence of Dicey's conception:

> The main purpose of constitutional conventions is to ensure that the legal framework of the Constitution will be operated in accordance with the prevailing constitutional values or principles of the period.[14]

It is worth unravelling this conception, for such an exercise will reveal, I believe, four essential features of constitutional conventions that are acknowledged by most constitutional writers, including Dicey's critics.

The first feature is that the constitutional function of conventions is to provide rules concerning the proper exercise of the legal powers of government. For example, the convention requiring that the Queen or her representative should act on the advice of ministers responsible to the elected branch of Parliament governs the way in which the Queen should exercise the vast powers vested in her by law. At *least* in this sense, conventions are closely related to laws. As many constitutional writers have pointed out, the existence of some legal powers—for example, section 9 of the BNA Act, which vests "the Executive Government and Authority of and over Canada" in the Queen—would be intolerable if these powers were not exercised in accordance with well-established constitutional conventions.

Secondly, conventions have a strong normative character. Conventions may arise through custom and practice, but unlike mere custom or earlier precedents, conventional rules have come to be regarded as obligatory by most of those who are active in the institutions to which the conventions pertain. It may not be easy to discern the extent to which a convention or a particular formulation of a convention has come to be accepted as obligatory. Take, for example, the conventions relating to the Crown's prerogative power to dissolve Parliament. In 1926, when Governor-General Byng refused Prime Minister King's request for a dissolution, not all of the political actors involved agreed that constitutional convention permitted a Governor-General to deny a dissolution in those circumstances.[15] But the existence of this dispute does not in itself constitute proof that the Governor-General was wrong. Even less does it prove that there is no constitutional convention permitting the Crown in certain circumstances to refuse a prime minister's request for a dissolution.

The three dissenting judges appear not to agree with this point. According to them,

> while a convention, by its very nature, will often lack the precision and clearness of expression of a law, it must be recognized, known and understood with sufficient clarity that conformance is possible and a breach of conformance immediately discernible.[16]

I think this is too exacting a test of convention. It would mean that the normative force of a convention could be destroyed by the mere existence of a dispute about its correct application. This is wrong because the normative force of a convention is derived from acceptance of the principle upon which it is based.

This brings us to the third essential feature of constitutional conventions—namely, that their justification depends on the prevailing political principles of the period. For Dicey, the validity of constitutional conventions depended on the fundamental principle of popular sovereignty. He endeavoured to show that the reason for following the conventions of responsible government was to ensure that the exercise of governmental power was, as far as possible, in harmony with the will of the nation.[17] This was a requirement of democratic theory, and democratic theory, by this time, was at the foundation of the British constitution. In this sense, the ultimate justification of constitutional conventions must be in terms of whether a convention serves what has come to be a fundamental principle of the constitutional system.

But note it is the prevailing principles of the period that justify convention. This points to a fourth essential feature of conventions—the dynamic element they bring to a constitution. The observance of convention may avoid the necessity for formal constitutional change or revolution by ensuring that the exercise of legally defined powers is not out of keeping with what the politically active people of the nation find acceptable. In Great Britain, the conventions of responsible and Cabinet government meant that the operation of the British constitution could be adjusted to the requirements of a political culture that demanded government do much more for the people and be much more responsive to them.

Conventions in a Federal State

While all nine judges appear to be, for the most part, in agreement on these basic Diceyan attributes of convention, the three dissenting judges on the convention question took the position that constitutional conventions must have a much more limited application in the context of a federal state with a written constitution:

> In a federal state where the essential feature of the Constitution must be the distribution of powers between the two levels of government, each supreme in its own sphere, constitutionality and legality must be synonymous, and conventional rules will be accorded less significance than they may have in a unitary state such as the United Kingdom.[18]

It is not entirely clear how this statement is meant to apply to the conventions of parliamentary and Cabinet government. In the very next sentence the dissenting judges equate "constitutionalism in a unitary state" with the "practices" within "the national and regional units of a federal state." These practices, as is generally acknowledged by Canadian constitutionalists, are based primarily on conventional rules, many of which are subsumed under the phrase in the preamble of the BNA Act which states that Canada is to have "a Constitution similar in principle to that of the United Kingdom."[19] If the dissenting judges were suggesting that these conventions are to be accorded less significance in Canada than in the United Kingdom, they were surely wrong. Canadians no less than Englishmen would regard a failure to comply with the rule that the Queen or the Queen's representative act on the advice of ministers responsible to the elected branch of the Legislature as a serious breach of constitutional convention. The conventions of responsible government are as significant in Canada as they are in the United Kingdom.

Nor can I understand a later passage in the dissenting opinion on convention in which "the Dicey convention" is distinguished from the convention at issue in this case on the grounds that the former "does not qualify or limit the authority or sovereignty of Parliament or the Crown" while the latter "would truncate the functioning of the executive and legislative branches at the federal level."[20] The rules which Dicey called conventions do qualify the authority of the Houses of Parliament and the Crown in that they govern in an ethical, if not a legal, sense how the legal powers of these institutions are to be used. The majority attributed no greater force to the convention of provincial consent in the amending process.

It may be that the dissenting opinion's down-grading of the significance of convention in the Canadian context was meant to apply only to those conventions governing federal-provincial relationships. Perhaps the point they were getting at was that because there is a written constitutional text governing most of the important features of those relationships, conventional rules must have less significance in this area. Now if "significance" in this context is meant to have only a quantitative meaning, no one could seriously quarrel with the point. In countries which, unlike Britain, have written constitutions, a smaller proportion of important constitutional rules will take the form of conventions. But I suspect the dissenters were thinking of "significance" in a qualitative as well as a quantitative sense. They were, I think, suggesting that where conventions concerning federal-provincial relationships exist, they must necessarily be given less normative weight than is normally given to conventions. This is a much more dubious proposition.

In constitutional systems that have a basic constitutional text as one of their ingredients, constitutional conventions are often needed to modify or supplement relationships fixed in the formal text of the constitution.[21] This point has been made by many constitutional writers. Colin Munro, one of the Supreme Court's most respected authorities on conventions, points out that Dicey himself came to acknowledge that conventions may play an important role in countries which, unlike England, have written constitutions. Munro goes even further by suggesting that,

> Indeed, it is at least arguable that convention should play a larger role in countries with written constitutions; the greater the degree of constitutional rigidity, the greater the need for the benefits of informal adaptation which conventions bring.[22]

Conventions have certainly played an important role in the development of Canadian federalism. For example, early recognition of the requirement that all regions of the country be represented in the federal Cabinet helped render tolerable the exercise of central government powers over a society marked by sharp regional differences and compensated for the weakness of the mechanism provided for this purpose in the constitutional text, namely the Senate.[23] Another example is the federal government's refusal in recent years to use its powers of disallowance and reservation over the provinces no matter how much it might be provoked by provincial legislation.[24] This pattern of refusal reflects the growing strength of the federal principle in the operative political ethics of the Canadian constitution.

The last example demonstrates how a formal constitutional text can limit the application of convention. Even those who believe that the non-use of disallowance and reservation should be regarded as a constitutional convention would, I think, agree with the Supreme Court of Canada's holding in 1938 that if such a convention exists, it could not legally nullify a power explicitly established by the BNA Act.[25] The incapacity of convention to have the *legal* effect of nullifying established legal powers is not confined to conventions relating to federalism. For instance, although by convention Royal assent should be given to bills passed by the Legislature, because Royal assent is a strict legal requirement courts will not give legal effect to a bill from which Royal assent has been withheld even though it has been withheld in defiance of constitutional convention.[26] But, of course, the overriding effect of explicit legal powers does not in itself destroy the normative weight of convention.

Also it is important to note that the legally overriding effect of explicit powers established in the constitutional text is not relevant in a context involving a constitutional power or relationship not explicitly provided for in the written constitution. Precisely such a context was involved in the case at hand. The conditions under which it was proper for the federal Parliament to address requests to the UK Parliament for amendments to the BNA Act were not spelled out in that Act. Indeed, no power to make such requests or effect amendments concerning legislative powers was explicitly established by the written constitution. So this situation must be distinguished from the disallowance or reservation situation.

The dissenting judges, with their insistence that in a federal state with a written constitution "constitutionality and legality must be synonymous," disagreed with the majority that a breach of constitutional convention is properly referred to as "unconstitutional" behaviour. Here they seemed to be maintaining that because in a country like Canada "unconstitutional" can have a distinctly legal meaning—a violation of the division of powers in the BNA Act—which it could not have in the United Kingdom, the word should be used exclusively for such violations. But this argument ignores the fact that there is much more at stake than mere semantic tidiness in deciding how the concepts of "constitutional" and "unconstitutional" are to be used. To deny that behaviour which is merely a breach of convention can be considered unconstitutional is to take most of the political sting out of the finding that it would be a breach of convention for the federal Parliament to proceed with the proposed constitutional Resolution without a substantial measure of provincial support.

The devaluation of the significance of violating conventions is reasonable if one is not prepared to attach importance to the principle upon which conventions are based. Dicey thought it appropriate for an Englishman to refer to conduct violating convention as unconstitutional and mean something different from and often deeper than calling behaviour illegal, because in his view these conventions were based on a fundamental principle of the English constitution—popular sovereignty.[27] By the same token, Canadians who regard the principle of federalism upon which the convention at issue in this case is based as fundamental to the Canadian constitution should agree with the majority that it is appropriate to refer to conduct violating the convention as unconstitutional even though such action might not be illegal.

Identifying the Conventional Requirement

Turning to the substantive issue of whether the majority were correct in finding that convention requires at least a substantial measure of provincial consent, it is essential to consider the methodology used by the court in answering this question. It may be that the court's elucidation and application of this methodology is the most significant contribution it makes in this case to Canadians' understanding of their constitution.

The methodology employed by both the majority and the dissenters follows logically from the Diceyan conception of convention. It is a test which they found neatly summarized in the following passage from Sir W. Ivor Jennings' *The Law and the Constitution*:

> We have to ask ourselves three questions: first, what are the precedents; secondly, did the actors in the precedents believe that they were bound by a rule; and thirdly, is there a reason for the rule?[28]

It is vital to appreciate the multi-facetted nature of this approach. Too often, debates about Canadian conventions have been carried on solely in terms of precedent—each side endeavouring to bolster its case with some historical precedents, however quaint, irrelevant or peculiar they might be. Such an approach may be attractive because it seems so thoroughly empirical and therefore objective, avoiding any "value judgements" about which practices are right. But that is precisely the weakness of such an approach. By leaving out of account the reason for following a particular practice—the principle on which the convention is based—it ignores the extent to which questions about conventions are not simply questions about historical facts, but are normative or ethical questions. But they are ethical questions of a peculiar kind. An historical component is involved in answering these questions inasmuch as an acceptable answer depends not on one's personal view of why a practice ought to be followed, but on being able to maintain that the reason for following the practice rests on a principle of government that has come to be an essential feature of the political community in question.[29]

While the majority and the dissenters appear to agree on the threefold test of convention—precedents, attitudes of political actors and principle—they come to very different conclusions in applying each part of the test. The majority opinion follows closely the report of the British Kershaw committee[30] and the submissions made to the Court by Dean Lysyk as counsel for Saskatchewan. The dissenters follow most of the major arguments put forward by Mr. Chrétien in his paper, which attempts to rebut the Kershaw committee.[31] Kershaw, Dean Lysyk and the majority have much the better of this argument.

Consider first the treatment of precedents. The threshold question here is what are the relevant precedents? For the majority, the relevant precedents are those involving amendments which "directly affected federal-provincial relationships in the sense of changing provincial legislative powers."[32] Using this criterion they find only five positive precedents: the 1930 amendment giving the prairie provinces control of their natural resources, the Statute of Westminster, and the amendments of 1940, 1951 and 1964 giving the federal Parliament jurisdiction in the fields of unemployment insurance, old-age pensions and supplementary benefits respectively. All of these amendments were approved by all of the provinces whose powers were directly affected. Furthermore, in negative terms they find that "no amendment changing provincial legislative power has been made since Confederation when agreement of a province whose legislative powers would have been changed was withheld."[33]

For the dissenting judges, on the other hand, "the real test of relevance" is the reaction an amendment provoked from one or more of the provinces.[34] Thus amendments concerning central government institutions or federal subsidies to the provinces to which at least one province objected count for the dissenters as evidence that there is not a convention requiring unanimous provincial consent.

Setting aside for the moment the question of unanimity, I think that the dissenters' criterion of relevance is much too wide. By including aspects of federalism outside the realm of intergovernmental relations, it goes beyond the reference in the questions submitted to the courts to amendments "affecting federal-provincial relationships or the powers, rights or privileges" of the provinces. Furthermore, such a criterion is not sufficiently sensitive to the question of principle at issue in this case—whether one level of government in the Canadian federation should be able unilaterally to alter the powers of the other level.

Secondly, in considering the attitudes of political actors—the second part of the test of convention—it is essential to consider the historical context in which words were uttered. The dissenting judges do not do this. In their view the existence of conflicting statements in the historical record "adds additional weight to the contention that no convention of provincial consent has achieved constitutional recognition to this day."[35] But if instead of attaching equal weight to all quotations, these judges had taken historical context into account, they would have found it much more difficult to maintain their agnostic position. For example, at the dominion-provincial conference of 1931, Prime Minister Bennett, in seeking the support of the provinces for the "Canada clause" in the Statute of Westminster exempting the amendment of the BNA Act from that statute, assured the provincial premiers,

> that there would be no amendment to the constitution of Canada in its federal aspect without consulting the Provinces which, it must be remembered, had the same powers within their domain that the Dominion has within hers.[36]

Now, if Prime Minister Bennett meant to commit the federal government here only to consult with the provinces while maintaining the right to proceed unilaterally with amendments directly affecting provincial powers over the opposition of most provinces, then his statement and general performance at this conference must rank as one of the great confidence tricks in modern history.

The majority's interpretation of two other statements of crucial historical importance is also much more convincing than the dissenting judges' treatment of the same material. I refer to Prime Minister King's 1940 statement in the House of Commons and the fourth principle as set out in the 1965 White Paper on Constitutional Amendment in Canada. Mr. King's statement was made on a critically important occasion—the first time since the enactment of the Statute of Westminster that the federal Parliament had considered a Resolution addressed to the United Kingdom requesting a constitutional amendment affecting the division of legislative powers. By obtaining the consent of all of the provinces for this amendment, Mr. King explained to the House that his government had,

> avoided the raising of a very critical constitutional question, namely whether or not in amending the British North America Act it is absolutely necessary to secure the consent of all the provinces, or whether the consent of a certain number of provinces would of itself be sufficient.[37]

In the majority's opinion the only point about which Mr. King was uncertain was whether unanimity was required. There was no doubt "as to whether substantial provincial support is required." The dissenting judges dismiss King's statement as showing merely that Mr. King thought it was "good politics" to obtain provincial consent.[38] But here they miss the point about convention: conventions are fundamentally about "good politics" in that they embody standards of political conduct that have come to be required by the prevailing sentiment of the political community.

The fourth principle in the 1965 White Paper to which the majority opinion gives great weight is described as follows:

> The Canadian Parliament will not request an amendment directly affecting federal-provincial relationships without prior consultation and agreement with the provinces. This principle did not emerge as early as others but since 1907, and particularly since 1930, has gained increasing recognition and acceptance. The nature and the degree of provincial participation in the amending process, however, have not lent themselves to easy definition.[39]

They rightly emphasize that this statement was carefully formulated by the federal government and accepted by all of the provinces. Again, the dissenting judges' denial of this statement's significance is unconvincing. They allude to a sentence in the White Paper referring to all of the principles governing the process of securing the UK amendments to the BNA Act as "not constitutionally binding in any strict sense."[40] But, of course, this statement only recognized that these principles belong to the conventional part of the constitution and are not in the written constitution. As the second Kershaw report points out, if this statement were taken to mean that the principles in the White Paper were not constitutional requirements even in a conventional sense, then Canadians could have no constitutional objections if the UK Parliament ignored the White Paper's first principle by amending the BNA Act on its own without any request from Canada.[41] But surely such an action would be regarded by the federal government and by the provinces as unconstitutional.

The minority also maintained that the two sentences following the fourth principle demonstrate an absence of the unanimity and certainty required for constitutional amendments. Taking unanimity first, and setting aside qualms I have about accepting unanimity as a necessary property of conventions (who must be unanimous? does one successful repudiation or breach of convention destroy the convention?), the fact that all the provinces and Ottawa accepted the White Paper as a correct statement of the principles governing the amending process shows that by 1965 the most relevant political actors all accepted the convention of provincial consent. As for uncertainty, again it is questionable to regard certainty as a necessary property of conventions. Whose formulations, for instance, of the conventions of parliamentary and Cabinet government are to be regarded as certainly the correct ones? As Dean Lysyk pointed out in his oral submission to the court, the absence of a precise and universally accepted definition of the conditions under which a Legislature's confidence in the government may be said to be lost does not prove that there is no convention requiring the government to maintain that confidence.[42] Besides, the uncertainty in question pertains only to the precise extent of provincial agreement required. That is precisely the issue about which Mackenzie King was uncertain, on which federal and provincial leaders over many years were not able to agree, and on which the majority wisely did not attempt to be definitive, but left open to resolution in the political arena. Lack of knowledge of exactly how much provincial consent is required does not preclude a firm belief that for the federal government to proceed against the wishes of eight of the ten provinces would be a violation of constitutional ethics.

The statements of the political actors are what provide the main basis for the majority's declining to find that convention requires unanimous provincial consent. As all of the relevant precedents, on their face, supported unanimity, without these statements the evidence might seem to favour unanimity. As for principle—the third part of the test for convention—it does not provide a firm basis for unanimity. There have certainly been many Canadian leaders who have regarded Confederation as a compact, the terms of which can only be changed with the consent of all the parties. That indeed was the position which seven of the eight provinces opposing Ottawa took in this case. But such a view of the federal principle implicit in Canada's constitution has not been accepted by federal leaders or by all provincial leaders.[43] Nor can a requirement of unanimous consent be derived from the general theory and practice of federalism. None of the classical federal systems requires that all of the units agree to amendments affecting their powers.[44]

Although the majority do not find that unanimity is required, neither do they reach a firm conclusion that unanimous consent is not required. Their conclusion is that "the agreement of the provinces of Canada, no views being expressed as to its quantification, is constitutionally required. . . ."[45] Thus it was still open for Quebec to argue that its consent is required on the grounds that unanimity is a conventional requirement. I think a stronger case would be based on the contention that the requirement of substantial provincial consent has not only a quantitative dimension but also a qualitative, dualistic dimension which requires the consent of the province in which most of Canada's French-speaking citizens reside. In considering this claim, not only must precedents be considered, but equally the extent to which federal and provincial leaders indicated that they felt obliged to observe a Quebec veto and the historical acceptance of cultural dualism as a fundamental principle in Canadian political life.

Finally, there is the question of principle—the reason for accepting a practice as binding. The majority looked upon provincial autonomy in matters constitutionally assigned to the provinces as basic to the federal character of Canada's constitution. That principle has been recognized as a fundamental principle of the Canadian constitution in a number of judicial decisions.[46] In the majority's view, that principle "cannot be reconciled with a state of affairs where the modification of provincial legislative powers could be obtained by the unilateral action of the federal authorities."[47]

It is no answer to this to say, as the dissenters, that "the BNA Act has not created a perfect or ideal federal state," or to point to provisions of the BNA Act that modify the federal aspects of the Canadian constitution.[48] For the majority position to be sound, it is necessary to accept only that as a minimum requirement of the federal dimension of the constitution one level of government not be able unilaterally to alter the powers of the other level. Unquestionably, the BNA Act contains provisions that were based on principles other than those of federalism. Alongside the federal division of powers are provisions derived from British imperial history more suitable to the constitution of a unitary state, with a senior level of government at the centre and inferior local governments.[49] These unitary or imperial elements of the constitution were, no doubt, welcomed by those Fathers of Confederation who, like Sir John A. Macdonald, did not care for federalism at all. Still, it is reasonable to assume that the Confederation coalition would not have held together had it been understood that the federal element in the new constitution was so weak that the provinces' powers could be altered unilaterally by the central government. It is even clearer that as Confederation evolved, the unitary-imperial provisions so valued by Macdonald's part of the Confederation coalition became increasingly unusable because their operation collided with the deepening and broadening acceptance of federal principles by the bulk of politically active Canadians. In Canada, "the prevailing constitutional values or principles of the period" are now such as to require that the federal principle be respected at least to the extent of ensuring that the provinces participate in making decisions on amendments affecting their own powers. Paradoxically, this is evident in the Trudeau government's commitment to an amending formula that would entrench in a patriated constitution the right of the provinces to participate in the amending process.

The best counter to the majority's position on convention was given not by dissenting judges, but by dissenting politicians. This is what one should expect given that conventions are established and developed in the political arena. Prime Minister Trudeau in his initial response to the Supreme Court decision (the televised press conference from Seoul, South Korea) acknowledged that a convention requiring provincial consent for amendments affecting provincial powers had existed.[50] However, he went on to argue that unless this convention was set aside, at least for the immediate period, its strict observance would perpetually frustrate the realization of another essential Canadian constitutional value—the full achievement of Canada's self-government. This response has the merit of recognizing that constitutional conventions are a dynamic part of the constitution, and furthermore, that a constitutional system is based not on a single absolute principle, but on a number of political values or normative considerations, the ordering of which may well be shaped by the political exigencies of the country. Mr. Trudeau, as it turned out, did not press this argument to the point of proceeding unilaterally with the patriation package without making one more effort to arrive at a consensus with the provincial premiers. But, I would submit, had the concessions he made in modifying his package not been reciprocated by concessions from a substantial number of premiers, he would have had a reasonably strong case in terms of constitutional ethics for proceeding unilaterally.

Law and Convention

While the Supreme Court justices did not agree whether a convention requiring provincial consent exists or whether violations of conventions in Canada constitute unconstitutional behaviour, they were unanimous that whatever the convention is, it cannot be enforced by the courts. This brings us to the most difficult question of jurisprudence in this case—the relationship between law and convention. On this issue the Supreme Court judges may speak as one, but the constitutional scholars clearly do not.[51]

There can be no serious quarrel with the court's starting point on this issue. The court was surely correct in drawing a distinction between convention and law. As their quotations from Dicey demonstrate, Dicey introduced the concept of "convention" precisely to distinguish two sets of constitutional rules—one set which he referred to as laws "in the strictest sense" and another which, although forming a "portion of constitutional law," he called conventions. Also it is true that for Dicey, as for the Supreme Court, the key difference between the two sets of rules was that whereas "constitutional laws in the strict sense" are enforced by the courts, constitutional conventions are not.[52] Conventions develop in the political arena, and the sanctions for breaching them are administered in that same arena by officials, politicians, and ultimately by the electorate.

But pointing out this difference between law and convention does not exhaust what can be said about the relationship between law and convention. As the Supreme Court itself acknowledged, conventions have frequently been recognized in judicial decisions "to provide aid for and background to constitutional or statutory construction."[53] Many cases were cited by counsel for the provinces (most systematically by D.A. Schmeiser, counsel for Manitoba)[54] in which Canadian and English courts have referred to constitutional conventions. However, the Supreme Court insisted that none of these cases constitutes an instance of a court enforcing convention or of a convention crystallizing into law, and that it was "an overdrawn proposition" to say that in the cases cited the court had "given force to convention."[55] The majority on convention went even further and denied that convention was part of constitutional law: "constitutional convention plus constitutional law equal the total constitution of the country."[56]

I have some difficulty with this portion of the court's jurisprudence. I see at least two problems in insisting on such an unbridgeable gulf between law and convention. The first is that some of the cases cited do suggest that in certain contexts courts will give legal effect to conventions. The second is the court's inference that what is not enforceable by courts is not law.

The cases that are difficult to reconcile with the court's position are those involving conventions which, far from being in conflict with the law, were used to interpret legal rights and obligations. The best known Canadian example is Chief Justice Duff's opinion in the Labour Conventions case that the practice of Dominions entering into agreements with foreign states "must be recognized by the Courts as having the force of law."[57] For the Supreme Court, this example does not really count as it belongs in the realm of international law which "perforce has had to develop, if it was to exist at all, through commonly recognized political practices of states. . . ."[58] So let us consider a completely domestic example, Arseneau v. The Queen.[59] In Arseneau, the Supreme Court held that a person charged under the section of the Criminal Code establishing the offence of bribing "a member of a Legislature" could not escape conviction by claiming that the person who accepted his bribe did so as a Cabinet minister rather than as a member of the Legislative Assembly. Justice Ritchie, writing for the majority, rejected this distinction because it was not in accord with "the generally accepted practice in this country whereby Ministers are accountable to the elected representatives of the people in Parliament or the Legislature."[60] A similar English example, cited by Mr. Schmeiser, is Liversidge v. Anderson,[61] where the House of Lords referred to the convention of ministerial responsibility as one of its reasons for not going behind a detention order. In these cases, conventions were given legal effect to the extent that they shaped the interpretation of legal powers and responsibilities, and the decisions recognizing the conventions became legal precedents.

Outside the context of statutory interpretation there are examples, at least in English law, of the courts giving legal effect to fundamental political principles and making them part of the common law. The most important example is the courts' recognition of the supreme authority of Parliament. In the words of Sir Ivor Jennings, "It is, therefore, *common law* that Parliament can do as it pleases."[62] A much more recent example of the English courts showing a willingness to incorporate convention into the common law is Attorney-General v. Jonathan Cape (the Crossman Diaries case).[63] In that case, the British government sought an injunction to prevent publication of an ex-Cabinet minister's diaries on the grounds that publication would violate the convention of Cabinet confidentiality. Against this claim the publisher contended that "whatever the limits of the convention of joint Cabinet responsibility may be, there is no obligation enforceable at law to prevent the publication of Cabinet papers and proceedings, except in extreme cases where national security is involved."[64] The government's claim, it should be noted, was not tied to any alleged breach of the Official Secrets Acts or of an oath of office, but was based solely on the essential importance of the rule of Cabinet confidentiality in maintaining Cabinet responsibility. After considering a great deal of evidence concerning the existence of the convention in question, Chief Justice Widgery concluded:

> The Attorney-General has made out his claim that the expression of individual opinions by Cabinet Ministers in the course of Cabinet discussions are matters of confidence, the publication of which can be restrained by the court when this is clearly necessary in the public interest.
>
> The maintenance of the doctrine of joint responsibility within the Cabinet is in the public interest, and the application of that doctrine might be prejudiced by premature disclosure of the views of individual Ministers.
>
> There must, however, be a limit in time after which the confidential character of the information, and the duty of the court to restrain publication, will lapse.[65]

Because nearly 10 years had elapsed since the Cabinet conversations recorded in Mr. Crossman's diaries had taken place, the Chief Justice thought that Cabinet solidarity would not be endangered and therefore refused the injunction.

The Supreme Court tried to explain away Jonathan Cape on the grounds that the court was simply "applying its own legal principles as it might to any question of confidence, however it arose."[66] But this does not adequately account for the fact that in this case the English judge stated that he was prepared in certain circumstances to give legal protection to Cabinet information in order to uphold an important convention of the constitution. Chief Justice Widgery's reference to precedents outside of the political context in which the courts had given protection to confidential communications (in commerce and matrimonial relations) does not detract from the fact that he was willing to give legal effect to the convention of Cabinet confidentiality in a situation where Cabinet solidarity would otherwise be endangered.

The process whereby judicial decisions give some legal effect to constitutional conventions may not be most aptly characterized as "conventions crystallizing into law"[67] or "the transformation of a conventional rule into a legal rule."[68] These expressions suggest that once the courts have pronounced upon a conventional rule it is no longer a convention, but that is surely not the case. The conventions of parliamentary and Cabinet government remain conventions even though they may be recognized from time to time in judicial decisions. Also, these expressions may suggest that once the courts have given legal effect to a convention in one context they would thereby be committed in the future to enforcing the convention in all contexts. But this, too, would be incorrect. The courts need only treat the cases recognizing convention as legal precedents in situations where similar rights and powers are at issue as were involved in the earlier cases. Also, of course, because conventions are established and changed in the political arena, they can be altered independently of judicial decisions. Thus, for example, if the politicians abandoned the convention of Cabinet confidentiality, the courts could not recognize it in subsequent decisions.

The second problem with the court's categorical distinction between convention and law is its implicit assumption that enforceability by a court is a necessary condition for the existence of law. This proposition, which, I take it, is a first premise of legal positivism, seems to be taken for granted by the court. But I find it difficult to accept this positivism as Canada's official philosophy of law without resolving a number of questions it raises. Among such questions are the following: what does enforceability mean? does it mean giving a remedy? any remedy, even a declaratory judgement? who decides what is enforceable? if it is the judges who decide, how are they to know before they have enforced a rule whether or not it is a law? or must all law originate in statutes or the written constitution, and if that is so, how do we account for common law?

Perhaps there are good answers to all of these questions. But until I find acceptable answers I am not persuaded that conventions must be denied any legal status because normally courts do not enforce them. Dicey, who as much as any other writer made a distinction between conventional rules and rules that "are in the strictest sense 'laws,'" did not go as far as the Supreme Court. While he distinguished constitutional conventions from the "law of the constitution," he referred to both as the "two elements" of the "constitutional law" of his country.[69] By recognizing that convention and the law of the constitution were organically related as twin sources of constitutional law, the court might have been better able to justify its decision as a court of law to answer the question on convention.

The Incompleteness of Canada's Constitution

Besides the contention that the convention itself was enforceable, there
were other legal arguments which the court (by a seven-to-two majority)
had to overcome to be able to conclude that provincial consent was not a
legal requirement for an amendment affecting provincial powers. These
questions had both a Canadian and a British side.

On the Canadian side, the central issue was whether the Canadian
Parliament was legally empowered to address resolutions to the United
Kingdom requesting changes in the provinces' power. In answering this
question, the majority rejected the implication in the second Quebec
question that the power of the House of Commons and the Senate must be
proven by remarking that "it would be equally consistent with constitutional precedent to require disproof."[70] Here they seem to be doing more
than asserting a presumption of constitutionality, for which there is
certainly precedent. They were also making the more fundamental point
that Canada's constitution is "incomplete" in that not all the powers of
government are specified and defined by statutes or the written constitution.[71]

Even if we concede this assumption about the incompleteness of
Canada's constitution, it does not follow that any branch of government,
including the House of Commons and the Senate, can act in relation to
those matters on which the constitution is silent so as to effect fundamental
changes with respect to those matters on which the written constitution is
quite specific. That is precisely the point emphasized by the two dissenting
judges (on the question of law) in insisting that under a system of constitutional government a legislative body cannot do indirectly what the
written constitution prevents it from doing directly.[72] As Justices Martland
and Ritchie point out, in other areas where the Canadian constitution
might be said to be incomplete, such as judicial review, the interdelegation
of legislative powers, and Canadian treaties,[73] the courts have ruled that
Legislatures are *ultra vires* if they act in a manner that would bypass or
defeat the federal division of powers in the BNA Act. This, I think, is a
powerful argument which is not adequately answered by the majority.

The majority's position rests on drawing a sharp distinction between
passing resolutions and enacting legislation. They accept the federal
government's contention that the passing of resolutions is not subject to
the division of powers in the BNA Act. Such an activity simply falls under
the power of the Houses of Parliament to govern their own internal
proceedings, a power they claim is on the same legal footing as that of the
British Parliament and which is therefore beyond judicial review.[74] But
nowhere do they consider the appropriateness of transposing this British
doctrine to a country like Canada with a written constitution and a federal
division of powers. Nor do they consider the implications of the Senate and
House of Commons Act, which limits the "internal" powers of these bodies

to what is "not repugnant to the BNA Act." It is the view of the dissenting judges that such a restriction precludes a resolution which would have the effect of curtailing provincial legislative powers under section 92 of the BNA Act.[75] Justices Martland and Ritchie, rightly in my view, go beyond legal formalism. Noting the federal government's repeated assertion that there is a "firm and unbinding convention" that the British Parliament must enact any amendment requested by a joint resolution of the House of Commons and Senate, they realistically find that the resolution at issue in this case, although only a resolution and not a legislative enactment, will have the effect of altering provincial powers.[76]

The British Parliament and Canada's Constitution

There was also a British side to the legal issues. The majority appear to deny this. Near the beginning of the majority judgement on law we find the following statement:

> Secondly, the authority of the British Parliament or its practices and conventions are not matters upon which the Court would presume to pronounce.[77]

Despite this statement, the opinion goes on to discuss at length whether the British Parliament's authority to amend the BNA Act is subject in law to a requirement of provincial consent. The court could not avoid this question if it was to deal with the provinces' argument that since the recognition in 1926 of the Dominions as "autonomous Communities within the British Empire,"[78] the British Parliament had relinquished its supremacy over the sovereign powers, federal and provincial, of the Canadian community. In answering this question concerning the independence of Canadian Legislatures from the British Parliament, the court, regardless of its protestations, was necessarily answering a question about the power of the British Parliament over Canada.

The majority rejected the provincial claims of sovereignty for their Legislatures and upheld the federal government's view that the British Parliament has retained its "omnipotent legal authority in relation to the British North America Act."[79] This conclusion is based entirely on interpretation of the Statute of Westminster. The majority, in a rather cursory manner, rejected any suggestion that where the Statute of Westminster recognizes the principle of the modern Commonwealth that laws made by the UK Parliament will not extend to a Dominion "otherwise than at the request and with the consent of that Dominion,"[80] the Dominion, in the case of Canada, means not the Dominion Parliament alone, but the federal state of Canada in which sovereign legislative power is distributed between the federal and provincial Legislatures. The majority do not explain why those who drafted the Statute of Westminster would have used such an ambiguous word as "Dominion" if their intention was to establish a

Dominion Parliament's request as the requisite antecedent condition for imperial legislation extending to an autonomous Dominion.[81]

The majority go further and, in effect, assert that Canada in law is—or was before April 17, 1982—a British colony so far as authority over her constitution is concerned. This, in their view, was the effect of section 7(1) of the Statute of Westminster, which exempts amendment of the BNA Acts from that statute. This exemption, they hold, left the British Parliament's power to amend Canada's constitution supreme and completely untrammelled. This finding means that not only was Britain free to impose constitutional changes on the Canadian provinces, but it was equally free to impose changes on the federal Parliament or to reject changes requested by that Parliament.

The majority's conclusion that Canada, so far as its constitution is concerned, was still, in law, totally subordinate to the UK Parliament seems wrong to me because it ignored the right to self-determination which Canada could successfully assert internationally. If Britain had imposed constitutional changes on Canada or refused to enact changes requested by the federal Parliament and all ten provinces, I am certain that Canada's rejection of this exercise of British power would have been upheld by her own courts and by the international community. In other words, it would appear doubtful that the enactment of changes in Canada's constitution by the British Parliament, regardless of the wishes of the autonomous Canadian community, was all that was needed to give such changes legal status in Canada. The Supreme Court majority, like many Canadians who were in a rush to achieve patriation, may have found it convenient to forget that the legal procedures agreed to at the constitutional conference of February 1971 for achieving patriation called for the passing of identical resolutions by the Parliament of Canada and all the provincial Legislatures endorsing the amending formula and any substantive constitutional changes. The British Parliament's authorization was then simply regarded as an extra step "to ensure the legal validity of the procedures."[82]

The point of such a ratification step in Canada would have been to recognize in a formal way that the legitimacy of Canada's constitution was based in both a legal and political sense on an act of the Canadian political community. This would have rooted Canada's constitutional autonomy more clearly in what K.C. Wheare referred to as "constitutional autochthony"—a constitution sprung from the land itself.[83] Because a majority of the members of Quebec's Legislature opposed the terms of patriation, it has not been possible to give the new constitution such an autochthonous base. As a result, the foundation of Canada's constitutional autonomy rests on an Act of the British Parliament which, from a narrow legal point of view, could be unilaterally rescinded by that Parliament. Canadians must continue to live with the unhappy fact that the social contract on which Canada's constitutional self-government should ideally rest has not yet been fully consummated.

Conclusion

Thus my own assessment of the strength of the arguments advanced by each side of the court on the questions of law and convention leads me to the conclusion that the provinces should have won the case on the basis of law alone. Although I think the opinions on convention also favour the provinces, still I believe that given the view put forward by the majority at the beginning of their opinion that convention is *entirely* political and in no sense legal, in strict logic the court should not have answered the question about the content of convention.

This is a troubling conclusion because, as I have suggested at the outset, it may be that the court's opinion had a beneficial effect in bringing about a resolution to Canada's constitutional impasse. If that is so, I would like to be able to congratulate the members of the Supreme Court, especially the four judges, Justices Dickson, Beetz, Chouinard and Lamer who anchored both majorities, for the wisdom of their statescraft. But to do so I am afraid may mean that I am subscribing to a "result-oriented" jurisprudence which assesses judicial decisions in terms of whether they support one's personal political preferences. Such a jurisprudence is scarcely jurisprudence at all, for in denying the relevance of rationality in the judges' reasons it denies that there is any inherent difference between decision-making by courts and decision-making by the political branches of government. And that is a conclusion which neither I nor, I am sure, the court could accept.

Notes

1. The question the Quebec government submitted to the Quebec Court of Appeal is as follows:

   Is the agreement of Quebec, by convention, constitutionally required for the adoption by the Canadian Senate and House of Commons of a resolution whose object is to amend the Canadian constitution in such a way as to affect:
   (i) the legislative authority of the Quebec legislature by virtue of the Canadian constitution;
   (ii) the status or role of the Quebec legislature or government within the Canadian federation;
   and, does Quebec's objection render such a resolution unconstitutional in the conventional sense?

   Re Attorney General of Quebec and Attorney General of Canada (1982), 134 D.L.R. (3d) 719.

2. *Toronto Globe and Mail*, Dec. 7, 1982.

3. Paul Weiler, "Two Models of Judicial Decision-Making" (1968), 46 *Canadian Bar Review*, p. 419.

4. The argument is set out at pages 29 to 31 of the Factum of the Attorney General of Canada submitted to the Supreme Court in this case.

5. [1980] 1 S.C.R. 54.

6. *Reference re Amendment of the Constitution of Canada (Nos. 1, 2 and 3)* (1982), 125 D.L.R. (3d) 1 at p. 17.

7. *Ibid.*, p. 107. It should be noted that Justice Hall of the Manitoba Court of Appeal refused to answer the second question put to the Court "because it is not appropriate for judicial determination." *Reference re Amendment of the Constitution of Canada (No. 1)* 117 D.L.R. (3d) 1 (Man. C.A.).

8. *Reference re Amendment of the Constitution of Canada (Nos. 1, 2 and 3), loc. cit.*, at p. 88.

9. *Toronto Globe and Mail*, Oct. 15, 1980.

10. For a good discussion of the pro's and con's of the reference procedure, see Barry Strayer, *Judicial Review of Legislation in Canada* (Toronto: University of Toronto Press, 1968).

11. This is based on my own record of these proceedings. There is no official transcript of oral hearings in the Supreme Court of Canada.

12. The first edition of Dicey's book was published in 1885. References to the book which follow are to the tenth edition, published by Macmillan in 1959.

13. A.V. Dicey, *Introduction to the Law of the Constitution*, p. 417.

14. (1982), 125 D.L.R. (3d) 84.

15. For a discussion of conflicting views see Peter W. Hogg, *Constitutional Law of Canada* (Toronto: Carswell, 1977), pp. 158-60.

16. *Reference re Amendment of the Constitution of Canada (Nos. 1, 2 and 3), loc. cit.* at p. 114.

17. The purpose of conventions, said Dicey "is to secure that Parliament, or the Cabinet . . . shall in the long run give effect to the will of that power which in modern England is the true political sovereign of the State—the majority of the electors or (to use popular though not quite accurate language) the nation." Dicey, *op. cit.*, p. 429.

18. *Reference re Amendment of the Constitution of Canada (Nos. 1, 2 and 3), loc. cit.* at p. 110.

19. For a discussion of the role and status of such conventions in Canada's constitutional system see R. MacGregor Dawson, *The Government of Canada*, 4th ed., Rev. by Norman Ward (Toronto: University of Toronto Press, 1963), ch. 4.

20. *Reference re Amendment of the Constitution of Canada (Nos. 1, 2 and 3), loc. cit.* at p. 115.

21. See K.C. Wheare, *Modern Constitutions* (London: Oxford University Press, 1951).

22. Colin R. Munro, "Laws and Conventions Distinguished" (1975), 91 *Law Quarterly Review*, p. 219.

23. See W.A. Matheson, *The Prime Minister and the Cabinet* (Toronto: Methuen, 1976). According to Matheson, "The practice of ensuring representation from provinces and groups (in the Cabinet) has now broadened into a rigid convention of the Canadian constitution . . ." p. 27.

24. Some constitutional scholars would still support the use of disallowance at least to protect civil liberties, but others view it as being rendered obsolete by convention. See Hogg, *op. cit.*, p. 39, note 37.

25. *Reference re Disallowance and Reservation of Provincial Legislation*, [1938] S.C.R. 71.

26. *Gallant v. The King*, [1949] 2 D.L.R. 425.

27. Dicey, *op. cit.*, p. 419.

28. *Reference re Amendment of the Constitution of Canada (Nos. 1, 2 and 3), loc. cit.* at p. 90. Jennings' three-fold test was proposed in Saskatchewan's factum. See p. 14.

29. In principle the task of ascertaining the answer to a question about convention is similar to Ronald Dworkin's characterization of the judge's task in deciding "hard cases" about legal rights, a task in which the judge must recognize that "what an individual is entitled to have, in civil society, depends upon both the practice and the justice of its political institutions." Ronald Dworkin, *Taking Rights Seriously* (Cambridge, Mass.: Harvard University Press, 1977), p. 87.

30. United Kingdom, Parliament, House of Commons, Standing Committee on Foreign Affairs, *British North America Acts: The Role of Parliament*, January 30, 1981.

31. Jean Chretien, *The Role of the United Kingdom in the Amendment of the Canadian Constitution* (Government of Canada, March 1981). The Kershaw committee produced a rejoinder to this paper. *Supplementary Report on the British North America Acts: The Role of Parliament*, April 15, 1981.

32. *Reference re Amendment of the Constitution of Canada (Nos. 1, 2 and 3), loc. cit.* at p. 93.

33. *Ibid.*, p. 94. The four negative examples were Ontario's and Quebec's refusal to support a proposed amendment on indirect taxation in 1951, the failure to agree on an amending formula in 1960, Quebec's rejection of the Fulton-Favreau amending formula following the 1964 first ministers' conference, and Quebec's rejection of the Victoria Charter in 1971.

34. *Ibid.*, p. 118.

35. *Ibid.*, p. 121.

36. *Ibid.*, p. 105.

37. *Ibid.*, p. 101.

38. *Ibid.*, p. 121.

39. *Ibid.*, p. 99.

40. *Ibid.*

41. *Supplementary Report on the British North America Acts: The Role of Parliament*, April 15, 1981, p. xvii.

42. A different point is developed in Saskatchewan's written factum. There it is argued (pp. 37-38) that traditionally in exercising judicial review, courts have ruled that in the particular circumstances of the case government activity violates the constitution without providing a comprehensive and precise formulation of a constitutional rule covering all circumstances. For example in *Reference re Anti-Inflation Act*, [1976] 2 S.C.R. 373, the court did not define a precise level of inflation that justifies use of the federal emergency power.

43. See Edwin R. Black, *Divided Loyalties: Canadian Concepts of Federalism* (Kingston: McGill-Queen's University Press, 1975), ch. 5.

44. See William S. Livingston, *Federalism and Constitutional Change* (Oxford: Clarendon Press, 1956).

45. *Reference re Amendment of the Constitution of Canada (Nos. 1, 2 and 3), loc. cit.*, at p. 107.

46. Numerous decisions were cited in the majority opinion on convention and in

the minority opinion on law. See especially *ibid.*, pp. 55-60 and 75-77.

47. *Ibid.*, p. 104.

48. *Ibid.*, p. 125.

49. The principal examples of these imperial elements are the federal government's powers of disallowance and reservation, of appointing provincial Lieutenant-Governors, of appointing the senior provincial judges, and the federal Parliament's power to declare local works to be under federal jurisdiction and to establish Canada's Supreme Court.

50. *Toronto Globe and Mail*, Sept. 29, 1981, p. D7.

51. Colin Munro's article, *loc. cit.*, is a strong statement of the view that law and convention are totally distinct. Sir Ivor Jennings' *The Law and the Constitution* provides a powerful statement of the opposing view.

52. Dicey, *op. cit.*, p. 24.

53. *Reference re Amendment of the Constitution of Canada (Nos. 1, 2 and 3), loc. cit.*, at p. 88.

54. See Factum of the Attorney General of Manitoba, pp. 30-36.

55. *Reference re Amendment of the Constitution of Canada (Nos. 1, 2 and 3), loc. cit.*, at p. 88.

56. *Ibid.*, p. 87.

57. *Reference re Weekly Rest in Industrial Undertakings Act*, [1936] S.C.R. 461 at p. 477.

58. *Reference re Amendment of the Constitution of Canada (Nos. 1, 2, and 3), loc. cit.*, at p. 24.

59. *Arseneau v. The Queen*, [1979] 2 S.C.R. 136.

60. *Ibid.*, p. 149.

61. [1942] A.C. 206.

62. Ivor Jennings, *The Law and the Constitution*, Fifth ed. (London: University of London Press, 1959), p. 109.

63. [1976] 1 Q.B. 752.

64. *Ibid.*, p. 765.

65. *Ibid.*, p. 771.

66. *Reference re Amendment of the Constitution of Canada (Nos. 1, 2 and 3), loc. cit.* at p. 26.

67. Sir Ivor Jennings attributes the "crystallization" language to the Chief Justice's use of this concept in *Reference re Weekly Rest in Industrial Undertakings Act*. But he states that Duff's use of the concept in this case was "not consistent with the practice of the courts, which is the common law. The constitutional usages which were incorporated into the common law were more of the seventeenth century." *op. cit.*, p. 127.

68. Professor Hogg, *op. cit.*, p. 8 suggests that "a judicial decision could have the effect of transforming a conventional rule into a legal rule." The minority opinion on convention appears to repudiate this possibility, (1982), 125 D.L.R. (3d) at 113.

69. Dicey, *op. cit.*, p. 24.

70. *Reference re Amendment of the Constitution of Canada (Nos. 1, 2 and 3), loc. cit.* at p. 31.

71. *Ibid.*, p. 41.

72. The BNA Act did not explicitly prohibit the federal Parliament from amending

238 / The Courts in the Constitutional Process

the BNA Act with respect to provincial powers. However, the fact that in 1949 Parliament obtained a limited amending power [section 91(1)] which explicitly excluded, among other things, amendments affecting provincial powers provided an overwhelming presumption that Parliament was not empowered to enact amendments affecting provincial powers. *Ibid.*, p. 61.

73. See cases discussed in *ibid.*, pp. 73-76 and 58-61.
74. *Ibid.*, p. 30.
75. *Ibid.*, pp. 70-73.
76. *Ibid.*, p. 69.
77. *Ibid.*, p. 21.
78. The phrase used in the Balfour Declaration which issued from the Imperial Conference of 1926.
79. *Reference re Amendment of the Constitution of Canada (Nos. 1, 2 and 3), loc. cit.* at p. 34.
80. This phrase is found in the preamble to the statute. Section 4 of the statute establishes the same rule.
81. *Reference re Amendment of the Constitution of Canada (Nos. 1, 2 and 3), loc. cit.* at pp. 39-40.
82. Canada, Senate and House of Commons, *Final Report of the Special Joint Committee of the Senate and of the House of Commons on The Constitution of Canada* (Ottawa: Information Canada, 1972), p. 8. For a discussion of this issue see Melvin Smith, "Patriation: A Myth or Reality?" 2 *Policy Options*, December, 1981.
83. K.C. Wheare, *The Constitutional Structure of the Commonwealth* (Oxford: Clarendon Press, 1960), ch. iv.

Part IV/Democracy and the Constitution

Chapter 12/Democracy and the Canadian Constitution
Reginald Whitaker

Canadians, we are told, are not very interested in the great constitutional debates which have so animated the politicians in recent years. Perhaps. Yet if ordinary Canadians are not much interested in the constitution, it has been equally true that the constitution has not been much interested in Canadians.

The constitution of Canada has been, from 1867 onward, an arrangement between elites, particularly between political elites. Constitutions are normally arrangements between people and their governments. The American constitution, for example, begins: "We, the people, in order to form a more perfect union . . . ," and then goes on to regulate the relations between people and the governments they were instituting. The preamble to the constitution of the Fifth French Republic (1958) begins: "The French people solemnly proclaims its attachment to the Rights of Man and the principles of national sovereignty as defined by the Declaration of 1789 . . . ," and goes on to state that the community shall be based on "equality" and "solidarity," that the republic shall be "democratic," and that "national sovereignty belongs to the people, which shall exercise it through its representatives and by way of referenda." The Basic Law of the Federal Republic of Germany (1949) begins with a preamble indicating that the "German people . . . are called upon to achieve in free self-determination the unity and freedom of Germany," and then immediately in the first 19 articles recognizes "inviolable and inalienable human rights as the basis of every community" and binds the state to "respect and protect" the enumerated basic rights. The British North America Act of 1867 was, as I shall presently show, almost entirely innocent of any recognition of the people as the object of the constitutional exercise.

If we go back further, we find that the seventeenth century social contract theorists such as Hobbes and Locke saw the fundamental basis of government as resting on an arrangement to maintain social peace between the individual members of a community. Canada may be the only country where the primary role of the constitution is to maintain peace between governments rather than between people, or between the people and their governments.

The British North America Act ignored individual Canadians, except as they qualified through membership in a church or a language group. The BNA Act was itself never submitted to a popular referendum for ratification, except when Newfoundland was asked if it wanted *in*, and when Quebec was asked if it wanted *out*. But to make matters worse, almost all of the commentary—whether political, judicial, or academic—on the nature and reform of the constitution has tended to ignore the question of the relation of people to government, or of people to each other, in favour of persistent attention to the relation of government to government, or of Crown to Parliament, or of Canada to the British Parliament.

This obsessive orientation has not only had the effect of making constitutional questions appear tedious and irrelevant to most Canadians, but it has contributed to one of the least attractive qualities of Canadian public life—a general level of illiteracy in political philosophy. That a major debate over constitutional revision in the 1970s and early 1980s should take place in apparent ignorance (apart from a few glimmerings from a few participants) of the profound questions of liberty, equality, authority and obligation, which any significant change in a national constitution must raise, is a sad commentary indeed. The irony is that these questions *are* inevitably involved. Canadians simply tend to sleepwalk their way through while remaining unconscious of the implications of their words and actions.

This is not some peculiar Canadian variant of original sin which we are fated to carry in our genes. It is a product of history and circumstance, and hence open to change. Indeed, there were faint indications in the great constitutional debate of 1980–82 that people are beginning to be included. It is said that a proverbial Irishman, coming upon a donnybrook in progress on a Dublin street, tapped one of the contestants on the shoulder and politely inquired: "Is this a private quarrel, or may anyone join in?" It is about time that the private quarrel of eleven governmental elites was extended to one which anyone can join in. But to do this it is necessary to retrace some of the roots of this mentality with regard not to the legalist language in which it has comprehended itself, but rather in the language of political ideas.

I propose to concentrate on the idea of *democracy*. We are told that we are a democracy. This is supposed to demonstrate our superiority to other systems, which are totalitarian or dictatorial or communist or barbaric—but certainly never democratic. When Paul Henderson scored the winning goal in the last minute of the final game of the first Canada-Russia hockey series, he confessed that he suddenly understood the "meaning of democracy." Lacking that luminous epiphany, the rest of us may still need guidance on the point, especially in Canada.

First of all, "democracy" has been reduced, in the Canadian case, to *representative* democracy; we exercise our sovereignty only to choose our governors. Of course there is an underground or dissenting tradition in this country of direct, populist democracy, evident in the farmer and progressive movements of the early twentieth century and in the extra-parliamentary, direct action, and citizen group activities of the last two decades, to give but two examples. But these have been sporadic and marginal to general practice. The United States has been much more given to such exercises of direct democracy as referenda, with "Proposition Thirteen" simply being a particularly spectacular example of a general tendency rarely followed in Canada. Prime Minister Trudeau, in his earlier, philosophical guise, even raised our practice to the dignity of theory: "at each election . . . the people assert their liberty by deciding what government they will consent to obey."[1] Rousseau, two centuries earlier, was more sardonic on the subject of English parliamentary government: "The English people thinks it is free. It greatly deceives itself; it is free only during the election of the Members of Parliament. As soon as they are elected, it is a slave, it is nothing. Given the use made of these brief moments of freedom, the people clearly deserve to lose it."[2] The theory of direct democracy has never been given full constitutional form in a liberal democracy, but some constitutions do recognize some elements of direct democracy, usually in the form of referenda.

Representative democracies formally substitute the national majority for the Rousseauian general will. But even this concept has its limits in a country like Canada. National majoritarianism as the legitimate expression of the popular will, resonant as it is in relatively centralized and unitary states, tends to become weakened and uncertain in a federal context. Obviously a national majority may here represent the enforced supremacy of one province or region over others. As long ago as the 1840s, John C. Calhoun began exploring the dangers of majoritarian democracy to sectional interests in his *A Disquisition on Government*.[3] As a Southerner, Calhoun formulated a theory of "concurrent majorities" to defend against a Northern anti-slave majority. In the event, the North ignored such theory and put the South's peculiar institutions to the torch in the Civil War. At the same time, Calhoun's argument raised another dilemma often associated with sectional defences against national majorities: the argument may actually be on behalf of a sectional majority wishing to deny rights to a sectional minority, in this case slavery of blacks. Suffice to say at this point that the tempering of majoritarianism with federalism introduces deep ambiguities and contradictions into democratic discourse—or at least ambiguities and contradictions peculiar to federal societies.

However complex the problem, it must be recognized that an acceptance of the federal principle does necessarily enforce distinct limitations on democratic theory. Any federal system worthy of the name, by dividing powers between co-ordinate governments and by recognizing or creating sub-national jurisdictions on regional lines (especially where such jurisdictions overlap more or less with distinct regional, ethnic, religious or linguistic cleavages), has in effect denied the universal efficacy of the national majority as the embodiment of the sovereign democratic will. In the Canadian case, federalism actually meant a more specific limitation on an older, non-democratic principle of sovereignty—the British doctrine of the supremacy of Parliament. By dividing powers between legislative jurisdictions in a written constitution, the BNA Act limited both the supremacy of any Legislature and the scope of national majority will.[4]

We will return later to the special case of federal democracies. But to assess Canada's place as a representative democracy, we will at this stage confine ourselves to a consideration of the principle of universal adult suffrage. By this yardstick, Canada today seems unexceptionable. Virtually all adult citizens can exercise their franchise to choose their governors. Exclusions from the franchise are relatively marginal. In the Canada Elections Act of 1970, all franchise restrictions on citizens eighteen years of age and over have been eliminated, save for convicts, the mentally incompetent, federal judges, and electoral and returning officers. It would be a brave reactionary indeed who would today dare publicly to urge the disenfranchisement of any group of citizens.

This democratic orthodoxy is, however, of comparatively recent origin. Native Indians were first allowed to vote in 1960. Canadians of Japanese origin were enfranchised for federal elections as recently as 1948. It was only in 1940 that the female population of Quebec was permitted to vote in provincial elections. Despite the rhetorical tendency of present-day politicians and commentators to read back into the past current conventional wisdom, Canada's origins have little to do with democracy and a great deal to do with a consciously anti-democratic ideology. Somewhere between the British North America Act of 1867 and the 1914–18 War (when Canadians were exhorted to die to "make the world safe for democracy,") *democracy* as a term of political discourse changed from a bad word to a good word. Such a change in discourse normally indicates an important change in the ideological structure of politics. In the case of Canada, it indicates a transformation in the relationship between citizens from hierarchy to at least formal equality. It also involves a crucial question about the legitimate source of sovereignty in the body politic.

The problem is that we have continued into the late twentieth century with a constitutional framework expressing eighteenth and nineteenth century British notions of sovereignty as derived from the Crown-in-Parliament, combining the three traditional elements of authority: the Crown (monarchy), the Lords (aristocracy), and the Commons (representative democracy). It was believed that a balanced constitution, mixing these three legitimate principles, was the wisest form of statecraft.

The earliest forms of government in the British North American colonies as drawn up by the British Colonial Office reflected a deep British distrust of the democratic potential inherent in American republicanism, a distrust hardened by conflict with the Americans and by the spectacle of a social and political revolution in France in 1789 and the subsequent Napoleonic wars. The influx of loyalist refugees and the determination of the British colonial administrators to build a "better America" as revenge for the loss of the thirteen colonies to the south meant that English Canada began its constitutional history in an atmosphere which could only be described as distinctly anti-democratic. The paternalistic colonial framework of authority was always present in the official ideology of loyalty to the British Crown. Within the colonies, the executive was crushingly dominant, backed by appointed officials from the local oligarchies, and not held responsible to the elected assemblies, which were themselves based upon a limited property-holding male franchise. To complete the picture, local strivings for self-government, such as American-style town meetings, were not only discouraged, but sometimes violently repressed. And in Lower Canada, ethnic conflict further deepened elite distrust of man in the mass, in this case involving a French-speaking majority facing an economically and socially privileged English-speaking minority.

The particular conditions of Canada's colonial genesis did much to contribute to a deeply-ingrained anti-democratic strain among the political elites, a strain reinforced by the decisive turn of the Americans towards democracy in the early nineteenth century, the War of 1812, and the American Civil War and its implications for Canadian autonomy. But Canadian elite opinion was only reflective, in a particularly sharp focus, of educated opinion in Britain. Not only was democracy an American and thus un-British aberration, but it was an ideological battle cry increasingly to be associated with the emergent urban proletariat spawned in the "dark satanic mills" of the industrial revolution. Trade unions and radicals challenged the stability of the bourgeois order and England's hegemony in the world economy, based as it was on starvation wages and vast capital accumulation. This image of democracy as a spectre haunting the middle classes led even such a fair-minded and liberal thinker as John Stuart Mill to devise elaborate franchise schemes for containing the potential influence of the lower orders. In this suspicion of democracy, conventional opinion was backed by the full weight of the respectable tradition of political philosophy, all the way back to Aristotle's espousal of the mixed regime as the best possible among imperfect men.

It should be specified that in the Canadian case, there was a kind of special populist twist to this anti-democratic argument. The idea that persons who sold their labour to others or who owned no property were not free and autonomous citizens and thus could not be trusted to exercise the franchise in a responsible fashion was widely accepted. On the other hand, it was a piece of more or less conventional wisdom in colonial Canada that by contrast to Europe, land was cheap and labour dear. The consequence was that propertyless immigrants found it relatively easy to become small farmers. In becoming small farmers, even if heavily indebted to merchants and banks, they were likely to qualify for the property franchise. Thus, the anti-democratic ideology did leave open the possibility that in frontier North America hard work could elevate those from the lower orders to the status of citizens participating in the public realm.

The actual situation in the various colonies before Confederation with regard to the franchise is difficult to summarize. Each colony had different rules; actual statistical information on the proportions of the adult populations that could vote is extremely difficult to come by, and the socio-economic structure of colonial society was itself always changing, thus altering the overall impact of the legal qualifications. It does seem likely, however, that as the century wore on, as the number of poor immigrants increased, and as land was more and more accounted for, the enfranchised proportion of the population actually declined. But this was subject to local variations and is not backed by conclusive empirical evidence.[5]

At the first federal election following Confederation in 1867, about 15 percent on average of the total population of the four original provinces was eligible to vote. By 1882, the last federal election held under variable provincial franchises, this proportion ranged from a low of 11 percent in British Columbia to a high of 35 percent in Manitoba. In 1891, all provinces except British Columbia showed enfranchised populations from one-fifth to one-quarter of the total. By the turn of the century, the progressive enfranchisement of adult males was slowly, but apparently inexorably, proceeding. Yet when the demand for *female* suffrage was raised, there was no shortage of anti-democratic arguments to justify the restriction of the vote to male heads of household who alone disposed of property and thus possessed true citizenship. Finally, however, following the war to "make the world safe for democracy," women were admitted to the franchise, and in the 1921 election the electorate accounted for 50.6 percent of the total population.[6]

This question of the extent of the franchise is a good index of the dominant political theory of the elites. It indicates that throughout the nineteenth century, there was a long ideological rearguard action fought against what Alexis de Tocqueville in the 1830s had described as the "irresistible," "universal" and "providential" rise of equality, a trend which was in his eyes endemic to modernity and impossible to reverse.[7] Moreover, an examination of the political discourse of the elites suggests that until very late in the century it was not even perceived as a rearguard campaign at all. Sir John A. Macdonald appears to have been blandly confident that democracy was just another American aberration, which sound and sensible British institutions would override. Indeed, Sir John— of whom his secretary wrote he had always held repellent the idea that a man should vote just because he breathed—once delivered himself of perhaps the most aphoristic distillation of the conservative anti-democratic view to be found anywhere: "The rights of the minority ought to be protected, and the rich are always fewer in number than the poor."[8] Nor was the Grit opposition to Toryism notable for its democratic sentiment. There was some such sentiment among the *Rouges* of Quebec, although here democratic sentiment can also be read as the nationalism of the French-speaking majority. The Ontario Grits sometimes sounded themes such as the famous "rep by pop" rallying cry, but on examination this had much more to do with asserting the primacy of Protestant English-speaking Ontario over Catholic Quebec, with the method of representation a handy weapon in the struggle. Representation of the "people" was thus distinctly secondary to representation of the interests of particular regional economic groupings, or the interests of particular religious, ethnic or linguistic groupings.

Let us now take stock of the distant relationship between democracy and the constitutional arrangements of 1867. First, the actual language of the British North America Act itself is revealing. Many constitutions use a preamble as a vehicle for discussion of the general political principles of the nation in question. Ours limited itself to noting that the *provinces* have "expressed their desire to be federally united into One Dominion," that such a union "would conduce to the Welfare of the Provinces and promote the Interests of the British Empire," and that it is thus "expedient, not only that the Constitution of the Legislative Authority in the Dominion be provided for, but also that the Nature of the Executive Government therein be declared." No mention of people, only of governments. Thus was set a theme which is carried through the rest of the exercise with only minor deviations.

People did make a first tentative appearance in section 14, where it is stated that, "if Her Majesty thinks fit," the Governor-General might appoint any persons to be his "Deputies," but this was quickly revealed to refer to those who held office. Governments, it appears, are actually composed of persons, but their importance derives from their office alone. This became obvious in the curious discussion of the House of Commons. Section 37 indicated in its original form that 181 members shall be "elected," but apart from an involved discussion of the respective weight of the provinces in the House, and even some detailed instructions on the distribution of seats geographically within provinces, there was little indication of *who* was supposed to elect the representatives of these provincial and geographic areas. Whatever franchise qualifications already existed in the provinces were to be adopted *holus bolus* by the new Dominion government, except for a clause in section 41 which boldly declared that at any election for the District of Algoma, "every Male British Subject, aged twenty-one years or upwards, being a Householder, shall have a Vote."

Section 51 dealt at length with the problem of "readjustment of representation," but solely in terms of balance between provincial contingents. Population changes were to be considered in relation to provincial strength, but such changes bore no relationship to the numbers of actual *voters*. In other words, people counted as components of provincial weight, but not in and of themselves.

Some of the legislative institutions were deliberately designed to be quite undemocratic. The non-elected Senate was to be Macdonald's safeguard for the wealthy minority. The property qualifications for a senator were highly specific: 4000 dollars of *net* worth in land and an equal amount in "Real and Personal Property." Given that the average annual income of a fully employed mechanic in the 1870s was about $450 *before* expenditures on food, clothes and accommodation for his family, it becomes apparent that the Senate certainly deserved its popular attribution as "rich man's club." Just to rub it in, section 31 specifies that if a senator loses his property or becomes bankrupt, he is to be removed.

Another sort of special privilege was written into the constitution with the provision for a second, non-elected chamber, the Legislative Council, in Quebec. Although the reason why Quebec, alone of the provinces, should have been saddled with a second chamber is not spelled out in the BNA Act, it is clear from the context of the debates. The Senate was to protect the wealthy minority, and the Legislative Council was to protect the English Protestant minority of Quebec. That similar councils were not set up to protect, say, the Catholic minority in Ontario speaks volumes about the nature of the bargain struck.

The concern about the Protestants of Quebec also led to one of the closest brushes with recognition of people to be found in the original Act. Section 93 speaks of protection of the "Rights and Privileges" of Catholic and Protestant subjects in education, of appeals to the national government against provincial Acts affecting the educational rights of religious minorities, and of "remedial Laws" to be made by the Parliament of Canada where such rights are judged to have been so affected. Without touching upon the tortuous and troubled history of this section in relation to Manitoba and Ontario, it might simply be noted that this unusual sign of recognition of the rights of citizens was not on the basis of individual citizenship at all, but rather on the basis that individuals had rights only as bearers of a recognized collective identity—in this case membership in a particular church. Similarly, section 133 gave limited recognition to the place of the French as well as the English language in the Legislature, laws and courts of both Canada and Quebec; once again, the singling out of Quebec among provinces indicates that it was actually the anglophones of Quebec who were the main objects of this attention. Once more, individual rights were given indirect and limited recognition through individual membership in a group—English or French speakers.

This brief inventory pretty well exhausts all evidence of apparent interest in the citizens of the new nation on the part of the BNA Act. For the rest, one has to suppose when taxes and revenues are discussed that they are to be derived from citizens, but the major thrust is to specify the fiscal relations between the provinces and the national governments in loving, and sometimes ludicrous, detail, including interest rates on outstanding intergovernmental liabilities fixed at 5 percent, and New Brunswick's right to continue to levy lumber duties.

If the BNA settlement were merely a document drawn up in a language which only inadequately expressed the reality of Canadian political relationships, we might pass over the matter in embarrassed silence. In fact the language of what was our fundamental constitutional document for over a century faithfully reflects the political philosophy of the political elites responsible for Confederation. That no popular ratification of the settlement was ever sought, indeed that any referendum or other such recourse was deliberately avoided, is a clear indication that the sovereignty of the people was a principle consciously rejected by the elites. Sovereignty was to continue in an unbroken chain of tradition in the person of the British monarch, to be exercised through her deputy in Canada with the advice of her ministers and the consent of the Commons and the Senate, and with certain powers further entrusted to Lieutenant-Governors and their provincial advisors: in short, the Crown-in-Parliament in a federal system of co-ordinate spheres of jurisdiction.

This traditional British concept of sovereignty has, to be sure, its own antiquarian charms. Yet even in England this ancient Whig notion has about as much relevance to the real world of today as the pomp of a royal wedding has to Britain's industrial decay. The rise of universal suffrage, political parties organizing the mass electorate, executive domination of policy making and other familiar aspects of twentieth-century life have emptied the concept of its original content. The Crown is limited to a largely ceremonial role, the Lords do an odd bit of sniping here and there on behalf of corporate interests, and even the Commons is normally subservient to the Cabinet and the higher civil service. These observations are the mere commonplace of current political science. Yet the theoretical implications for the theory of the "sovereignty of Parliament" are too often ignored by romanticists of the British way of life and the Mother of Parliaments. The fact is that the people exercise a kind of sovereignty by choosing every few years which lot of politicians they wish to put in, and which out. Once in, a party governs with an eye to a number of factors— from how their actions are going down with the business community to the public opinion polls. If this form of government should be raised to the dignity of a philosophy of sovereignty, which it perhaps ought not to be, then the best label one can attach to it may be the doctrine of majoritarian populism. The people are assumed to have a will which is expressed through the election of governments with legislative majorities.

The same changes have also taken place in Canada, with the equivalent transformation of the original, borrowed notion of sovereignty enshrined in the BNA Act. Thus, when Sterling Lyon, former premier of Manitoba, spoke with unaccustomed eloquence against the proposed federal Charter of Rights at the constitutional conference of September 1980 by invoking a traditional view of the supremacy of Parliament, he was in fact engaged in a deceptive discourse. Apart from the fact that federalism puts into question *which* Parliament is supreme, thus rendering the idea somewhat irrelevant in the first place, Lyon's words took on a double meaning. Formally, he was speaking of an old, pre-democratic concept of sovereignty; practically, he was engaged in a majoritarian populist argument that the Legislature of Manitoba should have an unimpeded jurisdiction over minorities, limited only by the conscience of the majority. This latter argument is by no means a traditional conservative view; rather, it is a particular kind of democratic argument, although one which many more liberal democrats would reject.

My point here is that when the content of the traditional notion of sovereignty has been transformed by the rise of universal suffrage and the acceptance of formal equality between all citizens, the retention of the trappings of the traditional constitutional structure tends to mystify and confuse the real political issues involved. This is not to suggest that parliamentary government is outmoded or inferior to presidential systems. It is simply to affirm that a lot of rubble has to be moved away to gain a clearer view.

Another aspect of the BNA settlement which has crucial relevance today is its particular concept of nationality. As a federal country with two main ethnic, linguistic and religious communities, it is now obvious that Canada could never have been a unitary nation such as France or even, perhaps, a relatively centralized federation such as the United States eventually turned out to be after the unpleasantness of a civil war. Yet it is also the case that the highly undemocratic nature of the Confederation settlement reinforced the centrifugal forces already at work. Sir John A. Macdonald and his Tory colleagues wanted a federation *more* centralized than that of the Americans. Whatever the Judicial Committee of the Privy Council later did to stand the division of powers on its head, there can be no serious argument that Macdonald's intention was to do other than to build as centralized a nation as was practicable. The award of all the important economic powers and all the important sources of revenue to the national government, the powers of reservation and disallowance, the declaratory power, and numerous other aspects of the BNA Act establish this tendency.

It is an old chestnut of examinations in introductory courses in Canadian politics to ask why a constitution, which on the surface is so centralized as to lead some students of federalism to deny that Canada can even be called a federation, has resulted in perhaps the most decentralized federation in the world, rivalled only by Switzerland. I do not want to go over the standard historical answers to this question. I do want to suggest, however, that the concept of building a national state was a peculiar and peculiarly limited one, and that some of its limitations are connected to its undemocratic nature.

Nation-building rested on two main foundations: formally, on the concentration of economic powers and fiscal resources at the national level along with the federal mission to colonize the prairies and integrate them into the national structures; informally, on the putative attraction of the various elites to accommodate each other on the prospect of mutual economic benefit. The relationship between the CPR, the Conservative party and westward expansion is highly illustrative of the political economy of a centralized federalism. The limitation of this lies precisely in its reliance on elites and on their exclusively economic motives. Even a federation—perhaps *especially* a federation—needs some mass attachmient of an emotional or sentimental nature to the national level. A functioning federal state must strike some stable balance between regional, provincial or subcultural identities, and an identity of citizens *qua* citizens with their national state. The recognition of the principle of the sovereignty of the people is a way of encouraging such attachment over more limited identities.

The Americans began with the notion of "we the people," and certainly this deeply-held belief in popular sovereignty has been associated with that powerful sense of American nationalism which has long since overridden sectional loyalties. Few Canadians perhaps would want to emulate that example, with its attendant intolerance of "un-American activities," its expansionary aggressiveness and its self-righteous evangelism. Nor is it at all likely that even the best will in the world could ever have sponsored a replica of American-style populist nationalism in the hostile conditions of British North America. What is not open to question is that the distinctly undemocratic nature of Confederation did nothing to encourage a potential sense of mass nationalism, and perhaps did much to discourage it. Certainly provinces, regions and above all, linguistic-cultural communities became the most persuasive centres of sentimental attraction, *faute de mieux*. Worse yet, the seating of sovereignty in the British monarchy and the powerful emotional attachment to Britain and the Empire, which had always been so strongly encouraged in English-speaking Canada, was increasingly viewed in French Canada as a device for symbolically reinforcing anglophone Protestant hegemony over Catholic French-speaking Canada. The monarchy was thus at one and the same time a unifying symbol to one community and a divisive one to the other. On the other hand, the recognition and endorsement of differences has always been at the root of French Canada's demands on the national political system. It is hence a uniquely Canadian achievement to possess a symbol of unity which divides, and a division which unites. In neither case, however, is there any real sense of a sovereign Canadian people.

The burden placed on economic nationalism as a focus for attraction to the national government revealed a crucial weakness: economic relationships change with technological changes and transformations in production. In Canada this has meant that Macdonald's dream of national unity based on a national bourgeoisie and national political elite bound to the nation by fundamental economic interests has attenuated over the twentieth century as changing economic interests have drawn elites into attachments to provinces, regions, and even to north-south continentalist links with American capital and the American state.

All this is an historical parallel with the circumstances in which the federal government's constitutional initiatives of 1980–81 were brought forward. Coupled with the major economic initiative of the National Energy Program and a renewed interest in regaining national fiscal capacity and autonomy in federal-provincial economic relations, the constitutional proposals suggested concerted and purposive moves on the part of the federal government on a series of fronts, the like of which has not been seen for some time. In effect, the Liberal Party—shut out of office in every single province, and with only one provincial member elected in the four Western provincial Legislatures—had perforce taken on the nationalist mantle of Macdonald's nineteenth century Tories at the national level. The defeat of the Parti Québécois' sovereignty option in the Quebec referendum of 1980 and the inability of the premiers in the same year to agree upon a constitutional formula for renewed federalism gave the Trudeau Liberals the historic opportunity to act unilaterally. And they seized the opportunity with the same determination which has characterized their attempted re-assertion of federal dominance over energy policy and fiscal federalism. In Trudeau's vehement rejection of Joe Clark's "community of communities," his passionate assertion that Canada is "more than the sum of its parts," and his government's national initiatives since its re-election in 1980, one can discern the elements of a new National Policy in the late twentieth century.

How does the constitutional reform fit into this renewed assertion of federal domination? In part—and it is this part which is relevant to our concerns—it does reflect a dawning, if imperfect understanding of the connection between the relatively low level of legitimacy of the national government and the weak constitutional basis for popular sovereignty in the BNA Act and in our constitutional practices since 1867.

The most controversial aspect of the initiative taken by the federal government in the fall of 1980 was its unilateralism, its assertion that a joint address to the British government by a simple majority in Parliament, with or without substantial provincial support, would suffice to create a new constitution. Much of the criticism of the method rested on the grounds of the violation of liberal procedural justice, a source of criticism to which Pierre Trudeau ought to have been especially sensitive given his philosophical convictions. Yet the government never argued that it was a *good* method, merely that it was a *necessary* one, all other avenues having been exhausted. Finally, when the Supreme Court handed down its judgement of Solomon on the matter, thereby sending all parties back to the bargaining table, the final compromise reached in November of 1981 indicated that perhaps unilateral patriation had always been more of a bargaining position than a final strategy in itself.

Whatever the Liberal government's motives and intentions, it is worth examining the opposition to unilateralism. This arose partly from traditionalism. In part, the provinces—including, no doubt, a substantial number of people as well as governments—saw the federal government as fundamentally unrepresentative of regional opinion, especially in the West, where the Liberals have very little support. This certainly weakened the legitimacy of a national government based on a national plurality of votes heavily skewed towards central and eastern Canada acting unilaterally on a matter so fundamental as constitutional revision. A question of concurrent majorities in a federal society is inescapable under the circumstances. On the other hand, the fact that the same forces bitterly opposed to unilateralism tended to be equally bitterly opposed to a popular referendum on the constitution raises another question of motives. Even a minority of the New Democratic Party, as well as some left-wing political observers,[9] argued that the proposed method was *undemocratic*. This calls for some discussion.

The argument that the bypassing of provincial government consent was undemocratic involves a curious definition of democracy. The consent of the governed is transposed to the consent of governments. This is squarely within the Canadian tradition, but seems of doubtful relevance to questions of democracy. Unilateral patriation *was* undemocratic, but so has been every other amendment of the BNA Act inasmuch as only governments, never people, have been consulted. And so was the final compromise, applauded by most of those who had fought unilateralism. The agreement hammered out in the kitchen of the conference centre was made by Messrs. Chrétien, Romanow and McMurtry, not by the people of Canada, who have not even been asked to ratify the agreement through any form of popular consultation. Finally, it must be said that there were some significant aspects of the proposed constitutional package which did recognize at least some elements of popular sovereignty. The federal and provincial oppositions sometimes ignored, but in many cases positively opposed, those elements, and in the end they succeeded in eradicating most of them. A strange victory, this.

Before examining each of the democratic elements of the constitutional proposals in turn, I should like to begin with an alternative model of democratic federalism to clarify the contrasts with the existing system. I assume a federal *society*, that is, one in which provincial diversity is not merely the reflection of provincial governmental activity and interest, but results from regional economic, cultural and linguistic bases which would persist in some form or other whatever the constitutional superstructure. National and provincial governments are co-ordinate, with their own spheres of jurisdiction. The main difference between the two types of government, apart from the specific allocation of powers and resources between them, would in my model rest on the two different electorates. The provincial mandate awarded to a party victorious in a provincial election would be the symbol of the sovereignty of the people of that province, just as the national mandate would be the symbol of the sovereignty of the

Canadian people as a whole. Both would be equally legitimate within their respective spheres, and both equally illegitimate when extended unilaterally into the other sphere.

Two implications follow from this. First, it is clear that a constitutional framework must, of course, order the specific division of powers and thus act as the final recourse over jurisdictional disputes. Here the familiar apparatus of federal-provincial conferences and judicial review of constitutionality will continue to be operative in much the same way as always. At the same time, however, the constitution should concern itself at least as much with the relations between citizens and the state. Here the framework must be national, universally applicable to all citizens, and concerned with relations with all governments, national or provincial. A clearly specified set of rights and obligations of citizens will act as a guide to legislators at all levels, but in the final analysis the courts alone can be the final judge, as they are already with the division of powers between governments. This does not involve the intervention of the national government *qua* government in the sphere of provincial jurisdiction, but merely the subjection of all governments to common standards of behaviour *vis-à-vis* their citizens and a common recourse for citizens against the actions of any government.

A second implication is that the national government is not a "government of governments," but a government of citizens. That is to say, it should be representative of the national electorate of a federal society. It should seek to maximize its *direct* representativeness of the constituent elements of this electorate through whatever institutional devices appear appropriate (proportional representation, a regionally representative second chamber, decentralized administration are some ideas). But it should minimize the interposition of provincial governments as "representatives" of provincial or regional citizens. Intergovernmental relations will continue on matters of federal-provincial concern, but within their own spheres governments should be in direct relationship with citizens only.

Some provincial proposals for constitutional change have been in direct conflict with this model. The Parti Québécois' White Paper on sovereignty-association suggested a transfer of powers from the federal government to a series of non-elected commissions and other bodies which would be responsible not to electorates, but to governments. The Quebec Liberal Party's Beige paper on renewed federalism recommended a second chamber in Ottawa replacing the Senate, with members appointed by the provincial governments. This latter suggestion, echoed with variations by some other provinces, would not only substitute governments for people, but would also introduce a radical asymmetry into federalism since no equivalent intrusion of federal government representatives into the institutions of provincial government has been contemplated.

There were three elements of the federal constitutional proposals which could be cited as democratic, by contrast with the views of the provincial governments, or by contrast with some of the federal opposition as well. Two of these are in the text itself, and one in the process whereby the proposal was arrived at.

First was the Charter of Rights and Freedoms. Quite apart from liberal arguments for guaranteeing individual rights, especially against administrative and judicial abuses, an entrenched Charter performs a basic democratic function of regulating relations between governments and citizens which was never performed by the BNA Act. That it does so by clearly and decisively enunciating the equality of all citizens in their rights and freedoms is a major step forward. Section 3 of the new Charter at least spells out that "every citizen of Canada has the right to vote in an election of members of the House of Commons or of a legislative assembly and to be qualified for membership therein." Even if this actually will not change anything, it at least gives a constitutional sanction to the fundamentally democratic nature of the Canadian political system.

Prime Minister Trudeau has for some time been an advocate of such a Charter, on traditional liberal grounds, of course, but as well on grounds specific to Canadian federalism—that a federally-guaranteed Charter of Rights offers a protection for individual Canadians which would tend to bind them directly to the national government, thus counteracting to some degree the centrifugal attractions of provincialism. This is equally true of his 1960s strategy for federal bilingualism to draw francophones to Ottawa as well as Quebec City, of his government's promotion of multicultural-ism, and of his argument that minority language rights are best protected by federal guarantees to individuals. This is why he had opposed provincial suggestions that provinces be allowed to "opt out" of the Charter. It would, after all, utterly undermine the concept of a national guarantee of individual rights of citizens if some citizens could have their protections waived by their provincial governments. Or so the prime minister argued—until the last moment.

The Charter does seem to command wide support among Canadians. A Gallup poll in the spring of 1981 indicated that 62 percent agreed that a Charter of Rights should be included in the patriation plan, with only 15 percent opposed. Support was pretty uniform across all regions.[10] Such support may, in part at least, reflect another democratic aspect of the constitutional debate, this time having to do with process. The televised and widely-reported hearings of the Special Joint Committee of the Senate and House of Commons attracted wide attention from various Canadian citizens and groups who testified, particularly on the Charter. Very exten-sive revisions were made, incorporating many of the suggestions concern-ing weaknesses and omissions from the initial draft. This popular consultation of a government with its citizens could be widely appre-ciated—in contrast to the views of the Progressive Conservatives in Parliament, who had bitterly opposed the closure of parliamentary debate and the referral to the committee as the "death of democracy." Why the consultation of people by the politicians should be considered undemocratic in contrast to debate among politicians is a question best left to opposition MPs.

One might also ask some questions about the result of the discussion over rights. While clearly identifiable groups—women, native people, handicapped persons, cultural minorities—are given various forms of recognition, the Charter is quite deficient in what might be termed *social* rights. A number of European constitutions drawn up with the participation of socialist and Communist representatives at the end of the war (Italy and the Fourth French Republic being the best examples) included such constitutional provisions as the right to strike and the right to a job, or the right of workers to participate in the decisions affecting the conditions in which they work. These social rights are notably absent from the text and even from the discussions and debates, within Parliament and without. That the Charter should reflect an image of liberal rather than social democracy is not particularly surprising given the structure of Canadian society, and the philosophical make-up of the governing party. What is rather more surprising is that the New Democratic Party, despite its vaunted alliance with the Liberals over the constitution, failed to force, or even to demand, any such concessions from their allies. Nor was it on these grounds that the Saskatchewan rebels broke ranks with the NDP caucus. The Canadian Labour Congress remained virtually silent during the debate, in part for fear of alienating its nationalist-minded Quebec wing. The NDP did win a negative concession when the entrenchment of property rights was withdrawn in the face of an NDP fear that such a provision could enable judges to prevent federal or provincial governments from nationalizing private corporations. On the whole, however, and even to the NDP and the CLC, democracy in Canada seems pretty well defined by liberal limits.

The final point to be pursued in this connection, and the one which had perhaps been most hotly contested by the premiers and other opponents, was the device of the referendum to amend the constitution. Carefully employing the same amending formula for provincial government approval (Ontario, Quebec, two Western and two Atlantic provinces), the referendum avoided the anti-federal dangers of majoritarian democracy, but for the first time instituted a recourse to direct popular consultation, something which had, as we have seen, been rigorously excluded from the original constitution-making process.

It is striking that it was this provision which drew the sharpest fire of the leader of the opposition and the premiers. The idea that provincial governments could be bypassed for direct consultation with the people was treated as almost an unthinkable suggestion contrary to our constitutional traditions. There is no doubt that it *is* contrary to our constitutional traditions. The point is that not all traditions are worth cherishing, and in this case there is an excellent case for dispensing with it. The case has been made best by the prime minister in a speech to law students at Osgoode Hall:

> Right now, alas, the fount of our sovereignty lies in the United Kingdom. When it comes home where will the fount of sovereignty lie? Will it be an assembly of 11 first ministers as Mr. Peckford claims, as I'm afraid Mr. Blakeney claims too? Or will it be the people of Canada? And if you are a democrat it seems to me the answer is clear. It is not the institutional leaders elected at a point of time. It is the people of Canada and, if the people of Canada are not prepared to assume that burden and duty of speaking their will over the heads of their elected premiers and prime minister, then I say they are not a nation.[11]

The tradition opposed to this is that politics is an affair for governments and politicians alone, a Canadian tradition perhaps, but not a very admirable one, not one that has done much to strengthen popular support for and attachment to the Canadian nation.

That the referendum procedure and machinery would have rested in the hands of the federal government was, in my view, entirely appropriate, as it is the only government that represents all Canadian citizens. Provincial fears that this would, somehow, have allowed the federal government to manipulate impressionable citizens were exaggerated to say the least. First, if elections are merely manipulation, then the provincial premiers owe *their* alleged right to monopolize the expression of provincial opinion to their ability to manipulate their voters in provincial elections. Secondly, the idea that voters can be browbeaten by clever manipulation of the referendum questions shows a deep contempt for voters—one which is not borne out by the result of the Quebec referendum on sovereignty when the Parti Québécois' own convoluted and ambiguous question was rejected by 60 percent of the voters. Nor is it borne out by the experience of the federations of Switzerland and Australia, which employ popular referenda as a means of amending their constitutions and have discovered that voters are generally very conservative about change and often tend to vote contrary to the desires of their national governments.

There was one glaring weakness in the Liberal government's espousal of the referendum device as an amending procedure, in fact the Achilles heel of the whole process. If Trudeau really had had the courage of his democratic convictions, the entire constitutional proposal should have been submitted to a national referendum, to be counted on the same regional basis as the original amending formula. Despite the Supreme Court ruling, if such a referendum had been passed by the concurrent popular majorities of all regions, any possible obstinacy or interference in Westminster would have been rendered wholly illegitimate and would have constituted nothing less than the gravest of insults to the Canadian people.[12] To be sure, such a course of action might have involved considerable risks; one or more regions might have voted "no," and the package would have sunk. To assess the extent of the risk involved, however, we must consider the compromise text which actually emerged from the final federal-provincial First Ministers' Conference.

It is hard to escape the conclusion that the final text reflects more concessions on the part of the federal government than on the part of the provinces, Quebec being the exception in all cases. From my present point of view, it is most striking that it was the democratic elements of the federal proposal which were bargained away. Although the prime minister did at one point suggest submitting two versions to the voters in a referendum— an option which gained momentary support from Quebec Premier René Lévesque—he just as quickly dropped it in face of unanimous disapproval from the English-Canadian premiers. There followed a compromise which, among other matters, included: (1) carving out some of the provisions of the Charter of Rights and then subjecting most of the remaining provisions to a legislative override, whereby Parliament or the provincial Legislatures might legislate "notwithstanding" the provisions of the Charter; (2) excising all references to referendum procedures for amendment; and (3) substituting a new formula for provincial ratification of amendments. Each of these will be examined in turn.

The *non obstante* or override clause is a compromise which raises considerable question whether Canadians actually will have an entrenched Charter of Rights at all. At best it is a quintessentially and uniquely Canadian device which in effect says we have entrenched rights if necessary, but not necessarily entrenched rights. The override is admittedly hedged with checks, and much is left, in effect, to public opinion to prevent Legislatures from using the power. The effects are therefore not all that easy to predict. Moreover, "democratic," "mobility," "language" and "educational" rights *are* entrenched, without potential override. "Democratic" rights, however, include no more than a statement that every citizen has a right to vote in federal and provincial elections, and provisions for the number of sittings and terms of the Legislatures. The "fundamental freedoms," "legal rights" and "equality rights" are all subject to legislative override. To the extent that the override is used, we will have witnessed a triumph of the Canadian tradition of elitism—governments over people. Even if it is sparingly employed, it constitutes a kind of potential constitutional denial of individual rights.

This contrast of perspectives was dramatically highlighted when the ten consenting first ministers (without exception male and white) cynically decided to jettison native rights and some important aspects of sexual equality from the Charter. In this case the spectacle was too much, even for Canadians. There followed one of the most extraordinary exercises of direct, spontaneous democratic pressure on governments that has ever been seen in this country. The campaign by women on both levels of government was partially successful, that of native groups less so. But here at least was ample evidence that elected politicians cannot and ought not be allowed to arrogate to themselves the exclusive right to speak in the name of the people, that a functioning representative democracy requires constant pressure by citizens directly if it is to remain truly representative. The point was brought home forcefully when Sterling Lyon, perhaps the strongest opponent of an entrenched Charter of Rights, was unceremoniously defeated by the voters of Manitoba within a week of arranging the Accord emasculating the Charter.

Yet the new constitution allows precious little scope for popular participation. The removal of the referendum procedure for amendment means that there will never be in the future any popular consultations for change. At most one might envisage one level of government calling an "advisory" referendum to make a point against the other level on a dead-locked attempt at change. But this would have no formal authority. Again, Canadian tradition has been vindicated—at the expense of democratic sovereignty.

Finally, something should be said about the new amending formula itself. The Trudeau proposals had recognized a *regional* basis for what were, in effect, concurrent majorities necessary for any constitutional change. Partly out of western indignation that Ontario should get a veto, the opposing premiers finally agreed upon a counter-proposal for amend-ment by two-thirds of the provinces representing at least 50 percent of the population. For reasons which remain obscure, Premier Lévesque agreed with this proposal, which withdrew Quebec's veto. When Trudeau finally agreed to accept the counter-proposal in the final agreement, Lévesque cited the denial of a Quebec veto as a major reason for refusing to sign the Accord. Exasperation at Lévesque's bargaining tactics ought not blind one to the dangerous implications of the loss of a Quebec veto. Given the binational character of Canada, and given the central role of Quebec in French Canada (Trudeau himself has described Quebec as *"le foyer et le centre de gravité de la nation canadienne-française"*), it is a direct challenge to the very essence of any notion of democratic federalism to deny Quebec a veto and thus potentially subject Quebec to a national majority will repugnant to it. To be sure, there are now "opting out" provisions for provinces which do not like a constitutional amendment approved by seven of their sister provinces; and in the case of changes touching on educational and cultural matters, fiscal equivalents will be granted to any province exercising this right. This clearly constitutes a tacit recognition of Quebec's "special status." In addition, contrary to some Quebec critics, the new constitution does recognize Canada's cultural duality in terms of the entrenched language and education rights—a duality of *individuals* as members of linguistic groups, although certainly not a duality of *states* as between Canada and Quebec. Having said all that, the fact remains that a constitution which does not recognize a concurrent majority in Quebec is a constitution which leaves a festering wound in the Canadian body politic.

One improvement which the final agreement did make over the federal text had to do with the Senate. Despite the democratic tendencies in the Liberal proposals, they had rather cynically agreed to offer the Senate a veto over changes to its character in order to smooth passage of the Resolution through that chamber. The Senate, that apotheosis of all that is undemocratic in our past, was not only spared change in the constitutional revision, but was to have its status further strengthened. Giving the senators a veto over Senate reform was the equivalent of putting alcoholics in charge of a detoxification centre. Happily, this vicious provision was dropped, given the interest of several premiers in major Senate reform. In the event, the senators did not dare restore the clause, perhaps sensing their lack of popular legitimacy.

Virtually all the recent proposals for a reconstituted second chamber have turned on the need for regional representation, given the growing unrepresentativeness of the national government when no political party can command support in all regions. That the Liberals can govern on the basis of a majority in Quebec and Ontario while excluded from the West reflects a serious deficiency, and one which could be partially alleviated by a second chamber with particular responsibilities for the federal-provincial questions. The idea of such a chamber being appointed by the provincial governments is not only undemocratic, but subversive of the national government's exclusive sphere of jurisdiction as well. More appropriate is direct regional representation within the national structures of government. One intriguing possibility here would be an *elected* Senate, chosen on a basis of provincial or regional equality as in the American case. Such a Senate could be elected on a basis of proportional representation, leaving the Commons as a constituency system. Party representation would be more reflective of actual popular support, meaning that a few Liberals would come from Alberta and a few Progressive Conservatives from Quebec. Thus, in the two Houses of Parliament the two kinds of representative principle appropriate to a democratic federation could be harnessed together: the national majority in the Commons and the concurrent, provincial majorities in the Senate. A recent national survey by the Canada West Foundation shows that almost two-thirds of Canadians would favour an elected Senate, and that less than one in three preferred the present Senate.[13] This may very well be one of the priorities for change now that the new constitution is in place.

In conclusion, the balance-sheet on the democratic basis of the new constitution is mixed to poor. The original federal proposals fell far short of an ideal democratic federal constitution, but at almost every point of difference with the BNA Act they must be judged as being more democratic. That it would be genuinely difficult to imagine them as less democratic is itself quite a comment on our constitutional history. Yet the premiers and the Progressive Conservative opposition in Ottawa revealed in the course of the debate apparent views about the sovereignty of the people which accord poorly indeed with that ritual rhetoric about "democracy" so familiar to political discourse. In the final crunch, with the encouragement of the Supreme Court, the Liberals compromised away most of the democratic content in order to get an agreement (*any* agreement?). Canadian traditions were preserved.

Of course, there are many other equally legitimate ways of judging the process of constitutional change. This way has the virtue of helping illuminate some of the unstated assumptions of political philosophy held by participants in the debate. The picture thus revealed is perhaps not all that flattering.

Notes

1. Pierre Trudeau, *Approaches to Politics* (Toronto: Oxford University Press, 1970), p. 77.
2. Jean-Jacques Rousseau, *The Social Contract* (London: J.M. Dent, 1973), Book III, chapter 15.
3. (New York: Poli Sci Classics, 1947).
4. I have explored these questions at greater length in "Federalism and Democratic Theory," paper presented to the Canadian Political Science Association, June 7, 1982.
5. F. John Garner, *Franchise and Politics in British North America 1755-1867* (Toronto: University of Toronto Press, 1968); Fernand Ouellet, *Lower Canada 1791-1840*, tr. Patricia Claxton (Toronto: McClelland and Stewart, 1980), pp. 24-26.
6. Norman Ward, *The Canadian House of Commons: Representation* (Toronto: University of Toronto Press, 1950), pp. 211-32; Gregory S. Kealey, *Toronto Workers Respond to Industrial Capitalism 1867-1892* (Toronto: University of Toronto Press, 1980), pp. 330, 367-68n.
7. *Democracy in America*, ed. J.P. Mayer and Max Lerner, tr. George Lawrence (New York: Harper & Row, 1966), Vol. 1, Introduction.
8. Quoted in Bruce Hodgins, "Democracy and the Ontario Fathers of Confederation," in Ontario Historical Society, *Profiles of a Province* (Toronto: Ontario Historical Society, 1967), p. 88.
9. For examples of such left-wing criticism, see John Richards, "Populism: A Qualified Defence," *Studies in Political Economy*, Vol. 5 (Spring, 1981), pp. 23-25, and Norman Penner, "The Left and the Constitution," *Canadian Forum* (June-July, 1981), pp. 10-13. Similar criticisms were raised by dissenting delegates to the NDP's national convention, July, 1981.
10. Canadian Institute of Public Opinion, *The Gallup Report*, May 13, 1981.
11. Quoted in the *Toronto Globe and Mail*, February 6, 1981, p. 10.
12. Edward McWhinney makes this democratic argument strongly in *Canada and the Constitution 1979-1982* (Toronto: University of Toronto Press, 1982), pp. ix-x, 102-114.
13. *Toronto Globe and Mail*, December 31, 1981, p. 9.

Chapter 13/The Constitution and Human Rights

Walter S. Tarnopolsky

As of April 17, 1982 we have a new constitutionally entrenched Canadian Charter of Rights and Freedoms. It forms Part I of the Constitution Act, 1982,[1] which is proclaimed to be part of the constitution of Canada. As such, it is "entrenched;" it cannot be amended by the ordinary legislative process, but only by the new amending formula in section 38 of the Constitution Act. Above all, because the Charter is part of the constitution, it is "the supreme law of Canada, and any law that is inconsistent with it is, to the extent of the inconsistency, of no force or effect." The Charter is the greatest achievement of the recent exercise in constitutional renewal.

To assess the possible impact of the new Charter, I propose first to discuss the significance of its constitutional status compared to that of the Canadian Bill of Rights; second, to compare the Charter with the bill to note the main changes in content; third, to discuss more fully some of the new provisions; and fourth, to consider the new enforcement provisions which have been introduced.

The Constitutional Status of the New Charter

The fundamental weakness of the Bill of Rights passed in 1960 was that it did not prevail over other legislation. One of the reasons given by various majorities on the Supreme Court of Canada for avoiding giving it an overriding effect over laws inconsistent with it is that it is not "constitutional;" that it is merely statutory,[2] or at most "quasi-constitutional."[3] If a bill of rights must clearly be a part of the basic constitutional text in order to be interpreted and applied so as to have overriding effect, then the Charter does constitute a major change.

As part of the Constitution Act, 1982, the Charter has the same status as any of the BNA Acts, 1867 to 1975 (now all renamed Constitution Acts). It should therefore be given the same consideration as that given by Lord Sankey to the BNA Acts in the famous "Persons" case:

> The British North America Act planted in Canada a living tree capable of growth and expansion within its natural limits. The object of the Act was to grant a Constitution to Canada. . . .
>
> Their Lordships do not conceive it to be the duty of this Board—it is certainly not their desire—to cut down the provisions of the Act by a narrow and technical construction, but rather to give it a large and liberal interpretation. . . .[4]

Two important ramifications of this status have been expressed in two other important Canadian cases decided by the Judicial Committee of the Privy Council. In British Coal Corporation v. The King, Lord Sankey suggested: "in interpreting a constituent or organic statute, . . . that construction most beneficial to the widest possible amplitude of its powers must be adopted."[5] Subsequently, in the Privy Council Appeals case, Lord Jowitt stated: "To such an organic statute the flexible interpretation must be given which changing circumstances require. . . ."[6]

Essentially, the statements of Lords Sankey and Jowitt suggest that a constitution, unlike an ordinary statute, is intended to last for decades, if not centuries. It cannot be given an interpretation that is "frozen" to concepts as understood at the time of its adoption. It has to be adapted by the judiciary to meet the needs and ideals of the time at which it comes to be interpreted, although obviously within the principles and standards written into it. As a remedial instrument—dealing with human rights and fundamental freedoms—it must be given a large and liberal interpretation. As a corollary, penal statutes and statutes limiting the life, liberty and security of the person have, under common-law principles of interpretation, been narrowly construed.

Furthermore, the courts cannot ignore the similarity between many of the clauses in the new Charter and such other domestic bills of rights as that of the United States, as well as such international bills of rights as the European Convention (which the United Kingdom has ratified, and therefore the interpretation of which has to be applied in the United Kingdom as a condition of membership in the Council of Europe), and the International Covenant on Civil and Political Rights (which Canada has ratified and is thus a binding obligation in international law, although subject to application through internal implementation procedures). The significance of a constitutionally entrenched Charter of Rights that adopts the language of international instruments was recently discussed by the Judicial Committee of the Privy Council. In Minister of Home Affairs v. Fisher, concerning the Bermuda constitution, Lord Wilberforce summed up what was required of the court in such constitutional interpretation:

> Here, however, we are concerned with a Constitution, brought into force certainly by Act of Parliament, the Bermuda Constitution Act 1967 United Kingdom, but established by a self-contained document. . . . It can be seen that this instrument has certain special characteristics. (1) It is . . . drafted in a broad and ample style which lays down principles of width and generality. (2) Chapter I is headed "Protection of Fundamental Rights and Freedoms of the Individual." It is known that this chapter, as similar portions of other constitutional instruments drafted in the post-colonial period . . . was greatly influenced by the European Convention for the Protection of Human Rights and Fundamental Freedoms (1953). . . . That Convention was signed and ratified by the United Kingdom and applied to dependent territories including Bermuda. It was in turn influenced by the United Nations' Universal Declaration of Human Rights of 1948. These antecedents, and the form of Chapter I itself, call for a generous interpretation avoiding what has been called "the austerity of tabulated legalism," suitable to give to individuals the

full measure of the fundamental rights and freedoms referred to. (3) Section 11 of the Constitution forms part of Chapter I. It is thus to "have effect for the purpose of affording protection to the aforesaid rights and freedoms" subject only to such limitations contained in it "being limitations designed to ensure that the enjoyment of the said rights and freedoms by any individual does not prejudice . . . the public interest."[7]

Even more important, Lord Wilberforce went on to elaborate what was suggested earlier, that a constitution cannot be interpreted in the same restricted way as an ordinary statute. It needs a large and liberal interpretation:

> When therefore it becomes necessary to interpret "the subsequent provisions of" Chapter I . . . the question must inevitably be asked whether the appellants' premise . . . that these provisions are to be construed in the manner and according to the rules which apply to Acts of Parliament, is sound. In their Lordships' view there are two possible answers to this. The first would be to say that, recognising the status of the Constitution as, in effect, an Act of Parliament, there is room for interpreting it with less rigidity, and greater generosity, than other Acts, such as those which are concerned with property, or succession, or citizenship. . . . The second would be more radical: it would be to treat a constitutional instrument such as this as sui generis, calling for principles of interpretation of its own, suitable to its character as already described, without necessary acceptance of all the presumptions that are relevant to legislation of private law.
>
> It is possible that, as regards the question now for decision, either method would lead to the same result. But their Lordships prefer the second. This is in no way to say that there are no rules of law which should apply to the interpretation of a Constitution. A Constitution is a legal instrument giving rise, amongst other things, to individual rights capable of enforcement in a court of law. Respect must be paid to the language which has been used and to the traditions and usages which have given meaning to that language. It is quite consistent with this, and with the recognition of the character and origin of the instrument, and to be guided by the principle of giving full recognition and effect to those fundamental rights and freedoms with a statement of which the Constitution commences.[8]

Even though constitutional status, of itself, provides paramountcy, a bill of rights overrides inconsistent laws *only if the actual terms so provide.* Constitutions do contain hortatory provisions, not judicially enforceable as such, but merely setting out legislative aims, such as the "Directive Principles of State Policy" in the Irish and Indian Constitutions, or the "Economic and Social Rights" in Quebec's Charter of Human Rights and Freedoms, though these are not included in its overriding provision.

One of the major defects in the 1960 Canadian Bill of Rights is that section 2, the "operative provision," merely provides that laws of Canada shall "be so construed and applied" as not to be inconsistent with the rights and freedoms recognized in the bill. It does not provide explicitly that legislative or administrative action found to be inconsistent should be invalid or inoperative, even though in the Drybones case,[9] the majority did so hold with respect to legislative Acts. In contrast, section 52(1) of the Constitution Act proclaims that:

> The Constitution of Canada [including, of course, the Charter of Rights and Freedoms] is the supreme law of Canada, and any law that is inconsistent with the provisions of the Constitution is, to the extent of the inconsistency, of no force or effect.

The timidity and obfuscation of the existing bill is replaced by the explicit primacy of the new Charter.

The second major defect of the Bill of Rights is that section 1 "recognized and declared" that the rights and freedoms listed "have existed and shall continue to exist." This has led to an interpretation involving the application of concepts "frozen" in 1960, when the Bill of Rights was enacted.

This principle of interpretation is rooted in a proposition which Mr. Justice Ritchie put forth in Robertson and Rosetanni v. The Queen.[10] It was then expanded by Mr. Justice Martland in the Burnshine case,[11] and Mr. Justice Ritchie returned to it in the Miller and Cockriell case.[12] It seems to have evolved from the view that, since the Canadian Bill of Rights refers to rights and freedoms which "have existed and shall continue to exist," reference must be made to the date when the bill was enacted in order to determine its meaning. Furthermore, since the opening paragraph of section 2 refers to the "rights and freedoms . . . herein recognized and declared," it was concluded that no new rights were created by the Bill of Rights. And since only "existing" rights were protected, any feature of our laws in existence at the time the Bill of Rights was enacted, such as the death penalty[13] or whipping,[14] could not possibly be found to be contrary to it.

If one turns to the Miller and Cockriell case, one sees that the assertion there of 1960s concepts had a rather odd result. Thus, Mr. Justice Ritchie referred to the fact that since the enactment of the Bill of Rights, Parliament had amended on three occasions the provisions of the Criminal Code defining the types of culpable homicide which were to be punishable by death, the first of these within a year after passage of the bill. In the light of this, and in the light of his "frozen concepts" interpretation, he came to a surprising conclusion. After noting that none of the amendments to the death penalty provisions contained the declaration to operate "notwithstanding the Bill of Rights," he observed that since Parliament "saw fit to retain the death penalty as part of the Criminal Code after the enactment of the Bill of Rights," this constituted "strong evidence of the fact that it had never been intended that the word 'punishment' employed in [the bill] should preclude punishment by death. . . ."[15]

Does this mean that the absence of the *non obstante* clause in legislation enacted after the Bill of Rights means not only that Parliament did not believe its own legislation was contrary to the Bill of Rights, but that the courts must so conclude? If so, we have reached the point where the Bill of Rights can never have any effect! On the one hand, according to the express terms of section 2, inclusion of the clause excludes the application of the bill. On the other hand, the absence of the notwithstanding clause in legislation enacted after the Bill of Rights would also, according to his reasoning, mean that no provision of the bill could possibly be contrary to such legislation because Parliament did not think so and therefore left the clause out.

The dilemma arising out of the majority decision in the Miller and Cockriell case illustrates the unworkability of an approach to the interpretation of the Canadian Bill of Rights which relies upon the "frozen concepts" of 1960. The Charter, in contrast, merely proclaims in straightforward manner that "everyone has the following fundamental freedoms" or that "everyone has the right to life, liberty and security of the person" etc. By use of the present tense, coupled with the principles of constitutional interpretation referred to earlier, the Charter should avoid the re-introduction of a "frozen concepts" interpretation. As the needs of our society change, so should our concepts of human rights and fundamental freedoms, and they should be interpreted in an evolving fashion by the courts.

A major weakness of the 1960 Bill of Rights is that it does not apply to the provinces. Although all ten have anti-discrimination statutes,[16] only Saskatchewan, Alberta and Quebec have bills of rights which cover the fundamental freedoms, and only Quebec and Saskatchewan have provisions guaranteeing legal rights (protection against abuse in the administration of justice), although the Saskatchewan provision is relatively narrow.[17] Therefore, considering that one of the fundamental principles of the Parliamentary system of government in Canada is that the Legislatures are supreme within their jurisdiction, there was, until the Charter came into force, absolutely no constitutional limitation on seven of the provinces from restricting fundamental freedoms, and on eight of them from restricting legal civil liberties, as long as the enactment was within provincial powers as set out in the BNA Act. The Canadian Charter of Rights and Freedoms does apply to the provinces, another critical change.

A Comparison of the Canadian Bill of Rights and the New Charter
Neither the Canadian Bill of Rights nor any of the provincial bills of rights, nor the human rights codes, are listed among the statutes in Schedule I of

the Constitution Act, 1982 that are repealed by section 53. Furthermore the Charter provides that, "The guarantee in this Charter of certain rights and freedoms shall not be construed as denying the existence of any other rights or freedoms that exist in Canada." Therefore, although all bills of rights and human rights codes are now subject to the constitutionally entrenched Charter, they will continue to operate to the extent that they are not over-ridden by it.

It is beyond the scope of this chapter to deal with all the ways in which the new Charter is a change from the Canadian Bill of Rights. However, some of the changes will be noted briefly, while more space will be devoted later to the "limitations" clause, the "override" clause, and to equality rights.

In the Canadian Bill of Rights, the War Measures Act[18] is exempted from compliance. The bill provided that anything done under the War Measures Act "shall be deemed not to be an abrogation, abridgement or infringement of any right or freedom recognized by the Canadian Bill of Rights." The Charter, on the other hand, does not mention the War Measures Act, but rather leaves it to be dealt with under section 1, which provides that the rights and freedoms under the Charter are, "subject only to such reasonable limits prescribed by law as can be demonstrably justified in a free and democratic society," or to section 33, which provides that Parliament may declare that an Act of Parliament or a provision thereof "shall operate notwithstanding a provision included in section 2 and sections 7 to 15 of this Charter." The result is, on the one hand, that each and every limitation taken by virtue of the War Measures Act can be tested under the Charter in light of section 1, but that on the other, any emergency measure enacted can be exempted from sections 2 and 7 to 15 by the use of the override power. Both the "limitations" clause and the override power will be discussed more fully later.

Whereas the Canadian Bill of Rights requires the federal minister of justice to scrutinize all proposed laws and statutory regulations in order to ascertain whether any provision might be inconsistent with the bill, there is no such responsibility under the Charter. Although this review responsi-bility will continue at the federal level with respect to the bill, it is not carried forward into the Charter and, of course, it does not apply to the provinces.

Although the new Charter expresses the fundamental freedoms in terms similar to those in the International Covenant on Civil and Political Rights and, therefore, more elaborately than was the case in section 1 of the Bill of Rights, there is probably no major substantive change. If the funda-mental freedoms are given greater application than is the case under the Bill of Rights, this will probably result from the constitutional status of the Charter and from section 52 of the Constitution Act. The actual scope of these freedoms will come through the interpretation of the "limitations" clause in section 1.

What is new in the Charter is the right of every citizen to vote in elections to the House of Commons and to the provincial Legislative Assemblies. Although this right seems to be obvious in "a free and democratic society," it must not be forgotten that women did not get the vote until World War I, that Asiatic Canadians did not get it until after World War II, and the native peoples not until after 1960. There is also provision to make explicitly applicable to all Legislatures what is essentially set out in the BNA Act concerning annual sessions and elections every five years.

Also new in the Charter are the "mobility rights," providing for a right of every citizen "to enter, remain in and leave Canada," and every citizen and landed immigrant "to move and take up residence" and "to pursue the gaining of a livelihood . . . in any province." These rights, however, are subject to laws of general application, and the right of affirmative action in favour of their own residents by provinces whose rate of employment is below the national average.

The Charter appears to leave out several legal rights which are to be found in the bill. The first of these is the provision of the bill which prohibits the arbitrary "exile" of any person. However, one must be able to argue that the "mobility rights" in the new Charter would also preclude the exile of a citizen. Second, the Charter contains no general rights to a fair hearing for the determination of one's rights and obligations, as does the bill. Section 7 of the Charter might cover the same area in its reference to "the principles of fundamental justice." However, section 7 would not seem to cover the most significant omission from the Charter, which is the "due process" protection of property in section 1(a) of the bill. Also, the Charter does not provide for a "right to counsel" when a person is compelled to give evidence, as does the bill, although this right might be asserted under section 7 and clearly forms part of the right to a "fair hearing" when one is charged with an offence.

The main lacunae that are filled by the Charter are the rights to be free from "unreasonable search or seizure;" to be informed of the right to retain and instruct counsel upon arrest or detention; to trial by jury for offences with respect to which the maximum penalty is imprisonment for five years or a more severe punishment; to be protected against retroactive punishment; and to be protected against double jeopardy. These and the other legal rights provisions in sections 7 to 14 are among the most likely to be raised most often in future adjudication.

Sections 16 to 19 provide that English and French shall be the official languages of Canada and New Brunswick. Essentially, the language rights in section 133 of the BNA Act are spelled out in greater detail in line with the federal Official Languages Act[19] and are extended to New Brunswick. Section 20 extends these rights to include communications with public institutions. Section 21 preserves the application of section 133 of the BNA Act to Quebec and of section 23 of the Manitoba Act to Manitoba, while section 22 preserves rights of other languages, whether such rights are pre-existing or acquired in the future.

Finally, there is a wholly new provision for minority language education rights for "citizens of Canada" who come within any of three categories: those "whose first language learned and still understood" is that of the English or French linguistic minority of the province in which they reside; those "who have received their primary school instruction" in those languages anywhere in Canada; those "of whom any child has received or is receiving primary or secondary school instruction in English or French in Canada." However, it appears that the first category will get those rights only when the Quebec Legislature or government so decides.

The right provided is that of having primary and secondary school instruction in the respective language as well as "minority language educational facilities" paid for out of public funds "where numbers warrant." This is a provision which could involve the courts in difficult questions concerning financial responsibilities of governments and even, perhaps, of supervision of the carrying out of these responsibilities: when will bussing suffice? Are separate classrooms in the same school building acceptable? Will separate buildings and grounds be required?

Finally, the Charter refers to "aboriginal rights and freedoms." These are not spelled out beyond acknowledging whatever rights or freedoms were recognized by the Royal Proclamation of 1763 or that may be acquired "by way of land claims settlement." Essentially, section 25 merely provides that these rights and freedoms, whatever they may be, are not affected by the Charter.

Two other provisions, however, which are not part of the Charter must be kept in mind. Section 35 of the Constitution Act recognizes and affirms the "existing aboriginal and treaty rights of the aboriginal peoples of Canada." Again, these are not spelled out and, since none have thus far been upheld by our courts against Parliament, probably have meaning only as a restraint upon the provinces. Perhaps the most important effect of this section is that the Métis have for the first time been recognized as one of the "native peoples of Canada." The second provision is section 37 of the Act, which requires that a conference be convened by April 17, 1983 between the "representatives" of the aboriginal peoples, the first ministers, and "elected representatives" of the Yukon Territory and the Northwest Territories to consider "constitutional matters that directly affect the aboriginal peoples of Canada, including the identification and definition of the rights of those peoples."

"Limitations," "Override" Clauses and Equality Rights

The "Limitations" Clause: One of the provisions that caused the greatest discussion before the Special Joint Committee of the Senate and House of Commons was the proposed section 1. The original federal version as submitted on October 6, 1980 would have provided:

The *Canadian Charter of Rights and Freedoms* guarantees the rights and freedoms set out in it subject only to such reasonable limits as are generally accepted in a free and democratic society with a parliamentary system of government.

Clearly, this was too wide an exception. Although such international bills of rights as the European Convention on Human Rights and the International Covenant on Civil and Political Rights do provide for limitations clauses, these are more narrowly framed. The limitations are only those which are "prescribed by law." The permissible limitations are only those which are proved to be "necessary" in a free and democratic society. Under both the European Convention and the International Covenant the permissible limitations do not apply to the legal rights during normal times. Even in times of officially proclaimed emergency, when legal rights might be limited, there are certain rights that cannot be taken away, such as that not to be subjected to cruel or unusual treatment or punishment.

The proposed section 1 clearly fell below these international standards. The permissible limitations were so wide that one could literally "drive a tank through them." How could one argue that a democratically elected Legislature that enacts a certain restriction by majority vote has not thereby enacted a piece of legislation that is "generally accepted?" Most of the actions in our history which we now look upon as infringements of human rights were certainly at least "generally accepted" at that time, if not overwhelmingly so. As section 1 was proposed, it was impossible to contemplate any limitation being placed upon the Legislatures and Parliament by the Charter.

In response to wide criticism, the government proposed a new version which reads:

The *Canadian Charter of Rights and Freedoms* guarantees the rights and freedoms set out in it subject only to such reasonable limits prescribed by law as can be demonstrably justified in a free and democratic society.

Although this version still suffers from the defect that it does not explicitly protect legal rights against limitation in normal times and does not provide that certain rights are non-derogable even in time of emergency, there is no question but that the present wording should permit that kind of argument to be put forth and accepted by the courts.

What is perhaps more important is where the onus of proof will lie. One would hope that the courts will not merely apply their own notions of which limits are "demonstrably justified." Furthermore, one could not expect the one who claims the protection of the Charter to justify limitations on his or her rights or freedoms. Clearly, the onus must apply to the one who claims that some right or freedom must be limited. For this purpose, because of a growing international jurisprudence on the matter, resort might be made to the jurisprudence of the tribunals under the

European Convention or the International Covenant for guides to such reasonable limits.

The "Override" Clause: The subject of limitations cannot be left without reference to the agreement to provide for a *non obstante* provision, section 33, whereby all the Legislatures and Parliament can specify that their statutes shall operate "notwithstanding a provision included in section 2 or sections 7 to 15" of the Charter. One might ask whether such a *non obstante* clause is necessary when section 1 of the Charter provides a wider limitations clause than that permitted under the International Covenant on Civil and Political Rights. Nevertheless, it should be pointed out that a limitation under section 1 might not be held constitutional when reviewed by the courts, whereas the enactment of a *non obstante* clause could not be overridden by the courts. On the other hand, a proposal to include the *non obstante* clause is a clear signal to the opposition, the media, and the electorate, that the governing party intends to override the Charter. This is not a step which would be politically easy.

Just such an overriding clause is found in all four of the existing bills of rights—the Canadian, and that of Alberta, Quebec and Saskatchewan. In the more than 21 years of the existence of the Canadian Bill of Rights, the *non obstante* clause was used only once, in the Public Order (Temporary Measures) Act,[20] which replaced the invocation of the War Measures Act in December 1970, and which lasted until April 1971. The Quebec government at one point proposed to include the *non obstante* clause in its first language bill (Bill 1), but the reaction was so strong, particularly from the *Commission des droits de la personne*, that it was dropped from the language charter that is now in effect (Bill 101).

Section 52 of the Quebec charter was used nine times, but it would appear that this was done out of excessive caution, and the courts might have upheld the limitations in any case. The first example is in the Jury Act,[21] in order to protect certain sections which required that jurors be Canadian citizens of full age and on the electoral list, and to disqualify members of the National Assembly, peace officers, practicing advocates or notaries, firemen, and judges' consorts. A second example is the Youth Protection Act,[22] to provide that certain hearings are to be held *in camera*. But section 23 already provided that hearings could be held *in camera* "in the interests of [inter alia] the protection of children." A third example is the Highway Safety Code,[23] which provides that any physician or optometrist is required to report to the Automobile Insurance Board the name and address of any patient 16 years or older whom he considers unable on medical grounds to drive a road vehicle. Again, despite section 9, which protects the "non-disclosure of confidential information," it is doubtful whether the provision would have been found to contravene the Quebec charter.

It should be noted that the Quebec National Assembly, in the summer of 1982, did enact an omnibus statute purporting to add the *non obstante* clause to all Quebec statutes. However, this was done with the obvious purpose of registering a protest against the whole process concerning the Constitution Act and not with the purpose of overriding protections of particular rights or freedoms. After all, even if the omnibus statute is upheld by the courts, Quebec laws will still be subject to the Quebec charter, which is as extensive as the new Canadian Charter.

Concerning the justifiability of a *non obstante* clause, I cannot but repeat what I suggested in 1976:

> Although I believe that the Supreme Court should be able to declare legislation inoperative if it is inconsistent with the Bill of Rights, nevertheless I believe that Parliament, cognizant of the fact that in the opinion of the Supreme Court a certain legislative measure is contrary to the Bill of Rights, should be able to decide that the legislation should operate notwithstanding the Bill of Rights. I do not believe that a Supreme Court, even with a written Bill of Rights in the Constitution, can ultimately stand in the way of a legislature determined to take certain action. All I ask of the Supreme Court and of a written Bill of Rights is that the legislature be conscious of the fact that an impartial tribunal, whose role it is to interpret and apply the law, has expressed its opinion that certain action is contrary to the Bill of Rights. Moreover, many of the cases which involve values protected by a Bill of Rights concern administrative, and not legislative, acts. Even in the United States, it is not so much acts of Congress or the state legislatures that have been invalid, as administrative actions taken pursuant to these acts. Therefore, in these cases the impediment of parliamentary sovereignty on judicial review is not often at issue.
>
> Because the legislature will ultimately have its way over the courts, and because civil liberties are best protected if the issues are clarified in a kind of public dialogue between the legislative and judicial branches of government, I believe a notwithstanding clause like the one in the present Bill of Rights may be the only restraint we need place on the legislature. I am not much concerned with the question of entrenchment against future deletion or amendment, because I do not believe that any future Parliament would be moved to amend the Bill of Rights except to strengthen it, and if times are so changed that I am proved wrong, even the Supreme Court and a written Bill of Rights would not stop such a Parliament. The electorate will. If it does not, then we will be in such a changed situation that Bills of Rights and Supreme Courts will be irrelevant.[24]

Equality Rights: The provisions which received the greatest attention from lobbying groups, particularly women and various associations of handicapped persons, were the three equality rights sections. The first is section 15, which provides:

15. (1) Every individual is equal before and under the law and has the right to the equal protection and equal benefit of the law without discrimination and, in particular, without discrimination based on race, national or ethnic origin, colour, religion, sex, age or mental or physical disability.

(2) Sub-section (1) does not preclude any law, program or activity that has as its object the amelioration of conditions of disadvantaged individuals or groups including those that are disadvantaged because of race, national or ethnic origin, colour, religion, sex, age or mental or physical disability.

In addition, the equivalent of an Equal Rights Amendment as debated in the United States is set out in section 28:

Notwithstanding anything in this Charter, the rights and freedoms referred to in it are guaranteed equally to male and female persons.

Finally, there is a provision which is peculiarly Canadian, namely section 27:

This Charter shall be interpreted in a manner consistent with the preservation and enhancement of the multicultural heritage of Canadians.

Although section 15(1) may seem to be the camel that a committee produces when attempting to design a horse, it is understandable in the light of the restricted effect given by the Supreme Court of Canada in interpreting the "equality before the law" clause in the Canadian Bill of Rights. First, in response to Mr. Justice Ritchie's judgement in the Lavell case concerning discrimination between men and women in the Indian Act[25] in which he implied a distinction between the "equality before the law" clause and unequal treatment "under the law," the Charter includes protection for equality "under the law." Second, Justice Ritchie had also confined the "equality before the law" clause to the Dicey definition of 1885 restricting it to equality before the courts of the land. Now, however, the legislative draftsmen have added the American "equal protection of the laws" clause. Third, since in the Bliss[26] case, dealing with unemployment insurance benefits, Mr. Justice Ritchie rejected a contention that distinctions made with respect to pregnant women contravened the "equality" clause on the ground that the distinctions "involved a definition of the qualifications required for entitlement to benefits," the Charter now also includes a clause providing for "equal *benefit* of the law."

Thus it is clear that section 15(1) governs every possible application of the law that affects individuals. On the other hand, it should not be expected that *no* distinctions will be permitted. The section 1 "reasonable limitations" provision applies. As a result, some distinctions will fall, while others will be upheld. In this line it might be useful to consider the way that the U.S. Supreme Court has applied the "equal protection" clause of the Fourteenth Amendment. It would appear that there are three levels of "scrutiny."[27] The highest, known as "strict scrutiny," applies to race, colour and religion. Distinctions made on these grounds are considered "inherently suspect." As a result, unless the government can show "an overriding state purpose, which could not be achieved in a less prejudicial manner," the distinction will fall. Probably because the U.S. Supreme Court had to consider statutes which were intended to protect women from some of the turn-of-century working conditions, "sex" was not included as an "inherently suspect" basis of distinction: hence, the U.S. Equal Rights Amendment proposal. In our case, particularly today, and also because of section 28 of the Charter, sex must be so considered. Also, because of the many years over which the various human rights codes have included these as prohibited grounds of discrimination, "national and ethnic origin" must also be included in this category.

At the opposite end of "strict scrutiny," the U.S. Supreme Court has applied "minimal scrutiny" to distinctions made on such grounds as indigence, residence, ability to pay taxes and similar economic and social characteristics. With respect to such distinctions there is a presumption of a "valid legislative purpose." Therefore, unless the one challenging the law can show that it has no "rational relationship to a valid legislative purpose," the distinction stands. In the case of section 15(1) of the Charter, such a test could be suggested for distinctions which are *not* listed in that provision.

In recent years the U.S. Supreme Court has evolved what has come to be known as "intermediate scrutiny" for distinctions made on the basis of sex and legitimacy. Under this test, the government must show "an important governmental objective" in order for the distinction to be held valid. In our case, under section 15(1), since "age" and "mental or physical disability" are listed, but since with respect to these grounds, *bona fide* qualifications and requirements are more readily evident, these might not be considered to be "inherently suspect," but rather subject to an "intermediate scrutiny" test.

There should be no question in Canada that "affirmative action programs" do not contravene the equality clauses. Even though both the American Bakke[28] case, which was concerned with racial quotas in a university admissions policy, and the Weber[29] case, which concerned a collective agreement that provided for affirmative action programs, were decided on the basis of the Civil Rights Act of 1964 rather than the Equal Protection Clause of the Fourteenth Amendment, and even though the Bakke case invalidated only strict quotas and not the plethora of measures which constitute affirmative action, there was enough suspicion in Canada that our courts might find such programs to contravene equality clauses that the draftsmen decided to eliminate any ambiguity.

Finally, I would suggest that section 15 will not be applied to "private action," but will rather be restricted to "government action." It is true that the Equal Protection Clause of the American Fourteenth Amendment has had a limited application to private action, but this must be seen in the context of a situation where there were no anti-discrimination (civil rights) Acts in fifteen of the states and very little at the federal level.[30] Even so, the U.S. Supreme Court only extended "state action" to a few areas, such as privately-owned but municipally-managed parks,[31] private restaurants in publicly-owned facilities,[32] and restrictive covenants, because they would be enforced only through court action.[33] When the Civil Rights Act of 1964 was enacted, it applied to the federal sphere, overrode any state civil rights Acts that were deficient, and applied to states that did not have their own. Therefore, resort to the Fourteenth Amendment became less crucial. Now, private discrimination cases are pursued under the various civil rights Acts; the Fourteenth Amendment is resorted to only for cases involving pure state action.

In our own case, three reasons suggest that section 15 should not be applied to "private action." First, the Charter states that it applies "to the Parliament and Government of Canada" and to "the legislature and government of each province . . . *in respect of all matters within the authority*" of the respective legislative body. This wording was specifically changed from the version proposed as late as April 24, 1981, which used the words "and to" in place of the words "in respect of." The intent seems clearly to restrict the application to legislative and government action. Second, section 15 refers to equality under and before the *law*, and equal protection and benefit of the *law*. The intent appears clearly to refer only to inequality arising out of any application of law. Third, every jurisdiction in Canada has an anti-discrimination (human rights) statute, and all of these apply to the Crown, that is, to executive action. Therefore, section 15 will clearly be applied where a discriminatory act is committed by legislative action and the jurisdiction concerned does not have an overriding clause in its human rights code, as do Alberta, Quebec and Saskatchewan. With respect to executive or governmental action, section 15 and the various anti-discrimination statutes will overlap. With respect to "private" discrimination, the human rights codes will apply, although they cannot contravene section 15. Finally, it has to be noted that this section does not come into effect until three years after the Charter comes into force.

Section 27 purports to constitutionalize a policy declared by the government of Canada in 1971 to promote the principle of "bilingualism within a multicultural" context. By the nineteenth century, it had become evident that the French-speaking inhabitants of Canada could not be assimilated. Later immigrants (whose descendants now number around 28 percent of the population) claimed equality of status with the two "founding" peoples. Native peoples had an even stronger claim on founding status. All these forces led to the official government policy of protecting the ethnic plurality of the country. It has been described as a "cultural mosaic," in contrast to the American "melting pot." Even though Canada's "mosaic" may be rather "vertical" to the advantage of those of British stock, section 27 of the new Charter now gives constitutional status to what was merely proclaimed government policy. It could play a role in the interpretation of section 15 to the extent that ethnocultural groups can show they are disadvantaged. It can certainly form the basis of claims for government funding of culturally-related programs.

Enforcement

If a Charter of Rights is to be truly effective, there has to be a means of enforcing it. However, in the famous Hogan case in 1975,[34] a majority of the Supreme Court held that although Hogan's "right to counsel" had been abrogated, there was no remedy set out in the Canadian Bill of Rights, and they would not create one.

In the original October 1980 version, the proposed Charter not only would have avoided the issue of a remedy, but would have prevented the development of one like the American "exclusionary" rule. That version of the Charter provided that:

> No provision of this Charter . . . affects the laws respecting the admissibility of evidence in any proceedings or the authority of Parliament or a legislature to make laws in relation thereto.

As with the proposed section 1, the reaction to this clause was so strong that the government proposed the following in substitution:

> Anyone whose rights or freedoms, as guaranteed by this Charter, have been infringed or denied may apply to a court of competent jurisdiction to obtain such remedy as the court considers appropriate and just in the circumstances.

Although it is not beyond the ingenuity of judges to find reasons why there is still no authorization for the provision of a remedy, one hopes that temptation has been removed. In addition, the final version of section 24 now includes a subsection:

> Where . . . a court concludes that evidence was obtained in a manner that infringed or denied any rights or freedoms guaranteed by this Charter, the evidence shall be excluded if it is established that, having regard to all the circumstances, the admission of it in the proceedings would bring the administration of justice into disrepute.

Because of limitations of space, it is possible to make only two points regarding this subsection. The first is that it is *not* an absolute exclusionary rule. The courts will be given room for discretion. Nevertheless, the second point is that it is a clear direction that the evidence *shall* be excluded "if admission of it would bring the administration of justice into disrepute." The big question is what would be the factors that could result in such a decision. Obviously one cannot today provide the answer. One could suggest that some kind of a "community standard" will be applied. In their consideration, courts will probably start from or at least refer to the following discussion of Mr. Justice Lamer in the 1981 Rothman case concerning the circumstances in which the administration of justice might be brought into disrepute:

> The judge, in determining whether under the circumstances the use of the statement in the proceedings would bring the administration of justice into disrepute, should consider all of the circumstances of the proceedings, the manner in which the statement was obtained, the degree to which there was a breach of social values, the seriousness of the charge, the effect the exclusion would have on the result of the proceedings. It must also be borne in mind that the investigation of crime and the detection of criminals is not a game to be governed by the Marquess of Queensbury rules. The authorities, in dealing with shrewd and often sophisticated criminals, must sometimes of necessity resort to tricks or other forms of deceit and should not through the rule be hampered in their work. What should be repressed vigorously is conduct on their part that shocks the community. That a police officer pretend to be a lock-up chaplain and hear a suspect's confession is conduct that shocks the community; so is pretending to be the duty legal aid lawyer eliciting in that way incriminating statements from suspects or accused; injecting pentothal into a diabetic suspect pretending it is his daily shot of insulin and using his statement in evidence would also shock the community; but generally speaking, pretending to be a hard drug addict to break a drug ring would not shock the community; nor would, as in this case, pretending to be a truck driver to secure the conviction of a trafficker; in fact, what would shock the community would be preventing the police from resorting to such a trick.[35]

Conclusion

This survey has been confined to the possible effect of the new Charter on the *courts*. However, it would be misleading to assess a Charter of Rights merely in the light of its application by the judiciary without taking account of the very important influence it can have regardless of the actions of judges. This would ignore the very important role of public opinion and of Legislatures and governments with respect to civil liberties. It would ignore the fact that most citizens, including agents of governments, tend to govern their activities in accordance with the law. Given a publicly-declared sense of values such as a Charter of Rights, few individuals are prepared to ignore a condemnation of their conduct when that conduct is deemed contrary to a proclaimed set of constitutional principles.

It should be acknowledged that most of the opposition to the adoption of the Canadian Bill of Rights in the first place, or to Prime Minister Trudeau's proposals to entrench a Charter binding on Parliament and the Legislatures in the written part of our constitution, *was based upon the distrust of the judiciary.* The fear seemed to be that the Supreme Court would become activist and conservative like the U.S. Supreme Court from 1890 to 1937, introducing a wide substantive due process interpretation, or activist and liberal like the Warren Court in the United States in the 1960s, giving an extensive procedural due process interpretation. However, an examination of the judicial interpretation of the Canadian Bill of Rights in the past twenty-one years must certainly quiet most of those fears. There is no evidence thus far that any of our courts, and certainly not the Supreme Court of Canada, are declaring legislation inoperative because of excessive zeal to protect our civil liberties against the legislators and administrators of Canada. Rather, as long as the Supreme Court of Canada continues in its cautious tradition, the fear is not that the judiciary will supplant the legislators as policy-makers in the field of human rights, but rather that they will abdicate that responsibility for protecting human rights which is contemplated in the new Charter.

Notes

1. *The Constitution Act, 1982*, is Schedule B of the *Canada Act, 1982* (1982 U.K.), c. 11.
2. See, e.g., Ritchie, J. in *Robertson and Rosetanni v. The Queen*, [1963] S.C.R. 651 at pp. 654-55; Martland, J. in *R. v. Burnshine*, [1975] 1 S.C.R. 693 at p. 702; Laskin, J. in *Curr v. The Queen*, [1972] S.C.R. 889 at p. 899: "Compelling reasons ought to be advanced to justify the Court . . . to employ a statutory (as contrasted with a constitutional) jurisdiction to deny operative effect to a substantive measure duly enacted by a Parliament constitutionally competent to do so, and exercising its powers in accordance with the tenets of responsible government which underlie the discharge of legislative authority under the *British North America Act*."
3. See, e.g., Laskin J. in *Hogan v. The Queen*, [1975] 2 S.C.R. 574 at 597: "The *Canadian Bill of Rights* is a half-way house between a purely common law regime and a constitutional one; it may aptly be described as a quasi-constitutional instrument."
4. *Edwards v. Attorney General for Canada*, [1930] A.C. 124 at p. 136.
5. *British Coal Corporation v. The King*, [1935] A.C. 500 at p. 518. This statement was noted by Martland J. in *Bogoch Seed Co. v. C.P.R. and C.N.R.*, [1963] S.C.R. 247 at p. 255.
6. *Attorney General for Ontario v. Attorney General for Canada*, [1947] A.C. 127 at p. 154.
7. *Minister of Home Affairs v. Fisher*, [1980] A.C. 319 at pp. 328-29.
8. *Ibid.*, 329.
9. *R. v. Drybones*, [1970] S.C.R. 282.

10. *Robertson and Rosetanni v. The Queen, loc. cit.*, at p. 654: "It is to be noted at the outset that the *Canadian Bill of Rights* is not concerned with 'human rights and fundamental freedoms' in any abstract sense, but rather with such 'rights and freedoms' as they existed in Canada immediately before the statute was enacted."

11. *R. v. Burnshine, loc. cit.*, at pp. 702, 705: "The Bill did not purport to define new rights and freedoms. What it did was to declare their existence in a statute, and, further, by s. 2, to protect them from infringement by any federal statute." He then went on to suggest that section 1, by its express wording, declared and continued "existing" rights and freedoms: "It was those existing rights and freedoms which were not to be infringed by any federal statute. Section 2 did not create new rights. Its purpose was to prevent infringement of existing rights. It did particularize, in paras. (a) to (g) certain rights which were a part of the rights declared in s. 1. . . ."

12. *Miller and Cockriell v. The Queen,* [1977] 2 S.C.R. 680.

13. *Ibid.*

14. *R. v. Dick, Penner and Finnegan,* [1965] 1 C.C.C. 171 (Man. C.A.).

15. *Miller and Cockriell v. The Queen, loc. cit.*, at p. 705.

16. For a detailed discussion of these see my book, *Discrimination and the Law in Canada* (Toronto: Richard de Boo, 1982).

17. It is s. 7, which provides: "Every person and every class of persons shall enjoy the right to freedom from arbitrary arrest or detention, and every person who is arrested or detained shall enjoy the right to an immediate judicial determination of the legality of his detention and to notice of the charges on which he is detained."

18. R.S.C. 1970, c. W-2.

19. R.S.C. 1970, c. O-2.

20. S.C. 1970-71-72, c. 2.

21. R.S.Q. 1977, c. J-2.

22. S.Q. 1977, c. 20.

23. S.Q. 1981, c. 7.

24. "The Supreme Court and Civil Liberties" (1976), 14 *Alberta Law Review* 58 at pp. 59-60.

25. *Attorney General for Canada v. Lavell,* [1974] S.C.R. 1349.

26. *Bliss v. Attorney General for Canada,* [1979] 1 S.C.R. 183.

27. For some of the numerous recent articles discussing current interpretation and suggesting new approaches see James A. Hughes, "Equal Protection and Due Process: Contrasting Methods of Review under Fourteenth Amendment Doctrine" (1979), 14 *Harvard Civil Rights–Civil Liberties Law Review*, p. 529. M.J. Perry, "Modern Equal Protection: A Conceptualization and Appraisal" (1979), 79 *Columbia Law Review*, p. 1023; L.A. Alexander, "Modern Equal Protection Theories: A Metatheoretical Taxonomy and Critique" (1981), 42 *Ohio State Law Journal*, p. 3; John H. Ely, *Democracy and Distrust; A Theory of Judicial Review* (Cambridge, Mass.: Harvard University Press, 1980); Symposium on Equal Protection, the Standards of Review: The Path Taken and the Road Beyond" (1980), 57 *University of Detroit Journal of Urban Law,* part 4.

28. *Regents of the University of California v. Bakke,* 98 S.C. 2733 (1978). See the

symposia on this case: (1979), 14 *Harvard Civil Rights–Civil Liberties Law Review*, pp. 1-327, and (1979), 67 *California Law Review*, pp. 1-255.

29. *United Steel Workers of America v. Weber*, 99 S.Ct. 2721 (1979).
30. *Brown v. Board of Education*, 347 U.S. 483 (1954).
31. *Evans v. Newton*, 382 U.S. 296 (1966).
32. *Burton v. Wilmington Parking Authority*, 365 U.S. 715 (1961).
33. *Shelley v. Kraemer*, 334 U.S. 1 (1948).
34. *Hogan v. The Queen*, [1975] 2 S.C.R. 574.
35. *Rothman v. The Queen* (1981), 59 C.C.C. (2d) 30 at pp. 74-75.

Chapter 14/Women and Constitutional Process
Chaviva Hošek

Women are generally perceived as having emerged among the winners in the process of patriating the constitution and entrenching a new Charter of Rights and Freedoms. A review of the history and outcome of that process, however, suggests a more qualified picture. Women had to wage a bitter battle to have their concerns recognized. At various points in the debate, gains that had seemed certain had to be fought for again. And even after the proclamation of the new constitutional provisions, there is justifiable scepticism about what has been achieved for women. The massive lobby effort in 1981 succeeded in securing a section guaranteeing all entrenched rights "equally to male and female persons." But the legal force of this section is unclear. Some see it as a symbolic and philosophical statement which will guide the interpretation of the Charter as a whole. Others reply that because the section is not part of some general statement of principles, it may well come into conflict with other sections in the Charter, and its force in such circumstances is uncertain. Clearly, any final assessment of the gains made by women in the constitutional wars will have to await the judicial and political developments of the next decades.

Nevertheless, the constitutional process itself tells us much about the position of women in the Canada of the early 1980s. This chapter examines the role of women's groups in the process of constitutional renewal from 1979 to 1982. The picture that emerges is a troubling one. It reveals the marginal role of women in Canadian politics and the forcefulness they must exert to avoid total exclusion. And this unsuccessful assimilation of women into the mainstream of politics raises some important questions about the quality of democracy in this country.

Canadian Women and Constitutional Rights
Until the spring of 1980, the women's movement in Canada had not focussed primarily on the fight for equal legal rights in the constitution. In this respect, Canada differed from the United States, where women's political energies were directed at the struggle to win passage of the Equal Rights Amendment (ERA) by Congress and the requisite number of states so as to entrench it in the constitution. The terms of the Equal Rights Amendment, which was first drafted in 1923 after women won the right to vote,[1] state that "Equality of Rights under the law shall not be denied or abridged by the United States or by a state on account of sex." If this amendment had been adopted, it would have become part of the American Bill of Rights, in effect becoming one of the defining principles by which American society is governed.

The status and power of the American constitution has made the history of social change in that country significantly different from that in Canada.[2] Major social reforms in the U.S. have been won through battles over constitutional rights, and the political rhetoric of rights has a powerful appeal in its politics. American feminism has absorbed this culture of rights; indeed, the entire history of feminism there is deeply entwined with the abolition movement in the nineteenth century and the black civil-rights movement in the 1960s. In such a context, fighting for an Equal Rights Amendment made a great deal of sense. Even then, however, the tight focus on the ERA issue throughout the 1970s had high costs. It has, for example, led to a comparative neglect of economic, health and social issues of concern to women on the national level, and so the failure of the ERA ratification effort may well presage a shift in the goals of American feminism. The decade to come may see the immense grass-roots organization, which the ERA struggle has created, mobilized for a much wider range of issues.

Canadian feminism has developed along a different path. While the American example has undoubtedly had a pervasive influence here, the Canadian movement has not developed in a political atmosphere highly charged with the rhetoric of political rights. From the outset, women's groups have pursued a wide range of economic and social objectives.

A crucial moment for Canadian feminism came in 1967, when pressure by traditional women's groups on the government of the day brought about the establishment of the Royal Commission on the Status of Women. In preparing for the hearings of that Royal commission, and in responding to the recommendations made in its report, the contemporary Canadian feminist movement discovered its own coherent goals. The early naiveté which assumed that the recommendations of the Royal commission would be implemented quickly and that women would easily achieve equality in Canadian society is long gone. Many of those recommendations, which are crucial to women, have yet to be enacted, and further political debate and research have since discovered and articulated new goals. Nonetheless, the Royal commission report remains a founding document of contemporary Canadian feminism.

The organized women's movement in Canada contains at least five identifiable types of women's groups. First, there are voluntary feminist groups devoted to improving the status of women on a large range of issues. These organizations, such as the Manitoba Action Committee on the Status of Women, *La Fédération des Femmes du Québec*, the Nova Scotia Action Committee on the Status of Women, and many others in each province and the territories, lobby primarily on the provincial level. The National Action Committee on the Status of Women (NAC) is an umbrella organization of over 200 such voluntary groups, and lobbies the federal government on a wide range of issues. Second, there are traditional women's voluntary organizations whose primary purposes are not explicitly feminist, but who lend their support to feminist causes at significant times. These include the Canadian Federation of University Women, the Imperial Order of the Daughters of the Empire, the Young Women's Christian Association, the National Council of Women, the Women's Institutes, women's church-affiliated groups, women's party-affiliated groups, and many more. Groups involved in the provision of specific services to women represent a third category. These may be largely voluntary, and include rape crisis centres, homes for battered women and their children, women's employment counselling centres, birth-control information centres, centres for immigrant women, collectives that publish books and magazines, and women's caucuses in unions. Fourth, there are advisory councils to the government in most provinces and in the federal jurisdiction. They are appointed by government and are meant to act as a means of liaison between government and women. Their members are always paid for their time, but their budgets vary considerably, as does their influence. The Canadian Advisory Council on the Status of Women has traditionally had a bigger budget than any other such group, and significant resources for researching policy areas of concern to women. The *Conseil du Statut de la Femme* in Quebec has also been given abundant resources. On the other hand, the Ontario Status of Women Council reported in 1982 that its research budget was $15,000. Since most other women's groups spend the little money available to them providing services to women, with little left over for lobbying governments on policy issues, the stable budgets of some advisory councils have given them substantial discretion in lobbying efforts. Finally, there are specialized national voluntary associations that lobby in areas of their own particular expertise and concern. These include the Canadian Congress for Learning Opportunities for Women, the Canadian Research Institute for the Advancement of Women, the National Association of Women and the Law, and others. These organizations also join coalitions to support causes outside of their own spheres of immediate concern.

These diverse organizations have lobbied on a wide range of important issues: legislated affirmative action; "equal pay for work of equal value" legislation; emergency services for women, such as rape-crisis centres and transition homes for battered women; access to affordable, quality child-care; access to birth-control information throughout the country; family law reform that recognizes the contribution of women to the property and income of the family; pension reform to accommodate women's patterns of participation in the work force; reproductive freedom of choice; access for women to education and training; occupational health and safety controls in the workplace. It is a long list, and has involved thousands of feminists throughout the country.

Until 1980, formal legal rights did not figure largely on this list. Indeed, insofar as Canadian women have worked for legal equality, they have been sorely disappointed. In the most notable constitutional matter affecting women, the Supreme Court of Canada ruled in 1928 that women were not "persons" in the law, and only the overturning of that ruling in Britain in 1929 made women legal "persons" in this country. In the 1970s, in the Bliss, Lavell, Bedard and Lovelace cases, the Canadian Bill of Rights proved to be a deficient legal instrument for women's equality. And the struggle to reform section 12(1)(b) of the Indian Act, which discriminates against Indian women who marry men who are not status Indians, continues without success.

Thus the drive for equal legal rights did not spring spontaneously from within the women's movement. Rather, it developed in response to the determination of the federal government to entrench a Charter of Rights and Freedoms during the patriation process. This was at once an advantage and a disadvantage. On the one hand, American women had to struggle for years to put equal rights on the political agenda, and it was not at all clear that Canadian women would have been any more successful on their own had the government not advanced the idea of a Charter. On the other hand, the terms of the Canadian debate and the timetable for its resolution were set by governments, and women were able to manoeuvre only within the narrow spaces afforded them by elected political leaders.

The Battle Begins

In the spring of 1980, the federal government announced its initiative to patriate the constitution, and the women's movement mobilized to develop a policy on this major development. On May 27, 1980, the National Action Committee on the Status of Women (NAC) wrote to the prime minister describing a plan for regional meetings of women's groups in most provinces across the country which would develop positions on aspects of constitutional change with which women were concerned. After the provincial meetings, women's groups would meet to agree on a national policy. In effect, it was a plan for a federal-provincial consultation process within the women's movement itself.

There was no obvious consensus on what women would want in a new constitution. Women were residents of different provinces, with various political party affiliations and different views on patriation, the amending formula, the division of powers and other issues. Like all other citizens of Canada, women had different approaches to the idea of an entrenched Charter of Rights. Women in Quebec, for example, largely wished to retain powers in the province, partly because the government of Quebec was perceived by many women to be more forward-looking on women's issues than the federal government of the day. Women in the Western provinces, and those with more traditionalist views, tended to believe that it was not in keeping with Canada's political history and political culture to have an entrenched Charter of Rights giving the Supreme Court final say on human rights. By comparison, women in Ontario tended to be the major supporters of the idea.

The recent history of constitutional negotiations between the federal government and the provinces put active feminists on the alert. They were most concerned to find a way to include women in the new round of constitutional discussions, since the consequences of women's previous exclusion might have proven seriously detrimental to their interests. At the February 1979 constitutional meeting, the first ministers reached agreement only on the transfer of divorce jurisdiction to the provinces, a change that would have had severely inequitable consequences for women.[3] Fortunately, massive lobbying by women's groups in Manitoba convinced their premier to oppose the change, which effectively put the issue on hold. In the spring of 1980, however, divorce jurisdiction remained a symbolic reminder of what could happen to women's interests when no informed women sat at the table where political deals between first ministers were struck.

Nevertheless, clear positions on the constitution had to be developed. To facilitate this, the Canadian Advisory Council on the Status of Women planned a conference for early September 1980. The timing was ideal because the first ministers were scheduled to meet one week later for what was billed as the last attempt to secure agreement among the governments before the federal government moved to patriate the constitution unilaterally. The women's conference was designed to pool information from women's groups across the country and to formulate a policy which could be fed into the federal-provincial process. The Canadian Advisory Council commissioned several papers on the constitution in order to focus the conference deliberations.[4] Once again, its stable budget proved critical, since no group in the voluntary sector would have been able to fund such research or provide the travel budget required to bring women's groups together. Among the topics to be considered at the conference were the entrenchment of rights, family law, the rights of Indian women, affirmative action, and overlapping jurisdiction in the provision of services to women.

Women's groups spent the summer in intense consultation about the constitution, and in great anticipation of the conference. The National Action Committee's contacts across the country that summer revealed extensive interest and a determination to ensure that legal equality between men and women would be one of the achievements of constitutional change. The publicity about the fight for the ERA in the United States helped to mobilize groups of women in Canada to fight for equal legal status, and even traditional women's groups were highly concerned. Thus, although constitutional change had not been the first item on the women's agenda, energy and commitment were available as soon as the opportunity presented itself. There was little sense that constitutional renewal alone was going to bring about all the changes necessary for women to have equal power in society. But since there was going to be significant change, women were going to make sure that their legal status would be stronger than it had been.

Regrettably, this early effort came to naught. In early September, the translators of the Canadian Union of Professional and Technical Employees (CUPTE) went out on strike for maternity-leave benefits. The CUPTE translators were supposed to be the translators for the women's conference on the constitution, and if the conference went on, women would have to cross a picket line made up almost entirely of women striking for a goal all feminist groups supported. That was impossible. The CUPTE translators were willing to translate for this conference *pro bono* in order not to force cancellation, but the Advisory Council was told by the Treasury Board that they could not have any dealings with CUPTE while it was out on strike. They could not make a separate deal with them, nor have any contact with them, until the strike was settled.

The Advisory Council cancelled the conference on Women and the Constitution, promising to hold another as soon as possible. But the disappointment, even despair, was palpable. The great concern was that the end of the strike would not coincide with a politically strategic time for another conference, and that a rare, historic opportunity might be lost.

Unilateralism and the Charter

The first ministers met on September 12, 1980 and were unable to agree. On October 2, the government released its proposed Resolution respecting the constitution of Canada and announced its decision to proceed unilaterally. The Resolution included a Charter of Rights and Freedoms, which the federal government proposed to entrench in the constitution, and women's groups began to study it intensely. At this point, however, many women were caught in a dilemma. Some women strongly opposed federal unilateral action and the circumvention of provincial powers that this involved. Nonetheless, an entrenched Charter of Rights would give those rights supremacy over the laws of the provinces, and some provinces had notably bad records on women's issues. Similarly, there were women who were very reluctant to give the courts greater power in the definition of rights, because the history of judicial decisions on women's rights in Canada was very poor. Since the judiciary in Canada is appointed by order-in-council, and judges have not traditionally felt any responsibility for making social precedent, there was concern that the judiciary was less likely than the Legislatures to move forward on equal rights for women. Nevertheless, such reservations were overridden by even more intense concerns about the draft Charter itself. Many of its clauses were distinctly ungenerous. The proposed Charter was not attractive enough or liberal enough to seduce people into supporting entrenchment without misgivings. On the contrary, the Charter had so many flaws that it frightened people and mobilized women and many other interest groups into action.

The government had underestimated the intensity and extent of popular concern with the proposed Charter. On October 18, the fifty-first anniversary of the declaration by the Judicial Committee of the Privy Council in Britain that women in Canada were "persons" in the law, the National Action Committee sponsored a day-long public meeting on the constitution. The meeting discussed those sections of the Charter that were problematic for women, agreeing on essential changes. That evening, the group was addressed by the minister responsible for the status of women. But the minister completely misread his audience, its understanding of the issues and the intensity of its concern. He simply told the assembled group to "trust" his government to come through with a better wording of the Charter. Most of the audience was outraged at being treated with such condescension. Clearly, in those early days the government was not yet aware of the strength of feeling in the country about the Charter. And certainly the demand for wider public participation in the process of constitutional change was to become far stronger than Ottawa had expected.

The Joint Committee Provides a Forum

Under pressure from the opposition parties, the federal government agreed to refer the constitutional Resolution to a Special Joint Committee of the Senate and the House of Commons for one month. Further pressure extended that period to five months. The deliberations of the Joint Committee afforded a crucial experience for women's groups, as it did for other groups of concerned citizens. The hearings raised the political consciousness of many people, and revealed the range and vitality of the opposition to the wording of the Charter and its approaches to human rights. Many people watched the televised presentations of the Joint Committee with fascination and a growing hope that the highly persuasive cases made by many civil libertarian groups would force the government to strengthen the Charter. It was a source of great encouragement simply to see how fine the work done by various concerned organizations was, and with what dignity and precision they approached the problem of turning the dog's breakfast before them into a Charter of Rights of which a democratic nation could be proud.

In the five months of hearings, the Joint Committee heard from a variety of women's groups in briefs and consultations. The recommendations of the major national women's groups had many highly specific concerns in common:

1. The "limitation section," which allowed rights and freedoms to be subjected to "such reasonable limits as are generally accepted in a free and democratic society with a parliamentary

system of government," was too broadly worded. It should have been deleted altogether, or at least re-worded to specify the permissible limitations on rights and freedoms. Women also argued that the guarantee of equality in another section of the Charter should never be subject to this limitation clause.

2. The Charter should have begun with a statement of purpose, guaranteeing the equal rights of men and women.

3. The word "person" should have been used throughout the Charter, since its meaning is legally defined. Instead, the Charter used terms such as "one," which had no clear legal meaning, and which could give rise to unnecessary legal arguments about the rights of the foetus.

4. The section that guaranteed that "Everyone has the right to equality before the law and to the equal protection of the law without discrimination because of race, national or ethnic origin, colour, religion, age or sex" was too narrowly stated. The section should have indicated that equality in the *content* of the laws was guaranteed, and not just equality in the procedure. Moreover, the list of grounds should have been open-ended to allow for the development of new categories, and marital status, sexual orientation and political belief should have been added at the outset. Finally, the courts should have been directed to use the "strictest" legal test when assessing the validity of laws that differentiate on prohibited grounds.

5. The section providing for affirmative action programs did not guarantee that women would qualify for such help.

6. The section that protected existing "rights or freedoms that pertain to the native peoples of Canada" was also a concern. This section would have permitted the Indian Act to continue to define band membership in a way that discriminates against Indian women who marry men who are not status Indians.

7. Another section stated that unlike any other part of the Charter, the equality rights would be subject to a moratorium of three years.

8. There was concern that a new section introduced in response to multicultural groups to ensure "the enhancement and preservation of the multicultural heritage of Canadians" would conflict with the section guaranteeing equality. Cultural values have been used to justify discrimination against women before, notably in the Indian Act, and women's groups were concerned that the new section could undermine women's general guarantee of equality.

9. Women are more than half of the Canadian population but at
the time were not represented at all on Canada's highest court.
The constitution should have guaranteed a representative
number of women on the Supreme Court of Canada.

Even though the Joint Committee gave these concerns some visibility,
it was not at all clear what the government would do with the presentations. Renewed political action would be needed to make the difficult
transition from submissions to the Joint Committee to decisions of the
federal Cabinet. In December, the Canadian Advisory Council told
women's groups that their conference would be held on February 14, 1981.
This appeared to be strategic timing, as the Joint Committee would then
have just finished its deliberations. The next stage of political action would
then have to begin.

Crisis in the Canadian Advisory Council

In January, before the Joint Committee had finished its private deliberations, the revised Charter was brought to the House. The changes tabled by
the Minister of Justice represented a partial response to the recommendations of women's groups, but left many crucial matters in a perilous state.
The "limitation" section had been partially tightened, but the general
guarantee of equality rights remained limited by the wording; there was no
general purpose section with a statement about equality of the sexes; the
purpose of affirmative action was partially tied to the prohibited grounds
of discrimination; although the section guaranteeing equality rights had
been revised in part, the word "person" was not used, but "one" was
changed to "individual" as in the Canadian Bill of Rights. The rewording
of the section to guarantee equality "before and under the law" also was not
strong enough, since it could still mean only equality in the administration
of the law and not in the laws themselves. Women's groups, along with the
Canadian Advisory Council, wrote the minister of justice and the minister
responsible for the status of women to insist that more changes in the
Charter be made.

On January 5, however, the Canadian Advisory Council constitutional
conference was cancelled, and a statement was issued saying that regional
conferences would be more appropriate. Rumors were rife that Lloyd
Axworthy, the minister responsible for the status of women, preferred this
arrangement as it would not embarrass the government at a critical juncture in the constitutional battle. Doris Anderson, then president of the
Canadian Advisory Council, called a meeting of her executive, together
with the minister, in an effort to reverse the decision, which had been
made in her absence. But the executive insisted on cancellation. Anderson
publicly accused the minister of interfering with the autonomy of the
organization, and convened the full council in the hope of getting from
them the support for the conference she had not been able to get from their

executive. The emergency meeting of the entire council also voted to cancel, however, and Doris Anderson resigned as president on January 19, 1981.

It is difficult to understand what advantage the government might have gained from the cancellation. The Joint Committee had already publicized the process of constitution-making. The opposition parties and the provinces were so insistent on having a say in the process that a conference of women was not going to make things much worse. The process was simply not going to be as neat and expeditious as the government had hoped and wished. The political advantages of allowing the conference to go ahead, on the other hand, could have been considerable. The Liberal Cabinet could have pointed to its financial support for the organization as proof of its commitment to wider public participation in constitution-making. More importantly, it might have used the conference to rally support for speedy patriation and entrenchment of the Charter. Instead, the political costs of cancelling the conference turned out to be high. The women's movement suddenly had a heroine, a villain and an event, all of which symbolized its exclusion from the constitutional process. The media had a field day. The complex issues involved were reduced to a dramatic fight between a woman and a man. And as a former editor of *Chatelaine*, Doris Anderson was a particularly potent symbol around which concern about the constitutional issue could crystallize.

The Ad Hoc Committee Takes Up the Standard

A few days after Doris Anderson's resignation, approximately a dozen women who were active in various women's groups met in Toronto to discuss strategy. Timing was a serious problem. Even if the voluntary women's groups decided to have conferences of their own, months of organization would be required and the chance to influence the process of constitution-making would have passed. There was a fear that after the Joint Committee adjourned, there would be no way for women's groups to have a further say.

An ad-hoc committee emerged as the best vehicle for resolving the contradictions experienced within women's groups on the constitution. Women who were active in the Liberal Party felt that informal influence would work best. However, the cancellation of the conference made other women suspicious about this back-door route. Without public pressure from large groups of women, informal lobbying might not be very effective. Major voluntary groups, wary of leaving other issues neglected as the American ERA groups had done, worried about putting all their people to work on the constitution. Some women's groups were adamant that entrenching the Charter in the constitution was a serious danger. Women's groups in Quebec, seriously in conflict internally about their stance towards the federal initiative, were not prepared to submit their internal coherence to the test of a clearly stated choice on constitutional policy.

In order to avoid internal dissension, an ad-hoc committee was formed to organize a conference on "women and the constitution" on February 14, precisely the same date as the conference that had been cancelled. Support for the ad-hoc committee mushroomed. Women were determined to have their meeting with or without the government's resources and support, and the ad-hoc committee poured all its energy into the conference. The women involved in the committee devoted all their efforts to it. What may be described as the training in "crisis management" that ordinary women's lives provide came into play, and a kind of feminist pride at making do with very little animated them. The group was surprised and encouraged by the astonishing response from women all over Canada.

For many, this was a time of political awakening. Women who had not been activists and had simply assumed that women in Canada were legally equal to men were profoundly insulted by the cancellation of the Canadian Advisory Council conference. There was a sense that this was a once-in-several-lifetimes opportunity in which one had to participate. The sense of historic urgency was powerful. Women were prepared to fight for their daughters' equality with men where they might not have been for their own. Some women were convinced that if enough of a political push were made, it might be possible to get a Canadian equivalent to the ERA in one fell swoop. As a result, the conference exceeded everyone's expectations, and the attendance reached 1300 women.

Because the members of the Canadian Advisory Council were seen as having traded women's concerns for party loyalty, the ad-hoc committee was careful to ensure that its conference would not be used for purely partisan purposes. The Progressive Conservatives were fighting entrenchment of a Charter of Rights, and there was a danger that putting the entrenchment issue first on the agenda might have the conference too neatly serve the Conservatives' needs. Discussion of entrenchment *per se* was, therefore, put off until discussion of the Charter took place so that the meeting could generate a position on its content first. Moreover, a resolution opposing entrenchment on any grounds, which could have been recommended to the meeting after the Charter had been discussed, was avoided by judicious handling in the resolutions committee. In addition, chairs and speakers at sessions were chosen to achieve balance in partisan representation. Flora MacDonald and Pat Carney, Progressive Conservative members of Parliament, and Pauline Jewett and Margaret Mitchell, New Democratic Party MPs who had worked hard and well on women's behalf in the Joint Committee, were not invited to speak on any panel.

The ad-hoc conference passed a number of resolutions on the Charter and on the process of constitutional patriation (see the Appendix to this chapter). After the conference, several key people stayed behind in Ottawa to lobby Parliament for the conference resolutions. They spoke to MPs,

House leaders, leaders of the opposition parties and the minister of justice, and they issued press releases on their progress. Women across the country contacted their MPs to make their support for the resolutions known. After initial resistance, the Department of Justice began to work with the ad-hoc committee members to draft what later became section 28: "Notwithstanding anything in this Charter, the rights and freedoms referred to in it are guaranteed equally to male and female persons."

At the annual meetings of NAC and the National Association of Women and the Law, the resolutions of the ad-hoc conference were further endorsed. Women were making their elected representatives declare their positions on women's equality, and the three parties finally moved to support the resolutions. The NDP moved to amend the parliamentary Resolution to include section 28, and it was passed unanimously in the House of Commons on April 23, 1981.

Many women were shocked to discover how hard they had to lobby to get section 28 into the Charter. They were astonished to find such resistance to equality rights for women. In the midst of an historic opportunity to make a statement about the basic principles by which Canadian laws were to be governed, equality for women still had to be negotiated, fought for and defended at every stage.[5]

The Supreme Court and the Infamous November Accord

The summer of 1981 was a quiet time on the constitutional front. People were tired, perhaps even shell-shocked. Everyone waited to see what the Supreme Court would say about the legal rights of the provinces in the patriation process. All along, the federal government had been wooing people interested in civil liberties and rights by claiming that it was the only level of government interested in giving Canadians rights, and that the provinces were backward, recalcitrant and otherwise unwilling to abide by liberal principles. In September, the Supreme Court decided that legality and convention could be distinguished, a decision which is examined fully elsewhere in this volume. The federal government chose to make a final attempt to reach agreement with the provinces, and the people in the women's movement became apprehensive. The process would be opened up to bargaining once more, and again no one around that federal-provincial table would be fundamentally committed to women's interests.

The fears were justified. In the final desperate negotiations to achieve substantial agreement between the federal and provincial governments, women's interests were sacrificed, almost by neglect. The federal minister of justice and his provincial counterparts put together a new override section which effectively confused the issue of whether the Charter of Rights was or was not entrenched. The supremacy of the Charter over all the laws of the country was now in question, and the override section could mean that Canadian laws would *not* have to apply equally to men and women. Here, the fact that section 28 had not been made part of a first-principles section began to show its fateful disadvantage.

Confusion reigned. The Accord was reached on November 5. But when the prime minister was asked in the House of Commons whether section 28 would be subject to the override, he was unable to answer. It was not until November 9 that he made clear that it was. Women's groups were appalled. It seemed impossible to believe that women had lost what had been won so recently and with such massive political effort. And it was incomprehensible that the prime minister should be so uncertain about what was, to women, a crucial matter. While Quebec's right to a veto and native people's aboriginal rights had clearly been traded away, women's rights were so invisible to the government that for several days they did not even know whether or not they, too, had been traded.

Back into the Fray

With a sense of weariness and outrage, the ad-hoc committee and other women's groups struggled to free the equality provisions of the Charter from the override. This time the federal government took the view that the provinces were the culprits, and women therefore focussed their lobbying efforts on the premiers. Because the pressure was on the provinces, some of the people in the federal jurisdiction were able to help. Judy Erola, the new minister responsible for the status of women, Flora MacDonald, a leading member of the opposition, and Margaret Mitchell of the NDP gave the ad-hoc committee access to telephones and other equipment. The ad-hoc committee and other women's groups called across the country to inform people of the various premiers' positions and to co-ordinate the pressure. Some women who felt that they had not done enough in the previous round of lobbying came forward. There was generalized concern about Quebec's loss of its veto, about the native peoples, whose aboriginal rights were in jeopardy, and about the whole concept of entrenchment. Canadians seemed to be getting the worst of both worlds in this particular federal-provincial agreement.

Media coverage in this period was interesting. There was elaborate reporting of the reaction in Quebec and a great deal of coverage of aboriginal rights. But although the women's lobby was working actively across the country, there was no coverage of its revival at all for at least ten days. Women were ignored with a "Catch-22" rationale: they were not seen as a group with political clout of their own, nor were they perceived as sufficiently weak and helpless to merit the concern of journalists. Women were neither powerful enough nor weak enough to get attention.

After the November 5 Accord, the women of the ad-hoc committee got promises of support from the opposition parties, particularly from the leader of the Progressive Conservatives. But the main targets were the provincial premiers. Telephone calls were made around the clock; questions were asked in every provincial Legislature; ads appeared in newspapers; petitions were signed; telegrams were sent; letters to the editor were written; MPs were lobbied. The ad-hoc committee and women's groups wished to remove the override from both the general equality provisions and section 28. However, since section 28 was the only one dealing exclusively with sex, the strongest push was made there. In effect, the federal government's statement on November 9 that the override did apply to section 28 narrowed the protest of women's groups. If section 28 had been declared at the outset to be outside the scope of the override, women's groups would have focussed on section 15(1) and might have succeeded, together with other interest groups, in removing the override from equality rights as a whole.

Nevertheless, the lobbying of the provinces served to reveal the political vulnerability of provincial governments on human rights issues, especially when they are not protected by the intergovernmental process. When first ministers negotiate as a group, no single one of them can be held responsible for the decision reached. The lobbying of women's groups shone a spotlight on each premier individually, and in that context no premier dared to refuse, as a matter of principle, to entrench equality for women in the constitution of Canada.

The mass lobbying by letter and telegram was reinforced by personal contacts around the country. Someone knew Premier Peckford's campaign manager and called her; she called the head of the Newfoundland and Labrador Advisory Council on the Status of Women and a former executive member of NAC; they all called the premier. While women's groups were demonstrating on the steps of the Newfoundland Legislature, others were talking to the premier. Newfoundland soon agreed to exempt section 28 from the override provisions. In Prince Edward Island, the Status of Women Council kept in constant contact with the ad-hoc committee. Both incoming and outgoing provincial premiers had to be lobbied as one premier had resigned from politics and was being replaced by a new party leader. In Nova Scotia, while individual women and women's groups were getting telegrams into the premier's office, Flora MacDonald, an old family friend of the premier, called him and urged him to exempt section 28 from the override. In New Brunswick, Senator Muriel Fergusson, the Speaker of the Senate, and Gordon Fairweather, head of the Canadian Human Rights Commission, talked to the premier, as did Madelaine LeBlanc, head of the New Brunswick Advisory Council on the Status of Women.

Quebec had refused to sign the Accord and was therefore not implicated in this action. But a network of women lawyers in Quebec City and the *Conseil du Statut de la Femme* got the premier to support removal of the override from section 28 and to state publicly that including section 28 in the override provision had never been discussed by the first ministers.

Ontario received a huge number of telegrams and telephone calls, and quickly agreed to exempt section 28 from the override. In Manitoba, women felt that there was no hope of persuading the premier. He was, however, in the middle of an election campaign, and women's groups made section 28 an election issue. The provincial NDP promised its support, and immediately after its victory, the new Manitoba government agreed to entrenchment of women's equality in the constitution. In Alberta, the support of the federal Conservative Party was crucial to women. All the Alberta federal Tories called the premier, as did a prominent Liberal Cabinet minister who was an old friend of the Progressive Conservative party whip in the Alberta Legislature. In British Columbia, women's groups' intensive lobbying and pressure from the NDP were powerful forces. Premier Bennett, in his role as chairman of the provincial premiers, was under heavy pressure, and in the end he bowed to the inevitable.

Curiously, Saskatchewan was the last hold-out. The material on section 28, which the ad-hoc committee had prepared for the lobby, had not reached Saskatchewan women's groups. These groups stood with their premier, and his officials trotted out old anti-ERA arguments that entrenching section 28 would mean that women would not be able to rent rooms to women only, or would endanger affirmative action for women. Indeed, at its annual meeting the Saskatchewan NDP defeated a resolution on freeing section 28. But the telegrams poured into the premier's office from across the country. When the actual text of section 28 and the override clause made their appearance in the newspapers there, the tide turned. Perhaps the closeness of women's groups to the premier and the government had initially prevented them from seeing the full implications of Saskatchewan's position. But this same closeness certainly became an asset when an influential group of women, who had previously supported his position, urged him to agree to free section 28 from the override. Their pressure was reinforced by the federal New Democratic Party and the federal minister of justice, and eventually the Saskatchewan premier agreed. In effect, Premier Blakeney traded women's rights for aboriginal rights by consenting to freeing section 28 only if aboriginal rights were restored to the Charter.

The lobbying of the provincial premiers reveals interesting contradictions. The premiers were convinced by a combination of mass political pressure in the form of letters, telegrams and telephone calls from across the country, and individual contacts made by people they already knew. The provincial advisory councils on the status of women came into their own, using their bridging relationship between non-governmental women's groups and the governments in power to great effect. Here, also, the incidental but pervasive personal connections between committed women and men in positions of political power are revealed in curious light. The personal connections would never have had the desired effect without the massive lobbying. However, the massive lobbying was given a human face by the intervention of women personally connected to the premiers.

The lobbying of the premiers also reveals the difficulty of believing that contact with men in political power alone will eventually give women legal and economic rights to equality. The personal and political acquaintanceships were already in place for the women's lobby to exploit. Nonetheless, the fact that women were their wives, mothers and daughters and, more crucially, their campaign managers, party officials, and government ministers did not prevent the first ministers from signing the November 5 Accord, as it had not prevented them from maintaining the status quo in regard to the position of women in Canadian society.

The Unfinished Agenda

In a typically Canadian compromise, we now have an entrenched Charter of Rights, but some of our rights are more entrenched than others. The question of whether Parliament or the judiciary has final say over rights in Canada has not been settled one way or the other.

The victory which let section 28 stand unimpeded by the override provision should not obscure the other changes in the Charter which women's groups fought for and did not get: (1) there is no statement of purpose or governing principles in the Charter within which the equality of the sexes is one of the guiding principles; (2) the power of section 28 in relation to other sections is not clear, and will surely have to be tested in the courts; (3) fundamental, legal and equality rights in the Charter can be overridden by Parliament and the provincial Legislatures; (4) equality rights generally are subject to a three-year moratorium and so cannot be tested before the courts until 1985. It is the only part of the Charter subject to the moratorium. Moreover, marital status, sexual orientation, and political belief were not added as prohibited grounds of discrimination; (5) the Charter does not use the word "person" throughout its wording. It is inconsistent and will clearly be grounds for battles on the legal rights of the foetus; (6) the multiculturalism clause remains problematic, since there is no statement that gender equality overrides cultural practice; (7) the fate of section 12(1)(b) of the Indian Act is unclear in relation to the Charter's equality provisions; (8) there is no constitutional right of representation of women in the Senate, the Supreme Court, and on government boards and commissions. In addition to these specific points about the Charter, the constitutional debate had raised a wide range of other issues of concern to women: overlapping jurisdictions and their impact on the availability and funding of services for women, the spending power of governments, family law, and the reform of government institutions.

Part of the story of women and the process of constitution-making in Canada is thus the progressive narrowing of the issues on which women have had a say. For the moment, the decisions on family law jurisdiction are suspended. No government institutions have been reformed, and jurisdictional matters have not yet been addressed in this round of constitutional reform. The political history of the development of the Charter of Rights and Freedoms shows women's groups addressing a steadily narrower range of issues as it becomes clear that fewer and fewer of their concerns will be met. It was necessary to choose the very few rock-bottom issues to address, without which the Charter would be wholly unacceptable on the issue of women's equality with men. This is also a story of the progressive exclusion of women from the process of constitutional change, and of the elaborate strategies required for them to break into the process.

Women must be centrally involved in any future constitutional change. Reforms in government institutions, decisions on the spending power and family law, changes in the division of powers between governments, cannot be made in a gender-neutral way unless women knowledgeable about the consequences take part in the process. The story of the proposed changes in divorce jurisdiction is a classic example of the problems caused by well-meaning people who simply do not, as a matter of course, consider the *differences* in impact on men and women of a given political decision. Unless the discussions surrounding such issues are open, governments will continue to make inequitable decisions and further erode the confidence of women in the responsiveness of Canadian political institutions. The many interest group representatives who testified before the Joint Committee on the Constitution expressed the legitimate concerns of the people they spoke for. Public interest groups do not usually emerge unless citizens feel that their needs are not being met by governments. The fact that women had to function as an "interest group" testifies eloquently to the failure of our national institutions to represent the specific concerns of women as women adequately.

In November 1981, in the midst of the struggle to free the equality rights provisions of the Charter from the override, the minister of justice suggested that women could deal with the dangers by being "vigilant." Women's groups are now preparing for further vigilance. Partly as a result of the political process traced here, they have become more sophisticated about rights and about the political power and strategies necessary to protect and extend them. The Canadian Advisory Council, the National Association of Women and the Law, and the ad-hoc committee, along with other concerned women, are considering legal action funds with which to test the new provisions of the constitution on behalf of women. They have examined models such as American civil liberties funds for women, the Canadian Civil Liberties Association, the consumer's associations and the environmental law associations. Women's organizations will have to battle in new forums, and with new tools.

Already barriers are emerging. The Supreme Court is being urged on many sides to approach the Charter in a strict and narrow rather than liberal fashion. One sign of this is the stance taken by the new Centre for Human Rights at the University of Ottawa, which has received a large grant from the Department of Justice to research the implications of the Charter and to advise judges on it. Already the centre has adopted the narrow view of the force of section 28; the symbolic or philosophical approach has been given no expression in that particular forum. But women's groups knew very early in the process of constitutional change that "entrenchment of rights would only be good for women if the wording provided women's right to equality in a way that the Supreme Court could not interpret narrowly."[6]

Major battles thus lie ahead. But the women's movement engages in them more strongly than before. Women and the women's movement have become more sophisticated in their understanding of what it takes to win a political victory against serious resistance. New lobbying strategies have been developed, and the networks connecting women across the country have been extended. Moreover, women's groups now have more specialized knowledge about the constitution and the implications of future changes for them. Politically active women lawyers will have a significant and growing impact in the women's movement, partly because of the opportunities for change offered by the Charter of Rights. With its professional base, the National Association of Women and the Law will be a key organization in women's rights politics in the next decade, and may shift increasingly into professional service for other women's groups, especially on constitutional matters.

The danger inherent in this state of affairs is the possibility of splitting the women's movement between groups interested in equality rights and the legal battles associated with them, and others interested in legislative and administrative change, including changes in the design and delivery of social services to women. It would not serve the best interests of the women's movement, or its traditions, to have women lawyers professionalize concerns about the Charter to such an extent that they will be removed from the scrutiny of other interested women. Yet there is an undeniable need for professional expertise in this area. One challenge the women's movement will have to face is to combine concern with rights with the longer and more varied list of problems that have not yet been adequately solved.

Representational politics have so far not served women's interests very well. On the one hand, the changes in Canada's constitution will make the legal system an increasingly important arena for social change that women's groups will exploit. On the other hand, the very process of constitutional change has brought into the women's movement many women who had previously believed that Canadian society was already egalitarian with respect to women. When the unwritten constitution came to be made explicit, a much less liberal set of assumptions held by Canadian governments, federal and provincial, was revealed. Because of this perception, the number of women who are willing to identify themselves as part of the women's movement has grown. In addition, partly as a result of the perceived success of the women's lobby on the constitution, political parties have become more interested in women as a voting group. Greater responsiveness to women's concerns in the area of representational politics may yet turn out to be the most important legacy of the process of constitutional change.[7]

Appendix

Resolutions Passed at the Ad-Hoc Conference, February 14, 1981

—"That this Conference endorse in principle the concept of an entrenched Charter of Rights as per the recommendations passed February 14, 1981, and that, unless the Charter reflects the amendments made here today, that it not be included in the submission to the British Government in order to provide time to incorporate these amendments."

—"That failing the full adoption of our amendments, incorporation of a Charter of Rights be accomplished by a constituent assembly of 50% women."

—"That the women of this Conference support bringing home the Constitution with an amending formula."

—"That the Women's Conference on the Constitution insist on a full and fair debate in Parliament on the Constitutional package before it, and oppose any closure on that debate."

—"That this meeting approves the principle of equitable representation of women throughout the political system. In the case of appointments to the Upper House, Boards, Commissions and the Bench, women should have equal access to appointments and positions and hold at least half the positions at all levels."

List of Required Amendments to the Charter as Agreed by the Ad-Hoc Conference

Clause 1   a statement of purpose should be added providing that the rights and freedoms under the Charter are guaranteed equally to men and women with no limitations

any limitation to clause (1) should follow the format and content of Article 4 of U.N. International Covenant on Civil and Political Rights

the word "person" should be used throughout the Charter, in lieu of any other word denoting human being

Clause 7   that clause 7 be amended to include the right to reproductive freedom

that clause 7 be amended to include the right to equality of economic opportunity

Clause 15 (1)   that the list of prohibited grounds of discrimination in clause 15 (1) be amended to include: (1) marital status (2) sexual orientation (3) political belief

that clause 15 contain a two-tiered test recognizing that there shall be no discrimination on the basis of sex, race, religion, colour, national or ethnic origin, mental or physical disability, age, marital status, sexual orientation, and political belief, and that there be a compelling reason for any distinction on the basis of sex, race, religion, colour, or national or ethnic origin, sexual orientation or political belief

Clause 15 (2)   affirmative action programs under clause 15 (2) should apply only to disadvantaged groups as listed under clause 15 (1) and not to individuals. Explanatory note: it is our opinion that individuals who are members of disadvantaged groups benefit under the programs listed above

Clause 26   clause 26 on multiculturalism be dealt with in the preamble

Clause 29 (2)   the three-year moratorium for the implementation of clause 15 be deleted from the Charter

Notes

1. Beth Atcheson, "Countdown to Equality," Newsletter of the Ontario Committee on the Status of Women, December 1981.
2. J.R. Pole, *The Pursuit of Equality in American History*, Jefferson Memorial Lecture Series (Berkeley, Calif.: University of California Press, 1978).
3. The laws for divorce would not be uniform throughout the country, and federal power over custody and maintenance would cease. This would lead to jurisdiction-shopping, with the more mobile spouse being able to choose a better deal, and after separation it is usually the male who is mobile. The problems of enforcing custody and maintenance orders are already great. Giving divorce jurisdiction to the provinces would exacerbate the problems of enforcement by adding to them the complexity of multiple legal jurisdictions. The legal costs of enforcement would mount significantly, as would the bureaucratic difficulties, and most of these would fall on the spouse seeking enforcement, who is usually the woman.

    If marital status were defined differently in each province, the payout of Canada Pension Plan survivor's benefits, veteran's pensions and private pensions would be affected. Women with the same history would have different marital statuses and different rights to pensions in different provinces.

    The usual argument for giving all matters in relation to divorce to the provinces is to allow for a more integrated approach to family law within provincial jurisdictions; and to allow for a more integrated approach within the civil and common law systems. The government of Quebec wished to get back power over marriage and divorce "to create true family courts, to update our

family law and to recognize the equality of Quebec women in all areas."
Quebec's family law provisions are equitable for women and therefore most
Quebec women's groups support provincial jurisdiction in divorce and family
law. However, women's groups in the rest of Canada tend to be opposed to the
transfer of jurisdiction in this area. See Mary Eberts, "Women and Constitutional Renewal," especially pp. 17-18, and Myrna Bowman, "From Bad to Worse
in One Easy Step: Proposed Transfer of Divorce Jurisdiction: An Assessment,"
in Audrey Doerr, and Micheline Carrier, editors, *Women and the Constitution in
Canada* (Ottawa: Canadian Advisory Council on the Status of Women, 1981).

4. *Ibid.*

5. In May 1981, after the Charter had passed through Parliament, the Canadian
Advisory Council finally held its conference on "Women and the Constitution."
The topics discussed largely concerned jurisdictional matters, and as a result of
the concerns expressed at the conference, the Council later presented a brief to the
Parliamentary Task Force on Fiscal Rearrangements, stressing the need for a
process of consultation with the consumers of social services, most of whom are
women. But two human rights issues were also addressed at the CAC conference:
the perennial section 12(1)(b) of the Indian Act, which discriminates against
native women who marry non-status men, and the Charter of Rights, with its
implications for the future. The concern about the Charter of Rights centred on
the possibility of using the three-year moratorium on implementation of parts of
the Charter to good advantage by providing information to the women's movement about legal action funds. After the conference, the Canadian Advisory
Council proceeded to fund and support a study of legal-action funds.

6. Beverley Baines, "Women, Human Rights and the Constitution," in Doerr and
Carrier, *op. cit.*, p. 60.

7. In the process of writing this paper, I have received valuable information and
assistance by Beth Atcheson, Rosemary Billings, Mary Eberts, Patricia Hacker,
Janet Hamilton, Penney Kome, Linda Ryan Nye and Alan Pearson. I thank
them all for their help; any errors or omissions are mine alone.

Chapter 15/The Indian Lobby

Douglas E. Sanders

Introduction

As the political struggle over patriation recedes into the past, it becomes clear that the least expected and most exotic part of the story was the Indian lobby. The constitution became the dominant political issue for Indians, Métis and Inuit in the years 1978 to 1982. They pursued a complex and expensive strategy which many politicians dismissed as naive and quixotic. They sought recognition as political actors within the Canadian state and piggybacked the campaign on a legal issue not of their making. In the effort to block or transform patriation, they sought to change their roles within Canadian federalism.

The Indian lobby occurred at a particular stage in the evolution of Canadian aboriginal policy. In the years since the Second World War, Canadian policy had progressed, particularly in the areas of legal equality and cultural rights. In the contemporary period the focus has shifted to special economic and political rights.[1] In the first decades after the war, Canada ended its formal discrimination against the Indian populations and began extending them normal social services. They gained the vote, access to liquor and family allowances. The church-state alliance in Indian education was ended, and students were increasingly integrated into provincial school systems. The ending of discrimination and the "normalization" of Indians within the Canadian state was accompanied by a partial dismantling of the special status of Indian reserve communities. While racism in Canadian society placed limits on this process, by the 1960s the right of Indians to equal treatment had been pervasively accepted in Canada, at least in theory.

The cultural dimension of Canadian Indian policy has a history of tremendous intolerance, symbolized most graphically by the campaigns against native languages in the Indian schools. While this intolerance continued in the years immediately following the Second World War, attitudes have now moderated. In the 1970s, the federal government officially approved Indian language instruction, Indian control of Indian education and the funding of Indian cultural-educational centres.

Progress on economic issues has been slower. Indian reserves were originally envisaged as a transitional arrangement designed to transform Indians into farmers; in practice, however, they perpetuated and increased Indian marginality. After the war, Indian economic development programs were individualistic or assimilationist in character. Gradually, however, as conditions on reserves became a public embarrassment, the government was forced to shift its concern to the plight of the reserve communities. Indian political demands focussed on special economic and social rights, using arguments based on treaty and aboriginal title. The government resisted these. The White Paper of 1969, which proposed the end of Indian special status in Canada, dismissed aboriginal title claims and trivialized treaty rights. But after a period of litigation and controversy, the government eventually developed a more accommodative policy towards Indian land claims. Aboriginal and treaty claims would be dealt with by a process of negotiation and settlement.[2] A major settlement occurred in 1975 in northern Quebec with the Cree and Inuit, thereby facilitating construction of the James Bay hydro-electric project. But progress in settling other claims has been stifled by legal issues, intergovernmental differences, bureaucratic delay and an insufficient politicization of the aboriginal population. The government response, political in its origins, became legalistic in practice.

The aboriginal organizations came to see that they had argued their case too narrowly. The new framework they proposed was explicitly political. The first major aboriginal political statement in the modern period was the Dene Declaration of 1975, asserting Dene nationhood within Canadian federalism.[3] The 1976 Nunuvut proposal envisaged an Inuit-controlled territory north of the tree line, and the Federation of Saskatchewan Indians pioneered the term "Indian government" in 1977. It quickly became national terminology, and political organization has adjusted accordingly. Between 1980 and 1982, the National Indian Brotherhood (NIB) was re-organized as the Assembly of First Nations (AFN).[4]

The federal government was apprehensive about this shift in ideas. Judd Buchanan, the minister of Indian affairs in 1975, rejected the Dene Declaration as "gobbledegook," and two years later the federal Cabinet rejected "political divisions and political structures based solely on distinctions of race."[5] In April 1980, Prime Minister Trudeau acknowledged an Indian demand for "internal native self-government," but refused to accept terms such as "self-determination" or "autonomy."

This progression in Canadian Indian policy since World War II forms the background to the constitutional issues of 1978 to 1982. While Canadian aboriginal policy had been changing, many Indian political demands were unacceptable to Canadian governments. In particular, any recognition of Indian governments as a distinct order of government within Canadian federalism was dismissed as inherently unrealistic. But this was the central thrust of Indian demands, and it underpinned the native strategy in the constitutional wars.

Getting in the Door

In 1978, it seemed unlikely that Indians, Inuit and Métis would play any substantial role in the Canadian constitutional reform process. After all, constitutional reform was basically a response to Quebec; the actors in the reform process were the first ministers, and no interest group participation was envisaged. Most politicians and bureaucrats assumed that aboriginal issues could be handled by legislation, and were not of a constitutional order; and they regarded the aboriginal group as factionalized and politically unsophisticated.

Governments were aware that some constitutional issues did involve Indians. The most persistent constitutional problem was the provision of social services. How could Indians, a federal responsibility, be included in the modern range of social services being provided to Canadians by the provincial governments?[6] As well, there were constitutional issues in the area of hunting and fishing rights.[7] The federal White Paper of 1969 proposed the repeal of section 91(24) of the British North America Act, which gives the federal government jurisdiction over "Indians, and Lands reserved for the Indians." But after strong Indian opposition, the White Paper was officially withdrawn a year later. The Clark government in 1979 recognized that Indian and Inuit land claims were a factor to be dealt with in any transfer of the ownership of off-shore resources to the coastal provinces; and the constitutional evolution of the two northern territories involved aboriginal questions as well. But there was little else. Indians, Inuit and Métis were not on any government's list of major constitutional issues.

Indians, on the other hand, had become interested in the constitution. They had traditionally argued that federal jurisdiction must continue, reflecting both the Indian focus on special status and a history of provincial indifference or hostility. As well, on the prairies there was a well-established tradition that the treaties were, in effect, constitutional documents which should be protected by or incorporated in the constitution. In 1978, the National Indian Brotherhood (NIB) identified constitutional reform as an Indian issue, transcending the traditional treaty and non-treaty divisions within the organization. In one sense, the Indian approach was rooted in history. Indians knew they had a special constitutional status and believed it was inadequately recognized by both federal and provincial governments. In addition, Indians asserted a special relationship with the Queen, which was to be a distinctive feature in their later arguments and strategies. But in another sense, they were free from history. As Noel Starblanket, the president of the NIB, testified in 1978, "We are now prepared to consider the negotiation of the terms and conditions upon which we will develop our relationship with Canada."[8] He also wrote to Trudeau saying, "our relationship with the rest of Canada remains to be defined."[9]

These initiatives were given at least vague symbolic recognition in constitutional discussions. The Trudeau government's constitutional amendment bill, introduced in June 1978, included a provision to ensure that its Charter of Rights did not erase Indian rights based on the Royal Proclamation of 1763. The accompanying White Paper, *A Time for*

Action, stated that "the renewal of the Federation must fully respect the legitimate rights of the native peoples."[10] Other studies and initiatives, such as the 1978 Canadian Bar Association study and the 1979 report of the Task Force on Canadian Unity, also identified Indian questions as part of the constitutional reform agenda. The Quebec Liberal Party's 1980 Beige paper, for example, said that the native people "must become the authors of their own destiny and not mere subjects of jurisdiction."[11]

In this context, the NIB formulated two basic and specific demands. First, a new constitution must entrench aboriginal and treaty rights; and second, the Indians must themselves be involved in the process of constitutional reform. At its general assembly in Fredericton in August 1978, the NIB threatened that if these demands were not met, it would travel to England to ask the Queen to block patriation of the constitution.

There was a limited, but accommodative response. Representatives of the three national aboriginal organizations were invited to the first ministers' meeting as observers in October 1978. The NIB represented status Indians, the Native Council of Canada (NCC) represented Métis and non-status Indians, and the Inuit Committee on National Issues (ICNI) represented the Inuit. Federal thinking insisted that the status Indians could not be invited without the non-status Métis and Inuit as well. The federal government was embarrassed by the distinction between status and non-status Indians even though it was the product of earlier federal Indian policies, and it could not understand the NIB refusal to co-operate with the NCC. Although the Inuit were as far from the understanding of federal politicians as Baffin Island, their right to be equally involved with the Indians was assumed as well. But the NIB was the major actor as far as governments were concerned.

Since the October meeting was public, the invitation to be observers simply meant that the aboriginal representatives had seats in the conference centre. As Noel Starblanket said later, he could have seen the proceedings just as well on television. Indian distrust of the reform process was clear. Noel Starblanket testified to the Task Force on Canadian Unity,

> The federal government has continually hammered the Indian people with as much vigour as it has the Parti Québécois. In Ottawa's minds, a move to undermine the special status of Indians is a move to undercut the special status of Quebec.
> The Indian people greatly resent this government's willingness to fight the Parti Québécois on the backs of the Indian people.[12]

Joe Dion, president of the Indian Association of Alberta, came away from the first ministers' meeting "concerned that treaty rights may not be safeguarded by a new constitution and that the ending of Canada's colonial status could also mean the ending of the Indian people's special relationship with the Crown."[13]

For the next first ministers' meeting in February 1979, the three national aboriginal organizations were again invited to send observers. The invitation was particularly meaningless, however, since most of the sessions were closed. At the meeting, Prime Minister Trudeau proposed a new agenda item, "Canada's native peoples and the constitution," to which all premiers agreed. The Prime Minister's Office insisted that "the federal government does not wish to abdicate its special trust relationship with native peoples," and emphasized the need for "frank discussions between all the parties concerned."[14]

Despite this, the NIB took the position that it was excluded from the constitutional reform process and proceeded with its plan to visit the United Kingdom and petition the Queen. Serious planning for the trip only began in March and April, though the trip was scheduled for July. The federal government, meanwhile, tried several strategies to avoid potential embarrassment. The minister of justice wrote to the NIB on May 8, offering participation in the fall meeting of the Continuing Committee of Ministers on the Constitution. Indians would be allowed to participate at the ministerial level, but not at the level of first ministers. Soon after, however, the Liberals were defeated in a general election. At its first Cabinet meeting, the new government had to decide what instructions should be given to the Queen about the brotherhood's trip to England. The Cabinet decided to instruct the Queen not to meet with the Indian delegation.

The decision to block the meeting with the Queen was curious. If the Queen had no power, as bureaucrats often reminded the NIB, a meeting was simply a piece of symbolic politics. And Indians, in full regalia, had always been part of royal visits to Canada. Prince Charles had been made an honourary Kainai chief in a special ceremony in southern Alberta. Indian leader Harold Cardinal had given a political speech to the Queen on a royal visit in 1973. The speech and the Queen's reply had been fully negotiated before the event. In 1976, a visit of Indians to the Queen in England on the occasion of the one hundredth anniversary of Treaties Six and Seven was described as follows:

> Six Alberta Indian chiefs and their wives, in full traditional dress, went to Buckingham Palace . . . for an audience with the Queen. The Queen, in jolly mood, entertained them in a groundfloor reception room overlooking the sweeping palace gardens. The chiefs conveyed greetings on the 100th anniversary of two important Indian treaties signed with Queen Victoria, "The Great White Mother." The Indian party was accompanied to the palace by Canadian High Commissioner, Paul Martin. The party was led by Lt. Gov. Ralph Steinhauer of Alberta, a Cree Indian chief. . . .[15]

The Clark Cabinet apparently had not wanted to convey the impression to Quebec that they regarded the Queen as having any real power. In addition, the government probably expected the London trip to be a failure and feared that a meeting with the Queen might save an otherwise failing strategy. Whatever the reasoning, however, the decision certainly embroiled the Cabinet in the event. While approval of a visit with the Queen would not likely have been attributed to the Canadian government, blame for blocking the audience was laid squarely at Clark's feet.

In a last-minute letter, Federal-Provincial Relations Minister William Jarvis seemed to offer substantial Indian involvement in reform. But it was too late. The letter was hand delivered to the NIB offices on July 3; the Indians had already left for England.

The trip to England was a success.[16] As many as two hundred Indians made the journey. Though they were not able to meet with the Queen, the prime minister or members of the Cabinet, they did meet the leader of the opposition, members of the House of Commons and the House of Lords, various High Commissioners and a senior official in the Foreign Office. Moreover, the event was well covered in the Canadian media. The Indians had a hidden card in the London strategy. The romantic notion of the noble red man has a deep hold in Europe: the Indians were the first and remain the classic victims of European colonialism. Labour backbencher Bruce George in particular had a life-long interest in North American Indians. He was active in a London-based group, Survival International, which was intensely involved with issues affecting South American Indians. His support was essential to the London trip, and it continued through to the final debate on the Canada Bill in 1982.[17]

The Clark government's promise of aboriginal involvement in the constitutional reform process was confirmed at a meeting between the executive council of the NIB and the prime minister in September 1979. Prime Minister Clark rejected the idea of having the NIB as "an 11th province at all discussion tables," but did contemplate having "the NIB or Indian representatives speak at the First Ministers' table on matters that have clear legal impact on Native people."[18] Starblanket was positive. "Our request for ongoing and full participation has been accepted."[19] Having achieved this breakthrough, Starblanket and the NIB pressed the point: almost everything on the first ministers' agenda affected aboriginal people, they argued, and therefore should come within the native agenda item. Starblanket argued:

> We are not willing to accept exclusion from debate on a matter simply because it affects everybody in the country and not exclusively Indians. Nor can we accept the idea that there can be an arbitrary separation of "Indian issues" on the one hand and non-Indian issues on the other hand.[20]

These federal initiatives took place without consultation with the provinces, however. At a meeting of provincial officials on July 31,

General concern was expressed that the Jarvis letter had pre-cast the nature of Indian/Native involvement and may preclude any recommendations from the Annual Premier's Conference. Some officials stated their belief that the Jarvis letter was not so much a policy statement but rather more so the product of a nervous, quick federal reaction to the NIB prior to the England trip by Indian chiefs.[21]

Some provinces were hesitant about the open-endedness of the aboriginal involvement in the constitutional reform process.[22] Howard Leeson, Saskatchewan's deputy minister of intergovernmental affairs, complained of unilateral federal initiatives in vigorous terms:

These meetings were ill-considered and unfortunate. The subsequent telexes from Arnold Goodleaf and Noel Starblanket give ample evidence of how quickly misunderstandings can develop. I wish to register my formal objection to the way in which federal officials have acted in this matter. The expectation level on the part of the native organization and their subsequent disappointment, can be directly traced to these previous federal initiatives.[23]

Linking the federal-provincial process to a government-Indian process clearly would not be easy.

Nor, in general, were the provinces well informed on aboriginal questions. The minutes of a meeting of provincial officials July 1979 concluded that "other than Saskatchewan, no provinces have a clear policy position regarding 'rights' of Indians by virtue of Treaties of 'special status.'"[24] As late as June or July 1980, a federal government internal background paper commented: "at this stage very little can be said about the positions of each of the Provinces on the various issues relating to Natives and the Constitution."[25] In all the detailed constitutional position papers put forward by the provinces, there was only one reference to the subject of native people and the constitution. Despite these problems, however, the provinces did agree to go along with the federal initiatives.

The national aboriginal organizations and Continuing Committee of Ministers on the Constitution met on December 3, 1979. The ministers spoke of the meeting as a significant advance. In contrast, Noel Starblanket spoke bluntly. He had agreed with the prime minister on full, equal and ongoing participation in the constitutional talks, limited only to the native agenda item. To meet with the continuing committee at all was itself a concession on the part of the brotherhood:

Let me now tell you gentlemen I do not appreciate dealing with you. I will advise you that we did not negotiate for this to meet you people.

He rejected any process of negotiation or compromise:

I am not here to negotiate. I cannot compromise the position my colleague, Chief Dion has espoused or anything mandated by our annual meeting resolutions. It is pure and simple. You must now go forward to your continuing committee and report that that is our position. There has been no compromise as far as we are concerned and you will report that accordingly.[26]

Starblanket asserted that the Indians should be involved in the constitutional negotiations as governments. Rather than negotiating on this point, he was prepared that they "disagree as gentlemen."

If negotiation and compromise were rejected, what was the brotherhood's view of the process? Starblanket talked of a Canadian Indian constitutional commission which would hold hearings and consolidate an Indian position. If no compromise or negotiation were to occur, the first ministers would eventually be faced with the package developed by the commission and an absolute demand for acceptance. Starblanket also made it clear that governments would have to deal separately with the three national organizations. While the Native Council of Canada clearly sought a unified front with government, the NIB followed its traditional rejection of common-front strategy. Finally, Starblanket predicted failure:

> Not a Liberal government and not a Conservative government, has not and will not in the near future anyway accede to treaty rights and aboriginal rights in this country . . . we know very well what your government's position will be, what it is, has been and what it is going to be.[27]

Starblanket's position on co-operation with NCC and ICNI would have come as no surprise to ministers. But the almost exclusive focus on meetings with first ministers, the rejection of negotiation or compromise and the prediction of failure must have seemed extreme. Places at the federal-provincial bargaining table had never before been opened to any but government executives.

Shortly after the December meeting, the Clark government fell and the constitutional renewal process stopped. After Mr. Trudeau regained office in February, the Quebec referendum on sovereignty-association became the overriding federal preoccupation. Meanwhile, the Task Force on Canadian Unity reported, recommending that,

> Both central and provincial authorities should pursue direct discussions with representatives of Canadian Indians, Inuit and Métis, with a view to arriving at mutually acceptable constitutional provisions that would secure the rightful place of native peoples in Canadian society.[28]

In April, the NIB held a national all-chiefs conference in Ottawa, which was attended by an estimated 376 chiefs and 2,000 other Indian people.[29] The assembly was called the "first nations' constitutional conference," and was held in the largest conference room in Ottawa. The federal government hosted a banquet on the second night, and Prime Minister Trudeau spoke of the "remarkable progress in mutual understanding which has taken place between native peoples and the federal government during the 1970s," including the "valuable and historic precedent" of involving aboriginal representatives directly in the constitutional reform process.[30] Trudeau was claiming credit for this innovation. But in fact his White Paper had made no reference to the "involvement of Indian, Inuit and Métis representatives," nor did the documents issued after the first ministers' conference of February 1979. In effect, Trudeau was distorting history to take credit for a policy initiated by former prime minister Clark. But at least all three federal political parties now had the same stated positions, and no federal or provincial politicians publicly opposed aboriginal participation in the reform process or the inclusion of aboriginal rights provisions in a new constitution.

The Short List: Participation Delayed

The defeat of the Quebec referendum on sovereignty-association in May was followed by new initiatives in the reform process. The first ministers met in June 1980 and agreed on a two-stage strategy. The Continuing Committee of Ministers on the Constitution would work on a list of 12 items over the summer and present their conclusions to a September first ministers' meeting. Other constitutional issues would be put off for a "second stage." Aboriginal issues did not make the short list.

The accelerated schedule with its deadlines worked against the aboriginal organizations. Extensive work had been done on constitutional questions such as a Charter of Rights, the Senate and family law, but no comparable work had been done on aboriginal questions. The National Indian Brotherhood and the Native Council of Canada proposals for commissions of inquiry needed a year or two to carry out. The strategy had made sense when Clark was in power; it could not respond to the new Trudeau agenda.[31] The government was aware of the dilemma in which it had placed natives. An internal federal memorandum, written probably in early July, commented:

> The short list, together with the agreed upon time schedule, leaves open the distinct possibility that Native interests and positions may be compromised or ignored in the rush to achieve general consensus under most of the items. It is this possibility amongst other factors that has led to increasing demands by the Native leadership (especially the NIB) for "full ongoing and equal" participation in all discussion relating to the short list items in addition to the "Natives and the Constitution" item. The fact that governments have issued no formal statements on the status of the item "Natives and the Constitution" has compounded this problem for the Native leadership.[32]

Nothing was done, however, to ease the problems. In only one token meeting did a subcommittee of the Continuing Committee of Ministers on the Constitution meet with the representatives of NIB, NCC and ICNI. The organizations were all concerned with the process being followed. Harry Daniels, president of NCC, stated that he was,

> puzzled at how this form of our participation in the constitutional review process has come to pass and why we are being asked to comment on a list of priority items distilled from over two years of federal and provincial meetings and negotiations from which we have been excluded.

Del Riley, the new president of the NIB, added:

> At no point have there been discussions about the process involved. In our view we should be invited to participate in the September meeting of First Ministers and in all future First Ministers' meetings. In addition, in our view, we should be given a seat on the Continuing Committee of Ministers on the Constitution, which would mean ending the need for a special subcommittee of the CCMC on native questions.

Jean Chrétien, representing the federal government, repeated the pledge that aboriginal representatives would be at the table with the first ministers when the time came to discuss the native agenda item. The fact that financial support to assist the aboriginal organizations in the constitutional process had just been paid was used to justify the delay in dealing with the aboriginal issues. But Chrétien clearly rejected the idea of Indian groups as a third order of government in Canada as a "non-starter" in constitutional discussions.[33]

While the first ministers were meeting from September 8 to 13, the NIB held a parallel conference rather than simply accept observer status. The NIB announced that it would "begin a systematic and timely dialogue with the provinces on our mutual constitutional interests." An advance team was mandated by the National Indian Brotherhood executive council to go to England to prepare for a systematic lobby of the Queen, parliamentarians, Commonwealth embassies, and the European Economic Community. The NIB also planned to join other indigenous nations in an international forum in Canberra, Australia in March and to lobby at the United Nations. "And we will attempt a much needed public education program in Canada."[34]

A Militant Reaction: Fall 1980

When the Trudeau government decided to move unilaterally, its Resolution contained only two sections affecting aboriginal groups. A general clause allowed affirmative action programs; and another provision protected "the rights and freedoms that pertain to the native peoples of Canada" from the Charter of Rights and Freedoms. The document was consistent with the federal position that aboriginal questions were for the second stage of constitutional reform.

Aboriginal organizations knew they had been left out of the action and out of the constitution, and there was an aggressive response. The Union of

British Columbia Indian Chiefs took on the cause with a vengeance. In September, the union initiated a lawsuit in Canada asking for a judicial declaration that Indian consent was necessary before the constitution could be patriated. The union also promised further actions:

> The Union of British Columbia Indian Chiefs is presently investigating the possibility of taking legal action in Great Britain and also within the terms of the United Nations. In Great Britain we are seeking to bring an action asking that the British courts declare that Britain is still in a trust relationship to the Indian people and cannot patriate the Constitution without Indian people's consent.
>
> On a world level, we are seeking to have world courts declare that the Treaties entered into between Great Britain and the Canadian Indians cannot be extinguished on the request of the Federal Government of Canada.[35]

George Manuel, head of the Union of B.C. Indian Chiefs, accused the federal government of trying to terminate Indian rights. He saw the egalitarian provisions of the Charter of Rights as designed to make Indian rights illegal.[36]

> The measures which are now underway to patriate and amend the Canadian Constitution appear to be designed to remove all constitutional impediments to an accelerated termination of the special status and rights of Indian Nations by eliminating Canada's administrative responsibilities now carried out on behalf of Britain. Canada seems intent on nothing less than the total assimilation of Indian peoples and the complete destruction of Indian Governments.
>
> Current Canadian intentions with respect to Constitutional amendment should not come as a surprise. The fact that a new Constitution appears geared to a termination policy, rather than to any recognition or enhancement of Indian rights, is entirely consistent with long-standing Canadian objectives and practices.[37]

In October, the union announced plans for a "constitution express," a protest train to travel from Vancouver to Ottawa. The federal government had established a Special Joint Committee of the Senate and the House of Commons to hold hearings on the constitutional proposal, and the NIB had called an emergency First Nations Assembly. The constitution express would arrive in Ottawa for both events. Then, a delegation would go on from Ottawa to New York to petition the United Nations. In addition, the NIB announced that it would establish an "embassy" in London.[38] At the urging of Bruce George and other British supporters, the term embassy was dropped in favour of the "Office of the First Nations of Canada." The NIB talked of establishing an office in New York as well.

Additional forums became available. The Foreign Affairs Committee (the Kershaw committee) of the British House of Commons began hearings on November 12 on British responsibilities for the Canadian constitution.

Indian groups sent briefs and asked to appear as witnesses, but the committee heard no witnesses from Canada. The fourth Russell tribunal was held in Rotterdam from November 20 to 24 on the situation of the Indians in the Americas. Briefs were submitted on the constitutional issue, and Indians from British Columbia, Alberta, Saskatchewan and Ontario attended.

Again, the federal government tried to counter the Indians' international lobby. The prime minister wrote to the aboriginal organizations on October 30, assuring them that patriation was not a threat to their rights and repeating the government's promise to involve them in the second stage of constitutional talks.[39] He also proposed a meeting in the spring of 1981 to discuss how to involve the aboriginal groups in the first ministers' meeting.[40] Clearly, aboriginal lobbying had placed the government in a difficult political and moral position, as an internal federal document written at this time reveals:

> There is likely to be a major effort by Canada's Native Peoples to win national and international support (especially at Westminster) for their stand against patriation. If the Native Peoples press forward with their plans and if they succeed in gaining support and sympathy abroad, Canada's image will suffer considerably. Because Canada's Native Peoples live, as a rule, in conditions which are very different from those of most other Canadians—as sample statistics set out below attest—there would well be serious questions asked about whether the Native Peoples enjoy basic rights in Canada.

There followed statistics on Indian health, life expectancy, unemployment, housing and rates of incarceration. Moreover, the document acknowledged the unreality of the government's second stage strategy:

> Native leaders realize that entrenching their rights will be enormously difficult after patriation, especially since a majority of the provinces would have to agree to changes which might benefit Native Peoples at the expense of provincial power.

Nevertheless, in public the government maintained its stated reason for a delay on aboriginal questions: the difficulty of formulating precise constitutional provisions. As the prime minister observed, "the simple claim of aboriginal rights, without anyone knowing exactly what it means, is not a matter which one can convincingly argue should be put in the Constitution at this time."[41]

The Indians' British strategy also hit a reef. On November 12, the Foreign Affairs Committee of the British House of Commons heard its first witness, Mr. J.R. Freeland, a legal advisor in the Foreign and Commonwealth Office. When Sir Anthony Kershaw asked if Britain retained treaty or other responsibility for Canadian Indians, Freeland replied, "In our view, all relevant treaty obligations insofar as they still subsisted became the responsibility of the Government of Canada with the obtainment of independence, which at the latest was with the Statute of Westminster of 1931.''[42] The report of the Foreign Affairs Committee the following January was to adopt Mr. Freeland's views on the treaty issue, and its judgement had great impact both in England and in Canada.[43]

In the meantime, however, five hundred Indians arrived in Ottawa on the constitution express in late November. Two days later, the Assembly of First Nations met, with perhaps two thousand Indians in attendance, again in the largest convention room in Ottawa. The Indians had established a remarkable presence in Ottawa at a crucial time in the constitutional reform process. But their presence confused observers and politicians. The Assembly of First Nations, rather than charting a war plan, drafted a general statement—the Declaration of the First Nations—which was presented to the Governor General:

> We the Original Peoples of this land know the Creator put us here.
> The Creator gave us laws that govern all our relationships to live in harmony with nature and mankind.
> The laws of the Creator defined our rights and responsibilities.
> The Creator gave us our spiritual beliefs, our languages, our culture, and a place on Mother Earth which provides us with all our needs.
> We have maintained our freedom, our languages, and our traditions from time immemorial.
> We continue to exercise the rights and fulfill the responsibilities and obligations given to us by the Creator for the land upon which we were placed.
> The Creator has given us the right to govern ourselves and the right to self-determination.
> The rights and responsibilities given to us by the Creator cannot be altered or taken away by any other Nation.

The Special Joint Committee had altered its schedule to hear both the NIB and the constitution express leaders. But at the last minute, both groups boycotted the committee hearings, and a delegation from the constitution express went to New York to the United Nations. The Native Council of Canada and the Inuit Committee on National Issues, on the other hand, did testify before the committee, as did regional groups such as the Council for Yukon Indians and the Nishga Tribe.

The lobbying in Ottawa and England produced some co-operation between the three national organizations. British supporters stressed that the aboriginal case would get greater support if the Canadian groups had a unified strategy there. In November, a single submission went to the British Foreign Affairs Committee on behalf of the NIB, NCC and ICNI. In addition, staff in the three national organizations developed a common position on constitutional provisions which would entrench treaty and aboriginal rights, recognize aboriginal self-government, and require aboriginal consent to constitutional amendments affecting their rights. But this co-operation quickly dissolved. A formal NIB executive council resolution of September 1980 had opposed co-operation with the Métis, and prairie leaders, particularly from Alberta, were furious that the NIB would defy their views in this way. Their organizations had long seen the Métis as rivals, and the following August the general assembly of the NIB resolved that the organization would "work alone on the constitution."

The thinking of one key group, the Union of British Columbia Indian Chiefs, had changed in an important direction during the constitution express. The idea of the entrenchment of Indian rights in a Canadian constitution was rejected as inconsistent with the national status of the tribes. As the union later reported to the NIB:

> If Indian people chose entrenchment, Indians are Canadian citizens forever, and the emphasis will be to get the best possible arrangements for citizenship, remembering that we will always be in a minority.
>
> If Indian people choose nationhood, and if we are unsuccessful in achieving a negotiation structure prior to patriation, the fallback position must be to lobby to keep section 91(24) and section 109 of the BNA Act in Britain, while the rest of the Canadian Constitution is patriated. We will then negotiate directly with Great Britain, on our own behalf, for our land, resources and for the settlement of the trust owing to us.[44]

As a result, the union, with a mandate from the NIB, began to explore the legal strategies open to Canadian Indians to achieve these goals. The union sought an opinion from Professor Ian Brownlie, an international law expert at Oxford University, on whether or not a case could be brought in England. They also explored the possibilities in the European Court of Human Rights, the International Court of Justice in the Hague and the Human Rights Commission of the United Nations.

"The Shortest Treaty in History"
The federal government's own strategy was encountering heavy weather. The Kershaw committee reported in January 1981 that the federal government was not constitutionally authorized to go ahead with patriation against the opposition of eight provinces. While Trudeau and Chrétien had consistently maintained that they had the power to petition the British Parliament without provincial consent, they had been, in fact, far less confident of their constitutional position. They faced more opposition from the provinces and the other federal political parties than they had expected. The Indian opposition was only one of many problems facing the government, but it was particularly troubling because of its combination of moral and legal arguments. The government knew that the Indian cause had significant appeal in Canada and in Britain.

The embattled federal government tried to broaden support for its position at the federal level.[45] The Joint Committee became a central vehicle for building that broader federal consensus, and aboriginal rights became a bargaining issue within that forum. The government told the National Indian Brotherhood that it would agree to positive entrenchment of aboriginal and treaty rights. Between January 28 and 30, the deal was struck by the three federal parties and the leaders of the national organizations. The key new section in the Resolution read:

> 34(1) The aboriginal and treaty rights of the aboriginal peoples of Canada are hereby recognized and affirmed.
>
> (2) in this Act, "aboriginal peoples of Canada" includes the Indian, Inuit and Métis peoples of Canada.

Section 25, protecting the rights of aboriginal peoples from the egalitarian provision of the Charter of Rights, was strengthened. A new subsection 35(2) required that a future first ministers' meeting involve the participation of aboriginal representatives and discuss aboriginal issues.

The amendments were in line with what the organizations had requested. The alteration of section 25 and the addition of subsection 35(2) came directly from the brotherhood's submission to the Joint Committee in December.[46] The section on aboriginal and treaty rights reflected the most persistent demand by the aboriginal organizations. The agreement was still a compromise, as there was no response to the aboriginal positions on self-government and a clause requiring their consent to future amendments. Nevertheless, it was seen as a dramatic reversal of policy. Indian, Inuit and Métis leaders declared they were beginning a new era in which they would at last take control of their own destiny. It was, said Del Riley, "an historic moment, a recognition of the right of native peoples to self-determination," and "a new beginning for Indian people in Canada." Native leaders announced they would join Prime Minister Trudeau in demanding that the British Parliament approve patriation. "I'll carry it back for him now," said Harry Daniels of the Native Council of Canada.[47] The emotional moment was shared by members of all parties, and the committee vote was unanimous.

The euphoria was short-lived. The breakthrough took place on a Friday, and by the following Monday Jean Chrétien was circulating additional provisions which would have allowed section 34 to be amended in the northern territories by the federal Parliament alone. In the provinces, the general amending formula would apply. Chrétien explained that these provisions were part of the Friday agreement. There were heated denials from the organizations and the opposition political parties. Although Chrétien withdrew the provision, there was a sense of betrayal. One brotherhood employee referred to the January 30 bargain as the shortest treaty in history. To the aboriginal organizations, the dispute emphasized the need for a consent clause on amendments. But a consent clause was unacceptable to the federal government.[48]

Ed Broadbent, leader of the New Democratic Party, advised the aboriginal leaders that the government would not move on a consent clause. He felt that the general amending formula gave the aboriginal groups sufficient protection. He feared that the demand of the Progressive Conservative Party and the majority of provinces for simple patriation without a Charter of Rights might succeed, and therefore asked aboriginal groups to accept their gains and support the government's package.

Nevertheless, within days the government was using the January 30 concession to build support. On February 6, Chrétien testified before the Joint Committee: having agreed to entrench rights for the handicapped, natives and Quebec anglophones, we cannot "play politics on their backs," he said.[49] In Britain, the Canadian High Commission quickly disseminated the news of the January 30 agreement, circulating a document rebutting "myths" about the Canadian constitution.

> MYTH: That the rights of the native people in Canada would be adversely affected by "patriation" of the Constitution.
> FACT: . . . The constitutional proposal actually marks a dramatic step forward in the relationship between aboriginal peoples and other citizens of Canada. For the first time, there would be a positive affirmation of aboriginal and treaty rights. In addition, the commitment of the Government of Canada to invite representatives of the aboriginal peoples to a Conference of First Ministers to discuss constitutional matters that affect them would be confirmed in the Constitution Act.[50]

But the January breakthrough quickly unravelled. There were hostile reactions from some of the member organizations of the National Indian Brotherhood. Alberta chiefs unanimously rejected the agreement, calling for Del Riley's resignation.[51] The executive council of the brotherhood forced the organization to reverse its stand. A moderate grouping, including the Dene of the Northwest Territories and the Council for Yukon Indians, lost in their bid for continued NIB support. In March, the Indian Association of Alberta withdrew from the NIB, alleging collusion with the federal government and with Métis and Inuit groups.[52] The Four Nations Confederacy in Manitoba severed its ties with the brotherhood on constitutional matters.[53] The NIB was discredited in the eyes of its member organizations. Actual leadership had shifted to organizations in the Western Provinces since at least October 1980, and any appearance of NIB co-ordination of the Indian strategy vanished.[54]

The London Lobby
The drive for international political support intensified. The Union of British Columbia Indian Chiefs announced a second constitution express, this time to Europe. Indians would visit Germany, France, the Netherlands and Denmark, gathering support on their way to London. The union also

called an emergency general assembly for May 14 and 15. President George Manuel warned:

> We are in a state of emergency. . . . We expect you to be at this meeting because the end of your Indian reserves, Indian governments and all your Indian rights is very close. . . . This is the final showdown.[55]

A delegation of Alberta Indians left for England in May. A Saskatchewan group left in June.

The Indians' legal and political initiatives increasingly focussed on the London lobby, which had begun as a continuous strategy that spring. The organizations did not participate in the litigation before the Supreme Court of Canada in the spring of 1981,[56] and the Canadian suit brought by the Union of British Columbia Indian Chiefs was not actively pursued. Canadian courts were the proper forum for Canadian governments and Canadian law. The Indians were better off litigating in England. The Union of British Columbia Indian Chiefs had given early leadership on the strategy of litigation in England, and over the summer there was co-operation between the union and the Alberta and Saskatchewan groups. In the fall, however, the co-operation dissolved. The Indian Association of Alberta initiated its own litigation. The Nova Scotia and New Brunswick organizations joined the Alberta suit, allowing both pre-Confederation and post-Confederation treaties to be involved in the arguments. The Union of British Columbia Indian Chiefs was joined by the Four Nations Confederacy in Manitoba and the Grand Council of Treaty Nine, a regional group in Ontario. The British Columbia and Saskatchewan groups continued to co-operate, though the Saskatchewan group launched its own suit.

Legal action was reinforced by political action. Lobbyists were in London continuously from June until the following March. The National Indian Brotherhood's London office was taken over by the western organizations, and from September 1981 to March 1982, the lobby met approximately two hundred and fifty members of the House of Commons and the House of Lords. There was, however, little media coverage of this activity in Canada.

An attempt to re-establish national co-ordination of the Indian strategy was made in July. The joint council of the National Indian Brotherhood and the Assembly of First Nations[57] hired Joe Dion, former president of the Indian Association of Alberta, and Wilton Littlechild, an Indian lawyer, to co-ordinate the lobby nationally and to report to the annual general assembly of the NIB. Dion and Littlechild spent a week in London meeting with significant actors in the constitutional drama. Their report gave an interesting picture of the thinking of various individuals at that time. Gilles Loiselle, Quebec's agent-general in London, apparently expressed interest in a joint Quebec-Indian court case in Britain—if they had similar positions. Sir Bernard Braine MP was planning "a short, sharp, rampant speech" in Parliament against the Canadian proposals. Bruce George advised them they could "lobby on the emotional side but [they] must also come up with a definite legal argument that the British Parliament has a legal responsibility."

Dion also wrote a paper "Indian Statehood," which proposed consolidating the Indian reserve communities in Canada into a national government with powers equivalent to a province. An executive or Cabinet would be composed of chiefs or ministers of various departments and agencies established to serve Indian people. It would report to an elected Legislature with possibly an additional chamber to accommodate a council of elders. There would be a judiciary and a public service staffed with people recruited by the Indian state to carry out the work of the various departments and agencies. Fiscal arrangements with the federal government "would be purely intergovernmental in nature," similar to those of the provinces, with equalization payments. Under the proposed plan, the Department of Indian Affairs and the Indian Act would cease to exist. Indians would no longer be identified by the province in which they lived, but rather as citizens of an Indian state.[58]

The idea of provincial status had been explored before. Nevertheless, the paper was a bold proposal which went well beyond any existing political consensus among Indians. In the general assembly of the NIB, the paper was supported by Indians from the northern territories. Opponents from Ontario and British Columbia argued that the paper dealt with post-patriation plans and was, therefore, tacitly admitting an Indian defeat in the fight against patriation. After a heated debate, the document was tabled for future discussion. It never came; this new effort by the NIB to co-ordinate the Indian strategy on the constitution had failed, and the initiative remained with the three western organizations.

Betrayal in Ottawa

The Supreme Court of Canada gave its decision on the federal unilateral strategy on September 28, 1981, setting the stage for the climactic first ministers' meeting in November. As the governments jockeyed for position, native leaders also began to organize.

The Union of British Columbia Indian Chiefs held a general assembly from October 28 to 30 to launch the second constitution express. The President of the union, George Manuel, circulated a letter he had written to the prime minister:

> Our indictment of your administration of our affairs can no longer be restrained. At this critical juncture in our relationship, your legacy of mismanagement and neglect coincides most remarkably with the hidden agenda of your government, which is to try to achieve the termination of our aboriginal title and our sovereign rights.

> In all the corruption and attempted destruction of our ideals by your government, we must point our accusing finger at you, Mr. Trudeau, as the Head of this government. It is impossible for us to disregard the hard evidence which is our daily companion. Daily, these assurances, promises and guarantees of your government are shown as lies.

British Columbia Indians flew to Europe on November 1. On the 2nd, a twenty-one member delegation of Saskatchewan Indians flew to London, the sixth trip to England by Saskatchewan Indians in two years. Indians from both Quebec and Saskatchewan met French officials in Paris. Later in the struggle, an Alberta Indian delegation met with the Pope.[59]

As the first ministers gathered in Ottawa for their fateful November meeting, the native groups supporting the government package, such as the Inuit Committee on National Issues, were fearful that section 34 might be traded off in some bargaining session. Jean Chrétien assured them the section was safe. But he was wrong. On November 5, a political compromise was announced at the end of the first ministers' meeting. The Accord was worded in such a way that it avoided any direct statement that section 34 was gone; and when Trudeau tabled it in the House of Commons, his speech did not mention the fate of the section. It was handled as a piece of dirty work.

There was immediate confusion. Who was responsible for the killing of section 34? Chrétien stated that the section had been dropped because the Indians had objected to it. Prime Minister Trudeau said that seven premiers had opposed it.[60] Mr. Broadbent understood that the prime minister had supported the removal of the section.[61] *Macleans* magazine wrote that Trudeau "tried briefly to reinstate native rights."[62] Another journalist reported that Trudeau had asked if aboriginal rights had been omitted by mistake. When told it was not a mistake, he "shrugged and moved on to the next agenda."[63]

The federal government had solved its main problem, but at some cost. On section 34, it lost at least one Liberal MP[64] and some opposition support. Both the Progressive Conservative Party and the New Democratic Party committed themselves to clauses on sexual equality and aboriginal rights. But only the NDP said it would vote against the package if these sections were not added. The government had been using the aboriginal and treaty rights section to assure Indian supporters in the United Kingdom that Indian rights were being respected. Indians had continually relied on conspiratorial arguments and challenged the good faith of the government. Now the conspiratorial arguments looked good. Canadian governments were prepared to gang up on Indian rights.

John Munro, the minister of Indian affairs, met with the National Indian Brotherhood on November 5. The strident Indian opposition had been deeply resented by the major federal politicians. Munro told the NIB leadership that they had "pissed and shitted" on him on the constitutional

issue. Ever the politician, however, Munro offered to meet with the Cabinet
the next morning to try to get section 34 restored at least to apply at the
federal level. But the NIB was uncertain whether it could support the rein-
statement of section 34 given the aggressive campaign of the provincial
organizations.

The political initiative was taken by others first. The Native Council
of Canada, the Inuit Committee on National Issues, the Native Women's
Association of Canada, the Dene Nation organization in the Northwest
Territories and the Council for Yukon Indians joined together as the
Aboriginal Rights Coalition. On November 9, the prime minister met with
Inuit leaders. Trudeau expressed his regret that the aboriginal rights
section had been dropped and suggested the possibility of restoring it for
the northern territories, where Ottawa had full jurisdiction. Charlie Watt
of ICNI rejected this proposal as unfair to other native groups and suggested
a three-year delay for a restored section 34, giving time for the governments
to negotiate specific provisions spelling out aboriginal rights. Trudeau
replied that if the aboriginal groups could agree on some proposals, the
Cabinet could consider them later in the week. Proposals were submitted.
They were considered and rejected at a Cabinet meeting on November 12:

> The Prime Minister and Cabinet would not restore section 34 even with a
> delay in coming into force; they would ask government lawyers to
> "study" the idea (which they themselves had earlier proposed to the
> Coalition) of applying section 34 to federal jurisdiction; they would
> make no attempt to persuade the provincial premiers to change their
> positions; they urged the natives to press the provincial premiers to
> change their positions; and they lamented the divisions in the native
> movement between the NIB and the Coalition   [65]

In the House of Commons on November 20, Mr. Chrétien offered to
entrench section 34 at the federal level if the NIB, NCC and ICNI indicated
their support for such an action by November 24. He repeated that section
34 could not be fully restored without the consent of the nine provinces that
had signed the Accord on November 5.

Lobbying in Ottawa was going nowhere. The Aboriginal Rights
Coalition and the NIB began to plan public protests. On November 16, the
anniversary of the execution of Louis Riel, Aboriginal Rights Coalition
supporters demonstrated in Ottawa, laying a wreath at the conference
centre where the Accord had been signed. The NIB declared November 19 as
National Indian Solidarity Day, and spent two days preparing a statement
of constitutional principles, which they presented to the Governor-
General.[66] November 19 saw Indian demonstrations in nine cities across
Canada. In Vancouver, Indians occupied the Museum of Anthropology.
Five thousand Indians demonstrated in front of the Alberta Legislature in
Edmonton. Premier Lougheed addressed the crowd, saying the province
supported existing Indian rights, which in his view were adequately

protected without section 34. If the aboriginal groups were seeking more rights, then the government wanted to know what additional rights were being sought.[67] On November 19, Premier Lévesque, referring to the deletion of section 34, called English Canada "hypocritically, fundamentally racist. . . ."[68]

The premiers gradually swung around. On November 17, Sterling Lyon was defeated in the Manitoba election and the new premier, Howard Pawley, announced his support for the restoration of section 34. On November 19, Premier Blakeney of Saskatchewan, in political trouble for his alleged opposition to a sexual equality section, offered to support that clause if other premiers agreed to restore section 34. That day, Premier Davis of Ontario stated his support for section 34. The next day, at the same time as Indians were addressing the provincial Social Credit convention, Premier Bennett announced British Columbia's support for the section. And the same day, Alberta Premier Lougheed, after negotiations with the province's Métis organizations, announced support for a modified section 34, limited to "existing" rights.[69]

The nine provinces agreed to the new wording. Mr. Chrétien stated in the House of Commons that his legal advisors had assured him that the addition of the word "existing" did not alter the meaning of the section. What had been implicit was now explicit.[70] Ten governments had agreed, and the matter was settled. In one sense, the massive pressure had worked. But remarkably, the new wording had the agreement of only one aboriginal organization: the Métis Association of Alberta. The Inuit, who had supported the government from January 30 to November 5, opposed the new wording. The three national aboriginal organizations were now fully united against the whole constitutional package.

The Final Drama in London

The very day Mr. Chrétien announced the new wording for section 34 (now re-numbered as section 35), the Indian Association of Alberta filed its action in the English courts. The association argued that the treaties had been signed with the Crown and therefore responsibility for them remained with the Crown in the United Kingdom. The suit directly challenged the testimony of Mr. Freeland to the Foreign Affairs Committee the previous November, which had been adopted as the position of the government of the United Kingdom. Freeland had taken an orthodox British constitutional position on the evolution of legal arrangements, which held that Canadian independence had evolved through custom and practice. At some point the authority over Indian affairs had shifted to Canada. It was not necessary to find a date or a document, so long as one could argue that the process of transfer was over.

Nevertheless, the Alberta association's claim had two strengths. It did not require arguments about Indian sovereignty or international law, both of which would have been difficult. Rather, it accepted that the treaties were "domestic," not international in character. The argument therefore only required asserting that the treaties were significant legal documents within Canadian federalism, an argument easily accepted in Britain. Second, there was a very straightforward argument that there had been imperial responsibility for Indian affairs, but never any explicit transfer of that responsibility to Canada.

Both the Saskatchewan and British Columbia groups were preparing legal arguments which asserted that Indian consent was necessary for patriation. Saskatchewan Indians were highly critical of the Alberta association for discarding any argument that the treaties were treaties in the international sense.[71] They based their arguments firmly on the status of the treaties. The British Columbia group, on the other hand, argued that the tribes were part of the constitutional order within Canada, and their consent, along with that of the provinces and the federal government, was necessary by the terms of the Statute of Westminster of 1931.

Underlying these legal arguments was a fundamental distrust of the Canadian government. Indians argued that while Canada was talking of entrenching aboriginal and treaty rights, it had an Indian Government Bill in the wings to undercut Indian self-government, and had introduced legislation hostile to Indian land claims in the northern territories. The larger threat was the terminationist policy espoused by the federal government in 1969, which was often alleged to be its hidden agenda. Canada, the argument went, did not have a free hand to terminate Indian rights so long as the treaty link to the United Kingdom existed and so long as the constitution contained its one provision on Indians, section 91(24) of the BNA Act. Patriation would both sever the treaty link and enable Canada to repeal that section.

The Alberta association's case was thrown out by a judge of the British Court of Queen's Bench on December 9. But on December 21, Lord Denning, the maverick chief justice of the Court of Appeal, granted leave to appeal. Denning, an elite populist Tory, a defender of the "little man," had taken jurisdiction on the plea of the red Indians of Canada. Denning was such an unusual figure that normal predictions of success meant little. The first reading of the Canada Bill took place in the British House of Commons on December 22, but the Thatcher government announced that second reading would be delayed until the Alberta association's appeal was completed. The appeal was argued on January 14 and 15, and judgement was given on January 28.

The decision was a disappointment to the Indians. Lord Denning upheld the treaties, but as Canada's responsibility. The Freeland argument accepted that the treaties were with the Crown in Right of the United Kingdom, but asserted that the U.K. had transferred its responsibilities to Canada. This was problematic in terms of the law of treaties. How could one party to a treaty shift its obligations to another state without the consent of the other party to the treaty? To avoid this problem, Lord Denning in the Court of Appeal ruled that what had been a unified Crown had divided into the Crown in Right of the United Kingdom and the Crown in Right of Canada. There had been no transfer. That part of the Crown with which the Indians had dealt had split off and continued to be the treaty partner of the Indians. Clearly, this was a mythical concept cloaking a non-explicit transfer of power. Lord Denning went on to note the Indian distrust of the Canadian government, but argued it was unjustified.

> There is nothing, so far as I can see, to warrant any distrust by the Indians of the Government of Canada. But, in case there should be, the discussion in this case will strengthen their hand so as to enable them to withstand any onslaught. They will be able to say that their rights and freedoms have been guaranteed to them by the Crown—originally by the Crown in respect of the United Kingdom—now by the Crown in respect of Canada—but, in any case by the Crown. No Parliament should do anything to lessen the worth of these guarantees. They should be honoured by the Crown in respect of Canada "so long as the sun rises and the river flows." That promise must never be broken.[72]

Judicial defeat left the British Parliament as the last forum. Sol Sanderson, President of the Federation of Saskatchewan Indians, proposed a legislative strategy to the other Indian organizations. His organization had drafted an "Indian Rights Amendment Bill" based on the treaty and aboriginal rights principles which had been agreed to by the National Indian Brotherhood–Assembly of First Nations (NIB-AFN) the previous November.

> The Amendment Bill [if] passed by the British parliament would make patriation of the Canada Act conditional upon recognition by Canada of Indian rights set out in the schedule. In other words, the British Parliament could pass the Amendment Bill in Britain and say to Canada, You can have your Canada Act if you recognize Indian rights and our Secretary of State is satisfied that you meet the conditions set out in the Indian Amendment Bill.[73]

The joint council of the NIB-AFN supported Saskatchewan's strategy in mid-February and approved lobbying both in Ottawa and London.[74] But time was running out. On February 17, debate began in the British House of Commons on the Canada Bill. The Parliamentary debate was a kind of victory for the Indian lobby:

> In the House of Commons, a total of thirty hours were devoted to debate on the Canada Bill over several days, and of these twenty-seven hours were on Indian matters. Approximately 90 percent of the time was exclusively spent on Indians. In the House of Lords, over 80 percent of the debate was concerned with our rights.[75]

But in the end, the bill was passed. The Queen came to Canada and gave Royal assent to the legislation on April 17, and later in the same month the British courts struck out the remaining Indian court cases.

The NIB declared April 17 a day of mourning. Robert Manuel said that any Indian participating in the celebration would be committing a "treasonous act against the Indian nations and their citizens."[76] The Queen, in her speech, referred to the Indian issue. She was pleased that "the rights of the aboriginal people are recognized with full opportunity for further definition."[77] Trudeau stated that the constitution "offers a way to meet the legitimate demands of our Native peoples. . . . The two orders of government have made a solemn pledge to define more precisely the rights of Native peoples."[78]

Patriation was over. In June, Prime Minister Trudeau met separately with the leadership of the three national organizations as part of the preparations for the 1983 First Ministers' Conference that would consider aboriginal questions.

Conclusions

From 1978 to 1982, the political initiatives on aboriginal questions came from the aboriginal organizations. There was important support from the various constitutional studies and from maverick MPs at Westminster. In Canada all governments, at least nominally, accepted the legitimacy of aboriginal provisions and aboriginal participation. But it was not obvious that this would produce anything more than pleasant words in a new preamble. In the real world of federal-provincial bargaining, surely the aboriginal organizations could not be real players.

The NIB took an aggressive line, interrupted only by the short-lived agreement of January 30, 1981. The aggressiveness of the stance seemed a cover for internal divisions and a lack of Indian politicization. If so, a process of political negotiation was never a real possibility, since a truly accommodative response from governments would have exposed the political weaknesses of the organizations. But almost predictably, the governments broke their promises of aboriginal involvement. The process became not reasoned negotiation, but public bargaining over symbolic provisions. In that process the aboriginal organizations *could* be real players. In the end, they achieved increased recognition in the new constitution without delivering any political agreement. It was surprisingly like the granting of the federal vote in 1960. Indians could later assert that any political implications of having the franchise had not been agreed to by the tribes. In the same way, no Indian political questions have been settled with the new constitution.

The Indian strategy, in retrospect, had serious problems. It was expensive. One estimate put the total cost of the London lobby at $4.5 million.[79] More importantly, the lobbying and litigation in the end could not succeed. The continuation of the strategy beyond January 1981 endangered the gain achieved with the original section 34 and resulted in a weakened section being restored. It severely antagonized the federal government, the only Canadian government likely to support Indian issues against other Canadian governments. It did not win allies among the provincial governments, which, while sometimes supportive, officially kept their distance. The strategy could have risked non-governmental support in Canada by its opposition to patriation.

Some blamed the Indians' strategy on their lawyers. Reeves Hagan, the federal government's representative in London on the constitution, was reported to have made this argument:

> While acknowledging that the Indian rights problem "can only be a source of regret and shame," he suggested that Indians lobbying in London "have been advised by very sharp lawyers and PR people who should probably be strung up by the heels."
>
> In Vancouver, Bob Manuel, president of the Union of B.C. Chiefs, countered with the observation that the Canadian government is getting some bad advice from shoddy bureaucrats.[80]

As well, two prominent Canadian constitutional authorities blamed the lawyers.[81] This analysis had the advantage of avoiding criticism of the Indians, but it was misguided. The Indian groups had obtained opinions from leading British academics and had hired leading counsel. From the information available to the writer, the lawyers consistently advised their Indian clients that it was unlikely or highly unlikely that they could win in the British courts. The Federation of Saskatchewan Indians estimated they had a 10 percent chance of victory.[82] Other estimates were somewhat higher, others lower.[83] While lawyers may have given conflicting signals, and Indians may have had undue faith in British justice, the basic reality is that the litigation in England was pursued as a political, not a legal, strategy.

What was the political strategy? In the controversy which has swirled around this issue, it is possible to discern a pro-aboriginal thesis and a pro-government thesis.

The pro-aboriginal view asserts that the aboriginal groups had a coherent and explicit set of demands. They were formulated in the briefs presented to the Special Joint Committee in December 1980, repeated in the treaty and aboriginal rights principles in November 1981, and re-worked again in the Indian Rights Amendment Bill in January 1982. The reality was not that the government was confused about what the aboriginal groups wanted, but that they were never really prepared to consider provisions on aboriginal self-government or a consent clause. This left the aboriginal groups with a simple choice between continued struggle and capitulation. Del Riley made an error by agreeing to the January 30 compromise, but it was soon reversed.

The pro-aboriginal view argues that it was the federal and provincial politicians who were disorganized and inconsistent over time. The politicians wanted to have it both ways. They wanted the political credit for involving aboriginal representatives, but they could never organize the reform process in a way that allowed them to live up to their promises. They promised participation, then denied it. They pledged that section 34 was non-negotiable, then negotiated it away. They responded not to principle, but to the federal political crisis of January 1981 and to massive Indian demonstrations in November 1981. In contrast, the aboriginal groups were much more consistent and principled in their approach to the reform process.

The pro-government analysis, on the other hand, asserts that the aboriginal leaders could not negotiate because their constituencies were not sufficiently politicized to enable a unified position to be developed or political agreement to be delivered. The unwillingness or inability of the groups to negotiate and accept compromise was a sign of political immaturity, not of principle. Why was consent delivered on January 30 and then withdrawn? That turnabout proved that Del Riley was an ineffectual leader. He could not deliver his constituency and did not realize that he could not deliver it. No coherent grouping would elect such a weak leader. How was the federal government to understand the ensuing campaign which focussed on a demand for a consent clause? Would a consent clause satisfy the groups, or would their demands simply escalate to recognition of aboriginal self-government? Some Indians were on record as saying that the Canadian constitution should not even mention them. They were parallel governments under the Crown, no more a part of Canada than Australia.

By the pro-government analysis, Indian activity was not simply disunited, it was chaotic. Del Riley was a startlingly weak leader. The London lobby was unco-ordinated. The provincial Indian leaders were all over the map. Sol Sanderson of Saskatchewan was smooth and deliberate. Eugene Steinhauer of Alberta played the radical and always avoided negotiations. Wayne Christian, the main organizer of the constitution express, called Trudeau a liar in a confrontation with the prime minister before television cameras, an act that did not encourage reasoned negotiations. On top of these divisions, the NIB would not co-operate with the NCC, and the Inuit were playing a different political game.

Both the pro-aboriginal and the pro-government views miss the mark. The aboriginal groups were seeking recognition as political actors within Canadian federalism. Their nationalist political positions had been developing since at least 1975. While governments had moved to some extent on questions of aboriginal and treaty rights, there had been little acceptance of the aboriginal re-definition of the character of the issues in Canadian aboriginal policy. Both the demands for a recognition of aboriginal self-government and for a consent clause were political demands that would have made aboriginal groupings actors equal to governments. The federal government's response to the politics of the situation was to offer a concession on the less controversial questions of aboriginal and treaty rights. That concession was not perceived as painless; it was delayed at length and only offered when the federal government felt it was in serious political trouble. But the government had already defined aboriginal and treaty claims in non-political terms. The Canadian legal system had delivered only limited recognition to these claims, and it was doubtful that section 34 would seriously alter the character of that recognition. Aboriginal title claims were uncertain with or without section 34.

The political goal was not to get and protect section 34. The goal was to achieve power by being political actors in the constitutional game. By this analysis, Del Riley was wrong in agreeing to section 34, though not because it was a compromise and not because he did not have the authority to bind the member organizations of the NIB. He was wrong because agreement ended the political role of the Indians in the constitutional game. By playing the game through to the end, the Indians were unmistakably political actors in the drama. They were the final domestic issue, along with women, in the November controversies. They were the final issue in England. Indian litigation there delayed patriation by two months, and the Indian issue occupied most of the time in the British parliamentary debates.

The Canadian government could dismiss the Indian lobby as incoherent. Prime Minister Trudeau said in exasperation "I honestly don't know what the Indians want. I just don't know."[84] But Bruce George, the romantic, knew:

> I believe that their campaign . . . will be seen by future generations as an important stage in their political development, and in the inevitability of the Indian nations of Canada playing an infinitely greater role in the governing of their affairs.[85]

Notes

1. Canada, Department of Indian Affairs, Indian Affairs Branch, *A Survey of the Contemporary Indians of Canada* (Queen's Printer, 1966–70), gives some background on Canadian Indian policy. S. Weaver, *Making Canadian Indian Policy* (Toronto: University of Toronto Press, 1981) is a valuable account of the development of the government White Paper of June 1969.
2. The policy was announced on August 8, 1973, and has been recently re-stated in two booklets: See Canada, Department of Indian Affairs and Northern Development, *In All Fairness; A Native Claims Policy*, (Ottawa: Supply and Services Canada, 1981), and *Outstanding Business; A Native Claims Policy* (Ottawa: Supply and Services Canada, 1982).

3. The Dene Declaration is reprinted in M. Watkins, *Dene Nation: The Colony Within* (Toronto: University of Toronto Press, 1977), p. 3.

4. The re-organization took place between April 1980 and the spring of 1982. In December 1980, an interim committee of the Assembly of First Nations (AFN) was formed. This committee met jointly with the executive council of the National Indian Brotherhood (NIB) to form the joint council. See also note 57.

5. Terms of Reference, Special Government Representative for Constitutional Development in the Northwest Territories, July 19, 1977, P.C. 1977-2227.

6. The issue was discussed at a conference of federal and provincial officials in 1963 and at a conference of ministers in 1964. See D. Sanders, *Family Law and Native People*, (Law Reform Commission of Canada, 1975), pp. 99-102. The Hawthorn report of 1966 and 1967 considered these problems and contained two chapters on constitutional and legal issues (*A Survey of the Contemporary Indians of Canada, op. cit.*). The 1969 federal White Paper aborted any continuing discussion of the issues of provision of services by proposing a termination of federal responsibility.

7. These issues entered the constitutional discussions of 1978-1982 in two ways. The federal government was conscious that the judicial decisions and the *Indian Act* meant that provincial hunting laws were limited by Indian treaty rights while federal hunting and fishing laws were not. The federal government was conscious that the provinces could fairly argue that the burden of these rights should be equally respected or equally ignored. Second, there was the real possibility of a transfer of jurisdiction over fisheries from the federal to the provincial level.

8. Noel Starblanket, Testimony to the Special Joint Committee of the Senate and House of Commons on Bill C-60, August 23, 1978, p. 4.

9. Starblanket to Trudeau, September 27, 1978.

10. Canada, Privy Council, Canadian Unity Information Office, *A Time for Action: Toward the Renewal of the Canadian Federation* (Ottawa: Canadian Unity Information Office, 1978), p. 8.

11. Constitutional Committee of the Quebec Liberal Party, *A New Canadian Federation* (Montreal: 1980), p. 84.

12. Starblanket, The National Indian Brotherhood presentation to the Task Force on Canadian Unity, March 2, 1978, p. 3.

13. *Kainai News*, Standoff, Alberta, November, No. 1, 1978, p. 3.

14. Office of the Prime Minister, Release, February 12, 1979, attachment Explanatory Notes Regarding the Eleven Items on the 'Second List', p. 6.

15. *Native People*, Edmonton, July 9, 1976, p. 1.

16. The only account of the trip is D. Sanders, "Indians, the Queen and the Canadian Constitution," *Survival International Review*, (Summer 1980), p. 6.

17. Bruce George became a controversial figure among Indians. He recommended to the Indians that they argue in terms of human rights and avoid talk of sovereignty. Duke Redbird of the Ontario Métis and Non-Status Indian Association accused him of paternalism, saying he wanted to be known as "Bruce of the Breeds." Other British MPs were involved. Sir Bernard Braine, known as a supporter of non-mainstream causes, was active with the Alberta lobby. Apparently he regarded Trudeau "as a communist who must be stopped" (Dion, "Report on Constitutional Lobby in London, England,"

August 5, 1981). He was described as the toughest critic on the Conservative side (*Vancouver Sun*, February 24, 1982), p. A14. MP Mark Wolfson had spent two years teaching at a Nishga school in British Columbia. MP David Ennals, a former Labour Cabinet minister, had supported the Indian cause from 1979. See "The Canada Bill in Westminster," *Saskatchewan Indian*, April, 1982, p. 16.

18. Meeting between Prime Minister Clark and Cabinet ministers and the National Indian Brotherhood Executive Council, September 28, 1979, Langevin Block, Ottawa (minutes probably prepared by the NIB), p. 5.

19. Starblanket to Clark, October 2, 1979.

20. Meeting of the Steering Committee of the Continuing Committee of Ministers on the Constitution with the representatives of the national aboriginal organizations, December 3, 1978 (Canadian Intergovernmental Conference Secretariat, Document 830-77/014) p. 15.

21. Provincial officials meeting, Winnipeg, July 31, 1979, minutes, p. 2.

22. Preliminary meeting of officials at the NCC offices, November 15, 1979, minutes taken by NIB.

23. Leeson to Nick Gwyn, December 13, 1979.

24. Continuing Committee of Ministers on the Constitution, *loc. cit.* (note 21), p. 6.

25. Background and Discussion paper, "Natives and the Constitution," written sometime after June 19, 1980, informally released.

26. Continuing Committee of Ministers on the Constitution, *loc. cit.* (note 20, pp. 54 and 89.

27. *Ibid.*, p. 56. The text of Starblanket's prepared speech was more positive than his comments at the meeting. The speech indicated hopefulness for mutual openness and trust and accepted involvement at all levels, and contained the positive statement: "Indians now have an opportunity to become partners within Confederation."

28. This theme of aboriginal participation in the reform process was repeated in a resolution passed by the National Liberal Convention in Winnipeg, July 4, 1980. It appeared as well in a background paper prepared by the Constitutional and International Law Section of the Canadian Bar Association for the bar convention in August 1980.

29. The idea of a national gathering of chiefs had been mooted within the NIB for a number of years. The meetings in London in 1979 had been described as an all-chiefs meeting, and a resolution had been passed there for the convening of another such meeting in Canada. That resolution had been approved by the general assembly of the NIB in September 1979.

30. Office of the Prime Minister, Release, Notes for Remarks by the Prime Minister at a National Conference of Indian Chiefs and Elders, Ottawa, April 29, 1980.

31. The NIB never established their commission of inquiry. In July 1980, the NCC established the Métis and Non-Status Indian Constitutional Review Commission. The President of NCC, Harry Daniels, acted as the commissioner, with other leaders acting as deputy commissioners for particular hearings. A report was published in April 1981, *Native People and the Constitution of Canada* (Ottawa: Mutual Press, 1981).

32. Background and Discussion paper: Natives and the Constitution, written sometime after June 19, 1980, informally released.

33. The sub-committee of the CCMC prepared a report on the August 26 meeting which the CCMC conveyed to the first ministers' meeting in September. The report recommended that the item "Canada's Native Peoples and the Constitution" be on the agenda in the future round of first ministers' meetings on the constitution, that native leaders meet directly with first ministers at that time, and that all parties accept the possibility that constitutional amendments in favour of native peoples could result from those discussions. See "Briefing Material on Canada's Native Peoples and the Constitution," approximately November 1980, informally released, p. 5 of the introduction.
34. *Kainai News*, Standoff, Alberta, September No. 2, 1980, p. 2.
35. "Legal Action," statement of the Union of British Columbia Indian Chiefs, no date, approximately September 25, 1980, 3 pages.
36. *Vancouver Sun*, October 15, 1980, p. B6.
37. Union of British Columbia Indian Chiefs, "Indian Nations: Self-Determination or Termination," October 1980, revised November 15, 1980, pp. 7-8.
38. *Vancouver Sun*, October 22, 1980, p. B6; October 30, 1980, p. B6.
39. Trudeau to Riley, October 30, 1980.
40. This is stated in "Briefing Materials on Canada's Native Peoples and the Constitution," approximately November, 1980 (informally released) p. 4 of the introduction.
41. Quoted in "Canada's Native Peoples and the Constitution, Background Material," (Federal-Provincial Relations Office, Government of Canada, November 1980) p. 3a; see also *Vancouver Sun*, October 31, 1980, p. A8.
42. Minutes of evidence taken before the Foreign Affairs Committee, Wednesday, November 12, 1980, p. 39.
43. Canadian constitutional expert Edward McWhinney later testified before the informal all-party committee of the House of Commons in London, rebutting Freeland's testimony. This seems to have been important in sustaining the Indian legal arguments in London. The Foreign Affairs Committee issued a second report in January 1982, arguing that with the agreement of nine provinces, it was proper for the British Parliament to pass the Canada Bill. The report referred to the first ministers' conference on aboriginal issues, promised in the Canada Bill, as the "proper forum" for the discussion of the concerns of the aboriginal people of Canada (*Vancouver Sun*, January 18, 1982, p. A1).
44. "Report to NIB Executive and First Nations All Chiefs Council re Canadian Constitution and legal action," Union of British Columbia Indian Chiefs, January 9, 1981, p. 4.
45. One account says that NDP leader Ed Broadbent informed Trudeau in December 1980 that he could not deliver one section of his caucus without a provision on aboriginal rights: James Lamb, "The dessert was native rights," *Vancouver Sun*, December 1, 1981, p. A4; see also Michael Valpy, "Mr. Broadbent has a problem," *Vancouver Sun*, January 26, 1981, p. A4.
46. The NIB brief to the Special Joint Committee on December 16, 1980, said "Section 32 formally institutionalizes the First Ministers' conferences and requires certain meetings to be held. A requirement of Indian participation, at least on matters affecting Indian people, should be included in any such provision."
47. *Ottawa Citizen*, January 31, 1981, p. 1.

48. *Ontario Indian,* March 1981, p. 16.
49. *Vancouver Sun,* February 6, 1981, p. A1.
50. "Canada—the facts," Canadian High Commission, London, no date.
51. *Kainai News,* Standoff, Alberta, February No. 1, 1981, p. 1; *Native People,* Edmonton, February 13, 1981, p. 1.
52. *Native People,* Edmonton, March 20, 1981, p. 1.
53. *First Citizen,* Winnipeg, May 1981, p. 1.
54. Del Riley came to deny that he had ever supported the January 30 package. Harry Daniels of the NCC came to describe the January support as conditional on a satisfactory resolution of the consent clause issue. On April 20, he announced the NCC's opposition to the package as it then stood ("Native Council of Canada withdraws support for constitution," *The Forgotten People* (Spring, 1981), p. 10; *The Native People,* April 24, 1981, p. 7).
55. *Coyote Prints* (newspaper, Williams Lake, B.C.) April/May 1981, p. 3.
56. The Four Nations Confederacy of Manitoba was represented in the Manitoba Court of Appeal and in the Supreme Court of Canada. No distinctively Indian legal arguments were presented.
57. From April 1980 to the spring of 1982 the National Indian Brotherhood went through a re-organization as the Assembly of First Nations. From December 1980 there was an interim committee for the AFN, which met jointly with the executive council of the NIB to form the joint council referred to in the text. This unusual transitional structure does not seem to have been a significant factor in the performance of the NIB leadership.
58. *Native People,* August 28, 1981, p. 1.
59. *Native People,* February 12, 1981, p. 1. See also November 13, 1981, p. 6.
60. *Vancouver Sun,* November 6, 1981, p. A15.
61. Stated on the CBC radio program "As it happens," Friday, November 6, 1981.
62. Anderson, "Cement for a nation," *Macleans,* November 16, 1981, p. 32.
63. Richard Gwyn, "The Premier's shame," *Vancouver Sun,* November 13, 1981, p. A6. Gwyn named the four western provinces, Newfoundland and New Brunswick. Gwyn's analysis is partly confirmed by Chrétien in the House of Commons *Debates,* November 9, 1981, p. 12,636.
64. Warren Allmand, former minister of Indian affairs, was a constant ally of the Indians.
65. P. Jull, "Canada: A Perspective on the Aboriginal Rights Coalition and the Restoration of Constitutional Aboriginal Rights," *International Work Group for Indigenous Affairs (IWGIA) Newsletter,* Copenhagen (April 1982), p. 89.
66. This document, "Treaty and Aboriginal Rights Principles," is reprinted in *The Saskatchewan Indian,* December 4, 1981, p. 5.
67. Excerpts from premier's address, *Native People,* November 27, 1981, p. 2.
68. *Vancouver Sun,* November 20, 1981, p. A14.
69. Meetings took place on November 16 and 19, 1981, and involved the premier, other provincial officials, leaders from the Métis Association of Alberta, Clem Chartier, legal advisor to the NCC, and Rod Hope, legal advisor to the Métis Association of Alberta.
70. There was a major controversy over whether the change in wording mattered. See *Financial Post,* December 5, 1981, p. 8.
71. *Saskatchewan Indian,* January 1982, p. 2.

72. R. v. Secretary of State for Foreign and Commonwealth Affairs; Ex parte Indian Association of Alberta, [1982] 2 All E.R. 118 (C.A.).
73. Saskatchewan Indian, January 1982, p. 28.
74. Saskatchewan Indian, February-March 1982, p. 2.
75. Opekokew, The First Nations, Federation of Saskatchewan Indians, 1982, p. 28.
76. Vancouver Sun, April 15, 1982, p. B8.
77. Native People, April 16, 1982, p. 1.
78. Native People, April 16, 1982, p. 3.
79. Keith Spicer, "Sarejevo-on-the Rideau?" Vancouver Sun, May 27, 1982, p. A5. The Canadian government has funded Indian, Métis and Inuit political organizations since the early 1970s. It was often assumed that this government funding went into the London lobby, though that was denied by some Indian leaders (Vancouver Sun, February 3, 1982, p. A1). Substantial funding came from the natural resource revenues of the Blood and Samson Bands in Alberta. The Federation of Saskatchewan Indians had negotiated a provincial tax rebate on gasoline taxation and asked Bands to donate the interest on the rebate amounts to the constitutional struggle. The two constitution expresses organized by the Union of British Columbia Indian Chiefs were largely paid for by the individual participants. The union also organized an auction sale of artifacts to raise funds. At the end of the campaign, in the spring of 1982, both the NCC and the NIB were seriously in debt. The debt of the NIB was estimated at $500,000 or $600,000.
80. Vancouver Sun, February 25, 1982, p. A17.
81. Edward McWhinney, Canada and the Constitution, 1979-1982 (Toronto: University of Toronto Press, 1982), p. 129; Professor Dale Gibson, one of the counsel for the federal government, was quoted as saying that the Indians were badly advised if they proceeded with litigation in England. Edmonton Journal, February 9, 1982, p. B4.
82. Saskatchewan Indian, January 1982, p. 3.
83. Representatives of the Union of British Columbia Indian Chiefs and the Federation of Saskatchewan Indians were told that the chances were "certainly less than even," perhaps 30 to 40 percent. The solicitor speculated that a judge might say that the Indians had rights, while ruling that no English court had jurisdiction to deal with them. Such a ruling could have "some political effect." Interview with J. Rosenheim, July 24, 1981, in Dion, "Report on Constitutional Lobby in London," England, August 5, 1981.
84. Quoted by Premier Lougheed in his speech on November 18, 1981 to the Indian demonstration at the provincial Legislature, Native People, November 27, 1981, p. 2. The statement was also quoted in the Saskatchewan Indian, January 1982, p. 26.
85. Quoted in the Toronto Star, reprinted in Saskatchewan Indian, February-March 1982, p. 4.

Chapter 16/Confederation as a World Example

George Woodcock

> No man becomes a great patriot without first learning the
> closer loyalties and learning them well: loyalty to the family,
> to the place he calls home, to his province or state or county.
> —Roderick Haig-Brown.

> The Fatherland, for us, is the whole of Canada, that is to say, a
> federation of distinct races and autonomous provinces.
> —Henri Bourassa

> I would not object to a little revolution now and again in
> British Columbia, after Confederation, if we are treated
> unfairly; for I am one of those who believe that political
> hatreds attest the vitality of the State.
> —Amor de Cosmos

> I suppose the Half-breeds in Manitoba, in 1870, did not fight
> for two hundred and forty acres of land, but it is to be under-
> stood that there were two societies who treated together. One
> was small, but in its smallness it had its rights. The other was
> great, but in its greatness it had no greater rights than the
> rights of the small, because the right is the same for everyone,
> and when they began by treating the leaders of that small
> community as bandits, as outlaws, leaving them without
> protection, they disorganized that community.
> —Louis Riel

The texts with which I begin will suggest the approach from which I embark on this essay. My political affiliations begin in anarchism, and however much experience may have frayed my adherence to that doctrine in its purer and more extreme forms, it has tended to strengthen my attachment to what still seem to me the great gifts of the anarchists to our political thought—Proudhon's plea for the federal society as opposed to the nation-state, Kropotkin's teachings of mutual aid as the natural uniting factor in human societies, and the decentralization that all anarchists have posed in opposition to the centralism which the Marxists inherited from the Jacobins.

My family myths led me back to Canada, and when I returned I found a country where regional feelings, which are the basis of any true federalism, are strong and persistent, but I also discovered that this country of intensely localized loyalties was governed by a political system some of whose features tended towards an institutional centralism that seemed strangely inappropriate in a land with Canada's historic and geographic con-formation.

My personal inclinations led me towards the minority cultures of the West—the Métis, the Indians, the Doukhobors—about which I eventually wrote what I feel are some of my better books.[1] I learnt from writing these books two interesting facts—not easy to reconcile—about Canadian society. There have been periods when the majoritarian concept of democracy, with its centralizing and homogenizing tendencies, has been intolerantly ascendant in Canada; it was this concept that provoked the Métis rebellions, that made the Coast Indian potlatch a crime, that deprived the Doukhobors of their lands because they would not subscribe to an oath of allegiance. One can easily extend the record of such crimes against minorities by recalling, for example, the sad history of the *Komagatu Maru* in 1914, or the unforgiveable exiling of the West Coast Japanese—including large numbers of the Canadian-born—in 1942. Often, looking at these lamentable events from a viewpoint that judged democracies according to their ability to contain minorities without attempting to assimilate them, I despaired of the Canadian system—until I realized that there was a compensating factor at work within it. It arose from the fact that in opposition to all that was centralizing and all that was intolerantly majoritarian in our political system, the moving social forces in Canada have been regional and centrifugal, shaped by the vast historical and geographical divergencies within this immense land. And this has meant that no minority has been permanently submerged. They have all in the end come forward to take their places not only in history but in the present. In principle at least, the claims of the Indians and the Métis to their aboriginal inheritance, and the claims of Doukhobors and other groups like them to live undisturbed as peculiar peoples are beginning to gain recognition, even if not complete satisfaction. And this change, I suggest, is due at least partly to a largely inarticulate recognition by Canadians of the necessary pluralism in the society that various histories and a varied geography have combined to give them.

This recognition exists. It affects our political attitudes, and over the century and more of Canada's existence as a nation it has prevented the country from ever becoming a completely unitary state. But it has played a surprisingly slight part in the recent controversies over the constitution, which have tended to be fought out on a legalistic level in terms of the narrow interpretation of the British North America Act, or on an equally narrow political level of federal-provincial conflict over areas of legislative responsibility and financial gain. What seems lacking is the sense of a historic occasion, of the feeling that in shaping a constitution for themselves, the Canadians are not only making an assertion of their national identity as it has developed since 1867, but also making a statement regarding the nature of the good society that will be of interest and perhaps of value to the rest of the world.

Such a sense of mission, extending outside their own immediate circumstances, did exist among the Americans when they made their constitution in 1787. They were giving the weight of a whole people's support to the kind of statements about a society of guaranteed freedoms that only individual philosophers had made before. The same applied to the French after the revolution of 1789. They were not only bringing an end to old injustices and symbolizing their act with the destruction of the Bastille. They were establishing a new system of relations between man and man, and they not only hoped it would be an inspiration to other peoples; in their mistaken enthusiasm they tried to export it by the force of arms. Other constitutional exercises have had a similar messianic quality, a similar sense of formulating the best political system not only for a single country but also for the world of its time. That sense certainly existed in India when, after 1947, Nehru and the other heirs of Gandhi sat down to shape, out of British parliamentary traditions and the memory of ancient Indian village republics, a kind of democracy that would be appropriate to countries emerging out of colonial servitude. And whatever has happened to the United States and to France and to India since they first set out to create these new political forms, their examples inspired and changed the world of their time, and for that reason were among the great milestones of history.

In Canada, as yet, there is none of this sense that our constitution-making is or may be historic in a world sense, though, God knows, we live in a time that needs examples. We have brought home a makeshift document cobbled together by colonial politicians and Westminster political draftsmen in the 1860s with little sense of the way in which the Canada their statute created might develop. It is an obsolete piece of legislation, many parts of which—such as the provision for a Senate—have never worked as the Fathers of Confederation intended, and obviously in the next few years we shall have to change it to suit a different country from that over which Sir John A. Macdonald presided, and a different world from that on which he looked out from the young capital of Ottawa. Yet nothing seems to be in the minds of Canadian political leaders, no matter what their party, except tinkering with the Act in such a way that it will either strengthen the central government, which Mr. Trudeau and his associates would like, or consolidate and if possible increase the powers of the provinces, which the premiers would like. The one mildly but genuinely fresh approach—the Task Force of Canadian Unity's report, *A Future Together*, published in January 1979—was so unattractive in its confederalist tone to the leaders of the Liberal government that it was quickly shuffled into oblivion. The desire for a new approach that transcends the present poorly-working duality of Canadian politics is certainly present among the people of this country, but no vision has yet emerged to carry the debate into a context other than the narrowly Canadian.

I suggest that this lack of inspiration among the leaders and of a demanding enthusiasm among the people is due more than anything else to the absence of a true insurrectionary tradition in Canada, to the fact that

Canadians have never been collectively and directly involved in the processes that brought their country into independence. The people-armed acted decisively in the American and French revolutions; the people-unarmed, participating non-violently in Gandhi's great campaigns of *satyagraha*, hastened the end of the British Raj in India. The constitutions that emerged out of these struggles were formulations of the ideals that had inspired the insurrectionary peoples, and the peoples in their state of acute politicization demanded them. So, for their time, they were revolutionary documents, and the beliefs and forms they represented were, like all revolutionary manifestations, regarded as transportable, as indeed the ideals of the American revolution were immediately transported to France.

In Canada, the people as a whole was at no time involved, as an insurrectionary movement of any kind, in the series of changes that transformed the country from a group of colonial dependencies into a self-governing dominion and finally into an independent nation. The few rebellions that did take place—the risings of 1837 and 1838 and the Métis outbreaks of 1870 and 1885—occurred out of the main stream of Canadian developments and involved tiny dissident minorities. Responsible government came into being, no matter how much popular support there may have been for it, through the fiat of imperial governors in Nova Scotia and Canada, and Confederation was achieved—in the face of considerable popular opposition in the Maritimes—by champagne-quaffing politicians gathered in Charlottetown and Quebec who never thought of putting the question to a vote of the people. Where a genuine popular movement for Confederation did appear, like that led by Amor de Cosmos and John Robson in British Columbia, it was sidestepped by Macdonald, who preferred to intrigue with the colonial officials.

And indeed, perhaps what now alarms political leaders of all Canadian parties is the idea of the voice of the people mingling in the debate over the constitution. None of them is genuinely enthusiastic over the idea of submitting constitutional proposals to a popular referendum, though such recourses to the public are part of the constitution-making and constitution-amending mechanisms in many countries. And though the proposal for a popularly elected constitutional convention has been made, the idea has aroused no enthusiasm among politicians of any party. Up to the present, the whole procedure of changing the way our country is governed has been treated as a matter to be decided like any other political business— by parliamentary representatives acting under their party disciplines—and no real attempt has been made to arouse the participation of the Canadian people as distinct from their acceptance of measures proposed, debated and ratified by the professional politicians. The feeling that the making of a constitution is an historic event, entirely transcending the everyday business of politics, which certainly existed among Americans between 1776 and 1787 and among the French shortly afterwards, has not been communicated to Canadians. This, I suggest, results from the

negative and passive aspect of our political life, and is one of the consequences of our lack of any popular revolutionary tradition.

But there is another aspect of Canadian political life that runs counter
to our inclination to accept the dictates of a national establishment and that
is linked closely to the strength of regional trends within the country. This
is the side of ourselves that elects different parties to provincial than to
federal office, that can bring about the dramatic reduction of the party of
government's strength in large areas of the country, as happened to the
Liberals in the West, and can raise powerful locally-oriented movements at
variance with national trends—Social Credit and the Progressive Party in
the West, the Parti Québécois in Quebec, the Co-operative Commonwealth
Federation in its early idealistic days. Such movements are not revolutionary, but they are movements of populist rebellion and rejection, and they
represent a longing among millions of Canadians for a changed political
system that would be more responsive to their immediate needs and local
attitudes. In the comparatively near future, if they are not channeled in
more positive directions, such trends may become in their own way even
more nationally divisive than Pierre Trudeau's search for an artificial unity
based on the authoritarian re-structuring of institutions. Separatism is
entrenched in Quebec and likely to remain so; Newfoundland, which
entered Canada by a marginal vote in 1949, is restive; the separatist
movements of the West may well be near the kind of takeoff point that
boosted Social Credit during a few years of the 1950s from 1.5% to 45% of the
British Columbia vote.

All these situations are threats to Canadian unity, as are the provoca-
tive stances of the federal government and the narrowly-focussed ambitions
of the provincial premiers. But with an imaginatively new approach to
Canada's political future, I believe that the dissident regional forces could
be harnessed into creating a new political form for Canada that would not
only suit the geographically dispersed and historically varied nature of our
land, but would also provide an inspiration in a world where the nation-
state as we have known it for two centuries is passing, not without a
struggle, into obsolescence, and a new, confederal model needs to be created.

The unitary nation-state was the product of a past revolutionary phase
in European politics. It arose out of the alliance between the kings and the
rising middle class against the power of the feudal lords. It resulted in
authoritarian regimes like that of Louis XIV under which political
boundaries were extended and consolidated, administration centralized,
local power centres destroyed. It set the stage for the French revolution,
which completed the formation of the modern nation-state by exchang-
ing national for dynastic loyalties and by introducing conscription, which
imposed on every citizen the duty to defend the Republic One and Indivis-
ible. Such a republic was obviously different from the product of an earlier
revolution that called itself the United States, and in departing from American confederalism in favour of the Bourbon-Jacobin centralization of

which Pierre Trudeau is such a belated defender, the French also rejected an earlier European revolutionary model, that of the Swiss, whose Everlasting League of the three forest cantons of Uri, Schwyz and Nidwalden provided in 1291 a surprisingly early example of confederate republicanism.

The French model triumphed in Europe. Whatever their attitudes towards the French revolution itself, the new powers that emerged during the nineteenth century—Germany and Italy—adopted the nationalist ideology of the French, their administrative centralization, their subordination of the individual will through conscription to the will of the state and, of course, the aggressiveness that constantly hungered to increase the prestige and the territory of the fatherland. Older nations such as Britain, Spain and the Austrian empire turned themselves in varying degrees into nation-states, dangerous to their neighbours and oppressive to those cultural minorities that did not accept the nationalist ideals—the Irish in the United Kingdom, the Bretons in France, the Catalans and the Basques in Spain, the Sicilians and Sardinians in Italy. Only smaller countries without the hope of achieving military power, such as confederal Switzerland and the northern marginal lands of Scandinavia, remained untouched by the fever of national aggrandizement. Sweden's willing relinquishment of territorial power when it allowed the Norwegians to create their own nation in 1905 was an example none of the major European countries of that time would or could have imitated.

Implicit in the guiding philosophy and in the very structure of the nation-state was hatred and distrust of "the other," whether manifest as a rival nation, as a nonconformity, as a disobedient individual. Out of this hatred of "the other" sprang on the one side the series of progressively more destructive wars that devastated Europe between the Franco-Prussian war of 1870 and the Second World War of 1939–1945, and on the other side the elaborately organized mass tyrannies of Nazism and Fascism, which sought to eradicate not only minorities of race and culture and opinion, but also the individual as an entity distinct from the state.

An unwilling recognition of the external dangers of the nation-state led, at the end of the last great war, to the re-organization of West Germany into a confederal rather than a centralized state. And an equally reluctant recognition of the nation-state's internal dangers has forced European nations since 1945 to undergo a measure of decentralization, so that the minority peoples of Spain are being given a measure of self-government, Italy has notably localized administration, Britain has given a little more say in their own affairs to the Welsh and the Scots than they enjoyed before, and even France, for so long according to one's tastes either the model or the appalling example of bureaucratic centralization, has at last, under President Mitterand, begun the long and Herculean task of administrative devolution.

But all these are piecemeal efforts to mitigate the worst aspects of the nation-state, which still, sick as it is, show its dangerous potentialities. The recent wars between Iran and Iraq, two Moslem states, and Britain and Argentina, two countries presumably close in their anti-Communist ideologies, show how strong the old nation-state urges to grab and defend territory have remained, and how dangerous such countries remain to the world's peace.The example of Spain, where the army poses as the guardian of national values and threatens both the newly-won regional rights of Basques and Catalans and the democratic rights of the people as a whole, shows how the urge remains to subordinate nonconformist groups and individuals to the uniformity of nationalist aims.

The most typical and the most dangerous example of the surviving nation-state is Russia, precisely because it is the least successful. Russia is not dangerous as the disseminator of Communism; that goal went out of the Kremlin window with Trotsky. The real significance of Russia in the modern world comes from the fact that the nation-state of the Western-European kind had only begun to develop there within the late mediaeval autocracy of the Tsars, encouraged by the rising middle class and by elements in the army and the civil service, when the revolution occurred.

The development of the nation-state did not cease at that point. The Bolsheviks took it over or, rather, it took over the Bolsheviks. After the first heady years of the revolution, the anarchists, the Social Revolutionaries, the Mensheviks, the Tolstoyans, the experimental artists, all the internationalist and idealist elements, were weeded out. Then came the turn of the real Bolsheviks, beginning with Trotsky's exile, ending in the Moscow trials of the late 1930s with the public purging of the men who had made the revolution in the October days of 1917 and with the vast secret massacres of all kinds of dissidents. There remained, in the graveyard Stalin had created, a nation-state not unlike the rest, ruled by the principles of a National-Communism that was almost a mirror-image of Hitler's National-Socialism.

Russia in the 1980s is a grotesque and bloated caricature of the classic nation-state. Desperately fearful of "the other," whether external or internal, it persecutes cultural and religious minorities, it tries to eliminate ideological and artistic dissenters (whose activities it condemns as crimes against the state), it anxiously defends its boundaries and expands them (as in Afghanistan) where it can, while it endeavours, with a notable lack of success, to administer as a centralized state its vast territory, a veritable empire—and almost the world's last—of different peoples. Russia is dangerous, not only because it is a nation-state with some very destructive weapons, but because its rulers realize how precarious and inefficient it has become in that role and how much it needs the support of like states. So it makes allies, not among those with genuinely revolutionary politics, but among those who share its outdated nationalist inclinations—the rulers of Syria, Indira Gandhi and, more recently, the military adventurers who rule Argentina.

The nation-state survives because, in an unsure world, people are not sure where a viable alternative may be found. Clearly, it must be the kind of society that is no longer closed externally or internally, and here we return inevitably to the rejected model which Pierre-Joseph Proudhon proposed in his seminal 1863 book, *Du principe fédératif et de la nécessité de reconstituer le parti de la révolution.*[2] In this book, Proudhon elaborated the idea he had already adumbrated in earlier works[3] of a decentralized society that would not be crippled internally by interlocking power structures since it would be built upon local and functional groups agreeing in their spheres of interest, but would also not be aggressive externally because its inner ease of relations would erode the frontier state of mind and it would move outward with the same ease and freedom that characterized its internal operations.

Proudhon's ideas, which were shared not only by the anarchists, but also by such varied political mavericks as Herzen, Tolstoy and Gandhi, and by such pioneer environmentalists as Patrick Geddes and Lewis Mumford, were formulated in a vanished France of peasant farmers and of the urban artisans who advocated his views in the First International and initiated the great split that divided, and still divides, the libertarian followers of Bakunin and Kropotkin from the authoritarian followers of Marx and Engels. But for the past century the ideas have remained alive as a possible alternative to the way of big states and big corporations that the world has followed. Now, in the last perilous days of the nation-state, it looks as though they may come into their own, and I suggest that it is not frivolous to propose Canada as the country that might lead the world in embarking on a confederalist reform of political structures and political aims.

My reasons for this proposal are firstly, that in geographical and historical terms Canada is a country peculiarly difficult to organize as a unitary state and correspondingly well adapted to an experiment in true confederation, and secondly, that history has already led us in Canada a long way down the road to the kind of confederal constitution whose implementation might not only revive the nation, but also inspire the world.

Canadian unity has always seemed a strange and paradoxical thing, based on a dialectic of apparent opposites. Even in the time of New France, there were the problems of reconciling the varying interests of settlement and fur trading, of the *coureurs de bois* and the *habitants*, of the *pays d'en haut* with its free half-Indian way of life and the priest-ridden and puritanical towns along the St. Lawrence. After the conquest, the diversity only increased until it became the very nature of Canada: the British peoples came and settlement spread along the trade routes, and the creation of the Dominion brought in the other already established colonial societies of the Atlantic and Pacific shores, and the final settlement of the West plunged into the heart of the country a vast new element of people who were neither French nor British and added a whole new spectrum of cultural attitudes. But by the time the post-1945 emigration had brought in yet other elements—from Mediterranean Europe, from the Caribbean, from Asia—and Canada had finally shaken itself down, round about the 1967 centennial, into something like the society we know in 1982, it was still, despite all the changes, the country of which I once said:

> The unity, one might almost say, depends paradoxically on the diversity, and Canada, socially and politically as much as geographically, is the diverse country which the settlers created out of their differences of origin as well as of environment.[4]

Because of these diversities, the pressing realities of Canadian life tend to be local, except in times of exceptional crisis. Abroad it is easy for Canadians to proclaim their national identity, because that is what distinguishes them from the people they meet, but at home it often becomes more fitting to define oneself as a Newfoundlander or a Québécois or a British Columbian, not only because one's region is, as Al Purdy once put it, the "place to stand on," the world of immediate experience, but also because in a country where communities are divided by such distances and often by such varying interests, it is the immediate society one shares with one's neighbours that is of the first importance.

In fact, there have always been two processes at work in Canadian history: the regional and particular, and the uniting (rather than unitary) and general. A view of our history dominated by Creightonian myths would stress the uniting elements—the great sweep of the fur trade up the St. Lawrence into the hinterland and on to the Arctic and Pacific Oceans; the construction of a nation *A mari usque ad mare*; the laying of the great transcontinental railroads; the vast westward push of immigration. This is the Canada of the explorers, the traders, the surveyors, the trainmen, the entrepreneurs, the National Policy statesmen. But parallel with this there has always been regional Canada, the Canada of growth *in situ* rather than movement over vast spaces, and the significant fact is that the uniting movements have in fact tended to foster rather than to prevent the development of new regional enclaves. The fur trade unwittingly established the communities that became nuclei of western settlement; as well as keeping together the French of Québec and the English of Upper Canada, Confederation brought in, one after another, already-formed miniature societies— the Red River, British Columbia, the Maritime provinces, eventually Newfoundland—that have retained their special identity over a century of change; eastern European immigrants emptied into the great plains by the new railways not only planted there a whole garden of new cultural traditions, but also generated the radical populism of the West that has made it so unassimilable for national parties centred on Ontario and Quebec.

Everywhere one looks in Canada one sees the interweaving action of these two urges, equally favoured by history and geography: the challenge to reconcile the diversities of a vast land, and the recognition that only in the diversities can the true nature of the land be understood. Unity in diversity; the search for it poses the very condition that confederalism as a political philosophy is designed to meet. And this is why I suggest that in a world that needs a new confederal model of national organization, Canada might at the same time meet its own constitutional needs and offer an inspiration to other nations by embarking on an experiment in thorough-going confederalism. It could not possibly be more costly in financial terms than the present system. It could not be more disuniting than the shabby political manoeuvres that on many sides attended the recent patriation of the constitution. And the chances are that it might introduce more economical and reconciliatory forms of administration by summoning the latent stores of Canadian idealism that in recent years have been too little called upon.

To develop a model of confederation as it might be developed in Canada would take more time and require more space than I now have on hand. And the brief plea I now offer is designed as much to show how far our present constitution falls short of true confederalism as to suggest what a possible confederal system might offer.

In fact, the constitution that has recently been patriated is no more than the British North America Act of 1867 with a few appendages, and the BNA Act is an unhappy hybrid of federalism and centralization. What the Fathers of Confederation actually had in mind is still obscure since no records survive of the crucial discussions in Charlottetown and Quebec, but internal and external evidence suggests that it was regarded as a compact between potentially sovereign provinces. The preamble talks of the federation coming into being at the "Desire" of the petitioning colonies, and even Macdonald talked of a "treaty" between the provinces, so that the Dominion was in fact the creation of its provinces, which presupposes at least an equality of status between the two levels of government. However, the great powers given to Ottawa, and especially the grant of residuary powers, meant that in law, as founded in 1867, Canada was not a confederation any more than it was a conventional nation-state.

Yet almost immediately the forces of regional autonomy began to work, and what emerged, aided by the decisions of the Privy Council in England and by the provisions of the Statute of Westminster, which in 1931 recognized the sovereignty of the provinces in their own jurisdictions, was a system in which the autonomy of the provinces was in practice recognized to be greater and the authority of the central government more limited than the exact wording of the BNA Act specified. It came to be accepted, moreover, without ever being written into law, that the provinces must be consulted on constitutional changes, which is why in 1981 the judges of the

Supreme Court declared that Trudeau was correct in law but defiant of accepted convention in seeking to force on the provinces his own constitutional plans.

Clearly, whatever practice and precedent have made it over more than a century, in legal terms Canada has not evolved into a confederation. On the other hand, the development of strong regional feelings over the same period has made it virtually impossible for the present hybrid system to be converted into the kind of centralized state which the Liberal leaders seem to favour. Yet it remains a political system that perpetually frustrates the regions and especially the hinterlands in the pursuit of their legitimate local aims.

A confederal system as I propose it in the following sketch would be devised to spread power, relating it more closely to needs, and at the same time to spread responsibility, in the interests not merely of greater participation but also of greater efficiency, on the theory—to which the record of the existing federal government gives a great deal of support—that an excess of authority concentrated in the hands of a single group inevitably compounds the effects of administrative ineptitude.

In terms of the distribution of power, the present Canadian system is deficient at both ends. The excess of authority given to the central government in specified and unspecified ways has hampered regional development in many directions—through the centralized control of communications which has inhibited the adequate development of local broadcasting in any region except Quebec, to give but one example. At the same time, the provincial administrations as they now exist have tended to create their own internal centralization by ignoring or suppressing the interests of the municipalities or of special areas within the province. Provincial governments also become narrowly local in the sense that in clinging to their rights too closely they sometimes imperil regional initiatives that involve areas wider than provinces but smaller than the nation. The present polarization between a federal government constantly seeking to extend its authority within the "residual powers" area, and provincial governments constantly seeking to prevent it, not only introduces an unnecessary acrimony into national relations but also further diverts attention from regional and municipal needs.

In an ideal confederational constitution, powers would be related to needs, so that matters of merely local interest would be decided by the people immediately involved without interference from above, and so on up the scale of spreading areas of interest. This presupposes something like a four-tier rather than a two-tier system of government. Switzerland has a three-tier confederational constitution, of the communes or municipalities, the cantons or provinces, and the confederal government with its rotating presidency; it is the larger area of Canada which suggests the desirability of a fourth, or regional level.

In such a constitution, the powers of the central administration would be strictly limited to matters affecting the whole nation, such as defence, foreign relations, inter-regional transport and communications, currency, and the assurance of uniformity in legal codes and civil rights. Institutions contributing to the increase of central power would be abolished or modified. The RCMP, for example, would be dismantled and replaced by local police forces, and the CBC would be obliged to share its mandate with regionally-centred broadcasting systems. A reformed and elected Senate would act as the watchdog of local interests; it would have the power of veto in the case of any legislation that might impinge on regional, provincial or municipal rights, and would approve or reject important appointments in the public service, such as the presidencies of Crown corporations. The auditor general would be an officer of the Senate, and would not only watch over public expenditures but would also have the power to veto expansions of the public service and extensions of bureaucratic power through orders-in-council. In other words, it would strictly limit the ability of the Cabinet to operate outside the framework of Parliament.

Since regional and provincial interests do not always coincide, the next level of government would be a group of regional councils to deal with the common problems of certain geographical areas of the country. Within such councils would be represented the provinces and the larger metropolitan areas, which have special interests of their own and which in this regional context would be given a free-city status rather like that of the old Hansa cities of Hamburg and Bremen in the German confederation. For example, a Pacific regional council would include the province of British Columbia, the territory of Yukon, Greater Vancouver and Greater Victoria. Such councils would have power to deal with all matters extending beyond the scope of the provinces into that of the region. For example, in the Atlantic area a regional council would be the appropriate body to take over the control of fisheries from the federal government. By virtue of their relations with both provinces and municipalities, the regional councils would also arbitrate differences between these two levels of government. Inter-regional relations would be developed, and aid between regions, where needed, would be arranged in this way. Thus, equalization payments would no longer be handouts from Ottawa; they would be replaced by freely-arranged co-operation between the more and the less prosperous hinterland areas for the development of employment-creating industries. Shipbuilding, for example, an area long neglected by centrally-oriented governments, would be encouraged through the co-operation of Maritimers, British Columbians and wheat-exporting prairie dwellers, who would share a common interest. Given their shared history of exploitation by central Canada, western Canada and Atlantic Canada should be able to reach understandings not marred by historic bitterness.

Finally, there would be the provincial and the municipal levels of government, corresponding roughly with the cantons and communes in Switzerland. The municipalities would be the ultimate guardians of local interests, and the ultimate recipients of residual power after the federal, regional and provincial powers had been defined in terms of scope of common interests. As long as they did not harm the interests of people outside their areas, and as long as they observed the civil rights common to all Canadians, the municipalities would be free to experiment in social structures and to encourage the lifestyles agreeable to their citizens. As for the provinces, in a situation where they were no longer forced into perpetual conflict with a power-hungry central government, it is likely that they would cease to act the strident and apparently greedy roles they have often been forced to assume. As Virginia McDonald recently remarked:

> In short, I would suggest that if we treat the provinces as fractious chil-
> dren they will behave accordingly—concerned only with their limited
> self interest. If, on the other hand, we treat them as legitimate and
> essential partners in the evolution of our society and understanding of the
> national interest, the provinces will respond generously by assessing
> their positions in relation not only to their own needs but also to the
> wider Canadian context.[5]

I have talked here of a four-level confederal constitution, as distinct from the three-level Swiss confederation. But in fact there should be a fifth level, as there is in practice in the Swiss system. For the ultimate element in any sane and just polity—unacknowledged though it is in so many political systems—is that of the individual citizen. It is he who—in a true confederation—should have the power of saying yes or no on important issues without waiting out a five-year electoral term. The populist devices of the referendum, the initiative and the recall are well known, and they certainly work in polities like Switzerland and in a number of the American states.

Merely as an instrument in the hands of political leaders, the referendum can be turned to bad uses; Hitler was an expert at manipulating plebiscites. But combined with the initiative, which is a vote demanded by a substantial group of citizens, it revives, on the modern level of mass politics, the best elements of Athenian direct democracy. Finally, the recall is not, in our age of arrogant and office-greedy politicians, a mechanism to be despised. As I write, the whole of Canada is seething at the pretensions and the bungles of what must surely be the most incompetent government in the country's history, but there is no way under the present system by which that government can be ended quickly without its own consent, which is unlikely to be given. A provision for a new election in the event of a petition being signed by, say, two million voters would be an assurance not only against the perpetuation of governmental incompetence, but also against the possibility of popular frustration erupting into violence.

For the great virtue of a working confederal system is the internal flexibility it offers through its devolution of powers, and the opportunities it offers for grievances to be voiced and rectified. With such internal flexibility there also goes, I suggest, a change in attitudes towards the rest of the world. The nation-state element in our present mixed constitution would be eliminated as soon as the structures of power were re-arranged, and the increasing internal tendency to replace coercion by co-operation would be translated in terms of external policy into an exchange of military alliances for economic compacts and co-operation in peaceful international initiatives.

Thus our country would at least have the international role Canadians have long desired: first, as an example of how to create a viable political alternative to the obsolete nation-state, and second, as an example of how international relations can be modified by the nation-state's disappearance.

Notes

1. *Gabriel Dumont* (Don Mills: Fitzhenry Whiteside, 1978); *Peoples of the Coast: The Indians of the Pacific Northwest* (Edmonton: Hurtig Publishers, 1977); and Ivan Avakumovic, *The Doukhobors* (Toronto: Oxford University Press, 1968).
2. (Paris: Éditions Brossard, 1921).
3. See for instance his *Idée générale de la révolution du XIXe siècle* (Paris: Ernest Flammarion, n.d.).
4. *The Canadians* (Don Mills: Fitzhenry Whiteside, 1979), p. 50.
5. "A Barrel of Fish for a Barrel of Oil," *Canadian Forum*, June-July, 1981, p. 22.

Part V/Conclusion

Chapter 17/Federalism, Democracy and the Future

Keith Banting and Richard Simeon

Any society that lives through dramatic experiences naturally looks to the future. The desire to anticipate the consequences of major events is universal, and speculation about the future of constitutional change in Canada is as inevitable as it is difficult. Given the provision of the Constitution Act of 1982 and the manner of its creation, what can Canadians expect in the next years and decades?

History often suggests that the past is the best predictor of the future, and in one sense this injunction is particularly apposite here. Because of its limited nature, the constitutional settlement will not alter profoundly the basic dynamics of Canadian politics, or even re-direct them into radically different channels. The authors in this volume correctly emphasize the surprising degree of constitutional continuity implicit in the Constitution Act. There is some satisfaction that the constitution has been patriated and a Charter of Rights and Freedoms entrenched in the basic law of the land. But the overwhelming sense is one of lost opportunities. There is no feeling of historic breakthrough in collective accomplishment, no conviction that Canadians have renewed their federation. None of the underlying conflicts that gave rise to the constitutional debate in the first place have been resolved, and no new framework has been put in place to manage them more effectively in the decades to come. There was no creative reconciliation among the competing visions of Canada. Dreams for the future were denied or compromised.

Within this shared disillusionment there are, naturally, critical differences. For most English-speaking contributors, the reaction is one of regret and disappointment: we could have done better; we left too much unresolved; the settlement does not reflect our perception of the strengths of the country. For Quebec contributors, the reaction is much deeper: the settlement was an historic defeat; English Canada ganged up not only to frustrate Quebec's search for autonomy, but also to weaken its traditional role in Confederation; the settlement is not simply disappointing, but fundamentally illegitimate, a betrayal which sows the seeds of future conflict.

This pervasive sense of lost opportunities might suggest that the Constitution Act will have little impact on the future, except perhaps to exacerbate our existing conflicts. From this point of view, we have failed the future. We have entrenched our discontents even more firmly in Canadian political life, and handed them on virtually intact to succeeding generations.

But disappointment with the outcome should not blind us to the importance both of what has happened, and of what has not happened.

The incremental innovations contained in the Constitution Act will have immediate impacts: a First Ministers' Conference with native participation to address native issues; a Charter, the impact of which will dominate much of the politics of the 1980s; and an amending formula, which may well alter the dynamics of subsequent constitutional change. More importantly in the longer term, the capacity of our largely unreformed constitution to contain our discontents remains very much an open question. In the aftermath of the Parti Québécois election in 1976, many voices insisted that only major constitutional change could prevent the tension between French and English, region and country, government and government, from leading inexorably to the collapse of Canada. What, then, is the longer-term viability of our as yet unreformed federal system? Once again, these themes can best be explored in each of the domains central to this book: federalism and democracy.

Federalism and an Unreformed Constitution

The constitutional reform process unleashed a flood of innovative proposals for change, few of which survived to be reflected in the outcome. In effect, these proposals now constitute an unfinished agenda for reform. The lengthy list of ideas left on the table cover two broad areas: reform of the institutions of the central government, and the division of powers between levels of government. The first includes a revised second chamber, changes in the electoral system, new controls over regulatory agencies, and reform of the Supreme Court. The second covers a wide range of controversies concerning the division of powers between governments, several of which—jurisdiction over pay-television, off-shore mineral rights, and the trade and commerce power—have been the subject of heated court cases recently.

This unfinished agenda reflected widespread criticism of Canadian political institutions. In the turmoil of the constitutional debate, a searchlight was trained on every aspect of our system of government, and none escaped unscathed. Cabinet, Parliament, political parties, the electoral system, the courts, the balance between levels of government—all were judged incapable of integrating Canadians into a cohesive political whole. The effectiveness—even the legitimacy—of our governmental structure was thrown in doubt, and radical reform was advanced in measured but ominous cadence.

All this might suggest that a massive "phase two" of constitutional reform is about to begin. But this seems most unlikely. Public distaste for constitutional wrangling is deeply entrenched, and the economic crisis preoccupies both citizens and governments. In addition, the sheer difficulty of successfully amending the constitution undermines what little political incentive remains on any side to re-open the debate. The federal government emerged with its own powers intact, and can be expected to test their limits—both politically and legally—as it seeks to restore its power and authority in the federal system. Ottawa also knows that under the new amending formula any proposals for further centralization will either be blocked or provoke the use of the opting-out clause, resulting in the "checker-board Canada" it so greatly fears. Similarly, the provinces are aware that the federal government retains the capacity and the will to block movement towards their traditional agenda of decentralization and a greater voice in central decision-making, so they have little incentive to renew discussions. Quebec leaders also know that only a dramatic political breakthrough, such as a massive renewal of support for independence, can force its concerns back onto the table.

These barriers to change will not completely still the debate. Ideas tend to be irrepressible, and proposals for further change will continue to bubble up. As the federal government seeks to rebuild a country-wide basis of support and re-assert its presence in Canadian life, it may be tempted to explore a variety of institutional innovations. One possibility would be an elected Senate, a device which could increase representation of smaller regions in Ottawa while bypassing provincial governments. But speedy adoption of such a proposal is doubtful. During the constitutional nego-tiations, those provincial governments with a view on Senate reform generally supported a provincially-appointed chamber, and in August 1982 Alberta published a discussion document which added its support to that camp. The federal government might be able to mobilize substantial public support for a popularly-chosen Senate, but winning requisite provincial assent would remain nonetheless a protracted and difficult process.

Thus, further broad-scale constitutional renewal is unlikely in the near future. While many would argue that such reform is desirable, even essential, they are likely to be disappointed. Any constitutional discussions are likely to be restricted to individual issues on which a consensus appears feasible.

Two features of the Constitution Act itself may offset this general disinclination to raise constitutional issues. First, the new amending formula may encourage a different process. In the past, the need for a collec-tive agreement of virtually all governments ensured that each government's particular constitutional priorities reached the bargaining table; and proposed agreements took the form of complex packages which could collapse if any key government rejected any part of them. The origins and fate of the Victoria Charter spring to mind here. In the future, however, constitutional issues may be disaggregated. An amendment concerning quite a limited issue might begin with passage in only one or two Legisla-tures, and then gradually be adopted by additional ones until, possibly after several years, the requisite majority is reached. Indeed, in the short term, various governments might use this technique to raise again issues that were ignored in the 1981 settlement. One sign of this came in September 1982, when the British Columbia Legislature unanimously passed a resolution initiating an amendment to add to the Charter of Rights and Freedoms the right to the "enjoyment of property" and urged other governments to do likewise.

Second, the larger constitutional role of the Supreme Court may stimulate defensive efforts at constitutional reform by Cabinets and Legislatures. Heightened conflict between governments has already led to an increasing tendency to refer cases to the courts. Recent cases, such as the Senate reference, control of off-shore resources and the reference on the federal constitutional Resolution, have increased the court's visibility as an ultimate arbiter, and that can only be enhanced by its new role with respect to the Charter. As in the United States, an increasing source of constitutional claims may well be found in efforts to "undo" court decisions.

Nevertheless, even when allowance is made for the possibility of such incremental changes, the basic prognosis remains that wholesale constitutional renewal is unlikely. Canadians must face the future with a constitution molded in the distant past. In the longer term, the central question remains how well our largely unreformed constitution will contain the linguistic and regional divisions that stimulated the reform process in the first place.

The settlement, we have seen, represents a partial victory for what might be called the integrationist view of Quebec and French-Canadians in Canada: the rejection of Quebec's claims to a distinct role as the political expression of a nation; the emphasis on securing rights for minority languages across Canada; and the assertion that the interests of Quebecers can be promoted as well in Ottawa as in Quebec City. But whether, in the long run, this result fuels a re-assertion of Quebec nationalism or, on the other hand, leads to acquiescence or even outright support for federalism depends on developments both within Quebec and within English-Canada.

From the Quebec perspective, the question is whether the election of the Parti Québécois and the referendum represented the high-water mark of Quebec nationalism. Among the contributors here, Daniel Latouche seems to come closest to this view in his pessimistic retrospective. Writers such as Dominique Clift have argued more directly that many of the most powerful interests supporting the secular nationalism since the 1960s have achieved their goals, and a new Quebec business elite is now much more firmly integrated into the national scene. Other factors might push in the same direction. The deep structural problems of the Quebec economy may make independence seem to be an increasingly unacceptable risk, an expensive luxury in a time of economic turmoil. An independence movement in this view must be supported not only by a strong sense of identity and powerlessness in the larger political system, but also by a sense of opportunity, a faith that the society has the resources to go it alone. In addition, the federalist success in the referendum may suggest that in the competition between the symbols of Canadian and Quebec identity, the pan-Canadian idea retains considerable force.

But the future remains open, and the same forces may ensure that there is only a temporary lull in Quebec nationalism. The virtually unanimous rejection of the constitutional settlement among elite Quebec opinion seriously undermines its acceptance in that community. The alternative vision of a bilingual Canada from sea to sea finds only partial reflection in the Constitution Act, and minority language education rights in Alberta, or even Ontario, have little impact in Quebec. More importantly, any long-run economic and political decline of Quebec within Confederation is likely to increase a sense of threat and grievance, and decrease the relative costs of going it alone. Major economic adjustments throughout the industrial world threaten important sectors of the Quebec economy, and the shift of economic power within Canada towards the West further tilts the balance. Quebec industry is not well-placed to take advantage of the economic trends of the next decades, and it is not at all clear how much the federal system can, or will, shield it. Political developments could exacerbate these tensions. Population changes are inexorably weakening Quebec's weight in Canada. For most of this century, Quebec has exerted considerable influence in Ottawa through the Liberal Party. But were Canada to enter an extended period of Progressive Conservative rule with a government owing its dominance to support from Ontario and the West, the political dynamics would be changed. If the challenge to the Liberals is to represent and accommodate the West, the Tory challenge is to do the same in Quebec. Neither party has had much success. Thus the economic and political marginalization of Quebec within Canada could provoke a renewed *indépendantiste* reaction. Most of our Quebec authors regard the constitutional settlement as stark evidence that such a process of marginalization of Quebec's concerns has already begun.

Whether independence is on the table again in the near future also depends on English Canada. English Canadians have a tendency to become excited about "the Quebec problem" during moments of crisis, such as October 1970 and November 1976, soon to lapse again into indifference. The referendum no doubt led many to conclude that the independence threat had disappeared. In addition, Quebecers are correct to argue that the primary focus of the post-1976 debate at the national level was not on how to respond to Quebec, but rather on how to deal with regional tensions within English Canada. This preoccupation would likely continue in any subsequent constitutional deliberations, and any drive for a federal system particularly responsive to French-Canadian concerns is likely to be blunted. Clearly, the federalist victory in mitigating the enduring tensions between English and French is a tenuous one at best.

The capacity of our largely unreformed constitution to accommodate regionalism is also uncertain. The 1981 settlement was an inelegant compromise between the federalist and provincialist forces, and once again the adequacy of the compromise remains controversial. Have we also seen the high-water mark of regionalism and provincialism? Are the forces impelling us towards centralization finally going to prevail, as they have in most other federations? Or will regional grievances, heightened by the constitutional wars themselves, further erode the bonds that hold the country together?

Some argue that the principal impetus for provincialism comes from provincial governments themselves, with relatively limited spontaneous support from the population at large, and that the constitutional settlement, together with the National Energy Program, represent the belling of the cat. Canadians, they argue, are responsive to pan-Canadian goals and could rally behind a central government that powerfully enunciated a "new national policy." Moreover, during past periods of crisis, the public has accepted firm national direction, and the present economic turmoil could encourage a similar reaction. All of this would suggest many possibilities for would-be nation-builders.

Yet Canadian history is littered with the broken dreams of centralizers. Regionalism is firmly rooted in our economic and social life, and the capacity of provincial governments to mobilize support was not diminished by the constitutional settlement. Indeed, in the aftermath of the 1981 Accord some governments came under strong public pressure for being too accommodating to Ottawa during the negotiations. While all Canadians may remain united in economic misery throughout the 1980s, the politics of scarcity easily becomes the politics of jealousy. The economic interests of different regions still diverge widely; the distribution of wealth and economic opportunity among them will continue to generate tensions, as relatively wealthy regions seek to maintain their advantage, and declining regions seek to establish their claims. The politics of such economic inequalities is easily exacerbated by differences in size. They are easier to deal with when the richest region is also the largest, as was the case during Ontario's period of dominance; they are much more difficult when the largest provinces become claimants and are seen by richer provinces to be using their weight of numbers to force large transfers of wealth. The politics of regionalism is not going to disappear. The only question is how these tensions are to be managed.

From this perspective, the combination of a largely unreformed constitution and a more assertive federal government could further heighten regional divisions. As Roger Gibbins argued eloquently, the *sine qua non* for a successful re-assertion of federal authority is the establishment of nation-wide legitimacy for the central government. Without political support, the exercise of authority is seen as tyranny. A central issue remains the ability of federal institutions successfully to represent and provide a forum for accommodation among competing regional interests. But as noted earlier, massive political barriers confront the wide-ranging reforms that have been proposed to ensure this. The federal government stands at the ready to veto any reforms that enhance the status of provincial governments as the representatives of Canada's regions, whether through a decentralization of powers or through granting them a formal role in the policy process of the federal government itself. The provinces are equally ready to veto changes that would create competing regional representatives in Ottawa. And changes that can be enacted by the federal government alone, such as electoral reform, will continue to crash against the entrenched electoral interests of all three national parties. Institutional reform may be necessary, but it is not necessarily possible.

As a result, the successful management of regionalism will depend, as in the past, on enlightened political practice. The actions of parties, Cabinets and executives will remain paramount. The first basis for winning support is through policy—through actions which demonstrate responsiveness to different regions and through promotion of issues which transcend the regional dimension. Changes in the formal rules might increase the incentives to do this, but ultimately quality and style in leadership is essential. Successful governance in a country as regionally divided as Canada seems to require a particular orientation to policy-making. The logic of parliamentary democracy is that of majority rule: once in power, there are few restraints on how Cabinets and governing parties exercise it. Indeed, some writers have called the system a "constitutional dictatorship." Regionalism, on the other hand, requires substantial modification of majority rule, not only in constitutional structures but also in the theory and practice of government. The "public philosophy" of federalism requires an acceptance of the legitimacy, indeed the value of both regional and national interests and identities, searching not for a choice between them, but for complementarity and accommodation. And at the level of practice, it requires among decision-makers the pervasive realization that policy must also be a compromise among regional interests. The search must be for broad coalitions or concurrent majorities, even if that means some sacrifice of majority rule, political boldness and economic efficiency.

Realism might suggest that such aspirations are pious at best, naïve at worst. As long as Canadian political parties lack a truly national character, this philosophy of governance asks governments to deny their political base, their staunchest friends and allies, in order to accommodate regions and interests not even present at caucus meetings or at the Cabinet table. Such self-denial may be possible in occasional symbolic gestures, but less so in the *realpolitik* of basic economic strategy. Exhortations to abstinence tend to be as effective in politics as in family planning. But in facing the future with a largely unreformed constitution, Canadians have nowhere else to stand.

While the prospects for Canadian federalism are not particularly reassuring, a sense of perspective is nonetheless essential. Constitutional discussions, especially since 1976, have been marked by hyperbole and apocalyptic visions: Canada was about to collapse into a thousand tiny pieces, in a hundred painful ways. But it has not happened, as yet at least. The future will see our historic discontents as profound as ever, perhaps more so. Our failure to reach new understandings or to agree on new mechanisms during the constitutional process guarantees that we will manage these discontents less effectively than we might have. But none of this necessarily means that Canada itself will fail. There is no evidence that the twin forces of language and region will deliver a body blow to Confederation. The existing constitution has shown remarkable resilience in the face of virtually universal denigration, and it may yet survive, battered and bruised, well into the twenty-first century.

Democracy and a Partially Reformed Constitution

This book has been almost as much about the quality of Canadian democracy as it has been about the constitution and Canadian federalism. The authors were frequently drawn away from what many regarded as an uninspired and petty wrangling among governments about power to another set of questions. The constitution, argued many observers during the constitutional debate, is more than just about federalism; it is equally as much about the basic rules of a democratic political system. For American constitution-makers in 1787, or French ones in 1789, these were *the* constitutional questions. Debate about the roots and quality of democracy has, by contrast, been a muted theme in Canadian political debate. Our constitutional discussion has been about federalism; and federalism in Canada has been primarily about the balance between regional and national communities rather than about preserving democracy and rights.

Nevertheless, the recent constitutional debate, as we have seen, revealed much about Canadian conceptions of democracy, and the settlement itself contributes more in an immediate way to democratic practices than to federal ones. Democracy was injected into the debate first by the federal government, which since 1968 had argued that a Charter of Rights should logically come prior to an analysis of power and institutions. Many non-governmental participants raised the question of democracy in other terms. For them, the constitution was too important to be decided by politicians alone; public groups should not be frozen out of the process; and the agenda should be broadened. Many called for greater public involvement, and others wanted to bypass traditional representative institutions in favour of an elected constituent assembly.

In fact, all participants phrased their arguments in terms of appeals to democratic values, but each based his or her claim on a different aspect of the protean concept. The federal government appealed to simple national majoritarianism, held to outweigh regional majorities, and to the protection of individual rights from the tyranny of the majority. Opponents of entrenched rights appealed to the rights of legislative majorities, and opposed increasing the authority of non-elected judges. Provincialists argued that when contemplating constitutional change in a federal system, simple majorities were not enough. Concurrent majorities were essential, and those majorities should be legislative ones. While Quebec actually held a popular referendum and Ottawa proposed referenda for the future, all other governments were hostile to any form of plebiscitarian democracy.

Although the settlement did not embody any one of these conceptions of democracy in a pure form, it did shift Canadian practices moderately, opening at least three new channels for political action by Canadians. First was the formal commitment to hold a First Ministers' Conference with native participation to address native problems. This commitment was important at two levels. The substantive issues posed by the position of aboriginal peoples in Canada mix moral and legal concerns in a compelling way, and challenge our conceptions of both social justice and democracy. A single meeting with first ministers could not have been expected to resolve all of the issues involved. But given the anger surrounding them during the constitutional debates, the commitment to start substantive discussion was important. At another level, however, the commitment was also important procedurally. It enjoined governments and natives to search for a way to open up the federal-provincial process—hitherto a closed and often secret world—to direct participation of affected groups. The importance of such experiments is heavily underscored by the frustrations of the constitutional process and the angry reactions of women and natives after the November Accord. The clear message was that not only the settlement but also the process were simply not good enough for a democratic society. The challenge, then, is to develop an effective model of policy-making in federal-provincial negotiations which enhances wider participation and reduces the tension between an elitist politics and an age of heightened democratic expectations. If natives are successful in cracking the federal-provincial mold, other groups will not be far behind.

While important, this task is extremely difficult. In the case of natives, major adjustments are required on both sides if the frustrations described by Douglas Sanders are to be avoided. Native communities need to develop greater internal political coherence, such that agreed approaches can be brought to the conference table. Given the incredible range of political views within the aboriginal peoples, some of whom deny totally the relevance of the Canadian constitution and nation to natives at all, this is not an easy task. On the other side, governments have to alter ingrained habits of federal-provincial bargaining. Any attempts to exclude natives from critical decision-making sessions will jeopardize the entire process. The starting point is therefore not encouraging. But for those committed to the cause of openness in government generally, such experiments are critical.

Second, the 1980s clearly will be the decade of the Charter of Rights and Freedoms. All of the contributors to this volume agree that the impact of the Charter, both on the actual rights of citizens and on the general political habits of Canadians, is uncertain. During the first year, there has been a blizzard of appeals to the Charter in the courts across the country, but it will be years before the full impact becomes clear, especially in light of the three-year delay in the coming into force of the equality rights provisions. The extent of legislative recourse to the override clause, the power of the limitations clause of section 1, the precise meaning of a whole set of terms new to Canadian law—all these critical aspects of the Charter will become clearer over the next decade. The Charter will also begin to reveal its broader consequences for our political culture. Will litigation through the courts become a prominent feature of Canadian politics? How much will interpretation of the universalistic provisions of the Charter find itself in conflict with deeply-held interests and cultural values, as in the case of Quebec's language law and perhaps aspects of our multicultural heritage? All that can be known with certainty at this point is that the political reaction of citizens and governments to judicial initiatives will be an increasingly important element within Canadian politics; for as Tarnopolsky warns, government and the public, not the courts, will inevitably remain the final arbiters of individual rights.

Third, the new amending formula may change the dynamics of populist politics in Canada. While direct citizen involvement through referenda has been rejected, the possibilities for an incremental and cumulative approach to constitutional change mentioned earlier does open more avenues for public influence. Groups can bring pressure to bear on individual governments to initiate "their" amendment, and then expand their efforts across the nation, much on the model of the American ERA movement. Groups with intense moral concerns, such as the "Right to Life" movement, might mobilize along these lines. Or Franco-Ontarians might push the federal government to initiate an amendment extending official bilingualism to their own province as a means of intensifying the pressure on provincial politicians.

Thus the commitment to native participation, the Charter and the amending formula do open up new possibilities for political action by Canadians during the 1980s. How aggressively citizens utilize them in the coming years will determine the extent to which the Constitution Act makes an important contribution to democratic government in Canada.

Nevertheless, despite the possibilities inherent in the Act, the settlement does not profoundly change the fundamental processes of government in Canada, and all of the traditional controversies about the quality of Canadian democracy will endure. In a federal system that relies heavily on intergovernmental bargaining among ministers and officials, there are powerful pressures against openness, and the problems of accountability and responsiveness characteristic of all complex modern governments are enhanced. The authority of Parliament and provincial Legislatures, already constrained by the strength of party discipline, is further eroded. Regional accommodation, predicated on exchanges among executives, stands in striking contrast to a system that channels adjustments through representative institutions of parties and Parliaments, and thereby challenges traditional conceptions of responsible government.

The same logic constrains the role of citizens and public groups. Even if a successful model of wider participation is developed during deliberations with native groups, governmental pressures against its incorporation into the mainstream of federal-provincial deliberations will be intense. Strong public pressure might ensure that in the future, critical policies are not formulated in a purely intergovernmental process. But as in other areas, it is equally plausible that the future will resemble the past, and that Canadian politics will remain an elite process tempered by occasional populist anger.

While these questions reflect the particular form of Canadian federalism, the final and inescapable question about democracy in a federal system remains *which* majorities rule. In any given case, is the relevant majority that of the country as a whole or that of each individual province? The former risks overruling and frustrating local majorities. If the same group is a minority every time over a long period, the potential for secessionist movements grows. But local majorities can also frustrate national ones. So the critical questions for federalism are, on what kinds of questions is the country-wide majority the appropriate one? on which ones should local majorities decide? and which ones should be decided only by concurrent majorities?

In Canadian political discourse, these issues about democracy manifest themselves primarily in the historic debate over centralization and decentralization. Advocates of centralization see democracy embodied most fully in the national majority. Localism is seen as anachronistic, regressive, parochial, selfish. Only large national units can mobilize resources and bridge differences sufficiently to enable governments to satisfy majority demands in a complex industrial society. This is the traditional position of the left; it was conventional wisdom among English-Canadian commentators on federalism during the 1930s and 1940s. But another tradition, represented in this volume by George Woodcock, holds that centralization and authoritarianism go hand in hand, and that true democratic citizenship can only be found in units small enough to be comprehensible to the citizen and to make a single voice count. Applied fully to the Canadian case, this might embody not decentralization to provinces, but rather to cities, neighbourhoods, and factories. Each position contains its own dilemmas. Centralization may permit greater efficiency and redistribution among regions, but at the cost of responsiveness and participation. Local democracy may maximize the potential for participation and responsiveness, but at the cost of effectiveness and the sharing of resources among regions.

These are the grand issues of the link between democracy and federalism. They are not unique to Canada, but they are inevitable in any federal system. Nor can they ever be finally resolved. Each generation must find its own answer to timeless questions.

Thus, underlying the continuing debates about institutions, rules, amending formulae, the division of powers, reform of federal institutions and all the other nuts and bolts of constitution-making are another set of questions which we have inadequately addressed—questions about community, democracy, the role of government. That the first ministers did not think them all through—and often used them in a purely rhetorical manner to cloak self-interest in principle—should occasion no surprise. Nor, of course, do these philosophical issues explain the constitutional debate or the future of Canadian federalism. Constitution-making, our experience has revealed, is not simple. It reveals the best and the worst in our political leaders and institutions. It mingles the search for power, the play of economic interests, and high principle. It highlights issues usually hidden or obscured in day-to-day political debate. So for all Canadians it was at once exhilarating and frustrating; a process full of both threat and opportunity, flawed triumph and perhaps temporary defeat, dreams and compromises.

APPENDIX

CONSTITUTION ACT, 1982

PART I
CANADIAN CHARTER OF RIGHTS AND FREEDOMS

Whereas Canada is founded upon principles that recognize the supremacy of God and the rule of law:

Guarantee of Rights and Freedoms

Rights and freedoms in Canada

1. *The Canadian Charter of Rights and Freedoms* guarantees the rights and freedoms set out in it subject only to such reasonable limits prescribed by law as can be demonstrably justified in a free and democratic society.

Fundamental Freedoms

Fundamental freedoms

2. Everyone has the following fundamental freedoms:
(*a*) freedom of conscience and religion;
(*b*) freedom of thought, belief, opinion and expression, including freedom of the press and other media of communication;
(*c*) freedom of peaceful assembly; and
(*d*) freedom of association.

Democratic Rights

Democratic rights of citizens

3. Every citizen of Canada has the right to vote in an election of members of the House of Commons or of a legislative assembly and to be qualified for membership therein.

Maximum duration of legislative bodies

4. (1) No House of Commons and no legislative assembly shall continue for longer than five years from the date fixed for the return of the writs at a general election of its members.

Continuation in special circumstances

(2) In time of real or apprehended war, invasion or insurrection, a House of Commons may be continued by Parlia-

ment and a legislative assembly may be continued by the legislature beyond five years if such continuation is not opposed by the votes of more than one-third of the members of the House of Commons or the legislative assembly, as the case may be.

Annual sitting of legislative bodies

5. There shall be a sitting of Parliament and of each legislature at least once every twelve months.

Mobility Rights

Mobility of citizens

6. (1) Every citizen of Canada has the right to enter, remain in and leave Canada.

Rights to move and gain livelihood

(2) Every citizen of Canada and every person who has the status of a permanent resident of Canada has the right

(*a*) to move to and take up residence in any province; and

(*b*) to pursue the gaining of a livelihood in any province.

Limitation

(3) The rights specified in subsection (2) are subject to

(*a*) any laws or practices of general application in force in a province other than those that discriminate among persons primarily on the basis of province of present or previous residence; and

(*b*) any laws providing for reasonable residency requirements as a qualification for the receipt of publicly provided social services.

Affirmative action programs

(4) Subsections (2) and (3) do not preclude any law, program or activity that has as its object the amelioration in a province of conditions of individuals in that province who are socially or economically disadvantaged if the rate of employment in that province is below the rate of employment in Canada.

Legal Rights

Life, liberty and security of person

7. Everyone has the right to life, liberty and security of the person and the right not to be deprived thereof except in accordance with the principles of fundamental justice.

Search or seizure

8. Everyone has the right to be secure against unreasonable search or seizure.

Detention or imprisonment

9. Everyone has the right not to be arbitrarily detained or imprisoned.

Arrest or detention

10. Everyone has the right on arrest or detention
(*a*) to be informed promptly of the reasons therefor;
(*b*) to retain and instruct counsel without delay and to be informed of that right; and
(*c*) to have the validity of the detention determined by way of *habeas corpus* and to be released if the detention is not lawful.

Proceedings in criminal and penal matters

11. Any person charged with an offence has the right
(*a*) to be informed without unreasonable delay of the specific offence;
(*b*) to be tried within a reasonable time;
(*c*) not to be compelled to be a witness in proceedings against that person in respect of the offence;
(*d*) to be presumed innocent until proven guilty according to law in a fair and public hearing by an independent and impartial tribunal;
(*e*) not to be denied reasonable bail without just cause;
(*f*) except in the case of an offence under military law tried before a military tribunal, to the benefit of trial by jury where the maximum punishment for the offence is imprisonment for five years or a more severe punishment;
(*g*) not to be found guilty on account of any act or omission unless, at the time of the act or omission, it constituted an offence under Canadian or international law or was criminal according to the general principles of law recognized by the community of nations;
(*h*) if finally acquitted of the offence, not to be tried for it again and, if finally found guilty and punished for the offence, not to be tried or punished for it again; and
(*i*) if found guilty of the offence and if the punishment for the offence has been varied between the time of commission and the time of sentencing, to the benefit of the lesser punishment.

Treatment or punishment

12. Everyone has the right not to be subjected to any cruel and unusual treatment or punishment.

Self-incrimination

13. A witness who testifies in any proceedings has the right not to have any incriminating evidence so given used to incriminate that witness in any other proceedings, except in a prosecution for perjury or for the giving of contradictory evidence.

Interpreter

14. A party or witness in any proceedings who does not

understand or speak the language in which the proceedings are conducted or who is deaf has the right to the assistance of an interpreter.

Equality Rights

Equality before and under law and equal protection and benefit of law

15. (1) Every individual is equal before and under the law and has the right to the equal protection and equal benefit of the law without discrimination and, in particular, without discrimination based on race, national or ethnic origin, colour, religion, sex, age or mental or physical disability.

Affirmative action programs

(2) Subsection (1) does not preclude any law, program or activity that has as its object the amelioration of conditions of disadvantaged individuals or groups including those that are disadvantaged because of race, national or ethnic origin, colour, religion, sex, age or mental or physical disability.

Official Languages of Canada

Official languages of Canada

16. (1) English and French are the official languages of Canada and have equality of status and equal rights and privileges as to their use in all institutions of the Parliament and government of Canada.

Official languages of New Brunswick

(2) English and French are the official languages of New Brunswick and have equality of status and equal rights and privileges as to their use in all institutions of the legislature and government of New Brunswick.

Advancement of status and use

(3) Nothing in this Charter limits the authority of Parliament or a legislature to advance the equality of status or use of English and French.

Proceedings of Parliament

17. (1) Everyone has the right to use English or French in any debates and other proceedings of Parliament.

Proceedings of New Brunswick legislature

(2) Everyone has the right to use English or French in any debates and other proceedings of the legislature of New Brunswick.

Parliamentary statutes and records

18. (1) The statutes, records and journals of Parliament shall be printed and published in English and French and both language versions are equally authoritative.

New Brunswick statutes and records

(2) The statutes, records and journals of the legislature of New Brunswick shall be printed and published in English

and French and both language versions are equally authoritative.

Proceedings in courts established by Parliament

19. (1) Either English or French may be used by any person in, or in any pleading in or process issuing from, any court established by Parliament.

Proceedings in New Brunswick courts

(2) Either English or French may be used by any person in, or in any pleading in or process issuing from, any court of New Brunswick.

Communications by public with federal institutions

20. (1) Any member of the public in Canada has the right to communicate with, and to receive available services from, any head or central office of an institution of the Parliament or government of Canada in English or French, and has the same right with respect to any other office of any such institution where
(*a*) there is a significant demand for communications with and services from that office in such language; or
(*b*) due to the nature of the office, it is reasonable that communications with and services from that office be available in both English and French.

Communications by public with New Brunswick institutions

(2) Any member of the public in New Brunswick has the right to communicate with, and to receive available services from, any office of an institution of the legislature or government of New Brunswick in English or French.

Continuation of existing constitutional provisions

21. Nothing in sections 16 to 20 abrogates or derogates from any right, privilege or obligation with respect to the English and French languages, or either of them, that exists or is continued by virtue of any other provision of the Constitution of Canada.

Rights and privileges preserved

22. Nothing in sections 16 to 20 abrogates or derogates from any legal or customary right or privilege acquired or enjoyed either before or after the coming into force of this Charter with respect to any language that is not English or French.

Minority Language Educational Rights

Language of instruction

23. (1) Citizens of Canada
(*a*) whose first language learned and still understood is that of the English or French linguistic minority population of the province in which they reside, or

(*b*) who have received their primary school instruction in Canada in English or French and reside in a province where the language in which they received that instruction is the language of the English or French linguistic minority population of the province,

have the right to have their children receive primary and secondary school instruction in that language in that province.

Continuity of language instruction

(2) Citizens of Canada of whom any child has received or is receiving primary or secondary school instruction in English or French in Canada, have the right to have all their children receive primary and secondary school instruction in the same language.

Application where numbers warrant

(3) The right of citizens of Canada under subsections (1) and (2) to have their children receive primary and secondary school instruction in the language of the English or French linguistic minority population of a province

(*a*) applies wherever in the province the number of children of citizens who have such a right is sufficient to warrant the provision to them out of public funds of minority language instruction; and

(*b*) includes, where the number of those children so warrants, the right to have them receive that instruction in minority language educational facilities provided out of public funds.

Enforcement

Enforcement of guaranteed rights and freedoms

24. (1) Anyone whose rights or freedoms, as guaranteed by this Charter, have been infringed or denied may apply to a court of competent jurisdiction to obtain such remedy as the court considers appropriate and just in the circumstances.

Exclusion of evidence bringing administration of justice into disrepute

(2) Where, in proceedings under subsection (1), a court concludes that evidence was obtained in a manner that infringed or denied any rights or freedoms guaranteed by this Charter, the evidence shall be excluded if it is established that, having regard to all the circumstances, the admission of it in the proceedings would bring the administration of justice into disrepute.

General

Aboriginal rights and freedoms not affected by Charter

25. The guarantee in this Charter of certain rights and freedoms shall not be construed so as to abrogate or derogate from any aboriginal, treaty or other rights or freedoms that pertain to the aboriginal peoples of Canada including

(*a*) any rights or freedoms that have been recognized by the Royal Proclamation of October 7, 1763, and

(*b*) any rights or freedoms that may be acquired by the aboriginal peoples of Canada by way of land claims settlement.

Other rights and freedoms not affected by Charter

26. The guarantee in this Charter of certain rights and freedoms shall not be construed as denying the existence of any other rights or freedoms that exist in Canada.

Multicultural heritage

27. This Charter shall be interpreted in a manner consistent with the preservation and enhancement of the multicultural heritage of Canadians.

Rights guaranteed equally to both sexes

28. Notwithstanding anything in this Charter, the rights and freedoms referred to in it are guaranteed equally to male and female persons.

Rights respecting certain schools preserved

29. Nothing in this Charter abrogates or derogates from any rights or privileges guaranteed by or under the Constitution of Canada in respect of denominational, separate or dissentient schools.

Application to territories and territorial authorities

30. A reference in this Charter to a province or to the legislative assembly or legislature of a province shall be deemed to include a reference to the Yukon Territory and the Northwest Territories, or to the appropriate legislative authority thereof, as the case may be.

Legislative powers not extended

31. Nothing in this Charter extends the legislative powers of any body or authority.

Application of Charter

Application of Charter

32. (1) This Charter applies

(*a*) to the Parliament and government of Canada in respect of all matters within the authority of Parliament including all matters relating to the Yukon Territory and Northwest Territories; and (*b*) to the legislature and government of each province in respect of all matters within the authority of the legislature of each province.

Exception

(2) Notwithstanding subsection (1), section 15 shall not have effect until three years after this section comes into force.

Exception where express declaration

33. (1) Parliament or the legislature of a province may expressly declare in an Act of Parliament or of the legislature, as the case may be, that the Act or a provision thereof shall operate notwithstanding a provision included in section 2 or sections 7 to 15 of this Charter.

Operation of exception

(2) An Act or a provision of an Act in respect of which a declaration made under this section is in effect shall have such operation as it would have but for the provision of this Charter referred to in the declaration.

Five year limitation

(3) A declaration made under subsection (1) shall cease to have effect five years after it comes into force or on such earlier date as may be specified in the declaration.

Re-enactment

(4) Parliament or a legislature of a province may re-enact a declaration made under subsection (1).

Five year limitation

(5) Subsection (3) applies in respect of a re-enactment made under subsection (4).

Citation

Citation

34. This Part may be cited as the *Canadian Charter of Rights and Freedoms.*

PART II
RIGHTS OF THE ABORIGINAL PEOPLES OF CANADA

Recognition of existing aboriginal and treaty rights

35. (1) The existing aboriginal and treaty rights of the aboriginal peoples of Canada are hereby recognized and affirmed.

Definition of "aboriginal peoples of Canada"

(2) In this Act, "aboriginal peoples of Canada" includes the Indian, Inuit and Métis peoples of Canada.

PART III
EQUALIZATION AND REGIONAL DISPARITIES

Commitment to promote equal opportunities

36. (1) Without altering the legislative authority of Parliament or of the provincial legislatures, or the rights of any of them with respect to the exercise of their legislative authority, Parliament and the legislatures, together with the government of Canada and the provincial governments, are committed to

(*a*) promoting equal opportunities for the well-being of Canadians;

(*b*) furthering economic development to reduce disparity in opportunities; and

(*c*) providing essential public services of reasonable quality to all Canadians.

Commitment respecting public services

(2) Parliament and the government of Canada are committed to the principle of making equalization payments to ensure that provincial governments have sufficient revenues to provide reasonably comparable levels of public services at reasonably comparable levels of taxation.

PART IV
CONSTITUTIONAL CONFERENCE

Constitutional conference

37. (1) A constitutional conference composed of the Prime Minister of Canada and the first ministers of the provinces shall be convened by the Prime Minister of Canada within one year after this Part comes into force.

Participation of aboriginal peoples

(2) The conference convened under subsection (1) shall have included in its agenda an item respecting constitutional matters that directly affect the aboriginal peoples of Canada, including the identification and definition of the rights of those peoples to be included in the Constitution of Canada, and the Prime Minister of Canada shall invite representatives of those peoples to participate in the discussions on that item.

Participation of territories

(3) The Prime Minister of Canada shall invite elected representatives of the governments of the Yukon Territory and the Northwest Territories to participate in the discussions on any item on the agenda of the conference convened under subsection (1) that, in the opinion of the

Prime Minister, directly affects the Yukon Territory and the Northwest Territories.

PART V
PROCEDURE FOR AMENDING
CONSTITUTION OF CANADA

General procedure for amending Constitution of Canada

38. (1) An amendment to the Constitution of Canada may be made by proclamation issued by the Governor General under the Great Seal of Canada where so authorized by

(*a*) resolutions of the Senate and House of Commons; and
(*b*) resolutions of the legislative assemblies of at least two-thirds of the provinces that have, in the aggregate, according to the then latest general census, at least fifty per cent of the population of all the provinces.

Majority of members

(2) An amendment made under subsection (1) that derogates from the legislative powers, the proprietary rights or any other rights or privileges of the legislature or government of a province shall require a resolution supported by a majority of the members of each of the Senate, the House of Commons and the legislative assemblies required under subsection (1).

Expression of dissent

(3) An amendment referred to in subsection (2) shall not have effect in a province the legislative assembly of which has expressed its dissent thereto by resolution supported by a majority of its members prior to the issue of the proclamation to which the amendment relates unless that legislative assembly, subsequently, by resolution supported by a majority of its members, revokes its dissent and authorizes the amendment.

Revocation of dissent

(4) A resolution of dissent made for the purposes of subsection (3) may be revoked at any time before or after the issue of the proclamation to which it relates.

Restriction on proclamation

39. (1) A proclamation shall not be issued under subsection 38(1) before the expiration of one year from the adoption of the resolution initiating the amendment procedure thereunder, unless the legislative assembly of each province has previously adopted a resolution of assent or dissent.

Idem

(2) A proclamation shall not be issued under subsection

38(1) after the expiration of three years from the adoption of the resolution initiating the amendment procedure thereunder.

Compensation   **40.** Where an amendment is made under subsection 38(1) that transfers provincial legislative powers relating to education or other cultural matters from provincial legislatures to Parliament, Canada shall provide reasonable compensation to any province to which the amendment does not apply.

Amendment by unanimous consent   **41.** An amendment to the Constitution of Canada in relation to the following matters may be made by proclamation issued by the Governor General under the Great Seal of Canada only where authorized by resolutions of the Senate and House of Commons and of the legislative assembly of each province:

(*a*) the office of the Queen, the Governor General and the Lieutenant Governor of a province;

(*b*) the right of a province to a number of members in the House of Commons not less than the number of Senators by which the province is entitled to be represented at the time this Part comes into force;

(*c*) subject to section 43, the use of the English or the French language;

(*d*) the composition of the Supreme Court of Canada; and

(*e*) an amendment to this Part.

Amendment by general procedure   **42.** (1) An amendment to the Constitution of Canada in relation to the following matters may be made only in accordance with subsection 38(1):

(*a*) the principle of proportionate representation of the provinces in the House of Commons prescribed by the Constitution of Canada;

(*b*) the powers of the Senate and the method of selecting Senators;

(*c*) the number of members by which a province is entitled to be represented in the Senate and the residence qualifications of Senators;

(*d*) subject to paragraph 41(*d*), the Supreme Court of Canada;

(*e*) the extension of existing provinces into the territories; and

(*f*) notwithstanding any other law or practice, the establishment of new provinces.

Exception

(2) Subsections 38(2) to (4) do not apply in respect of amendments in relation to matters referred to in subsection (1).

Amendment of provisions relating to some but not all provinces

43. An amendment to the Constitution of Canada in relation to any provision that applies to one or more, but not all, provinces, including

(*a*) any alteration to boundaries between provinces, and

(*b*) any amendment to any provision that relates to the use

of the English or the French language within a province, may be made by proclamation issued by the Governor General under the Great Seal of Canada only where so authorized by resolutions of the Senate and House of Commons and of the legislative assembly of each province to which the amendment applies.

Amendments by Parliament

44. Subject to sections 41 and 42, Parliament may exclusively make laws amending the Constitution of Canada in relation to the executive government of Canada or the Senate and House of Commons.

Amendments by provincial legislatures

45. Subject to section 41, the legislature of each province may exclusively make laws amending the constitution of the province.

Initiation of amendment procedures

46. (1) The procedures for amendment under sections 38, 41, 42 and 43 may be initiated either by the Senate or the House of Commons or by the legislative assembly of a province.

Revocation of authorization

(2) A resolution of assent made for the purposes of this Part may be revoked at any time before the issue of a proclamation authorized by it.

Amendments without Senate resolution

47. (1) An amendment to the Constitution of Canada made by proclamation under section 38, 41, 42 or 43 may be made without a resolution of the Senate authorizing the issue of the proclamation if, within one hundred and eighty days after the adoption by the House of Commons of a resolution authorizing its issue, the Senate has not adopted such a resolution and if, at any time after the expiration of that period, the House of Commons again adopts the resolution.

Computation of period

(2) Any period when Parliament is prorogued or dissolved

shall not be counted in computing the one hundred and eighty day period referred to in subsection (1).

Advice to issue proclamation

48. The Queen's Privy Council for Canada shall advise the Governor General to issue a proclamation under this Part forthwith on the adoption of the resolutions required for an amendment made by proclamation under this Part.

Constitutional conference

49. A constitutional conference composed of the Prime Minister of Canada and the first ministers of the provinces shall be convened by the Prime Minister of Canada within fifteen years after this Part comes into force to review the provisions of this Part.

PART VI
AMENDMENT TO THE CONSTITUTION ACT, 1867

Amendment to Constitution Act, 1867

50. The *Constitution Act, 1867* (formerly named the *British North America Act, 1867*) is amended by adding thereto, immediately after section 92 thereof, the following heading and section:

"Non-Renewable Natural Resources, Forestry Resources and Electrical Energy

Laws respecting non-renewable natural resources, forestry resources and electrical energy

92A. (1) In each province, the legislature may exclusively make laws in relation to

(*a*) exploration for non-renewable natural resources in the province;

(*b*) development, conservation and management of non-renewable natural resources and forestry resources in the province, including laws in relation to the rate of primary production therefrom; and

(*c*) development, conservation and management of sites and facilities in the province for the generation and production of electrical energy.

Export from provinces of resources

(2) In each province, the legislature may make laws in relation to the export from the province to another part of Canada of the primary production from non-renewable natural resources and forestry resources in the province and the production from facilities in the province for the generation of electrical energy, but such laws may not authorize or

provide for discrimination in prices or in supplies exported to another part of Canada.

Authority of Parliament

(3) Nothing in subsection (2) derogates from the authority of Parliament to enact laws in relation to the matters referred to in that subsection and, where such a law of Parliament and a law of a province conflict, the law of Parliament prevails to the extent of the conflict.

Taxation of resources

(4) In each province, the legislature may make laws in relation to the raising of money by any mode or system of taxation in respect of

(*a*) non-renewable natural resources and forestry resources in the province and the primary production therefrom, and

(*b*) sites and facilities in the province for the generation of electrical energy and the production therefrom,

whether or not such production is exported in whole or in part from the province, but such laws may not authorize or provide for taxation that differentiates between production exported to another part of Canada and production not exported from the province.

"Primary production"

(5) The expression "primary production" has the meaning assigned by the Sixth Schedule.

Existing powers or rights

(6) Nothing in subsections (1) to (5) derogates from any powers or rights that a legislature or government of a province had immediately before the coming into force of this section."

Idem

51. The said Act is further amended by adding thereto the following Schedule:

"THE SIXTH SCHEDULE

Primary Production from Non-Renewable Natural Resources and Forestry Resources

1. For the purposes of section 92A of this Act,

(*a*) production from a non-renewable natural resource is primary production therefrom if

(i) it is in the form in which it exists upon its recovery or severance from its natural state, or

(ii) it is a product resulting from processing or refining the resource, and is not a manufactured product or a product resulting from refining crude oil, refining upgraded heavy crude oil, refining gases or liquids derived from coal or refining a synthetic equivalent of crude oil; and

(*b*) production from a forestry resource is primary production therefrom if it consists of sawlogs, poles, lumber, wood chips, sawdust or any other primary wood product, or wood pulp, and is not a product manufactured from wood.''

PART VII
GENERAL

Primacy of Constitution of Canada

52. (1) The Constitution of Canada is the supreme law of Canada, and any law that is inconsistent with the provisions of the Constitution is, to the extent of the inconsistency, of no force or effect.

Constitution of Canada

(2) The Constitution of Canada includes
(*a*) the *Canada Act, 1982*, including this Act;
(*b*) the Acts and orders referred to in the schedule; and
(*c*) any amendment to any Act or order referred to in paragraph (*a*) or (*b*).

Amendments to Constitution of Canada

(3) Amendments to the Constitution of Canada shall be made only in accordance with the authority contained in the Constitution of Canada.

Repeals and new names

53. (1) The enactments referred to in Column I of the schedule are hereby repealed or amended to the extent indicated in Column II thereof and, unless repealed, shall continue as law in Canada under the names set out in Column III thereof.

Consequential amendments

(2) Every enactment, except the *Canada Act, 1982*, that refers to an enactment referred to in the schedule by the name in Column I thereof is hereby amended by substituting for that name the corresponding name in Column III thereof, and any British North America Act not referred to in the schedule may be cited as the *Constitution Act* followed by the year and number, if any, of its enactment.

Repeal and consequential amendments

54. Part IV is repealed on the day that is one year after this Part comes into force and this section may be repealed and this Act renumbered, consequential upon the repeal of Part IV and this section, by proclamation issued by the Governor General under the Great Seal of Canada.

French version
of Constitution
of Canada

55. A French version of the portions of the Constitution of Canada referred to in the schedule shall be prepared by the Minister of Justice of Canada as expeditiously as possible and, when any portion thereof sufficient to warrant action being taken has been so prepared, it shall be put forward for enactment by proclamation issued by the Governor General under the Great Seal of Canada pursuant to the procedure then applicable to an amendment of the same provisions of the Constitution of Canada.

English and
French versions
of certain
constitutional
texts

56. Where any portion of the Constitution of Canada has been or is enacted in English and French or where a French version of any portion of the Constitution is enacted pursuant to section 55, the English and French versions of that portion of the Constitution are equally authoritative.

English and
French versions
of this Act

57. The English and French versions of this Act are equally authoritative.

Commence-
ment

58. Subject to section 59, this Act shall come into force on a day to be fixed by proclamation issued by the Queen or the Governor General under the Great Seal of Canada.

Commence-
ment of
paragraph
23(1)(a) in
respect of
Quebec

59. (1) Paragraph 23(1)(a) shall come into force in respect of Quebec on a day to be fixed by proclamation issued by the Queen or the Governor General under the Great Seal of Canada.

Authorization
of Quebec

(2) A proclamation under subsection (1) shall be issued only where authorized by the legislative assembly or government of Quebec.

Repeal of
this section

(3) This section may be repealed on the day paragraph 23(1)(a) comes into force in respect of Quebec and this Act amended and renumbered, consequential upon the repeal of this section, by proclamation issued by the Queen or the Governor General under the Great Seal of Canada.

Short title
and citations

60. This Act may be cited as the *Constitution Act, 1982,* and the Constitution Acts 1867 to 1975 (No. 2) and this Act may be cited together as the *Constitution Acts, 1867 to 1982.*